"This engaging book is both scholarly and personal. It incorporates the most recent scholarship on the Jesus of history and presents it in a way that is readable and understandable, even for beginners. The author's excitement for the topic is evident throughout, inviting the reader's own intellectual and spiritual response."

—**Michael J. Dodds**, OP, professor of theology, Dominican School of Philosophy and Theology

"Father Morris integrates scholarship and comprehensive analysis in this contemporary volume of Christology which provides clarity to the kingdom of God—past, present, and future—confirming our shared humanity with Jesus as revealer and intermediary whose life embodies a sacred universal focus on love. This book is an invitation to readers to know the authentic Jesus of Nazareth creating a concurrent fresh understanding of faith and theology."

—**Kathleen Shannon Dorcy**, director of research, scholarship, and ethics, Fred Hutchinson Cancer Center

"In *Jesus: The Person and the Mission*, Fr. John Morris beautifully accomplishes his stated goals to (1) simplify the challenges of reading the vast amount of contemporary research on the subject, (2) present challenging questions for the reader, and (3) assist in the development of our own personal understanding of Jesus' vision for the world. Written for a general audience, Fr. Morris supplies us with an accessible yet scholarly work that is sure to both illuminate as well as inspire."

—**Ed Tywoniak**, professor emeritus, Saint Mary's College of California

"This book—at once highly erudite and yet imminently readable—is the fruit of a lifetime of study, teaching, pastoral ministry, and personal devotion. Father John Morris offers us a rich feast of thoughtful intellectual discourse on the person and mission of Jesus, who has indeed been the center of Father John's life. I am pleased and honored to have this opportunity to endorse Father John's fine work."

—**David Gentry**, professor of theology, Pontifical Beda College

Jesus: The Person and the Mission

Jesus: The Person and the Mission

A Search for the Jesus of History

John R. Morris, OP

WIPF & STOCK · Eugene, Oregon

JESUS: THE PERSON AND THE MISSION
A Search for the Jesus of History

Copyright © 2024 John R. Morris. All rights reserved. Except for brief quotations in critical publications or reviews, no part of this book may be reproduced in any manner without prior written permission from the publisher. Write: Permissions, Wipf and Stock Publishers, 199 W. 8th Ave., Suite 3, Eugene, OR 97401.

Wipf & Stock
An Imprint of Wipf and Stock Publishers
199 W. 8th Ave., Suite 3
Eugene, OR 97401

www.wipfandstock.com

PAPERBACK ISBN: 979-8-3852-0509-7
HARDCOVER ISBN: 979-8-3852-0510-3
EBOOK ISBN: 979-8-3852-0511-0

VERSION NUMBER 06/13/24

Unless otherwise noted, Scripture texts in this work are taken from the New American Bible, revised edition © 2010, 1991, 1986, 1970 Confraternity of Christian Doctrine, Washington, D.C., and are used by permission of the copyright owner. All Rights Reserved. No part of the New American Bible may be reproduced in any form without permission in writing from the copyright owner.

Scripture quotations marked (NRSV) are from the New Revised Standard Version Bible, copyright © 1980 by the Division of Christian Education of the National Council of the Churches of Christ in the U.S.A. Used by permission. All rights reserved.

Scripture quotations marked (NJB) are from the New Jerusalem Bible, copyright © 1985 by Darton, Longman & Todd, Ltd. and Doubleday, a division of Bantam Doubleday and Dell Publishing Group, Inc. All rights reserved.

Scripture quotations are from the Revised Standard Version of the Bible, copyright © 1946, 1952, and 1971 National Council of the Churches of Christ in the United States of America. Used by permission. All rights reserved worldwide.

Scripture quotations are from the New King James Version®. Copyright © 1982 by Thomas Nelson. Used by permission. All rights reserved.

Contents

Preface | vii
Acknowledgments | xvii
Abbreviations | xix

Introduction: Our Goals | 1
1 Images of Jesus in the Gospels | 19
2 The Search for the Jesus of History | 33
3 The Baptism of Jesus | 47
4 The Kingdom of God: Preliminary Considerations | 76
5 How Jesus Understood the Kingdom of God | 84
6 The Kingdom of God: A Theological Reflection | 108
7 Miracles: Preliminary Considerations | 131
8 Jesus as a Worker of Miracles | 142
9 A Critical Appraisal of the Miracle Tradition | 158
10 The Parables: Preliminary Considerations | 177
11 A Theological Evaluation of the Parables | 194
12 How Jesus Understood Himself | 216
13 Jesus the Teacher: Authentic Themes and Sayings | 237
14 Jerusalem: The Final Act | 262
15 The Passion and Death of Jesus | 289
16 Afterword: Concluding Comments | 297

Works Consulted | 317
Index | 323

Preface

Introduction

THE DISCUSSION OF JESUS of Nazareth, whether for reasons of faith and devotion or for theological reflection, is always of interest to the committed Christian. In more recent times, however, this discussion has absorbed the attention of believers as well nonbelievers alike. There are significant reasons for this development.

The point-of-departure for the first phase of these exciting times was born out of the publication of the encyclical letter *Divino Afflante Spiritu* of Pius XII in 1943. One could never have imagined its impact. The development of Catholic scripture scholars and the results of their study of the Bible were the first fruits of the encyclical, which became recognized as the Magna Carta of biblical studies in the Catholic communion. Today we are blessed with an incredible amount of scholarship as well as a significant number of gifted scripture scholars, many of whom are from the United States. Not long after this epic event, Catholic theologians celebrated the 1,500th anniversary of the Council of Chalcedon in 1951. The interest in the most important christological event in the life of the church produced a plethora of accomplished theologians writing on the subject. It also produced a major shift in theological thinking. It has been noted that there was much more that belongs to Jesus' life than the dogmatic definitions of Chalcedon, important as these are.[1] When

---

1. This text deals with many of the concepts or ideas that consider Jesus from a soteriological perspective and not just a dogmatic perspective. By soteriology we mean the study of Jesus' saving acts. Soteriology considers what Jesus said and did, his words and works. The dogmatic perspective deals with the person of Jesus, his identity, and not his mission.

PREFACE

John XXIII convened the Vatican Council II (1962–1965) it was greeted by a host of talented theologians and biblical scholars at its service. The council was a Copernican change for the church as anyone who lived through this historical period can attest. Who could have anticipated the impact that these twenty-two years from 1943 to 1965 would have had on the life of the church?

The second phase of these exciting times can be described as an assimilation of the results of the council into the life of the church and the lives of Christians. It also promoted a more open contact with the secular world. All of this was by design. What makes this second phase so interesting and exciting is that theologians began the prospect of assimilating this continuing biblical research into systematic theology. In the Catholic tradition there has always been a close union between Scripture and theology. What set this era apart from all previous eras were the results of Catholic biblical scholarship and its use of contemporary methods of interpretation. This has had a profound impact on the study of Jesus of Nazareth, whom we identify in faith as Jesus the Christ.[2] Today we are still far from accomplishing this task of assimilation. We are now experiencing the more fully developed and acceptable historical Jesus of which much more will be said later. While Raymond Brown had anticipated that this assimilation would be completed by the turn of the twentieth century,[3] the task is far from complete. He missed the mark in thinking that the biblical scholars would have completed their work by the last third of the twentieth century in preparation for theologians to begin theirs. But that work continues, and this is what is so exciting. Rather than undermining the faith, the results to this point have given support and grounding to the traditional faith of the church. This will be explored more fully below.

---

2. Jesus of Nazareth, also understood as the historical Jesus, will be conceptually distinguished from the Jesus of faith or Jesus Christ. This distinction will be sharply made as we progress. See chapter 2.

3. Raymond Brown thought that the twentieth century could be conveniently divided into thirds. The first third provided us with little useful results in terms of Catholic biblical scholarship. The second third, under the influence of *Divino Afflante Spiritu*, would provide us with the results of present-day Catholic biblical scholarship. The third part of the century would witness the assimilation of this biblical scholarship into speculative theology. The idea proved correct, but the predicted timing was not at all accurate. See Brown, *Virginal Conception and Bodily Resurrection*, 3–6.

PREFACE

The Justification or Reason for This Text

Before we enter into the subject matter of our investigation, a few observations concerning the purpose or goal of this text would be profitable. At a time when there is so much written about Jesus the Christ, some of it excellently researched and written, is there room for one more tome on the subject? Wouldn't we be better served looking for that major text that begins a new development or direction in our search? There needs to be some justification for another text although it might be said at the outset that *the more the merrier*. Can there ever be too many?

My intention in moving this work forward is fairly simple. First, it is an attempt to introduce a subject matter very dear to the mind and heart of all Christians. Second, it is an effort to make more manageable a huge amount of literature that can be intimidating to the beginning or casual reader. This work also attempts to raise challenging questions, but makes no attempt to supply all the answers. Its goal is much humbler, but one which is much needed. This text is an attempt to explore our personal vision or understanding of Jesus as well as Jesus' vision for the world. It is about Jesus as a historical person; what this Jesus of history did and taught. It is also about how the primitive community understood the Jesus of history in its faith and how it expressed that faith in the Scriptures and its lived experience. The work's ultimate goal is to examine how this vision of Jesus might now be expressed in the lives of contemporary Christians. It is an attempt to account for the most recent biblical research as it takes its rightful place in theological and christological reflection. Finally, this text endeavors to discover something of the Jesus of history, of how he is expressed in the Scriptures and how he impacts Christians today as the Christ of faith. The central question it wants to answer is how Christ and Christianity make a difference to individuals and the world they live in. The vague response that "Jesus is the Savior of the world" or other similar statements is too distant for most of us. While dogmatic discussions of Jesus are needed, his relationship to the individual and to the world in a real, concrete way is just as important. The question is why should anyone be a follower? Why does anyone need Jesus? This is what we intend to explore.

Another important consideration is to determine who this book is for, who would find it useful. This project did not begin with a specific audience in mind. It was originally designed and written for its author, with the hope that others might also find it profitable.[4] It is the distillation of notes prepared for classroom lectures over many years. No claim is made for originality. In organizing and synthesizing this material, it became clear that this work was an intrinsically personal enterprise. It should readily be admitted that many of us write for ourselves—and we hope that others will find the fruits of our contemplation useful. This work is not intended to be the last word, but rather a productive first word on the subject. My hope is that the end product presents a clear and useful overview of the intended material, which is both readable and intelligible.

This text is written for the young intellectual, the neophyte theologian, as well as for the educated reader searching for a deeper understanding of Jesus of Nazareth. The busy preacher, one who has finished his theological studies and is too busy to pursue further formal studies, might also find this work of interest. It is for anyone who has an interest in this subject matter and who has the energy to read carefully.[5] It may prove useful for parish discussion groups. The text may require some effort and will certainly require engagement. My challenge has been to develop a text that satisfies both the beginning theological student as well as my inquisitive friends and colleagues who question whether the work will ever be completed! There is need for a theologian to introduce the beginner to the thought of serious biblical and theological scholars. This is the book that I would have cherished at the beginning of my theological career.

This book is designed to introduce the reader to the study of *Jesus*. It is intended to serve both faith and theological enquiry. Admittedly the text must remain a work in progress.[6] My intention is to develop an educational tool to guide students on their journey of discovering who Jesus is and what he means to both believers and nonbelievers in the world today. My goal is to produce an up-to-date, readable text employing the most recent biblical and theological scholarship that is relatable in a contemporary

---

4. This is probably true for all books. They are indeed the children of their authors.

5. I would suggest reading it carefully and slowly. In many cases it would prove helpful to read the notes. They are often instructive and include material that did not seem to fit the general text. The text ought to be read with a Bible close at hand for ready reference.

6. My hope is that the ideas expressed here will become the source of the reader's personal reflection, intellectual curiosity, and further development. It remains a work in progress for the reader since we can never exhaust the richness of our faith in Jesus Christ.

context.[7] Sources have been chosen so the reader may verify the conclusions put forth and judge them on his or her own terms.

What we must account for in our present age is the shift that has taken place in our understanding and expression in contemporary scholarship. There has developed a new vigor in understanding Jesus as a Jew. This development began in the seventies, and it has now become commonplace to explore Jesus in his religious and cultural context.[8] Additionally, we must acknowledge the Copernican shift that has taken place in the historical-critical method. Sanders and many others now claim that we can determine the "almost indisputable facts" in the life of Jesus.[9] John Meier has greatly expanded this methodology. There is much about the Jesus of history that is available to us.[10]

The first purpose of this study is to understand Jesus as he has come to be believed in, the Jesus who is understood as the Christ. Its focus is the articulation of Jesus as the object of Christian belief. This is the Jesus who is God's Son, the very presence of God in the world. The second task is to embrace that tradition and reveal what we can discover about Jesus of Nazareth who precedes Christian faith but stands at its foundation. This is Jesus as he was understood by his first disciples in

7. In this regard, my intention is to be faithful to the tradition as we have received it over twenty centuries. It will also require the assimilation of contemporary biblical studies into the work of Christology. This is no mean task but one that is necessary to write a successful contemporary Christology.

8. For works that explore this in depth see Vermes, *Jesus the Jew*. Vermes has written extensively on the subject. See Sanders, *Jesus and Judaism*.

9. Sanders, *Jesus and Judaism*, 11. The "almost indisputable facts" enumerated by Sanders are (1) Jesus was baptized by John the Baptist; (2) Jesus was a Galilean who preached and healed; (3) Jesus called disciples and spoke of there being twelve; (4) Jesus confined his activity to Israel; (5) Jesus engaged in a controversy about the temple; (6) Jesus was crucified outside Jerusalem by the Roman authorities; (7) after his death Jesus' followers continued as an identifiable movement; (8) at least some Jews persecuted at least parts of the new movement. Sanders enlarges this list in his *Historical Figure of Jesus*, 10–11. William R. Herzog modified this list. See his *Prophet and Teacher*, 2–3. Sobrino has also proposed a synopsis of historical facts from the life of Jesus. See his work *Jesus the Liberator*, 61. Crossan, *The Historical Jesus*, and Meier, *A Marginal Jew*, are also worth examining. These sources are a testimony to the confidence that contemporary biblical scholars have that they can identify considerable amounts of historical information about Jesus of Nazareth.

10. The historical-critical method, after several failures, came into its own somewhere in the mid-twentieth century. Those mentioned above wrote in the last quarter of the century and accomplished a great deal in employing this method. The most brilliant expression of the historical-critical method, however, is Meier, *A Marginal Jew*. The first volume was published in 1991. More will be said of this when we examine the historical-critical method.

PREFACE

Galilee before he was professed or proclaimed as the Christ. This exercise should prove both exciting and rewarding. Our program, then, is educational, devotional, and perhaps even inspirational.

The Importance of This Study

Why should one be interested in this study and dedicate the time and effort necessary to profitably engage it? Can the subject matter justify itself as having significant importance? In part, the answer depends upon the reader's subjective state of mind and his or her personal interests and faith convictions. There is something about the subject matter, regardless of one's particular faith commitment, that makes it worthwhile to explore with both enthusiasm and intellectual curiosity. This study is certainly meant to address the questions of faith that are central to understanding who Jesus was. How does the person of Jesus impact human beings today? How does this two-thousand-year tradition permit Jesus to address a contemporary audience? How have people understood Jesus during the last two thousand years?

This work engages in a significant part of a very ancient, rich, and influential tradition which has impacted countless millions of individuals as well as society and culture in general. If there has been a greater historical, cultural, or societal influence on the development of humankind, it would be difficult to imagine what it would be. Christ and Christianity have shaped the world as we know it for the better. Having said this, we should be able to formulate several good reasons for examining this tradition and its founder.

As to the general influence of Jesus, almost one-third of the world's population, nearly 7.5 billion people, are at least nominally Christian. This number in itself offers some indication as to the influence that Christianity has had in its two-thousand-year history. The central question is why over two billion people, influenced by their belief in Jesus Christ, live their lives as they do? What magnetism or attraction in the life and person of Jesus Christ leads to faith? Just as pertinent to our interest, what was the historical person of Jesus, Christianity's founder, really like? Can we recover something of his originality and charism? Can we associate and equate Jesus' teaching and life with revelation from God? The preliminary answer is a confident yes. Contemporary Christology, the theological study of Christ, has made great strides in helping us

PREFACE

assess more fully than ever before, the person of Jesus of Nazareth, who we have come to recognize as the Christ.

Furthermore, Christianity possesses an extremely rich intellectual tradition. From its inception, the Christian community was required to catechize new adherents to the faith. It also needed to defend its belief system to those who raised objections against it. These two approaches are referred to as catechesis and apologetics. The following centuries led to the development of theology proper, that is, the rational reflection on the faith to understand it more deeply. This particular reflection also exposes us to an extremely rich spiritual tradition rooted in the remarkable prayer life of Jesus himself. From its inception, Christianity received a profound liturgical, sacramental, and spiritual life from the teaching and activity of Christ. Over the centuries, this has resulted in an extraordinary spirituality experienced by both individuals as well as communities of people who joined together to express in a communal way the life lived by Christ himself.

Christ is also the source and inspiration of a rich tradition of religious art, architecture, liturgical and devotional practices, music, literature, and film. The art tradition which began in the first-century catacombs has found expression in every subsequent century. Biblical literature, the foundation for Christian life, found its artistic expression in illuminated manuscripts. This artistic form has delighted believers and nonbelievers for centuries. Biblical literature has also served as the foundation for other forms of literature based upon a belief in Christ. Our examination of the life and significance of Jesus Christ will reveal a connection, albeit distant, between many other human institutions. The influence of Christ and his believers led to the formation of hospitals in the middle ages, as well as the concept of the modern university, which finds its origin in the monasteries, cathedral schools, and universities of the eleventh, twelfth, and thirteenth centuries. There are other institutions which we now recognize as a part of both our religious and civic lives today. Perhaps more significantly, our study should help us more fully understand the impact of Jesus' life on humanity and its cultural, moral, and social teachings. Ignorance of the ancient tradition in which Jesus stands at the center is an impoverishment of our lives as humans.

What is important for us to understand is that our historical works of art, architecture, music, literature, and important social institutions were all influenced by Christians who saw an intimate and integral connection between their faith in the person of Jesus Christ and their social and private lives. It is a living tradition whose origin is found in Jesus of Nazareth. Our study will not trace out all of these connections, but should provide a framework for understanding the formational ideas that touched and prompted others in a special manner to make their mark in the world.

There are good reasons for pointing out these accomplishments. First, it is to indicate the positive impact Jesus has had on societal, cultural, and historical norms. And second, it is to counteract a narrower view of Christianity that focuses primarily on the church's sins: the bad popes; the Inquisition; the negative aspects of the Crusades; the sexual abuse scandal in the contemporary church; historical and contemporary criticism of the church's structure; and so forth. The positive accomplishments of Christianity are significant, and are a more authentic gauge of the impact of Jesus on the world than are the sins of some of his followers.

The Expected Goals or Outcomes of This Study

Our primary goal is to recover as much as is intellectually or rationally possible from the pertinent tradition of Jesus of Nazareth, the Jesus of history. While we will employ other methods, the historical-critical method will prove invaluable in our attempt to access the Jesus of history. The reasons for this will become clear as we proceed. During Jesus' lifetime there were numerous different responses to his life, teachings, and activities. Thus, we recognize Jesus as a contingent human being who does not exhaust the God question for us, and we understand that whatever his personal presence and message might have been to those who encountered him, it did not compel or force belief in him.[11]

We are most interested in discovering the primitive community's response to Jesus. What did the earliest followers of Jesus believe about him both before and after his death and resurrection? We want to understand the most primitive expressions used by the Christian community to express their faith in Jesus the Christ. How did his early followers express their understanding? What images did they use?

This has considerable importance for future studies. It will form a basis for examining how later, more developed ecclesial groups, from the second to the fifth centuries, expressed their understanding

---

11. Schillebeeckx, *On Christian Faith*, 2. All four chapters of this collection of a lecture series are well worth reading.

of Jesus. How did the authoritative, normative statements of the later church develop? These authoritative affirmations can be properly understood only with reference to the development and enculturation of the early church, which attempted to make the primitive gospel message intelligible within a cultural context other than the one in which it was originally preached. But the original message is its basis. This examination tracks the various ways that contemporary men and women express their understanding of Jesus. How does their response to Jesus shape their understanding and response to discipleship? In all of this, we want to be faithful to the Scriptures as well as the Christian tradition. Both of these are normative for this study.[12]

Conclusion

The prefatory remarks above aim to properly prepare the reader for the study of Christology. These remarks briefly explain the subject matter under consideration and offer a motive for why our undertaking is important and useful. The prefatory remarks briefly address the impact Jesus of Nazareth had on the cultural, intellectual, and moral lives of humans over twenty centuries. Briefly, we have laid out several important presuppositions to provide clarity to this study and to articulate the methods to be used and goals and outcomes to be achieved. All will be clarified further as we proceed.

This is both an important and exciting study which we hope will be well worth the time and effort it demands. It should serve both intellectual curiosity and the requirements for a lively faith. My hope is that you, the reader, will find it as exciting and rewarding personally as it has been for me in developing it.

This work is a Christology, an interpretation of the person of Jesus Christ. It is my personal attempt to address one of the richest treasures of the Christian tradition. This study attempts to explore in a special and personal way a tradition that is two thousand years old and yet as fresh and alive today as it was at its inception.[13] It is the tradition of the person of Jesus Christ. This text is based upon considerable empirical experience, and reflects the distillation of forty-five years of classroom teaching

---

12. In this regard see the works of Raymond Brown, Edward Schillebeeckx, and John Macquarrie.

13. As stated above, it remains a work in progress and must necessarily remain so.

PREFACE

and preaching. It is by grace and great privilege to have experienced such a career, spanning one of the most exciting times in church history and theological speculation. This work was born out of a personal effort to discern a deeper meaning of our common faith. In developing, organizing and revising this text, I owe a deep appreciation to the many students who have participated in bringing this work to what I hope is a successful conclusion. But I do share Fr. Pierre Mandonnet's sentiments in this work. "To read, joy; to think, delight; to write, torture." It is a sentence penned by Mandonnet on a piece of paper at the end of his life. It explains why he never completely finished his monumental *St. Dominic and his Work*.[14] I hope that I am able to avoid the same predicament although writing is never such a delight as reading and thinking.

---

14. This quote is from M. H. Vicaire's forward to Pierre Mandonnet, *Saint Dominic and His Work*, vii.

Acknowledgments

THIS BOOK BEGAN MANY years ago as a survey course in Christology. Both students and friends were instrumental in my continued effort to develop a well-researched and readable text. My students always provided me with inspiration; my friends provided me with motivation. Their common refrain was "when will it ever be finished?" Thanks be to God, my efforts have now reached fruition.

There were many scholarly works that proved invaluable to me on this path. Theologians such as Schillebeeckx, Rahner, Kung, and Kasper, and far too many others to mention supplied a foundation. Scripture scholars such as Brown, Fitzmyer, Perkins, and many others provided a structure. Numerous Protestant scholars such as Jeremias, Dodd, and Fuller made very important contributions. However, it was the seminal work of John P. Meier that gave my research its final direction. His five volumes, *A Marginal Jew*, will be the seminal work for the historical-critical method for years to come. I owe a great debt of gratitude to him and his research. It redirected my personal search for an understanding of the Jesus of history and Meier's hand can be seen on every page. Without his scholarship this book would never have been written. My earnest hope and intention are to be faithful to his scholarship.

I am forever grateful to those who assisted me on this long journey. The Christian Brothers at Saint Mary's College of California read and commented on every chapter. Their contribution in making my ideas much clearer was invaluable. My sincere appreciation and thanks also to the many librarians at Saint Mary's College, too many to name, who

ACKNOWLEDGMENTS

were instrumental in putting the scholarly references, the notes and bibliography, into superb academic order. They were brilliant and their contribution gave this book a more attractive and readable appearance. Finally, my deepest thanks to my friend Chris Sweeney who put the final touches on the written text. It reads so much better than it would have without his devoted editing.

For all of these scholars and friends I am forever grateful. It is to them and especially to all of my former students that I would like to dedicate this book.

Abbreviations

AAS	*Acta Apostolicae Sedis*
ABRL	Anchor Bible Reference Library
JAAR	*Journal of the American Academy of Religion*
L	Scripture found only in the Gospel of Luke
M	Scripture found only in the Gospel of Matthew
NABRE	New American Bible Revised Edition
NJB	New Jerusalem Bible
NJBC	*New Jerome Biblical Commentary*
NKJV	New King James Version
NRSV	New Revised Standard Version
Q	Source: primarily parallel sayings found only in the Gospels of Matthew and Luke

Introduction: Our Goals

The Point-of-Departure for This Study

"Who do people say that I am?" (Mark 8:27b).[1] Jesus first put this question to his disciples. It is informational. There were then (and are today) a variety of answers to it. Some were grounded in faith, others were not. This reveals that most of the people contemporaneous with Jesus' life did not understand him. The answer to this question requires careful thought and study. It is an intellectual endeavor. To his disciples, Jesus later put the question in a more personal way. "But who do you say that I am?" (Mark 8:29). This question is an invitation and requires both faith and a personal response.

Numerous Christologies begin their study of Jesus by proposing this later question of Jesus to his disciples.[2] This question refers to Jesus' personal identity.[3] Christology, as the study of Christ, attempts to enlarge

---

1. Gospel parallels to the question of Jesus' identity can be found in Mark 8:27–3//Matt 16:13–20//and Luke 9:18–21. All biblical references will be taken from the New American Bible, Revised Edition (NABRE). They will be compared frequently with the New Revised Standard Version (NRSV).

2. To the question "who do you say that I am?" the reader should not be looking for an answer from some (other) theologian, but from one's personal attachment to the Lord who always challenges us. Joachim Jeremias expresses a remarkably similar idea in *Problem of the Historical Jesus*, 12.

3. To complete this brief discussion, we ought to note that Peter did not get his response completely accurate. See Mark 8:31–33. At this point in his discipleship, Peter did not understand the type of messiah that Jesus was, that he had to suffer, be rejected, and then be put to death. Nevertheless, the moment captures his incipient faith. While his answer was partly correct, it also partly failed to discern and properly understand Jesus' identity. Only after the resurrection did Peter understand it correctly. We might associate this with the messianic secret so prominent in the Gospel of Mark. The true

the answer given by Peter: "You are the Messiah" (Mark 8:29). At the same time the episode recorded in the Gospels indicates that not all of Jesus' contemporaries responded in the same manner.

Notwithstanding the power of the Gospel question regarding Jesus' identity, my preference in choosing a point-of-departure for our investigation is a statement attributed to Fr. Paré, a French Dominican: that Christianity is not simply a set of commandments (moral norms) to control our behavior. Neither is it merely dogma that guides our belief. Christianity is first and foremost an attachment to a person, the person of Jesus Christ. Pope Benedict XVI expressed this same idea in a slightly different way. "Being Christian is not the result of an ethical choice or a lofty idea, but the encounter with an event, a person, which gives life a new horizon and a decisive direction."[4] Benedict's predecessor, John Paul II, expressed a similar idea. "We are certainly not seduced by the naïve expectation that, faced with the great challenges of our time, we shall find some magic formula. No, we shall not be saved by the formula but by a Person, and the assurance which he gives us: I am with you!"[5]

The operative part of Father Pare's statement is the reference to an "attachment to a person."[6] At its root, Christianity calls for a personal relationship with Jesus of Nazareth who, in faith, is recognized as the Christ. This personal relationship for Christians is based upon the conviction that Jesus is the unique pathway to experience God. It presumes that Christianity is a historical religion with an historical founder. It also presumes that Christianity is more than a dogmatic or moral teaching passed from one generation to the next, although teaching is certainly included in the tradition. It is noteworthy that when the Second Vatican Council spoke of welcoming individuals into the church, it pointed out that "the catechumenate . . . is not a mere exposition of dogmatic truths and norms of morality, but a period of formation in the whole Christian life of sufficient duration, during which the disciples will be joined to Christ their teacher."[7] Christianity cannot be

---

identity of Jesus is not revealed until the end of Mark's Gospel. The centurion, standing at the foot of the cross, exclaims, "Truly this man was the Son of God!" (Mark 15:39).

4. Benedict XVI, *Deus Caritas Est*, no. 1.

5. John Paul II, *Novo Millennio Ineunte*, no. 29.

6. This definition goes beyond dogmatic belief or moral behavior. Dogma and morals are the consequence of something that is more fundamental.

7. Flannery, *Ad Gentes Divinitus*, no. 14.

reduced to, or based upon, anything external to Jesus Christ. This is an important presupposition for our study of Christology. It recognizes that the basis of everything Christian, including the Scriptures, is the person of Jesus of Nazareth. Christianity is dependent upon the Scriptures as its most important source, but it is not determined by it. That determination comes from Jesus of Nazareth.

Recent Developments That Influence This Study

One of the first tasks of Christology is to understand the difference, as well as the identity, between the man Jesus and the Christ of faith. The expression *Jesus of Nazareth* refers to the Jesus of history. He is the person about whom we ultimately make our faith statements but who existed prior to our faith in him. In this we recognize him as an objective, historical human being. *Jesus Christ* is the Jesus of history who comes to be affirmed as the Christ, the Son of God and Lord. These affirmations are made in faith.

We presume an identity between the Jesus of history and the Jesus of the gospel. The faith statements made about the Jesus of history are not creations in the strict sense, an invention or fabrication of the early church made out of whole cloth.[8] They are interpretations or understandings of the person of Jesus made in faith. This identity is foundational for those engaged in Christology. We need to be clear from the outset that Jesus of Nazareth is the central focus of christological study because it is he who grounds the faith statements of both Scripture and tradition.

For centuries Christology was almost exclusively approached from a dogmatic perspective. Jesus was understood, not just as an integral human being, but as the *perfect man* united to the divine logos. Over the centuries this understanding became the matrix for examining his human existence. This focus was almost universal until the 1,500th anniversary of the Council of Chalcedon in 1951. Since then, Christology has benefited from a new emphasis on the humanity of Jesus and his saving words and deeds.

---

8. As we proceed in this study, we will note that the Scriptures, most especially the Gospels, contain considerable apologetic and interpretive statements which are assigned to the evangelists. We may refer to these as *creations* of the evangelists or the primitive church, but by doing so we do not mean that these are anything more than a conceptual understanding of Jesus made in faith.

Furthermore, recent developments in the academic world help us to speak of Jesus in a way different from that previously available to us. As a result, these developments have transformed contemporary Christology into an exciting academic discipline.[9] There are four areas of study to which we must be especially attentive in order to understand the changes which have taken place in recent years: the recognition that the New Testament contains numerous Christologies; the recovery (or proper understanding) of the mythological in the life of Jesus; the recovery of the Jewishness of Jesus; and recent developments that have shaped the historical-critical method.

The Recovery of the Mythological

In the recent past, much of the gospel retelling of the story of Jesus was perceived as having been expressed in mythological terms. This was especially true of the influential twentieth-century Scripture scholar Rudolph Bultmann and the scholars who immediately preceded him. Bultmann's predecessors had treated much of Scripture as mythological and rejected those parts as historical, often proposing that it was a total invention of the early Christian community and therefore had lost its validity in establishing anything about Jesus with historical certainty. Bultmann proposed *interpreting* the so-called mythological rather than simply dismissing it. But in so doing he gave short shrift to the historical events which grounded the scriptural expression of Jesus. The contemporary recovery of the mythological in the New Testament has made possible the affirmation of a much fuller, more developed picture of Jesus as a historical figure than in the past. In this sense the mythical is not understood as a falsehood or as a literary invention or convention, but rather as a literary genre that encapsulates a method of communicating the truth.[10] Consider for a moment the miracles attributed to Jesus. Bultmann understood the biblical reporting of miracles as mythological. It was meaningful but not historical. Myth and history touched one

---

9. There have been numerous developments in scriptural studies in recent times (the last century) to make the study of Christology an incredibly exciting venture. Among these methods or criticisms are literary, redaction, source, and form criticism. In addition to these, there are many other methods used to explore the Scriptures. We are presently in one of those critical periods and are in the process of assimilating a considerable amount of recent biblical scholarship into theology and Christology. See the preface.

10. See the discussion of myth in the preface.

another tangentially; they came together, embraced and became disconnected. Today, scholars understand these mythological expressions as material worthy of being examined by the historical-critical method. Jesus of Nazareth stands as their foundation.

The Recovery of the Jewishness of Jesus

The gospel clearly affirms that Jesus was born a Jew though his birthplace is disputed.[11] He is recognized as the Son of David both in a theological and a biological sense. He was immersed in his own culture, accepting fully the faith of Israel. This perception places Jesus within his historical and social context and does not understand him as a unique being standing outside his social, cultural, and religious roots. He may be a marginal Jew, as John Meier describes him, but he is nonetheless a Jew.[12] This affirmation will become much clearer as we proceed and will help us develop a better description of Jesus as he actually existed. This feature of Jesus, his Jewishness, is intrinsically intertwined with his history.

The Historical-Critical Method

The contemporary use of the historical-critical method has led to the recovery of a significant part of the Jesus of history and his authentic teaching. This has proven elusive in the past. Present scholarship is confident in affirming that it has indeed established a much more significant amount of the history of Jesus than past scholars have been able to develop, thanks in large part to the use of various critical tools. While this might seem inconsequential to novices in the study of Christology, we need to realize at the outset that our principal sources, the Gospels, were primarily written from a perspective of faith and not of history. The

---

11. One of the "almost indisputable facts" is that Jesus was a Galilean, which clearly implies his Jewishness. For an explanation of "almost indisputable facts" see the preface, xin9. This form of pagination refers to the page number (xi) and the footnote number (9) on that page. This form will be used throughout this text.

12. Meier, *Marginal Jew*. This five-volume work is destined to become the classic source for studies dealing with the Jesus of history. I owe Meier an enormous debt of gratitude for my frequent use of his outstanding scholarship. He is often quoted alone when there are many other authors who also propose supportive evidence. Without Meier's work this text would not have been possible. The reader should know that my understanding of Meier shines forth on every page of this text. Joachim Jeremias will also be appealed to often as an authority on the Jewishness of Jesus.

reporting on the Jesus of history is overlaid with the faith convictions of those who first understood the meaning of his life.[13] The sources are actually reflections upon the life of Jesus as seen through the eyes of faith; therefore, they are not history in the usual sense. The historical-critical method has made it possible for us to understand more fully the Jesus of history who is the basis of the early Christian kerygma.

Preliminary Remarks: Foundational Ideas

The foundational material for the reflections that follow address four central points: the experience of God as primary; Scripture and tradition as faith's expression of that experience of God; theology as a reflection on faith; and Christology as a particular part of theology.[14] These four points will be explored in the order articulated here.

The Experience of God

Because of his infinite nature, God stands outside created nature. He is spoken of as being transcendent. In spite of the vast difference between God and his creation they do share something in common.[15] We speak of God in an analogous manner, and we do so in images and metaphors.[16]

God is also immanent in the world, and this is an integral insight in the Jewish-Christian tradition. God has been experienced in a series of special relationships, first with Abraham, then with the Israelites through Moses, then with others, and ultimately through Jesus. The immanence of God presupposes that we experience God in the world, not simply in an intellectual way but in a personal, experiential way.

---

13. The Jesus of history is not necessarily the *real* Jesus. There is much more to be said for the real, actual Jesus than can be discovered by historical methods. For a discussion on this see Meier, *Marginal Jew*, 1:25.

14. I am especially indebted to Luttenberger largely because of the fortuitous manner in which he has defined Christology as well as the suggested foundational topics for this introduction. I have rearranged his material for convenience and to suit my particular reflection. See Luttenberger, *Introduction to Christology*, 12–28.

15. Both God and his creation are related by the concept of being or existence.

16. Even in faith we are restricted or limited to speak of God in metaphors, analogies, or symbols. Of historical interest is the position of Arius, a pious priest from Alexandria, who believed that the infinite gulf between God and humans could not be bridged. Consequently, he denied the possibility of the incarnation. This position was condemned at the Council of Nicea in AD 325.

The story of Moses' encounter with God in the burning bush on Mount Horeb is illustrative.[17] In whatever way one might understand or interpret the literary expression of this event, it seems obvious that it is intended to relate Moses' personal experience of God. It is this religious experience, mediated in a very human, natural fashion, which permits Moses to speak of God in faith. The plagues or miracles which ultimately liberated the Hebrews from slavery could also be seen largely as natural events.[18] This does not militate against the notion that God was experienced in these events. Natural, secular, or political events can also be the means by which God is experienced and in which he reveals himself. This idea is important in our understanding of the notion of Christology. It is in the person of Jesus the Christ that God and his revelation is experienced in a special, or as some say unique, way. Furthermore, God is a gift freely given to humanity; a gift that is not forced upon us.[19] We have the ability to accept or reject this personal relationship with God. Faith is our positive response to the experience of God. When this unique, personal relationship is accepted, it becomes transformative for the individual. The world is seen in a new light.

Scripture: The Community Retells the Story of Jesus

Faith in God through Jesus Christ is personal, but it is not private. The revelation of God is received by a community, and ultimately all theology must be brought back to the community to test its validity. As a consequence, when we speak of *tradition*, we are referring to the preservation and transmission of the community's experience of God. This is true both for Judaism as well as Christianity. Revelation is received in and by the community. Thus, when we refer to the tradition, we are pointing to a community of believers who receive the message and communicate it on to others. It is passed on both orally, in written form, and in liturgical actions.[20]

---

17. When Moses returned to this very mountain with the Hebrews to receive the covenant it is referred to as Mount Sinai (Exod 19:1).

18. See the notes on Exod 7:14–12:30 in the NABRE.

19. See Hos 11:4. Many believe that Hos 11 is a high point in Old Testament theology.

20. The notion of tradition as interpretation needs to be developed. Scripture itself contains tradition and is formed by tradition. For example, the parables and Q source (sayings) were a tradition received by the community and then codified in Scripture.

Scripture is the normative expression of the experience of God for faith. It is the fundamental source for our examination of Jesus as the Christ. The scriptural message is two-fold: it is partly from God and partly from humans. The initiative and content of the message is from God, but it takes human effort and language to articulate the experience in a manner which makes it capable of being received by the community. And it takes human effort aided by God's grace to recognize it.

Concomitant with our study of the Scriptures is the importance of establishing and maintaining the context in which Jesus undertook his ministry. This is also true for the postresurrection period in which the disciples proclaimed Jesus as the Christ. The Jesus of history lived in a context quite different from that in which the primitive church proclaimed him as the Christ. This context also differed during the time in which the Scriptures were written. These stages will be discussed at length in chapter 1. Very briefly, the first stage encompasses the period of the Jesus of history. The second stage encompasses the postresurrection period, during which the early church lived its experience of Jesus and proclaimed him as the Christ. The third stage is that period which follows during which the written Scriptures take shape. By themselves, these stages are important for helping the reader better understand the message contained in the Scripture. It is exceedingly important that these three stages be maintained within their proper contexts. Neglecting to account for the context will prevent us from obtaining a complete and accurate view of the events or narratives; it leaves behind material that is interpretive. We are mindful that we must not decontextualize the events of Jesus' life and death.

Theology: Reasoned Reflection on the Data of Faith

This study is properly named Christology, which is a part of theology. Both the nature of theology as well as Christology will be explained in the paragraphs below. But before we indicate more thoroughly what we intend to do in this study, we need to explain what we do not intend to do.

Theology, apologetics, and catechesis have as their subject matter the statements of faith, but they approach this common subject matter

---

The post-Reformation argument about Scripture and tradition has given way to a more sophisticated understanding that Scripture itself was a developing tradition.

INTRODUCTION: OUR GOALS

in quite different ways. By way of example, let us propose a general statement of faith: "I believe in God the Father." *Catechesis* proposes this statement for belief. It educates the catechumen that this statement belongs to the content of faith, explaining what the terms mean so that they can be understood and accepted in faith. *Apologetics* has a different aim. It does not prove the truth of these faith affirmations, but rather defends the affirmation as not being contradictory to truth or reason in general. "God the Father" is a possible, intelligible statement. Therefore, apologetics defends its reasonableness against those who would reject the statement. *Theology* has a different work: it presupposes the statement of faith as true, but it explores it for a deeper understanding. What can our statement *mean* and what impact does it have on believers? How does it relate to life? In this sense, theology is distinguished from catechesis and apologetics. This study is an endeavor to do theology.

The foundation of Christology is theology; therefore, a brief digression on the nature of theology will be helpful.[21] The classic definition of theology belongs to Anselm of Canterbury.[22] He defines theology as *fides quaerens intellectum*, faith seeking an understanding.[23] For theologians in general, God is the object of their study but not in the same way as it would be for a philosopher. A philosopher relies on his experience of the world in itself. A theologian would perceive God as a revealed object of faith.[24] Theology is the application of reason to the revealed

---

21. As has been mentioned above, Christology is a specific part of theology. We will take it up as soon as we have clarified what we mean by theology.

22. Anselm of Canterbury (1033–1109) is a doctor of the church and is often referred to as the founder of Scholasticism. He is known as proposing the ontological argument for the existence of God. The bulk of his academic life occurred while he was the prior of the Abbey of Bec, Normandy.

23. The study of the development of theology is interesting in itself. Peter Abelard wrote his invaluable work *Sic et Non*, in which he collected the seemingly contradictory statements in Scripture. It was the work of theology to explain that these were only apparent contradictions and reconcile them. In the mid-twelfth century, Peter Lombard organized and systematized the theological questions in his famous *Sententiae (Book of Sentences)*. This became the standard theological textbook and was commented on until the sixteenth century. In his *Summa Theologiae*, Thomas Aquinas refers to theology as *sacra pagina* (the sacred page/Scripture) or *sacra doctrina* (sacred teaching). This indicates the tight connection between theological reflection and the content of faith. The method of theology as conceived by Aquinas can be found in the *Summa Theologiae*, I, q. 32, a. 2, ad 2. Aquinas articulates his theological method (ways of argumentation) in his treatment on the Trinity. The discussion within Catholic circles in the early twentieth century was most informative but takes us beyond our present task. And in some way, it was a footnote to all that went before.

24. It should be noted that theology also uses the reasoning and conclusions of

content of faith, and it uses whatever disciplines that can help shed light on the particular subject matter.[25]

The classic definition of theology as articulated by Anselm has served theologians well for centuries. In spite of its pride of place, other theologians have proposed an updating of the definition largely because our theological expressions have evolved from the more static categories once employed by theologians of the past to more contemporary, dynamic categories. Luttenberger proposes the following definition of theology, and it has much merit given the way he frames it. "Theology is the process of interpreting one's faith-experience (knowledge, awareness) of God."[26] The term *process* as used in this definition, indicates that the conclusions of theology are not a fixed body of knowledge, nor is it something that is approached in a neutral manner. Just as there is development in doctrine so also there is a growth, a development, in theology. Our insights deepen. We see things from different perspectives because we have more academic disciplines at our service. Theology is rooted in a faith-experience of God which distinguishes it from a philosophical or rational study of God. The faith-experience of God is subject to interpretation. The notion of interpretation requires involvement. It is a stronger word than the *understanding* of the definition of Anselm.

This definition makes clear that theology is not faith. It is human reflection upon the object of faith.[27] This reflection has a definite purpose. It is not simply an abstract exercise done out of curiosity. It is not something to be found only in the academy or university. It is an exercise open to both the humblest person as well as the most highly gifted.

A word about method is in order. Scientific method constructs models or hypotheses whose purpose is to explain the given data.[28] It attempts to make sense of its data. The hypothesis or model is an explanation. Theological method is similar to the scientific hypothesis. It also constructs models or hypotheses in order to explain or understand the data of faith. Some of these models will be explored later in this book. Thus, the

---

philosophy within the boundaries of its own methodology.

25. It will become apparent how important other disciplines can be in helping us understand the various themes from the life of Jesus which we will examine in later chapters.

26. Luttenberger, *Introduction to Christology*, 14.

27. Some theologians (Rahner, liberation theologians) speak of first order and second order reflections. These correspond respectively to faith and theology.

28. See McIntyre, *Shape of Christology*.

theological explanation is changeable, subject to development. The best hypothesis or theological explanation is whatever explains the faith best. In the language of Aquinas, it "saves the appearances," that is, it satisfies or explains the data. Aquinas used an example from astronomy to illustrate his point.[29] He compared the theories used to explain the planetary motion. One theory applies epicycles, the other ellipses, to the data of planetary motion.[30] Each requires a different location for its focus or point of reference: the first uses the earth as its point of reference, the second uses the sun. The advantage of the second is that it explains the data in a manner that is simpler than the first. Thus, we do not speak about which theory or explanation is true or false, but which one explains the data better. Theological method is similar to this. The theological hypothesis is as good as it explains, clarifies, or interprets the data of faith.

The Definition of Christology

Having established a working definition for theology, we are now in a position to explain or define Christology, which is a part of the general study of theology. It should come as no surprise that Luttenberger's definition, which will be given here, uses many of the elements found in the definition of theology. His definition of Christology is as follows: "Christology is the process of interpreting one's faith-experience of God, alive for us in and through Jesus, the Christ."[31] Christology, like theology, is not merely study but requires personal involvement. The operative portion of Luttenberger's definition of Christology is the "faith-experience of God in and through Jesus, the Christ." The transcendent God is experienced in the person of Jesus Christ who stands as the point of departure for the experience of God. It is in his person that we come to know God.[32] Jesus Christ is the unique, principal mediator between God and humanity. This notion is especially resonant with a sacramental church such as

---

29. Aquinas, *Summa Theologiae*, I, q. 32, a. 1, ad. 2.

30. The first hypothesis, proposed by Ptolemy, is the geocentric model. It considers the earth as stationary, and the sun and all the planets rotate about it. The second, proposed by Copernicus and developed by Kepler, is called the heliocentric model. The sun is the stationary point of reference, and the planets move about it. This is the way we normally consider planetary motion today.

31. Luttenberger, *Introduction to Christology*, 12.

32. This is clear and explicit in Jesus' response to Philip: "Whoever has seen me has seen the Father" (John 14:9).

Catholicism which readily accepts mediators acting for God. It extends this beyond individuals (prophets, teachers) to creation itself (God acts through water, bread and wine, historical and natural events) and ultimately to Jesus Christ as the center of salvation history.

It is clear then that Christology is dependent upon human experience.[33] Christology is the interpretation of the experience of God which is acquired through Jesus. It explores the person of Jesus and his saving acts. Finally, we should note that Christology, like theology in general, is a process. It is never fully completed. We continue to examine our experience for its deeper meaning or to see how this faith in Jesus Christ is to be understood and lived in a contemporary context or situation.[34] Thus, though the faith remains constant, theological or Christological statements may possibly replace another when they can explain or interpret the faith more adequately.

Behind these affirmations regarding faith, theology, and Christology are several presuppositions which will be explored more deeply in subsequent chapters. The first of these is that God acts in the world for people. God's purpose is humankind's purpose; he is the God of human beings.[35] This establishes a very special understanding of God and will reflect the God of Jesus Christ as it is expressed in the Gospels. The second affirms that Jesus does what God does. His actions, his deeds, his teaching are an expression of God acting in our midst.[36] Jesus is the human face of God. He is the presence of God in our midst, and he makes it possible in a real way for us to know God and live in his presence. Finally, Jesus not only reveals God to us, but he also reveals what it means to be a truly authentic human being. Vatican Council II expressed this when it affirmed that "in reality it is only in the mystery of the Word made flesh that the mystery of man truly becomes clear."[37]

---

33. Liberation theology and other forms of contemporary theologies place special attention on human experience as its point-of-departure. Examples of this are the experience of the poor, the experience of women, etc. It is understood that these experiences can be easily located within the Scriptures and lend themselves to theological reflection.

34. A fresh and productive addition to traditional theological categories is the contemporary attention given to the context in which our sources are written as well as the context in which the events take place. Similarly, theology is required to pay attention to the context in which it is done.

35. Schillebeeckx, *Church: The Human Story*, 122.

36. Schillebeeckx, *On Christian Faith*, 42.

37. Flannery, *Gaudium et Spes*, no. 22. Jesus is further described in this paragraph

Introduction: Our Goals

Just as past theology has focused on orthodoxy, that is, right belief, so contemporary theology/Christology focuses much of its attention upon orthopraxis in conjunction with or in relationship to orthodoxy.[38] In doing so it is counteracting the past neglect to stress the consequences of a genuine, lived faith. Contemporary theology more clearly draws the connection between faith and life, that is, a lived tradition. As we will make clear later, this focus gives a new emphasis on soteriology, the study of the saving acts of Christ. It does not limit itself to past expressions of Christology, which focused on the person of Christ and responded to questions about Jesus' identity but not his salvific acts.[39] Contemporary theology/Christology attempts to unite the questions about Jesus' identity and his saving activity.

Conclusion

So far, we have noted that our point-of-departure for this study is an attachment to the person of Jesus Christ. We have defined Christology, which is the subject of our study. And we have situated contemporary scholarship and articulated several foundational concepts and first principles. It now remains for us to clarify what we intend to accomplish in the following pages.

Significant or Foundational Presuppositions

We will first identify several presuppositions which are necessary in order to accomplish the goals of this study. As we proceed, we will be mindful that any presuppositions that are not articulated here will be identified when they arise. This will be an important part of our reflections.

Scripture is the principal source of our faith. It is also an accurate reflection of the message preached by the Jesus of history. Scripture is

---

as the *perfect man*.

38. We need not digress here with a consideration of the Catholic/Lutheran discussion on the relationship of faith and works. Suffice it to say that the Catholic position is that works (orthopraxis) have merit and do play a role in salvation. Luther taught that works followed automatically upon one's faith, but they were not a factor in salvation.

39. Though we refer to this text as *Christology* we do not do so unmindful of the subject matter we refer to as *soteriology*. We are simply following an older scheme in which Christology was understood as subsuming both "who Jesus was" and "what Jesus did" without dividing this study into two distinct disciplines.

written for faith and not as a historical narrative. Meier points out that there is no way to establish a chronological sequence of events as they are reported in the Gospels. This is the result of the way the sources were collected and ordered in their written form. There is also obvious, and some not so obvious, editing by the evangelists. In this new context it is easy to identify insertions of church polemics against their opposition into the text.[40]

We recognize a development between the context of Jesus' public life and the context of the lived experience of the community that followed his death and resurrection. We presume that there is both continuity and identity between these stages, between the Jesus of history and the written Scriptures. The Scriptures faithfully and truthfully express or record the disciples' experience of the Jesus of history and his words and deeds. This is simply a rejection of the position that the early church invented what it has recorded. This requires a careful examination to avoid a simplistic reading of the Scriptures. It requires an understanding of the conceptual development that has taken place both in the oral tradition as well as the written tradition.

In our examination of Scripture and tradition we propose to remain faithful to the faith convictions expressed by the church, most especially the definitions of the Council of Chalcedon. We accept what has been proposed for our belief. This is always in our minds even when we are searching for the ground of that faith. We will often attempt to get behind the faith expressions, to discover the experience of the early disciples of these events. This is an effort to ground the faith in history and experience. There will also be a serious attempt to remain faithful to the theological tradition which followed and has been a treasure of the church for centuries. It is also important to establish and maintain the context in which the scriptural events narrating Jesus' life take place. There is no intention whatsoever to replace the Jesus of the Gospels with the Jesus of history. No new Christ can ever be expected, and no rewriting of the Scriptures will be attempted. Our goals will serve the gospel picture of Jesus and our faith in him.

---

40. What is often narrated as a fight between Jesus and the Pharisees, Sadducees, and scribes is often an early church conflict with what is described as the synagogue. There can also be found a few examples of historicizing events (Luke does this with the event following the resurrection) and the addition of theologoumenon (Matthew and Luke do this in the infancy narratives). Historicizing is to narrate something as appearing to be historical when it is not. Theologoumenon is defined and explained in chapter 3, 48n9.

INTRODUCTION: OUR GOALS

What Does This Study Hope to Accomplish?

The presuppositions noted above point to several objectives that we want to accomplish. These are significant since they determine the goal or purpose of this text. Four are enumerated here.

The first goal of this study is to continue the assimilation of the contemporary biblical data into the christological reflections. This is something that was not available in past theological efforts. Biblical studies have greatly advanced since the promulgation of *Divino Afflante Spiritu* by Pope Pius XII in 1947.[41] We understand that we are now in the position to assimilate a large body of biblical scholarship into systematic theology. To this point in time, theology, and therefore Christology, has not yet entirely assimilated it. In fact, it is only in its beginning stages.

Our second goal is to explore the Scriptures for whatever might deepen and ground our understanding of Jesus as historical. We want to create a fresh look at Jesus of Nazareth from the perspective of faith and recent scholarship. We are going to apprehend as much of the Jesus of history as possible which we distinguish from the Christ of faith. It seems clear that in our study we are sometimes concerned with the historical and authentic Jesus; at other times we are concerned with what the Scriptures narrate about him. There is a consistency between what Scripture proposes and what Jesus taught and did. The discovery of the Jesus of history, what can be attributed to him with some historical authenticity, will prevent us from interpreting Scripture in a way that is not faithful to his actual ministry. Meier makes an important distinction that will govern the effort of this study. He says, "In my opinion, there is certainly a place for a Christology that is historically informed, that seeks to absorb and integrate the quest for the historical Jesus into its understanding of the faith."[42] In the footnote to this quote Meier continues by saying, "I consider this book [*A Marginal Jew*] not an example of the quest of the historical Jesus as such, but rather a prime example of how one goes about appropriating results of the quest for a larger theological/Christological project."[43] This is support for a Christology that is historically founded. I

---

41. The Pontifical Biblical Commission's *Instruction Concerning the Historical Truth of the Gospels* (April 21, 1964) was tantamount to give full emancipation to Catholic biblical scholars. It is clear that this was influential in the development of the historical-critical method. An English translation can be found in Fitzmyer, *Theological Studies* 25.3 (1964) 402–8.

42. Meier, *Marginal Jew*, 4: 6.

43. Meier, *Marginal Jew*, 4:23n17. Meier favorably mentions two scholars who are

agree totally with this sentiment, and it defines one of the principal goals of this study. We are searching for the historical Jesus that underpins our faith statements.[44] It should be noted that it is only in recent times that this search would have been available to us. We are confident that it will yield considerable illumination of our chosen subject. This study depends heavily upon the work of John P. Meier.

The dogmatic statement of Chalcedon proclaimed that Jesus was a true, integral man. It intended to stress the human nature of Jesus. Irenaeus saw Jesus as bringing together in his very being that which was important to humans. He says that "the glory of God is a living man; and the life of man consists in beholding God."[45] Leo the Great was the principal architect of the Council of Chalcedon and speaks eloquently of Jesus' humanity.[46] The medieval theologians also addressed the human nature of Jesus.[47] Vatican Council II, in its Pastoral Constitution, *The Church in the Modern World*, spoke of Jesus as the perfect man. It declares that he, in his human nature, "fully reveals man to himself."[48] The church has always focused on Jesus as fully human.[49] Jesus is often spoken of as the human face of God. He should also be recognized as the true face of humanity. Jesus, in his humanity, tells us what it is to be a human being.[50] The human nature of Jesus Christ relates to our human nature. In this regard our study is not only about Jesus as a

---

in line with this project: N. T. Wright, *Jesus and the Victory of God*, and James D. G. Dunn, *Jesus Remembered*.

44. It is important to understand the relation between Scripture (faith) and the historical. We might consider Scripture in large measure as the poetical expression of faith. Aristotle tells us that "poetry is a more philosophical and serious business than history: for poetry speaks more of universals, history of particulars." Aristotle, *Poetics*, 33. We conclude that the truths of faith are contained in Scripture. But the historical provides us a base for the poetry of Scripture.

45. Roberts et al., *Apostolic Fathers*, 490.

46. Leo I, *Letters and Sermons*, 128–43, 165–81.

47. Jesus was often referred to as a *perfect man* in past theological discussions. This was true in the medieval discussion as well as with the scholastics of the early twentieth century. It appears clear that the older use of the term possessed a different connotation than does the contemporary use.

48. Flannery, *Gaudium et Spes*, nos. 22, 38.

49. This is not to deny that there are many who in their personal reflections are often more docetic or adoptionist than orthodox Christian teaching. Docetism is the position that emphasizes the divinity of Christ to the detriment of his humanity. Adoptionism is the position that understands Christ as human but not as divine. Both positions fail to do justice to the declarations of the councils.

50. Iranaeus saw him as summing this up.

man, but it is also, in a most profound sense, about what Jesus tells us about ourselves. Jesus reveals to us the true nature of a human being. His message is not simply a revelation from heaven abstracted from our human condition. Rather it addresses the deepest aspiration of our human existence and experience. This justifies the focus of this study on the human Jesus, the Jesus of history.

There is a second reason for our focus on the humanity of Jesus. Faith in Jesus affirms that he is the Christ, the Son of God. Nevertheless, there is an inclination or a temptation to understand Jesus' teaching as unique, as coming directly from God.[51] Our faith in Jesus as the Son of God should not be a justification to deny that revelation in general comes to us through intermediaries, both human and natural events. As a human, we must understand him as finite, limited, and free.[52] He shaped his vision of the kingdom from his personal human experience.[53] A focus on his humanity preserves us from Docetism, that is, an uncalled for dependence upon the divinity of Christ.

This study will not be undertaken in an ivory tower. Therefore our third goal will be to look for the consequences of the kingdom for contemporary life. In anticipation of this future discussion, we will show that the kingdom of God, central to Jesus' preaching, is not only a future reality but is also present, here and now. Jesus taught an ethics or moral behavior required for participation in the kingdom. The Christian life in the world is based on this. It is what is meant by living in the presence of God. Jesus also addressed the human condition. This speaks to the society in which we live, in our cultural surroundings. Presuming that the kingdom is present, we shape our environment (political, social, cultural, etc.) to account for the presence of God. In other words, Christians are committed to shaping the world to match their faith vision. This is another way of speaking of the kingdom as partial in the world. Jesus did not in fact directly preach for social changes. But it may be implied in God's rule. Consider the narrative in the Gospel of Matthew (25:31–46) in which all will be judged. The early Christians responded

---

51. Jesus is a unique person and his relationship to his Father is unique. Nevertheless, he chose the means in which his mission would be accomplished. That is the nature of human freedom.

52. As will be pointed out later, in his humanity, Jesus did not exhaust the God question. He may be unique, but he does not exhaust everything that is revealed about God.

53. There is a delicate balance between the human Jesus acting as a human and the influence of grace, which does not exclude full and true human activity.

in a positive way in helping their neighbors as individuals in need. It took a long time to see this articulated in terms of social structures. This development will certainly be a part of the explorations below. In any case, Jesus calls upon his disciples to live an ethical life in order to fulfill the requirement of belonging to the kingdom of God.

Finally, our fourth and principal goal is to begin a personal Christology. As has been mentioned in the preface, this project is aimed at the interested beginner, the neophyte theologian, as well as for those educated readers who search for a deeper understanding of Jesus of Nazareth. No attempt is made to disguise the difficulty awaiting someone who is willing to accept the challenge. Nevertheless, the intention of this study is to provide the reader with resources and references for personal study. It is to provide a road map for in-depth study and the formation of a personal Christology. This is foundational to a fully formed Christology. This is not an attempt to give the last word on our subject but rather a good first word, a good foundation for further development and growth. The purpose of this study is to uncover Jesus as he was experienced in his own time and translate that understanding in a contemporary context. This is propaedeutic to any future Christology.

1

Images of Jesus in the Gospels

Introduction

FOR 1,500 YEARS CHRISTOLOGY focused principally on the results of the Council of Chalcedon (AD 453). This was certainly appropriate, and we all benefited from the discussion of the divine and human in Jesus Christ. It is foundational to our faith. In the middle of the twentieth century a Copernican shift occurred. The 1,500th anniversary of the Council of Chalcedon (1953) ushered in a new way of researching Christology.[1] While not neglecting the results of the council, theologians began to focus on many areas of the life of Jesus that were not discussed at the council and were often neglected in later centuries. This led to a plethora of books and articles which proved to be a great enrichment of past Christology. It seems clear in hindsight that this development was based on a new emphasis on biblical studies within the Catholic community. In 1943, ten years prior to the anniversary of the Council of Chalcedon, the church was blessed with the publication of the encyclical letter *Divino Afflante Spiritu,* now recognized as the Magna Carta of Catholic biblical studies. Theology is still in the process of assimilating the results of this new approach to biblical studies. Another significant

---

1. Much of this history was discussed in the preface. The council resolved an earlier question about whether Mary should be referred to as *theotokos*, that is, the mother of God. The substance of the council's declaration is that Jesus Christ is truly God and truly man. He possesses both natures united in one person. What the council declared is absolutely central to the Christian faith. Our task is to theologically develop much of what it did not address.

event assisted the promotion of this scholarship. Vatican Council II commenced on October 11, 1962. Its impact on Catholic life in general and Catholic theology in particular cannot be underestimated. Theologians became enthused to address the world visualizing Jesus' place in it in a new way. These three events were joined by another that had a profound impact on the way in which theology and Christology is now done. The development of the most recent phase of the historical-critical method yielded significant results for the study of the Bible in general and of Jesus of Nazareth in particular. We have somewhat arbitrarily set the date for this event as around 1970.[2]

This far-too-brief history is given here to introduce the reader to the examination of our sources, the Scriptures. Recent scriptural studies have provided contemporary Christology with an opportunity to reflect anew on the person of Jesus Christ. The past seventy years have shown that there is more to be discussed than the results of the Council of Chalcedon, important as they are. During this time scripture scholars have given us a more profound understanding of the Scriptures. This will help us as we search for a deeper understanding of Jesus in the following chapters.

The Sources for Our Study

The historical sources used to establish the Jesus of history are very limited. Yet, we have more information about Jesus than we do any other figure of the ancient world.[3] The references to Jesus are found both from within and without Christianity. Nevertheless, useful sources are limited in number.

---

2. There were three phases to this development of the historical-critical method: phase one occurred in the nineteenth century and ended at the beginning of the twentieth; phase two began with Bultmann. It continued and developed largely by the work of his students who found themselves uneasy with the results of their teacher. The third and most recent phase began in the 1970s and the results have proven most felicitous for both biblical scholarship and theology in general. Raymond Brown situates this closer to 1980. The actual date is of little consequence to the point made here.

3. See Meier, *Marginal Jew*, 1:196–200.

Secular and Noncanonical Sources

Some of the more important secular writers of the ancient world who make some reference to Christ or Christians are Pliny the Younger, Lucian, Suetonius, Tacitus, and Josephus.[4] The first three give us little useful information. They simply report someone else's witness to the fact of Jesus' existence. Josephus wrote somewhere at the end of the first century.[5] John Meier claims that there are only a few salient facts about Jesus in the works of Josephus and he rejects his works as a source for a history of Jesus.[6] He says, "With Josephus and Tacitus we exhaust the early independent witnesses to Jesus' existence, ministry, death, and ongoing influence."[7] John Dominic Crossan is less critical of some of these sources than Meier. He believes they can be helpful to create what he calls trajectories to help reconstruct the earlier period in which Jesus lived. This is a useful technique, but it is more concerned with describing the sociological context than with describing Jesus the Nazarene. Crossan sees similarities between peasants living at any stage of human history. Codes of honor and shame are similar in any age. While this understanding has merit, it does not go directly to discerning the Jesus of history. For one thing, as will be pointed out in chapter 3, Jesus was a *tektōn*, a woodworker.[8] Some describe his coming from a peasant artisan family.

Crossan also proposes his theory of the Cross-Gospel, which stands behind the passion narratives of Mark and those upon which Matthew, Luke, and John (supposedly) depend. Meier rejects this theory on Crossan's own principle: "The simplest theory that explains the most data is to be preferred."[9] Meier finds Crossan's theory very complicated and sometimes self-contradictory. Such complexity is not necessary, he thinks, to explain the origin of the sources for the canonical Gospels. "There was no period when individual bits of tradition about Jesus floated about in a church bereft of the larger grid that the life, death, and resurrection of Jesus provided."[10]

---

4. See Bettenson and Maunder, *Documents of the Christian Church*, and Barrett, *New Testament Background*.

5. *The Antiquities of the Jews* was written around AD 93–94.

6. Meier, *Marginal Jew*, 1:68.

7. Meier, *Marginal Jew*, 1:89.

8. Brown, *Introduction to the New Testament*, 67.

9. Meier, *Marginal Jew*, 1:116.

10. Meier, *Marginal Jew*, 1:118.

Meier also rejects Crossan's theory because of the use of the apocryphal gospels to support it. In Meier's judgment, the apocryphal gospels postdate the canonical Gospels and therefore can offer little in our search for the historical Jesus. Furthermore, many of the apocryphal gospels are gnostic texts. This philosophy is not consistent with what we know of Jesus' teaching.[11] Crossan relies upon the apocryphal Gospel of Peter in his Cross-Gospel theory. The difficulty is that most scholars place this apocryphal gospel after the canonical Gospels. The same can be said of the Secret Gospel of Mark and the Gospel of Thomas.[12] Their composition is too late to be useful from a historical perspective. Meier believes that apocryphal gospels are dependent upon other sources; therefore, they are rejected for purposes of history. Crossan, on the other hand and contrary to most exegetes, believes that the Gospel of Thomas predates the canonical Gospels and that it forms a cornerstone for much of the hypothesis he proposes. Correctly dating this and other apocryphal documents is critical for this discussion. Such material as the Gospel of Thomas and other apocryphal gospels, rabbinical material, agrapha (sayings of Jesus that are not found in the canonical Gospels), are not totally abandoned by Meier but they should be used as a check on the canonical Gospels and not as an historical source.

In this very sketchy description of the noncanonical sources, one can see some major disagreements that will in some small way influence the results of the search for the Jesus of history.

---

11. Gnosticism is not a unified philosophical system; therefore, we must use caution in our judgments about it. Nevertheless, there is some commonality found in its various manifestations. Gnosticism incorporated fragments of Christianity into its philosophical structure in the second century. It proposed a personal spiritual knowledge (gnosis) for its adherents in opposition to the communal, authoritative teaching of the church. It proposed a supreme god who was independent of the material universe which was created by a lesser divinity (a malevolent god). It understood that the material world and matter was evil. Because of this, Gnosticism demanded absolute sexual continence of its adherents. This brought it into conflict with the early church's understanding of the incarnation as well as its understanding of marriage. Both gnostic cosmology and theology was rejected by earlier Christians as being incompatible with a faith in Jesus Christ.

12. There is no extant copy of the putative Secret Gospel of Mark. It is of no historical value to us.

The Canonical Writings.

While the secular and noncanonical writings do not provide us with useful information in our search for the Jesus of history, the same cannot be said of the canonical Scriptures. While the Hebrew Scriptures say nothing of Jesus directly, they do provide us with background. As we proceed, their importance will become clear. Jesus was immersed in the Jewish tradition and its Scriptures. Our principal source to establish the Jesus of history, however, is the New Testament. While this appears obvious, even here we are limited. Saint Paul's authentic Epistles and the writings other than the four Gospels provide us with a great deal of the community understanding and faith statements of the early church. Their use for our historical search is useful but limited.

The only writings with significant historical data for the life of Jesus are the canonical Gospels. There is little in the other writings of the Scriptures with historical value. Though the authentic Epistles of Paul predate the Gospels, he was not an eyewitness to Jesus' activity, nor does he refer to Jesus from an historical perspective.[13] The Gospels are not history as we commonly understand it. They are faith documents written for a faith community. They are the lived memory of the person of Jesus Christ as seen through the eyes of believers. We need to distinguish the evangelist's polemical or literary editing from the record of the historical Jesus. We acknowledge that there are a number of scriptural passages for which our criteria are insufficient to establish their historicity. We will deal more carefully with the sayings of Jesus that are problematic and explore those which have a better chance of being historically authentic. We will ground our reading of Jesus' words and deeds to the degree that we are able. We remind ourselves of the difficulty of this task. At best, we can be satisfied with a high degree of probability that we can establish the historicity of Jesus' sayings, his parables, his miracles, and

---

13. Paul wrote his authentic Epistles between AD 50 and 60; The Deutero-Pauline Epistles are given a range of composition from AD 70 to 100; the Pastoral Epistles were composed somewhere around AD 100; the Gospel of Mark was written around AD 70; Matthew and Luke were composed around AD 80; the Gospel of John is thought to have been redacted about AD 90 or even later. The earliest book of the New Testament, 1 Thessalonians, was composed around AD 50 and the earliest Gospel account of Jesus was about AD 70. This is to remind ourselves that we are not dealing with first-hand accounts of Jesus' life. One can understand that the apocryphal gospels, normally considered to have been written in the second century or later, would not be good sources for discovering the Jesus of history.

other deeds.[14] We will use proven criteria to accomplish this.[15] And we will point out the contribution of the primitive church whenever we can differentiate it from authentic Jesus material.[16]

We will attempt to gather and identify as much of Jesus' history, his authentic words and deeds, as we are able.[17] We do this for two significant reasons. First, as has been mentioned earlier in this study, discovering the historical Jesus prevents us from imposing our own thoughts and presuppositions into the biblical story.[18] We cannot turn Jesus into an empty cipher by making him say and do what we want him to.[19] Equally important is our recognition that the historical Jesus will serve as a very convenient and practical interpretive tool in our examination of the Scriptures. It will give us another way of reading the scriptural accounts of Jesus' life, death and resurrection as described by the evangelists that will be more authentic and truthful.[20]

The development of the Gospel sources follows the path from Jesus earthly life, death, and resurrection to the oral tradition that developed after the disciples' experienced Jesus raised from the dead, until finally the written tradition came into existence. The Gospels are written to explain the *meaning* of Jesus for the faithful. They are also

---

14. Meier, *Marginal Jew*, 2:413.

15. These criteria are articulated in chapter 2. They are worth careful study.

16. With this in mind we remain mindful that all Scripture, not simply what can be determined to belong to the historical Jesus, is revealed truth. Whatever can be established as most probably authentic can assist us in our understanding of the entire scriptural accounts of Jesus' mission and ministry.

17. The principal sources for this are the four Gospels, that is, the inspired record of the life, death, and resurrection of Jesus Christ. The other writings of the Scriptures will not be entirely neglected in our search. We are attempting to establish the words and deeds that can actually be identified as coming from Jesus and not those attributable to the evangelists or other editors. That is not to denigrate parts of the Gospel or any part of the Christian Scripture. The words and deeds of Jesus, the historicity of which cannot be reliably established, are of no less value to us than those whose historical authenticity can be established.

18. Our attempt is to obtain a sound, solid exegesis of the text and thus we avoid every temptation to engage in eisegesis. By eisegesis we mean an interpretation of the biblical text by reading our own ideas into it.

19. Meier raises this issue in several places in his work. Reading one's personal philosophy into the scriptural accounts was the accusation against the earlier eighteenth-century life-of-Jesus movement.

20. Meier will serve as our primary source for discovering the historical Jesus. We have chosen to be as faithful to his outstanding contribution to the search for the historical Jesus in *A Marginal Jew*.

addressed to a particular community in a Hellenistic environment, and reflect the religious needs of the communities. They cannot be expected to recount the words and deeds of Jesus and his contemporaries in a purely historical fashion.

Summary on the Sources[21]

There is scarcely any source outside the canonical New Testament that helps us in our pursuit of the Jesus of history.[22] The canonical Gospels alone offer large blocks of material for our study. The remaining books of the New Testament, including the Pauline corpus, offer little useful information. The only independent non-Christian source is Josephus, and he once again offers very little. Tacitus reports that Jesus Christ was executed by Pontius Pilate during the reign of Tiberius. Rabbinic material, the agrapha (sayings of Jesus that are not found in the canonical Gospels), the apocryphal gospels, and the documents from Nag Hammadi do not offer reliable historical material regarding Jesus.[23]

The Proper Understanding of Our Sources

As has been stated above, the Gospels are very important, but they are not the only source for the study of Christology. Catholics understand that tradition, such as the sacraments and liturgical practices, often supplies us with the hermeneutical tools to better understand the written revelation.[24] The Gospels, however, will provide us with a basis for dis-

---

21. See Meier, *Marginal Jew*, 1:139–141.

22. Crossan does not share this view.

23. We often hear of the newfound gnostic gospels (Nag Hammadi, Egypt, 1945) as being sources which give us more information about the Jesus of history. Sanders refers to these apocryphal gospels as legendary and mythical. See Sanders, *Historical Figure of Jesus*, 64. As we mentioned earlier, Meier believes that the apocryphal gospels are too late to be of significant use in determining anything about the Jesus of history.

24. The members of the Abbey of Saint Victor in Paris, commonly known as the Victorines, taught at the University of Paris in the twelfth century. The most famous Victorines were Peter the Chanter (+1197), Peter Comestor (+1178), and Stephen Langston (+1228). The Victorines proposed that the liturgy was a lived tradition of that which is contained in the Scriptures. They were the first to propose the liturgy as an exegetical tool for the Bible. It is of some interest to note that in 1227, as archbishop of Canterbury, Stephen Langston introduced the current chapters to the Bible.

covering the way Jesus was understood both by his contemporaries as well as the disciples who survived his death and resurrection.

The Gospels as Sources for the Study of Christology

The Gospels are the appropriate place to discover what belongs to the Jesus of history.[25] They are not the only source regarding our understanding of Jesus as the Christ, but they are a privileged place in general and the proper place for a historical inquiry.[26] The Epistles of Paul are excellent christological sources. The notion of Christ as preexistent is presupposed throughout Paul's Epistles and he spends a great deal of time and effort supporting the central place of Christ in salvation history.[27] But our study will focus principally on the Gospels because their subject matter is Jesus as experienced by his first disciples.[28]

A word of clarification is needed about the Gospels as sources. The Gospel of Mark is an independent written source. We have come to understand that the Gospels of Matthew and Luke are dependent upon the Gospel of Mark therefore much of what they wrote is not an independent source. The Gospel of John is also an independent written source. Besides these independent sources, both Matthew and Luke share another common source (apart from their main reliance on Mark) which is referred to as Q (*quelle*).[29] Both Matthew and Luke possess material proper to each of them, but not contained in any other Gospel. We refer to these as "Special Matthew" and "Special Luke" as a way of identifying them. This study will refer to them as M and L.

---

25. This expression, *the Jesus of history*, will be examined in itself and distinguished from other similar expressions in chapter 2. Throughout this study, when we use the name Jesus, we are referring to the Jesus of history.

26. Even though we will attempt to discover history, we are not able to determine a chronology of events in the life of Jesus.

27. The most obvious references to the preexistence of Christ in the authentic Pauline Epistles are the hymns in Phil 2:6–11 and Col 1:15–20. Some dispute whether Colossians is an authentic Pauline Epistle, but it clearly testifies to the postresurrection belief in the preexistence of Christ. Other references are in Rom 8:29, 1 Cor 8:6, and 2 Cor 1:19. See Dunn, *Theology of Paul*, 265–93.

28. The distinction between the names Jesus and Jesus Christ was mentioned in the introduction, 3, and chapter 2, 34–35.

29. Q is a shorthand way of referring to the German *Quelle* which means source. This source (Q) is the material shared by the Gospels of Matthew and Luke and is not found elsewhere. It is speculated that this source was originally an oral tradition of the sayings of Jesus and was probably a written source as used by Matthew and Luke.

Thus, as we proceed with our examination we consider Mark, Q, M, L, and John all as independent sources. These designations will be used throughout this text, and the distinction between these independent sources will become clear as we proceed. Needless to say, we will also discover numerous distinct literary genres within these sources.

The Gospels are Christologies[30]

The four Gospels are not merely sources of Christology, but they are themselves Christologies. Each evangelist has reflected upon the life of Jesus as he received it and formed a distinctive Christology according to the context in which the Gospel developed. This is the very reason for four Gospels. To clarify this notion of the Gospels as Christologies, refer to the definition of Christology already proposed.[31]

The Gospels give us the possibility of examining the historical life of Jesus so that we may attain an understanding of how the community moved from its particular experience of Jesus during his lifetime to its understanding and expression of him as the Christ after his death and resurrection. While the Epistles and other canonical sources contain important christological statements, they do not assist us in understanding their development. Therefore, we will put our emphasis on the Gospel stories which yield four distinct Christologies, or four distinct views of Jesus as the Christ.[32]

These Gospels were reflected on by the early church in its own proper context, and it was not until much later that the church formulated the normative statements of the Creeds.[33] As an interpretive adjunct to the Gospels, we will pay special attention to the lived practice and tradition of the church. It will prove invaluable as a source for our study.

---

30. When we reflect upon the nature of our data, the New Testament, we discover that there are two beginnings: the historical and the theological. Much of the New Testament is already an interpretation of the life and death of Jesus, that is, a theological reflection upon those events that the earliest disciples perceived as most important in the life of Jesus. And this reflection came about in its fullest only after they had experienced the risen Lord. It was only after this event, and in terms of this event, that they understood both Christ's life and death.

31. Earlier in the introduction we gave the following definition: Christology is the process of interpreting our faith experience of God through Jesus Christ.

32. Compare this to four siblings each of whom has a particular view or memory of a parent. There are likely differing Christologies within each Gospel.

33. These normative creedal statements came about in the fourth and fifth centuries.

The Composition of the Gospels

In understanding the Scriptures, principally the Gospels, as sources for the study of Christology we need to be aware of the manner in which they were composed. As has already been alluded to, the Gospels have an interesting history. Before the development of their written form a significant time transpired accompanied by considerable reflection on the events of Jesus' life.[34] The oral tradition and the gathering of oral and written materials finally gave way to a written form of the Gospels. This development occurred in particular social, political, and cultural situations. Each Gospel has its own history and context, that is, each reflects not only the story of Jesus but also something of the community situation and its response to that story. Therefore, we need to pay attention to several questions.

What in the Gospels belongs to the Jesus of history?[35] Can we discover it? Contemporary Scripture scholarship seems more inclined presently to affirm that we can discover significant information about the Jesus of history and with some degree of historical certitude. It believes that we are able to discover his authentic teaching and praxis.

Similarly, what in the Gospels serve as an authentic reflection or interpretation of the community of believers who experienced Jesus during his lifetime and came to call him the Christ, the Son of God? Are there any retrojections of the primitive community into the life of Christ as it is recorded in the Gospels? It seems clear that some Gospel texts do go back to Jesus as their immediate source and are authentic Jesus statements. Others are communal reflections that are postresurrection but are authentic memories.

Stages of Development of the Gospels[36]

Between Jesus' public ministry and the formation of the New Testament writings there were three distinct contexts or stages that must be accounted for in this reflection.[37] The recognition and study of these

---

34. These written traditions were given above as Mark, John, the Q source, Special Matthew (M), and Special Luke (L). These designations will be used throughout this text.

35. See Sanders, *Historical Figure of Jesus*, and Meier, *Marginal Jew*.

36. See Brown, *Introduction to the New Testament*, 107–11.

37. In his *A Marginal Jew*, 1:167–84, 619–31, Meier notes that there are three stages

stages has proven important in coming to a better understanding of our search for the Jesus of history in our study of the Scriptures. We distinguish these stages as follows. The public ministry of Jesus is the first stage. Jesus of Nazareth lived in a specific historical context or environment. During his public ministry he gathered followers, and he preached the kingdom of God. He invited those to whom he preached to share in table fellowship (his festive meals), and he worked his marvelous deeds in their presence. During this stage, the community experienced him as he proclaimed the kingdom of God. They were witnesses to his mission, to his words, and deeds. What is important is that the first stage forms the foundation for the other two. Jesus' public ministry constituted the living memory of all that the primitive community had experienced. This public ministry, briefly considered above, came to an end with Jesus' death. This is the basis of the community's preaching of Jesus as the Christ after his death and resurrection.

The second stage is the period following Jesus' death and resurrection. The community began to preach Jesus of Nazareth, the historical Jesus, as the Christ, the Messiah.[38] Other christological titles were also attributed to Jesus as recognition that he was the expected Savior. The images found in the Gospels were shaped by the context in which they developed. It was during the oral tradition that the story of Jesus was told. This was a shift from Jesus' own preaching, for he did not preach himself as Christ but rather preached the kingdom of God. The community of disciples identified Jesus with the kingdom. We presuppose continuity or identity between the Jesus who was preacher and the Jesus who was preached.

The oral tradition lasted for an extended period of time and was followed by the collection of stories, anecdotes, sayings, and parables which were crafted into the four Gospels.[39] These began to be written

---

of development. Stage I (AD 28–30), the life of Jesus; stage II (AD 30–70), the oral tradition of the early Church; and stage III (AD 70–100), the redaction of the sources by the evangelists. This is further developed in another place in these notes. See also Fitzmyer, *Christological Catechism*, 24–26. This is a very clear and easily read description of the three stages.

38. The names Jesus and Christ were discussed in the introduction. The name Jesus refers to the man from Nazareth. It is how his neighbors would have recognized him. Christ is a christological title affirmed of him. It recognized Jesus as the anointed one, the Messiah. These distinctions are important for our study.

39. Note that the authentic Epistles of Paul were all composed prior to his death in AD 66. Mark, the first Gospel, was not composed until AD 70.

by the community in an effort to these precious memories. The passion narrative was the first written stage of the Gospels. The second stage, the ministry of Jesus, was appended to the passion narrative. It was grounded in the collective memories of the community. The following stages were composed of the resurrection narrative and the infancy narrative.[40] The Gospel images of Jesus were influenced by the situation or context of each community for whom the particular Gospel was written.

The Christian Scriptures take shape in the third stage. The oral material expressing Jesus' words and deeds from the preceding stage was collected and formed the basis for the written Scriptures. The church preaching of Jesus as the Christ (second stage) and the later written expression of it (third stage) must be carefully distinguished. Even more importantly, we must be mindful that the first and third stages are not identical. A common mistake is to reduce the Gospels to a series of snapshots of Jesus' history. However, the Gospels are the written reflection and interpretation of the experience of God through Jesus Christ. They are history, but they are an interpreted history. As such, there is not a one-to-one congruence between the Jesus of history and the written reflection of his first century followers. A conceptual development took place, one that expresses more fully the content of the Christian community's faith in Jesus while remaining faithful to the original experience of the Jesus of history. Recognizing this is important because the Jesus of history is the foundation of the experience of the disciples. It is this faith experience of those who knew the Jesus of history that forms Scripture and tradition. We presuppose that there is continuity between these stages. This brief study will examine them more carefully.[41]

Several Presuppositions about Our Sources

As we begin our examination of the Gospels to uncover the data for our Christology, it is necessary to clarify a number of presuppositions regarding the text. They are as follows:

---

40. See Fitzmyer, *Gospel According to Luke*, 1:305. Fitzmyer has more to say about this in 2:1533. He refers to the infancy narrative, the passion narrative, and the resurrection narrative as subforms of the literary genre gospel.

41. We presuppose that this development continues to the present time. We continue to reflect upon our sources and interpret Jesus for our own time. We do this to make the life of Jesus accessible to contemporary men and women.

IMAGES OF JESUS IN THE GOSPELS

Continuity Between History and the Written Text

Preservation of continuity in the data between the Jesus of history and the Jesus expressed in the Gospels (motivated by faith or belief) is presumed. If there is no continuity between Jesus of Nazareth and the written word about him after his death, there is no reason to proceed further.[42] This means that the trustworthiness of the text is accepted as a given. The community, in expressing its belief about Jesus as the Christ, is not inventing or creating anything that is not conceptually identical with him in his public life. It has correctly identified him.[43] There is always the theoretical possibility that the community was mistaken, that its faith in Jesus was misplaced. While present-day Christians trust the primitive community and its expression of the meaning of the person and work of Jesus Christ, the nature of the evidence is not immediately and automatically compelling. It can be empirically denied. It can only be accepted in faith. The primitive community is describing and interpreting its experiences of Jesus through the eyes of faith.

When compared to one another, the Gospels reflect a difference in the description of Jesus in his ministry. This should come as no surprise. By way of explanation, all of us know someone well enough to describe him or her reasonably well. And if we are accurate and truthful, we will describe that person correctly. But we won't describe that person exactly as someone else will. Parents, grandparents, siblings, and relatives will all see a particular family member differently and truthfully. Several descriptions can differ and still be accurate. This is somewhat akin to the way siblings remember parents or as family members remember a special occasion. Each person has his or her own understanding of the event even though the event is identical for all. Differing expressions are not a falsification of the event. They simply point to the richness of an event that a single description alone can never accurately or adequately capture.

---

42. This does not mean that there is no difficulty in acquiring the historical underpinnings of the faith statements.

43. This does not deny that some pericopes were actually created by the evangelist. For example, the Golden Rule (Matt 7:12) was the handy work of Matthew. The parable of the good samaritan (Luke 10:25–37) is thought to be the creation of Luke. This sort of editing by the evangelist will be addressed later.

The New Testament Contains a Plurality of Faces of Jesus

The New Testament does not contain a single, unified, simple image of Jesus. It contains many differing images of him. Each evangelist has his particular understanding and interpretation of the Christ event.[44] We recognize that the primitive communities expressed their belief in Jesus according to their particular situation and circumstances. The attempt to make a unified Christology is impossible because that was never the original objective or intention of the evangelists. The practice of attempting to harmonize these differences has been replaced largely by interpreting them. We are better served by attempting to understand their theological purpose in expressing the faith statements about Jesus. We do so by offering a theological reason, that is, we explain the tradition by a hypothesis. We attempt to discover the meaning intended by the author.

Conclusion

We have now examined how our sources (the Gospels) developed. It is imperative that we have this information foremost in our mind as we proceed, because without it our reading of the sources would be extremely superficial.

This study will now focus on the major sources for discovering the Jesus who was affirmed by the Christian faith as the Christ. Traditionally these sources would mean the Scriptures and tradition, but we will focus on the four Gospels. Our intention is not to slight the other canonical sources, especially the authentic Pauline Epistles. However, the Epistles of Paul are simply not good sources for discovering the Jesus of history. They are only moderately useful for establishing Jesus' authentic teaching. The person of Christ is central to Paul's authentic Epistles. However, the "Jesus of history" plays an insignificant role in his Epistles. There is scant reference to the preaching and praxis (words and works) of Jesus' earthly life. The other New Testament letters, the Acts of the Apostles and the Apocalypse (Revelation), do not contain much in the way of Jesus' earthly ministry. The Gospels alone contain the bulk of Jesus' preaching and healing and the formation of his close disciples. The theology expressed in the other canonical sources, however, is important and will be incorporated into our study as we proceed as they are needed.

---

44. Each evangelist writes from his own perspective. Mark describes Jesus as a healer. Jesus is also the suffering servant. Matthew describes Jesus as a Jew within the Jewish tradition. Jesus is the new lawgiver. Luke describes Jesus as the social justice prophet. John writes from a high Christology. Jesus is the Word of God; he is Wisdom.

2

The Search for the Jesus of History

Introduction

WE ARE NOW IN a position to explore the principal subject matter of this work. First, however, we must distinguish between the name Jesus with reference to a historical figure and the name Christ which designates Jesus as the object of faith.[1] The proper name Jesus designates his human nature. We are referring to the man known as Jesus of Nazareth.

The origin of the name Jesus is *Yesu* (Aramaic), which is derived from *Yehoshua*, the Hebrew for Joshua.[2] The name means *Yahweh Helps*, but popular etymology claims it to mean *May Yahweh Save*, or *Yahweh Saves*. It was a common name during Jesus' lifetime, which explains the scriptural use of *the Nazarene* as a means to identify and distinguish him from others. The name became less popular in the century following Jesus' death.

Christ is the English equivalent of *Christos* (Greek) or *Christus* (Latin). The origin of this designation is *mashiach* (anointed one) and it is frequently used in the Hebrew Bible. The English translation is *messiah*, which refers to someone, such as the king or priest, who was consecrated or designated for a particular role by an anointing.[3]

---

1. See Meier, *Marginal Jew*, 1:205–207.

2. The origin of the English name Jesus is derived from the Latin *Iesus*, which in turn is derived from the Greek *Iesous*.

3. This most important title for Jesus, the Christ, takes on the character of a proper name. This occurs very early in the history of Christianity.

The historical Jesus is a scholarly construct which requires a critical reading of the Gospel text by employing modern criteria. We presuppose that this is possible and that there is continuity between the disciples' historical experience of Jesus of Nazareth and the written record of the early church designating him as the Christ. This search for the Jesus of history will not neglect the faith expression or affirmation of the Scriptures. The reader should know in advance that this study is heavily dependent upon John P. Meier and his magnum opus *A Marginal Jew*. He is foundational in the search for the Jesus of history and all that can be attributed to him as authentic.

The Significance of the Jesus of History

The search for the historical Jesus has a long and fascinating history, but has achieved limited success. In spite of this checkered academic history, contemporary biblical scholars express optimism that the Jesus of history is accessible from our sources. There is confidence that with the correct employment of the historical-critical method we can achieve more acceptable results than in the recent past. This optimism is justified.

The Jesus of History Explained

How should we understand the expression the *Jesus of history*? We will proceed by way of negation and begin by excluding what we do not mean. Then we will clarify the expression as it should be understood in this study. We will address three general portraits of Jesus and explain our choice for accepting or rejecting them.

The Jesus of history is not identified with what might be referred to as the *real Jesus*[4] or the *actual Jesus*.[5] The terms real and actual in this context are synonyms; they express the same idea. Brown describes the actual Jesus as everything of interest to us. It would include his height, hair color, and his daily activities such as work and hobbies. Realistically there are simply insufficient sources available to arrive at such a description. No modern-day biography is possible.[6] The real or actual Jesus of history is lost to us forever and it is beyond recovery.

---

4. Meier, *Marginal Jew*, 1:21–24.
5. Brown, *Introduction to the New Testament*, 105.
6. There was an effort to do this with Luther, but it failed. See Erikson, *Young Man*

THE SEARCH FOR THE JESUS OF HISTORY

On the jacket of John Dominic Crossan's *The Historical Jesus*, he states that the historical Jesus reveals the *true Jesus*.[7] Precisely what this statement intended to convey is not clear. Should we identify the historical as the true?[8] The full understanding of this statement need not concern us. It should, however, caution us to make clear what we mean by history. The Jesus of faith is more than likely to be identified with the true Jesus, since it contains the meaning for those who believe. It is a mistake, however, to claim that the historical Jesus is the true Jesus, most especially since it is not a matter of truth but a hypothesis or a reconstruction from the scriptural data.

The term *earthly Jesus* is also employed by scholars, but this can also be misleading. Meier promised that he would not use it as a major category.[9] As faithful as tried to be to this promise he could not refrain from using the term completely and it slipped back into his vocabulary within twenty pages.[10] The difficulty in equating the earthly Jesus with the historical Jesus is because Jesus did not cease being completely earthly with his ascension. He did cease being historical with his ascension, however. The Jesus who ascended to the Father is the Jesus who continues to be present to us today. As described above, scholars have indicated that their search is for the actual Jesus or the real Jesus. Others have indicated that it is the true Jesus or the earthly Jesus. These explorations have proven quite impossible since we do not possess sources that will permit such a discovery. This vocabulary will not be employed in this study because it is either inadequate or misleading.

There are two expressions which will be employed frequently in this study: the *Jesus of the Gospels* and the *Jesus of history*. Both require an explanation.

Luther. Erickson believed that he could explain Luther's life by events that occurred in his early years. The biblical texts simply do not provide us with suitable material to write a biography. For the real or actual Jesus, the problem remains the same.

7. Crossan, *Historical Jesus*.

8. History is not facts but the interpretation of (historical) facts. It requires the construction of a hypothesis or model, a theory. Aristotle thought that the poetic metaphor was closer to the truth than history. It was a matter of discovery and not the reconstruction of what might be. "Poetry," he says, "is a more philosophical and serious business than history: for poetry speaks more of universals, history of particulars." Aristotle, *Poetics*, 33.

9. Meier, *Marginal Jew*, 1:26. Meier discusses several of these important concepts on pages 21–31.

10. Meier, *Marginal Jew*, 1:45, 47.

The Gospel Jesus is the Jesus portrayed in the Scriptures.[11] They provide us with the authoritative evidence for our faith. We shall not forget this in our search. At times we will refer to the *Synoptic Jesus* or the *Johannine Jesus*. These evangelists have described Jesus from their personal perspective using the sources available to them. Needless to say, these portraits are the object of faith.

The Jesus of history is a scholarly construct dependent entirely on the Jesus described in the Scriptures. The expressions *the historical Jesus* and *the Jesus of history* are understood as identical in this work. Because of the challenges posed by the search for the historical Jesus and its failings, we will employ or at least prefer the expression *Jesus of history*. We hope that this will avoid any confusion with past efforts to discover the Jesus of history. The scholarly construct we are attempting to establish requires that we examine the foundation of the Gospels to recover the Jesus of history. The rules used to accomplish this will be articulated later in this chapter.

The Jesus of history is not to be equated with the Jesus of faith.[12] The expression refers to Jesus of Nazareth during his public ministry. The Jesus of history is arrived at by use of the historical-critical method, abstracting from all considerations of faith. Faith is intentionally bracketed in this quest but is not totally abandoned.[13]

The Jesus of history is that which we can retrieve from the available sources with a considerable degree of historical certainty. The canonical Scriptures, which are our major sources, were written from faith and therefore theologically suffused. Thus, they make the task of retrieving the Jesus of history a considerable challenge. However, Meier is very persuasive in his argument that there is more historical data available for Jesus than any other ancient figure.[14] That does not of itself mean that discovering the Jesus of history is an easy task. Even though there is optimism that a significant understanding of the Jesus of history can be acquired, agreement among scholars as to the results is far from assured.

---

11. This presupposes three stages of Gospel formation. See Brown, *Introduction to the New Testament*, 107. The development that takes place between the three stages is conceptual and continuity between them is presupposed.

12. John Meier, Raymond Brown, John Dominic Crossan, and E. P. Sanders all agree on this point. Nevertheless, the Jesus of history is the basis for the formation of our faith statements.

13. The Jesus of history is not the object of Christian faith. Meier, *Marginal Jew*, 1:197.

14. Meier, *Marginal Jew*, 1:196–200.

Our understanding of the Jesus of history is pre-theological, that is, it is what the historian or exegete can ascertain as having historical validity concerning Jesus of Nazareth. It does not mean, if we agree with the method articulated below, that this is all that can be affirmed about Jesus. It means that we can attain with a degree of certitude a historical understanding of Jesus of Nazareth. This is by no means insignificant. There is sufficient evidence to help us sketch a historical picture of Jesus that is both informative and useful to Christology. The reasons for this are articulated below.

The Importance of the Jesus of History for Christology[15]

Christology, as a part of theology, begins with the data of faith. Therefore, its primary interest is doctrinal not historical. However, that does not mean that Christology has no interest in the Jesus of history. How is the Jesus of history related to the Christ of faith? This is a major question that will be addressed but it seems obvious that the Jesus of history of necessity precedes faith in him. There is a significant relationship between the historical and the faith. We note the following: Christianity is a historical religion, and it has a historical founder. Its faith is rooted in the historical figure of Jesus of Nazareth. It was in this historical experience that the postresurrection primitive church was able to express its faith in its proclamation, its liturgical life, and its written Scriptures.

The nature of Christianity is such that it is not merely a belief system or a system of ideas. Christianity is an attachment to a person.[16] It is a way of life. It is the following of a historical personage, Jesus of Nazareth who, in faith, is proclaimed the Christ.

Furthermore, we are interested in Jesus' authentic praxis, what he actually did in his public life. We need to know the setting or context, the situation, and the Jewish culture, to understand the earliest Christian community's understanding and interpretation of Jesus.

Finally, Jesus has a present, historical importance to the life of the church. We consider him present to us now (although this presence is not historical in the literal meaning). It is experienced in the sacramental life of the church in which the presence of Christ is understood as more than

---

15. See Meier, *Marginal Jew*, 1:196–200. These thoughts are culled from Meier.

16. See the statement of Fr. Paré, OP, as well as those of recent popes in the introduction, 2.

a mere remembering. It is a real, actual presence here and now.[17] The understanding that Jesus is present to the community is rooted in the earliest consciousness of that community and it perdures to this very day.

These reasons suggest a sufficient motive for wanting to recover the Jesus of history from the Scriptures, our faith documents. Joachim Jeremias tells us that "we must go back to the historical Jesus and his message. We cannot bypass him."[18] It is not to deny the faith; it is to enrich it and to preserve it.[19]

The Historical-Critical Method

The inception of the historical-critical method came in the eighteenth century as a method to address the historicity of ancient documents in general. Until recently it has achieved mixed results for biblical studies.[20] Today, however, the method has developed to the point where scholars feel confident in what has been attained.

What methodologies or criteria are employed in the historical-critical method that permit us to recover something of Jesus of Nazareth? Meier has articulated the rules for the historical critical method extremely well.[21] He notes that there are three stages of development to consider. Stage I, the life of Jesus (AD 28–30); stage II, the oral tradition of the early church (AD 30–70); and stage III, the redaction of the sources by the evangelists (AD 70–100).[22] The question is this: How can

---

17. Some would argue that this presence is also found in the church's proclamation or evangelization.

18. Jeremias, *Problem of the Historical Jesus*, 12.

19. Meier suggests that he would be delighted if systematic theologians would pick up his search for the Jesus of history and continue with it in their speculations. Meier, *Marginal Jew*, 1:6. He tells us that "this entire work is, in a sense, a prolegomenon and an invitation to theologians to appropriate from this particular quest what may be useful to the larger task of a present-day Christology" (1:13–14). This present study is an acceptance of his invitation even though it must be considered as baby steps toward a full-blown Christology.

20. See Brown, *Introduction to the New Testament*, 817–30. This is an excellent overview and evaluation of the search for the historical Jesus.

21. Meier, *Marginal Jew*, 1:167–84. He repeats this list in each of the succeeding volumes. These "Rules of the Road," as he calls them, are a refresher on methodologies in 2:4–6, 619–31; 3:9–12; 4:11–17; and 5:8–21.

22. The other writings of the Scriptures (Acts of the Apostles, the Pauline Epistles, etc.) are not neglected; however, the Gospels are the foundational sources for the discovery of the Jesus of history.

we discern what came from each stage? Meier suggests both primary and secondary criteria.[23] As we shall see, these are easily understood and make eminently good sense.

Not all of the criteria proposed need be met to determine the authentic historicity of an event or narrative. The general rule has to do with the likelihood that a text or an event is indeed historical. The text which is under consideration must be found in the earliest level of the composition of the Scriptures. The reason for this is easy to understand. The earlier the text the more confident we can be that it was not a development of the community. These community developments are usually found in the later levels of redaction as we can well imagine. Thus, we should understand that we are looking for historical and not absolute certitude.

The rules are given below so that the reader might understand that this process is reasonable. The use of this method requires that we willfully suspend our faith commitment. The rules are as follows:[24]

The Primary Criteria[25]

Meier enumerates five primary criteria which are required for discovering the historical. He also enumerates five secondary criteria which support the conclusions. He offers the clearest articulation of these rules and for this reason we will expound them here and follow his order.

The Criterion of Embarrassment[26]

The principle of embarrassment indicates that passages that are surprising or that we would think ought to be excised from the text are

---

23. Reginald Fuller also gives an excellent enumeration of the principles. It is essentially the same as Meier's list with one major difference. His list of criteria is as follows: it must be in the earliest level of editing; criterion of multiple attestations; criterion of discontinuity; criterion of embarrassment; criterion of coherence or continuity; and criterion of an Aramaic flavor. See his *Interpreting the Miracles*.

24. Fitzmyer has given a very brief summary of these rules in *Christological Catechism*, 15–16. Most of the criteria can be found distributed throughout Fuller's book *Interpreting the Miracles*. They compare well with those articulated by Meier and Fitzmyer.

25. Meier is rigorous in his application of these principles to the themes of the kingdom of God and the miracle tradition. He is more liberal in his application of them to the parables. This is an interesting study in the application of these important rules.

26. Meier, *Marginal Jew*, 1:168.

probably authentic and are not eliminated. In short, when a text seems to potentially call into question the authenticity of an event by admitting something challenging or embarrassing, then the source is unlikely to have been invented or fabricated.

This criterion suggests that there are statements that create difficulty in understanding or explaining for the original community. For example, the baptism of Jesus by John the Baptist places Jesus in a subordinate position. Also, the cry of despair on the cross may be embarrassing since we prefer not to think that the Savior was in doubt of the outcome of his own death.[27] These situations seemed to have created difficulties for the evangelists and their communities.

There is a conserving force that preserves difficult passages because of their authenticity. If they were not thought to be authentic, the early community would have expunged them. Therefore, those embarrassing statements are more than likely to be authentic.[28]

The Criterion of Discontinuity

The criterion of discontinuity means that the words and deeds of Jesus cannot show any indication of being borrowed from another source if they are to be accepted as authentic. They cannot appear to have been derived either from the Judaism of his time, from the early postresurrection church, or from the Hellenistic world in which the Gospel was preached. To express the criterion of discontinuity in a more positive manner, the words and deeds of Jesus that are discontinuous from the above-mentioned sources would lend authority to their historical authenticity. An appearance of being borrowed or dependent upon another source suggests a lack of historicity. This criterion requires an understanding of the first century context of Jesus' public life. One must also keep in mind that Jesus was a man of his time and was influenced by Judaism. He was also the prime influence on the early church. Therefore, the above stated criterion has limited value and must be used cautiously.

---

27. This example actually has more the character of a literary device which will become clear in a later discussion regarding the death of Christ.

28. This is similar to the textual criterion *lectio difficilior potior* (the more difficult reading is stronger). Its point is that the more difficult reading of a manuscript is often the best. If it were not, the copyist would have corrected it or simplified it to make better sense.

Meier also suggests that rather than looking for what is unique about Jesus, which may be extremely limited, it might be better to look for that which is strikingly characteristic or unusual about him.[29] We need to identify the sort of things Jesus did and are attributed to him in general. To focus on a particular deed or event may present difficulties in determining its historicity. This is especially true of the miracle tradition. Jesus was known to have cured. About his healings there is little doubt. But can we, with historical certainty, identify what actually transpired in any pericope that reports a particular miracle?

The Criterion of Multiple Attestations

Multiple attestations indicate that an event is reported in more than one independent literary source and in different literary forms. A single text does not permit a comparison to discover any possible editing or change. An example of multiple attestations is the notion of the kingdom of God which is found in Mark, Q, M, L, and John. It is found in parables, beatitudes, prayers, aphorisms, and miracle stories. Meier finds that there is similar attestation among sources for Jesus' words over bread and wine as well as the prohibition of divorce. That an event or narrative is found in various sources and literary forms gives weight to its historical authenticity.

The Criterion of Coherence

This criterion is also referred to as the principle of consistency or conformity. Does the activity in question agree with the activity normally engaged in by Jesus? If not, it is suspect and should be rejected as historically authentic. For example, there are sayings and deeds of Jesus that fit well with the historical words and deeds previously established by other criteria. These may bear historical weight. An example of words of Jesus that are inconsistent with his way of conducting his mission is his apparent cursing of the fig tree (Mark 11:12–14). We will discuss this in chapter 8.

---

29. Meier, *Marginal Jew*, 1:174.

The Criterion of Rejection and Execution[30]

Jesus' violent execution and death are among the "almost indisputable facts" of Jesus life.[31] Meier points out that "Jesus met a violent end at the hands of Jewish and Roman officials."[32] The question that we must ask is what deeds or words can explain Jesus' execution? How did he infuriate the authorities to such a degree as to provoke his death sentence? The recognition of this criterion would lead to support authenticity. Jesus was certainly not a passive preacher who told interesting parables. His teaching was often provocative. What was there in Jesus' words and deeds that led to his death?

Meier concluded that these five primary criteria are extremely valuable and if used properly will help us discover the Jesus of history.

The Secondary Criteria

Meier also lists five secondary or dubious criteria.[33] Of the five secondary criteria, three are helpful to support previous findings, and two are useless. The three which have value are the criteria of Aramaic traces; the criteria of Palestinian environment; and vividness of narration. The convergence of different criteria is the best indicator of historical reliability. They are not definitive in themselves but add to the support of the historicity of the text. This work finds only the criterion of an Aramaic flavor helpful. The texts which indicate familiarity with the Aramaic language would lend support to authenticity.

All the other secondary criteria offer little help. They are not definitive in themselves but add to the support of the historicity of the text. No one individual principle establishes historicity. It requires a convergence of evidence, that is, the more principles that can be satisfied, the more likely it is that the event can be judged historical.

---

30. Meier, *Marginal Jew*, 1:177.
31. These "almost indisputable facts" are discussed in the preface.
32. Meier, *Marginal Jew*, 1:177.
33. Meier lists his secondary criteria in *Marginal Jew*, 1:178–183. They are the criterion of traces of Aramaic; the criterion of Palestinian environment; the criterion of vividness of narration; the criterion of the tendencies of the development of the Synoptic tradition; and the criterion of historical presumption.

Jesus and Christ—History and Theology

What has been said above is singularly important to our study. The significance of Jesus stands on its own and is accepted by all Christians. A word of clarification is needed as to our sources and the schematic history of Jesus. It has been pointed out above that the scriptural sources are not history as such. They speak to us of faith, and it is from them that our Christology finds its foundation. In that sense I do not search for the Jesus of history to discover something missing from our faith in Jesus. Nothing new in this regard will ever be discovered. But knowing something of the context and the history of Jesus gives us a better, a deeper, understanding of our faith conviction.[34]

The Importance of Searching for the Jesus of history

Meier asks, "Why bother with this venture to discover something about the Jesus of history?"[35] Christianity does not appeal to Jesus of Nazareth but rather to the Jesus proclaimed as Christ, who is the object of faith. Furthermore, the sources are extremely meager and fragmentary, and are colored by theological reflection so as to make a portrait of Jesus all but impossible. So why bother? Meier's answer is outlined below.

Bultmann believed that the Jesus of history and the Jesus of faith come together only tangentially. He has no personal interest in history because he does not think it is important. He thinks that Jesus' history cannot be discovered. It is the Christ of faith found in the Scriptures who demands our attention. Fundamentalists, on the other hand, accept the Christ of faith described in the Scriptures to be identical with the Jesus of history. This is a simplistic reading of the texts.

Meier disagrees with both Bultmann (from the left) and Fundamentalists (from the right). At this point in his investigation, Meier puts on his theological hat. The Jesus of history is not the object of Christian faith.[36] The object of faith is not, and cannot be, an idea or a scholarly

---

34. A word about context. Too often in the past theology has neglected the context of the words and deeds of Jesus. This decontextualizing can no longer be justified. The context is in itself interpretive. It is needed for a proper understanding. This will become clearer as we proceed.

35. That is, why not simply keep to the religious meaning? Meier brilliantly responds to this question. See Meier, *Marginal Jew*, 1:196–200. This short chapter is well worth the few minutes required to read it.

36. Meier, *Marginal Jew*, 1:197.

construct. The object of faith is the living person.[37] The Christian life is a way of life; it is the following or imitation of Jesus Christ.

Then what is the usefulness, or utility, of looking for the Jesus of history?[38] What safeguards does the Jesus of history offer us? Previous theology most often operated without including the Jesus of history.[39] Contemporary theology needs to incorporate this quest. Meier suggests several reasons why the Jesus of history serves theology which are elaborated on below.

Four Ways This Quest Serves Theology/Christology[40]

Recovering the Jesus of history prevents the Christ of faith from being reduced to a contentless cipher which will accept whatever meaning we wish to impose on it. Fidelity to the written record is demanded. Our faith is rooted in a historical figure.

It also counters docetic descriptions of Jesus. Such attempts tend to diminish or deny his humanity. The divinity of Christ swallows up the humanity of Jesus providing it with little or no importance. The conciliar teaching moved against this position and so should contemporary Christology. Jesus is truly human and not a mythical figure.

Recovering the Jesus of history counters a domesticated or tame Jesus. The Jesus of history was anything but tame. Jesus had a prophetic consciousness which led him to move counter to his culture and the political and religious authorities of his day. It cost him his life.

It also counters Jesus as a political or religious revolutionary. Jesus is remarkably silent on the social and political issues of his day.[41] He was not a social or religious reformer. That does not mean that social ethics is not to be found in his teaching. The preaching of the kingdom

---

37. This is reflected by the statement previously made by Fr. Paré. What is important is that Christianity is not merely a belief system or a system of ideas. Christianity is first and foremost an attachment to a person. See the introduction.

38. The following reasons can be found in Meier, *Marginal Jew*, 1:198–200.

39. It has been proposed that medieval theology was ahistorical. It applied philosophical categories in its investigations. This shift in using contemporary categories is well known. At the present time, historical categories have become available in a most useful and beneficial way.

40. This material depends on Meier whose reflection on this subject is extremely important. His justification for the application of the historical-critical method is foundational. See Meier, *Marginal Jew*, 1:198–200.

41. Meier, *Marginal Jew*, 1:199.

of God indeed addresses social issues. Jesus was in line with the Old Testament prophets. Their message was decidedly social. And it was not individuals who put him to death: it was the political and religious establishment of his day. As we shall see, Jesus was personally committed to the Jewish Tradition.

The Jesus of history subverts all ideologies.[42] The historical Jesus is a safeguard against turning theology or Christology into a system of ideas or ideals.[43] Meier mentions liberation theology in this regard. This is an interesting observation on his part, and it deserves further scrutiny. Does it mean that he does not believe that this theological enterprise, liberation theology, is grounded in the New Testament? Or is it merely that Jesus of history does not seem to support it?[44] The same judgment can be made for feminist Christology. This will have to be examined more closely at a later time. It seems clear, however, that the Jesus of history should imperate all modern attempts at Christology. It is my judgment that the historical Jesus will enrich all attempts to do Christology, and this includes liberation and feminist Christology.

Conclusion and Resume

This brief exposition provides us with the motive for employing the historical-critical method in our Christology. It justifies the search for the Jesus of history to provide us with the basis for theology or Christology not available until recent times. History anchors us. Jesus' words and deeds cannot be decoupled from his history. They must not be decontextualized. Nevertheless, the search for the historical and the authentic is not a limitation of the Scriptures with all of the development which took place after the life and death of Jesus. Neither is this a criticism of popular piety or devotion, which is often far from the historical.

Traditional theology appealed to a number of disciplines to help achieve its goals. We have now arrived at the point of discovery of the history of Jesus in his ministry, what he did and what he said. The Jesus

---

42. Meier, *Marginal Jew*, 1:199.

43. The affirmation that Christianity is an attachment to a person, the person of Jesus Christ, is another way of rejecting Christ and Christianity as an ideology.

44. See Meier's address at the forty-third annual CTSA meeting in Toronto, Ontario, 1988. The address is entitled "The Bible as a Source for Theology." He challenged liberation theologians and their critical reflections of the historical Jesus. This needs to be thoughtfully engaged.

of history logically precedes the Jesus who is the Christ of our faith. History grounds our conclusions.

In summary, we are encouraged to be aware of and to incorporate the Jesus of history into our theological thinking. It is one more important scholarly discipline to help us discover more about the Christ in whom we put our faith. This construct is not in itself the norm for our faith, but helps us to not misconstrue the statements of faith which are normative for us. Thus, in a very shorthand way we make several important observations. First, Jesus' message and conduct are important to our investigation. We are interested in what is referred to as his words and deeds, his preaching, and his praxis. What can be discovered of their historical nature? And second, the experience of this message as salvation here and now is important.[45] What is the salvation that Jesus brings? What are the good tidings about Jesus Christ that the gospel announces? The first point is of christological interest, the second is of soteriological interest. We will keep in mind that although we call this study Christology, by no means do we intend to exclude soteriology, that is, the saving acts of Jesus Christ. In fact, our use of the historical-critical method will permit us to discern the activity of Jesus just as philosophy helps us establish who he is.

---

45. Soteriology or salvation will be treated with the message of the kingdom of God, which is the offer of salvation. We need to look especially at the Old Testament antecedents. The captivity with the Egyptians, Assyrians, and Babylonians, the prophetic literature as well as the psalms contain indications of the meaning of salvation. The notion of the reign of God is more than the forgiveness of personal sins. Jesus' prayer, the Our Father, asks that God's will be done on earth as it is in heaven. It is a serious mistake to remove salvation from life as lived here and now. Salvation in the Christian dispensation is holistic, not something that is overly spiritual or otherworldly. It considers the whole person in his or her lived experience.

3

The Baptism of Jesus

Introduction

THERE IS NOT A strictly logical or chronological order to the public ministry of Jesus which is apparent, or which can be reconstructed from the Gospels.[1] The evangelists did not receive their traditions in any chronological order. They arranged their received source material in the Gospels according to their own theological reasons or literary designs.[2] Nevertheless, the Baptism of Jesus is logically the first introduction to his public life which of necessity precedes his itinerant ministry.[3] Prior to this event, the life of Jesus is hidden from view. Numerous fanciful and imaginative works describe Jesus' early life.[4] Some have speculated that he traveled to

---

1. The public ministry of Jesus is that recorded period between his baptism and the last week of his life. John Meier determined the dates as AD 28 to AD 30.

2. Meier, *Marginal Jew*, 2:237. It is Meier's position and one in which most scholars concur that there is no way to establish a chronology of events between Jesus' baptism and the last week of his life.

3. The baptism of Jesus is the first established historical event in the life of Jesus. Logically it belongs first. See the preface for a list of "almost indisputable facts" of the life of the Jesus of history. John Macquarrie tells us that "this [Jesus' baptism] is one of the best attested happenings in Jesus' career." Macquarrie, *Jesus Christ in Modern Thought*, 394.

4. Several apocryphal gospels that are of interest in this regard are the Infancy Gospel of Thomas written in the second or third century and the Protoevangelium of James (The Infancy Gospel of James) written mid-second century. Many other apocryphal gospels propose a fanciful life of Jesus. While interesting in themselves, they are written well after the events recorded in the canonical Gospels and are of little use in

India or perhaps some other eastern locale where he learned his wisdom or received his vocation. One contemporary novel describes Jesus and his family's return to their home in Nazareth from Egypt where they had fled to avoid the fate of the Holy Innocents.[5] There is not a scintilla of evidence available to reveal anything of Jesus' life prior to his baptism.[6] It is obvious that the events surrounding Jesus and John the Baptist must have occurred prior to Jesus' itinerant mission in Galilee and must be considered a preparation or prelude for it. Jesus' public ministry in Galilee more than likely did not occur until after the imprisonment of John the Baptist. The Synoptic Gospels witness to this.[7]

The Beginning of Jesus' Public Ministry

Beginnings are always important. In some way they portend what follows. Most studies of Christology devote far too little time to the beginning of Jesus' public life or John the Baptist's role in its formation. We intend to avoid that mistake. A careful study of the beginning of Jesus' public life will help us to understand his ministry much better and will give us a more accurate impression of his person.

The Infancy Narratives

Before we begin our examination of Jesus' public life a few words on the infancy narratives are in order.[8] The infancy narratives must be counted as a part of the gospel tradition, but it belongs to the latest written stage. Its literary genre has been referred to as a Jewish-Christian midrash, a story, a legend, fiction, fable, parable, history, and a theologoumenon.[9]

---

maintaining an authentic historical memory.

5. Rice, *Christ the Lord*.

6. We can reconstruct an imaginative picture of a first-century Jew based on social and religious information, but it would not be historical in the sense that we are trying to establish.

7. See Mark 1:14//Matt 4:12. Luke's version of the beginning of the Galilean ministry situates it in Nazareth and makes no mention of the imprisonment of John the Baptist (Luke 4:14–15). Mark, our primary source, and Matthew seem to place it in the environs of Capernaum.

8. The infancy narratives are found in Matt 1:1—2:24 and Luke 1:5—2:52. For a concise explanation of the infancy narrative problematic see questions 54–60 in Brown, *Responses to 101 Questions*, 76–84.

9. Theologoumenon is defined as a theological interpretation that is suggested as

The reason so many different literary genres are suggested for this narrative indicates the difficulty in identifying it. It does not fit any of the ordinary categories of form criticism. Both Raymond Brown and Joseph Fitzmyer made an exceedingly useful examination of the Infancy Narratives.[10] Brown tells us that "All of this (previous discussion) means that, in fact, we have no real knowledge that any or all of the infancy material came from a tradition for which there was a corroborating witness."[11] The purpose of the infancy narratives is theological, not historical. There are few things we can say about the infancy narratives with any certainty. It seems certain that they are an outgrowth of the primitive kerygma. They are definitely not intended to be a historical recounting of Jesus' infancy and hidden years. For example, Luke teaches about Jesus as a young boy in the Temple, asking questions and teaching the elders. Several theologians consider this episode to be an actual historical event, but it is recorded in Luke's Gospel alone.[12] It fails to satisfy the requirements of the historical-critical method proposed earlier in this study. It is in fact a theological or literary interpolation into the Gospel. Although they are not historical in the strict sense, Matthew and Luke share a number of historical details in their versions of the infancy narratives.[13] Nevertheless, their purpose is not historical; it is theological. The infancy narratives are theological constructs to indicate the high Christology of the New Testament. They were developed in the early church as expressions of its belief more than history in the strictest sense. The intention was to declare that the child Jesus is the Son of God, the Messiah. This belief was part of the original primitive kerygma.[14] We can also affirm that they tell us nothing of the psychological state of Mary upon receiving

---

a possible, but not a decisive, call to belief. It points to a doctrine. Meier defines theologoumenon as "a theological insight narrated as a historical event." Meier, *Marginal Jew*, 1:217. The theological intention of the infancy narratives appears to be the affirmation that Jesus is the Son of God. This is a doctrinal position offered for belief. The category of history does not satisfy as a genre for the infancy narratives. See Schillebeeckx, *Jesus*, 752.

10. Brown, *Birth of the Messiah*. Fitzmyer, *Gospel According to Luke*.

11. Brown, *Birth of the Messiah*, 33.

12. Elizabeth Johnson assumes the historicity of this event. See Johnson, *Consider Jesus*, 43. Because this episode is attested to only once in the life of Jesus, its historicity cannot be established. Luke was not expressing history. He was expressing a theological concept concerning the person of Jesus.

13. Brown, *Birth of the Messiah*, 34–35. Fitzmyer, *Gospel According to Luke*, 2:307.

14. See Dodd, *Apostolic Preaching and its Development*, 17–35. This lecture was delivered in 1935 at the University of London, Kings College.

the news she is to be the mother of Jesus; the purpose is to express a faith doctrine for the reader. For the true nature of the infancy narratives, see Brown's magisterial work on the subject.[15]

The Baptism: The Beginning of Jesus' Public Life

Jesus' public life can be conveniently divided into two parts: his ministry with John the Baptist and his itinerant ministry that followed. The former is a prelude to the latter. Jesus' baptism is the first historical event which can be firmly established, and this event begins the transition from his private to his public life. Therefore, it is essential to understand the meaning of Jesus' baptism as well as what it signifies. It is also important to understand the relationship between John the Baptist and Jesus. Both the event of Jesus' baptism and his relationship with John the Baptist are keys to understanding Jesus' life and ministry.

John the Baptist[16]

John the Baptist was already conducting his prophetic ministry prior to the baptism and public life of Jesus.[17] It is apparent that Jesus sought out John and not the other way around. It would be more than a little useful to examine the character and role of John the Baptist to discover what Jesus found religiously attractive in him. It is within the ministry of the Baptist that Jesus' ministry takes its point-of-departure.

---

15. Brown, *Birth of the Messiah*.

16. John the Baptist is recognized as extremely important in the tradition. The Solemnity of the Nativity of John the Baptist is celebrated liturgically on June 24, six months before the Nativity of Jesus. The date was obviously chosen to coordinate with Luke 1:36. This Solemnity was celebrated as early as the fourth century. The Martyrdom (Passion) of Saint John the Baptist is celebrated as a Memorial on August 29. John the Baptist is honored by all Christian sects. He is especially honored by the Mandeans, a gnostic sect.

17. Meier determined that the date for Jesus' first encounter with John the Baptist was AD 28. It is impossible to determine how much earlier John had initiated his ministry, but Meier thinks that it was not much before this. Thus, according to Meier's calculation, John the Baptist began his ministry around AD 28 and Jesus joined him shortly after. See Meier, *Marginal Jew*, 1:386. Jesus' public life is thought to be a little over two years, ending in his death in AD 30. See Meier, *Marginal Jew*, 1:402.

THE BAPTISM OF JESUS

What Sort of Person was John the Baptist?

John the Baptist was an enigmatic character. Luke alone describes him as coming from a priestly family and yet he seems strangely anti-cultic.[18] He is in no way associated with the temple or its priesthood. He appears more cut from the cloth of an Old Testament prophet than its priesthood.[19] No indication is given of his education. He is very charismatic. His name designates him as the only one who baptizes and there is no reference to his disciples baptizing.[20]

The place of his ministry is described as a desert region along the Jordan River, traditionally thought to be the area east of Jericho.[21] It might be better described as a desert wilderness. There would have been no permanent inhabitants in this region. It is described as being near a source of water.[22] The desert (wilderness) was the traditional place where the Israelites encountered God. Moses and the Israelites wandered in the desert for forty years and at the beginning of this period Moses, for a second time, experienced God. It was in the desert that the Israelites were formed into a people.[23] It is no accident that John chose a desert place for his ministry. And it is no accident that Jesus was later described as being led into the desert after his baptism. The desert possesses considerable religious significance.

---

18. This information is from Luke 1:5, the first line of the infancy narrative, and therefore it is more likely theological than historical. Traditionally the home of Zechariah and Elizabeth is situated in Ein Karem, an ancient village on the western slope of Jerusalem. Its location was convenient for Zechariah to carry out his priestly duties in the temple. It is the place in which the visitation of the Blessed Mother to Elizabeth would have taken place.

19. John's manner of dress and diet is described in Mark 1:6//Matt 3:4. The clothing made of camel's hair and his belt is reminiscent of Elijah's clothing described in 2 Kgs 1:8.

20. Interestingly enough, there is a singular reference that speaks of Jesus' disciples baptizing (John 4:2). This will be discussed at greater length below.

21. Multiple sites are claimed to be the area in which John baptized. The earliest tradition, dependent on John 1:28, identifies the site as Bethany, now known as Bethabara, on the west bank of the Jordan River. A later tradition places the site on the opposite side of the River Jordan, or on the Jordanian side. In 2015 UNESCO declared the western site as a world heritage site.

22. The description is historically certain. It is supported by multiple attestations of sources. See Mark 1:4 and Q (Matt 3:1–3//Luke 3:2b–4).

23. The desert place also resonates with the experience of Jesus being led into the desert for forty days after his baptism. Much of this replicates the Mosaic experience.

The Preaching of John the Baptist

John was not an apocalyptic although the context of his preaching might have suggested he was. He is better described as an eschatological prophet.[24] He was charismatic, able to draw large crowds.[25] His message, addressed to all of Israel which had gone astray, was the need for repentance for sin to prepare for God's coming judgment.[26] John preached the need for a change of heart, a metanoia or conversion. Matthew describes John as preaching in the desert saying, "Repent, for the kingdom of heaven is at hand!" (Matt 3:2). The expression is a reference to God's reign or rule over his people. Interestingly enough, this is the only record of the expression *kingdom of heaven* found on John's lips.[27] John preached the coming judgment of God, the day of the Lord.[28] It was a future-imminent judgment on all of Israel.[29] This was the definitive end of God's people, but it was both an end and a new beginning.[30]

Besides the formal call to repent, John instructed the crowds on the need to reform. John called men and women to better moral behavior. They thought that God's judgment was to come sometime in the near

---

24. See Meier, *Marginal Jew*, 2:31. Meier describes John as "an eschatological prophet tinged with some apocalyptic motifs."

25. Meier, *Marginal Jew*, 2:40.

26. It is interesting that Jesus did not preach repentance in the manner that John did. The Abba that Jesus preached was the God of grace. This is reflected especially in Jesus' joyous festive meals. We shall see that they were proleptic of the heavenly kingdom.

27. As we shall see in the following chapter, Jesus may have been the first to employ the expression *kingdom of God* regularly. It could well have been unique to him. Meier, *A Marginal Jew*, 2:244.

28. The day of the Lord is an Old Testament concept. It was first used for God's judgment and punishment on Israel's enemies. It shifted its meaning to include an unfaithful Israel. It is prominent in the prophets and good examples can be found in Amos 5:18–20; Isa 2:10–17; 30:27–28; and Zeph 1:14–18. The entire book of Zephaniah is a threat to Judah and Jerusalem. The concept was current during the time of John. The day of the Lord was preached as an imminent-future reality. The concept is also expressed as *the end of the age*. This expression is uniquely Matthean, found only in Matt 13:39, 40, 49; 24:3; and 28:20. Three chapters in the Synoptic Gospels are heavily apocalyptic. These are Mark 13, Matt 24, and Luke 21 and they refer to the end time or God's judgment. These three chapters are parallels.

29. We will see that Jesus preached the future-imminent coming of the kingdom of God. This is also expressed in the early Epistles of Paul.

30. John never preached that he was an intermediary for the day of Judgment. A significant part of his message is that "the one who is coming after me is mightier than I" (Matt 3:11).

future. After baptism they would return home to live normal lives while awaiting God's judgment and forgiveness.

John also gathered disciples who had a genuine commitment to him.[31] The job description of the disciples is not clear from our sources, but they stayed with John and were instructed by him. There is no reference that indicated that they baptized anyone.

The Praxis of John the Baptist: Baptism

Unlike Jesus, John the Baptist was not an itinerant. The crowds came to him. His practice of baptizing and the call to repentance (metanoia) place him squarely in the Old Testament prophetic tradition.[32] To his preaching, John added a symbolic baptism. His baptism and its associated preaching were one of repentance for the forgiveness of sins (Mark 1:4; Luke 3:3) but it did not offer this forgiveness.[33] It was not an offer of salvation. It was a new way of expressing metanoia or a commitment to prepare for God's judgment. It was inexpensive and anti-cultic or anti-temple. It did not require a pilgrimage to Jerusalem, the center of Jewish worship, to bring it to fulfillment. This is a major deviation from standard Jewish devotion and piety. Baptism was a special part of John's call for repentance. His tag name, the Baptist, supports this.

Several contemporary scholars associate John with the Essenes because they see similarities between them and John's ministry of baptism.[34] While it is possible that John may have had some contact with the Essenes because of the location of his ministry, it seems almost certain that he was not a member of this separatist group. The superficial resemblances are too minor to assign this role to John. John was not a

---

31. This is supported by Mark, Q, Luke, John, and Acts. See Mark 2:18; 6:29; Matt 11:2//Luke 11:1; John 1:35; 3:25; and Acts 19:1-7.

32. Meier, *A Marginal Jew*, 2:29. Meier places Jesus squarely within the same tradition. Both John and Jesus are understood as Israelite prophets.

33. John's baptism is known as a prophetic act. Prophetic acts are more fully explained later in this chapter.

34. The Essenes separated themselves from society and took up their residence in the desert waiting for the coming of the Messiah. They did have a form of baptism. See Fitzmyer, *Impact of the Dead Sea*, 23-43. The central location of the Essenes was at Qumran, less than ten miles from the northwestern shore of the Dead Sea. The site of John's ministry would not have been too far north of Qumran. Thus, some contact with the Essenes was certainly possible.

separatist. The frequent use of washings by the Essenes is not replicated by John's baptism which was a singular once-for-all event.

The Baptism of Jesus

Prior to his public life, Jesus lived in Nazareth, a humble village which lacked any prominence. It is not mentioned in any source until the New Testament. It was held in disdain by some (John 1:46). The number of inhabitants has been estimated to be anywhere between five hundred and well under two thousand. We can presume it had a synagogue. All three Synoptic Gospels refer to one. From our sources we cannot determine that there was anything remarkable about Jesus prior to his public life. This seems verified in the Scriptures for on his return to Nazareth after he had begun his public ministry, the villagers greeted him with incredulity and rejected him.[35]

While living in Nazareth where he conducted his occupation, Jesus must have heard something of the prominence of the baptist and made the journey to the Jordan where he was baptizing. We can presume that Jesus listened to John's preaching and was moved by it. What can be made of the fact that Jesus was baptized by John the Baptist? On its face it appears to be an odd thing for one who is confessed by Christians as sinless and who is identified as God's Son to submit himself to this symbolic act of repentance. John preached the need for metanoia for the forgiveness of sin. From a faith perspective Jesus had no real need for metanoia. Why then would Jesus have submitted to a subservient role to John and to have accepted his baptism?

Jesus' Baptism: An Accepted Historical Fact

The historical critical method leads us to accept the event of Jesus' baptism as historical.[36] Multiple sources attest as much (Mark and Q).[37] It is

---

35. We are told that "they took offense at him" (Mark 6:3b) because of his teaching. The villagers saw nothing distinctive about him. See Mark 6:1–6//Matt 13:54–58//Luke 4:16–30.

36. Meier asserts that the baptism of Jesus is "hardly a fiction created by the Church." Meier, *Marginal Jew*, 2:101. Jeremias says that there is no reason to doubt the historicity of Jesus' baptism. Jeremias, *New Testament Theology*, 55.

37. The baptismal event is recorded in Mark 1:9–11 and the Q source (Matt 3:13, 16–17; Luke 3:21–22). In the Gospel of John, no direct reference is made to Jesus'

also supported by the criterion of embarrassment. It is highly unlikely that, given its faith in Jesus, the early community would have invented this narrative or even kept the tradition if it were not factual.[38] That Jesus submitted to John's baptism has perplexed theologians, commentators, and Christians in general for centuries.

Accepting this event as factual, several puzzling incidents must be accounted for. First, the baptism placed Jesus in a subordinate position to John. Why then did Jesus adopt this subordinate position?[39] What is its significance? Theologians have resisted accepting this position for centuries because of dogmatic considerations: Jesus is the Son of God, the Christ. This dogmatic position would preclude, it was thought, a subordinate position of Jesus to John. Contemporary Christology, however, is not so timid in asserting that Jesus, in spite of the assertions of faith, had a serious commitment to John the Baptist. Jesus followed John as his disciple for a time. And second, from a faith perspective, Jesus is sinless and therefore does not require a conversion, a metanoia, which is called for in the baptism of John. Both of these puzzles will be addressed below. The scriptural evidence does not provide us with Jesus' motive. Past theology, however, has suggested several reasons.

Among the many theological interpretations of Jesus' Baptism, one is quite ancient. Many of the fathers of the church proposed that Jesus' baptism was a prototype or symbolic action to be imitated by Christians; it was an exemplar. An exemplar is not merely an example to be imitated. It is considered to be the first of its kind in the order of causality.[40] Jesus' baptism is the model and source of the Christian sacrament. This explanation has minimal merit; it does not give full weight to the action itself, which has such a prominent place in the New Testament. It fails to adequately satisfy the data.

---

baptism. See John 1:29–34.

38. Meier, *Marginal Jew*, 2:103, 105. Meier includes multiple attestation, discontinuity, and embarrassment as criteria that argue for the historicity of Jesus' baptism.

39. In being baptized by John, Jesus is subordinating himself to another person. In its context this action is also subservient. It bypasses the temple and the synagogue and takes on an altogether different authority. As we shall see, Jesus' ministry often led him to the synagogue to preach. John's Gospel describes him as visiting the temple several times. While Jesus is often portrayed as being in conflict with Jewish authorities his break with the temple does not occur until the last week of his life.

40. In the *Summa Theologiae*, III, q. 1, a. 2. Aquinas proposes that the sacrament of baptism received its efficacy from the baptism of Jesus. This would correspond to the description of Jesus' baptism as an exemplar. The resurrection of Christ is often considered an exemplar of the resurrection of Christians.

Another explanation is to identify Jesus' baptism as a prophetic act. A prophetic act is a prophecy in action, something more than mere verbalization of the message. A prophetic act is a symbolic action joined together with explanatory words. The Old Testament is replete with prophetic acts.[41] It is the way the prophet engaged others in his prophetic ministry.

During his lifetime, Jesus was known as a prophet, and he performed a number of prophetic acts.[42] The explanation that Jesus presented himself for baptism as a prophetic act has some merit in that it maintains the understanding that Jesus was sinless and did not require such a submission. The symbolic meaning to his baptism carries a message of repentance for Israel, and by association, all men, and women.

An interpretation that more closely explains what Jesus' motive might have been, is that his baptism reflected a conversion experience, a metanoia. This reflects the Gospel description of John's baptism. Mark identifies John's baptism as "a baptism of repentance for the forgiveness of sin" (Mark 1:4).[43] That Jesus would submit to this symbolic act seems highly unlikely if he were sinless as later Christology argues. The argument that Jesus required baptism has never had any support in the church. It seems unlikely that Jesus needed baptism for any personal reasons. This is not to argue that his baptism was not a religious experience. As true man, Jesus was capable of all things human. Was this a particular moment of grace for Jesus, a moment of his deepening

---

41. The prophet Jeremiah carried a yoke as a symbol of God's message that Israel should be submissive to the kings of Babylon (Jer 27:2). Later the yoke was broken by the prophet Hananiah who boldly prophesied that he would break the yoke of the Babylonians (Jer 28:10). Hananiah was punished for being a false prophet. There are many other similar examples of prophetic acts in the Old Testament. See Isa 20:3–6 (Isaiah walked naked and without sandals for three years), Jer 18:1–2 (the potter's vessel), Jer 19:1–13 (the potter's flask). It is the way the prophet engaged others in his prophetic ministry. Sanders gives a short list of prophetic acts in *Historical Figure of Jesus*, 253. He points out that these symbolic acts require some verbal interpretation by the prophet. See "Introduction to Prophetic Literature," 11:23, and "Ezekiel," 20:24, in Brown et al., *New Jerome Biblical Commentary*. This source will be referred to as *NJBC* in the following pages.

42. It will be argued in chapter 14 that the temple incident is best understood as a prophetic act. It fits the description of a prophetic act described above extremely well and understanding it as such gives a better explanation for this event than is commonly proposed. The entrance into Jerusalem is also a prophetic act.

43. Luke 3:3 affirms the same message as Mark 1:4 while Matt 3:11 refers to John's baptism as a baptism of repentance.

relationship with the Father?⁴⁴ Or was this a turning point, a becoming aware of his vocation? If Jesus were not conscious of any personal sins his submission to the baptism of John could well have been to show his solidarity with a sinful people.⁴⁵ This is similar to the consideration of baptism as a prophetic act as explained above.

Jesus' Baptism: His Personal Experience (The Theophany)

Whatever Jesus' personal motive for presenting himself for baptism might have been, what did he personally experience? The baptism of Jesus as described in the Synoptic Gospels is intimately connected to the descent of the Spirit upon him immediately after he exits the waters. All four Gospels agree that the Spirit came down like a dove (Matt 3:16; Mark 1:10; Luke 3:33; John 1:32). The historicity of the theophany has been challenged.⁴⁶ It seems likely that the declaration that Jesus was the Son of God could be a retrojection from the early Christians who believed he was the Son of God in their experience of Jesus raised from the dead. Meier proposes that the theophany is a Christian midrash, an employment of Old Testament references to interpret the true identify of Jesus.⁴⁷ Its purpose is to counter the understanding that Jesus is subordinate to John. The theophany is a "Christian composition interpreting the significance of Jesus person and mission."⁴⁸ Equally important, Meier proposes that "the theophany does not mirror some inner experience Jesus had at the time."⁴⁹ Nevertheless, he admits that others believe, with good reason, that Jesus did receive an inner experience. He quotes D. G. Dunn who proposed that Jesus underwent a consequential experience becoming aware of his sonship and the Spirit.⁵⁰ Jeremias

---

44. See Meier, *Marginal Jew*, 2:108–109.

45. Fitzmyer, *Christological Catechism*, 42; Viviano, "Gospel According to Matthew," in *NJBC*, 42:18.

46. It seems evident that Matt 3:13–15 and Luke 3:21–23 are dependent on Mark 1:10–11. The message is that Jesus is the Son of God. In the Gospel of John, John the Baptist sees the Spirit like a dove descend upon Jesus and he testifies that Jesus is the Son of God (John 1:32–34).

47. Meier, *Marginal Jew*, 2:106. Viviano, "Gospel According to Matthew," in *NJBC* echoes this notion.

48. Meier, *Marginal Jew*, 2:107.

49. Meier, *Marginal Jew*, 2:107. Fitzmyer is skeptical that we can determine the nature of that experience. See Fitzmyer, *Christological Catechism*, 41.

50. Meier, *Marginal Jew*, 2:107. See Dunn, *Jesus and the Spirit*, 63.

agrees with Dunn. He says that Jesus "experienced his call" in his baptism.[51] Jeremias asserts that this becomes even clearer when Jesus' authority is challenged later in his ministry (Mark 11:27–33 par.). He paraphrases Jesus' reply to his challengers. "My (Jesus') authority rests on what happened when I was baptized by John."[52] These arguments are worthy of further discussion. The question is this: What was Jesus' self-understanding at his baptism? Jeremias is inclined to believe that Jesus is conscious of his call to be God's servant promised by Isaiah.[53] His call is to be God's messenger, his eschatological prophet. Meier is less sanguine about this. It is not so much whether or not Jesus ever had a revelatory experience but when. Meier claims that "Jesus no doubt developed intellectually and experienced existentially these key insights into his relationship with God as Father and the powerful activity of the spirit manifest in his own life."[54] It is clear from the Gospel presentation of Jesus' mission that he was confident in his work.

Among these challenging interpretations is the suggestion that the baptism (theophany) of Jesus was a vocation experience, a call. Elizabeth Johnson writes that "the gospels use images such as a voice from heaven and a dove descending to signify the revelation of his vocation."[55] We saw above that this was Jeremias' position.[56] To put this in contemporary terms, Jesus engaged in a discernment process. It was his time to decide about his vocation. Jesus understood himself to have been called to preach the kingdom of God and that he possessed the principal role in its initiation. Did this calling, this vocation, come to him over an extended period of time?[57] Or did it come all at once and suddenly, that is, did it occur at his baptism? The question is actually about the timing of Jesus' personal self-understanding. How did he understand himself at his baptism? Could the baptism event have been the moment when he came to the realization of who he was and what his mission was? It is certainly possible. However,

---

51. Jeremias, *New Testament Theology*, 55.
52. Jeremias, *New Testament Theology*, 56.
53. Jeremias, *New Testament Theology*, 55.
54. Meier, *Marginal Jew*, 2:108. We have referred to this as his Abba experience.
55. Johnson, *Consider Jesus*, 44.
56. Jeremias, *New Testament Theology*, 55.
57. John Macquarrie imagines that Jesus' vocation came to him as a young man before he sought out John the Baptist. At John's baptism the vocation was intensified possibly with a messianic consciousness. This consciousness deepened during his ministry. Macquarrie, *Jesus Christ in Modern Thought*, 395.

Jesus' experience of God, his Abba experience, his deep conviction of his relationship with God can be established earlier in his nonpublic life. We have no solid evidence to support when his Abba experience occurred or when he understood his personal role in preaching the kingdom. It may well have occurred during the time he was with John the Baptist. It is also possible that this understanding could have developed during the entire time of his public life. There does not seem to be any way that we can adequately determine this with any certainty.

It may be that the argument will never be answered satisfactorily. It seems clear, however, that Jesus experienced God at some point, either before, during or after his baptism. This religious, charismatic experience might have developed over time. We are still left with the challenging question. Was the theophany a revelatory or disclosure experience, or was it an ecclesial confession? If it were a personal revelation to Jesus, then he must have been the source of this event. Its written expression in the Gospel would not be literal.

There is one more difficulty that we need to resolve. How do we harmonize the notion of Jesus' revelatory experience, whatever that revelation might have been, with the possibility that Jesus continued to follow John? Perhaps. It is possible that the experience described in Jesus' baptism actually came later, that is, after Herod had imprisoned John (Mark 1:14). Or, even more likely, the insight was not clear either at Jesus' baptism or earlier in his private life. It could have taken time for the true meaning of the revelation to develop and become apparent, which is true for every discernment process. Only later was this revelatory experience inserted into its present place in the Gospels.

The Relationship between John and Jesus

The relationship between John the Baptist and Jesus is much more complex and nuanced than is usually thought. John the Baptist holds a significant place of honor in all Christian faiths, most especially in Catholicism.[58] Jeremias indicates that the relationship between John and Jesus was not a fleeting one.[59] It is likely that Jesus received his call at his baptism and understood that his authority rested upon his baptism.

---

58. See above, page 50n16.
59. Jeremias, *New Testament Theology*, 46.

The relationship which Luke attributes to Jesus and John is one of kinship.[60] This is found in Luke alone and not in the other Synoptics or the Gospel of John. Neither John nor Jesus described their relationship as one of kinship. It is more than likely that the relationship of kinship is the creation of Luke.[61] The relationship which was formed between Jesus and John the Baptist because of their shared ministry is much more profound than a relationship of kinship.

Jesus: A Disciple of John the Baptist?

What was the relationship between Jesus and John the Baptist? Was Jesus independent of John or did he initially have a commitment to John as did his disciples, at least for a time? In the past our personal answer to this question depended upon dogmatic considerations regarding Jesus as the Christ. This would have excluded any subservient role for Jesus. Recent theological reflections more scripturally oriented have speculated as to whether Jesus might have been a disciple of John. It does appear from the scriptural text that Jesus may indeed have been a disciple of John the Baptist.[62]

Not a single verse in any of the Gospels claims explicitly that Jesus was a disciple of John the Baptist. It is unlikely that this relationship can be determined historically. The Synoptic narratives give no indication that Jesus was a disciple of John. Neither do they make any allusion that Jesus baptized others during his mission in Galilee.[63] They are completely silent on this matter. This silence, however, may have been a literary attempt to distinguish Jesus from John. Did the evangelists knowingly leave out a part of the tradition? There are three blocks of

---

60. Luke actually informs us that Mary and Elizabeth are related but he does not tell us exactly what that familial relationship is. Mary is told that her relative is with child (Luke 1:36). Mary stayed with Elizabeth three months, and we can presume she did not return to Nazareth until after the birth of John. John and Jesus are often spoken of as cousins.

61. Brown, *Virginal Conception and Bodily Resurrection*, 54. See also See Vermes, *Nativity: History and Legend*, 143.

62. Meier, Brown, Fitzmyer, Dunn, and Jeremias all believe that Jesus had some commitment to John after his baptism, at least for a brief time.

63. Jesus is never described as baptizing during his ministry. There is no record that he did, however, Meier believes that he did. It is clear that, after the resurrection, the disciples baptized. It was a large part of the early tradition as it is today. The postresurrection pericope of Matt 28:16–20 commissions them to baptize.

THE BAPTISM OF JESUS

material, however, which help us make a provisional determination. These will be examined below.

The first block of material is from John 3:22–30; 4:1–3. The Johannine tradition differs from that of the Synoptics in as much as Jesus is described as baptizing contemporaneously with John after his baptism: Jesus is in Judea and John is in Aenon near Salim (John 3:22–30). This scene was repeated in John 4:1–3. In John 4:1, Jesus is described as making and baptizing more disciples than John.[64] John 4:2 corrects this position. It reads, "(although Jesus himself was not baptizing, just his disciples)." However, John 4:2 is thought to be an editorial note or insertion, hence the brackets are inserted around the text to indicate this.[65] It seems clear that the Johannine tradition reports that Jesus did indeed baptize.

The first block of material given above strongly indicates that Jesus baptized alongside John. The second block of material (John 1:35–37) indicates that, after Jesus' baptism, several of John's disciples seem to have followed him. This indicates that Jesus spent time with John and did not leave immediately for Galilee as the Synoptics suggest. In the Synoptic tradition the call of the disciples takes place at the Sea of Galilee far from the area in which John baptized. In both traditions, Peter and Andrew are among the earliest disciples called. After the resurrection, when a successor to Judas Iscariot is chosen, the text in Acts indicates that Jesus had attracted followers of John to himself (Acts 1:21–22). Peter makes a speech to the first community in Jerusalem in which the qualification of the one to replace Judas is to have accompanied Jesus "from the baptism of John until the day on which he was taken up from us, become with us a witness to his resurrection" (Acts 1:22). Is this job description historical? From a postresurrection faith perspective, it makes sense. Jesus begins his mission and chooses apostles (the Twelve) to participate in his mission. But it is also likely, if there is a development in Jesus' personal understanding of his ministry, that being followed by some of John's disciples might have occurred after his baptism, even after John was imprisoned.

The third block of material is from the Q source (Matt 11:2–19// Luke 7:18–35). While in prison, John sends emissaries to Jesus to ask him, "Are you the one who is to come?" (Matt 11:3//Luke 7:20). It seems

---

64. Was there rivalry between the disciples of Jesus and John? Was there competition between John and Jesus? The question is provocative, but we have no way of determining the truth.

65. See Meier, *Marginal Jew*, 195n74. See Brown, *Gospel According to John*, 2:164. John 4:2 is clearly from another hand; that is, it is an editorial comment.

apparent because of his question that John did not know that Jesus was the mightier one even though they may have shared a common ministry. It is significant that John appears ignorant of Jesus' role as eschatological prophet both during Jesus' public ministry and while he was imprisoned. After the messengers from John had left him, Jesus declares that "Among those born of women, there has been none greater than John the Baptist" (Matt 11:11//Luke 7:28).[66] This statement is quite enigmatic. Why would Jesus praise John so highly? Was he indebted to John as his former disciple? Does Jesus praise John as his former teacher? This is certainly possible. This understanding deserves thoughtful consideration. Jesus completes the statement by saying, "Yet the least in the kingdom of God is greater than he" (Matt 11:11//Luke 7:28). Meier understands this as high praise for John, that Jesus is positioning himself as the prophet situated before the coming of the kingdom of God.

From these arguments we conclude that it is highly probable that Jesus had a commitment to John after his baptism. And he participated in John's ministry of baptism as his disciple. The Gospel of John indicates as much. Jesus began his public ministry baptizing with John but later changed to become an itinerant preacher.[67]

If Jesus was a disciple, his later self-understanding puts him in a privileged place. Jesus' response to John's disciples concerning his own identity contains an implicit reference to a prophecy of Isaiah (Matt 11:2–6; Luke 7:18–23). The passage indicates that Jesus identified himself with the one sent by God. This clearly explains his mission. Did he gain this insight into his mission after his baptism? This seems possible given the context. But it also indicates that Jesus recognized himself as the eschatological prophet, a position superior to that of John the Baptist.

John, the Forerunner of Jesus

John appears not to have understood his role as an agent of God's judgment which would come at some future-imminent time. He proclaimed

---

66. These references are from the Q source. The actual statement from Matthew is "amen, I say to you, among those born of women there has been none greater than John the Baptist" (Matt 11:11). This is an authentic, historical saying.

67. See John 3:22–24 and 4:1–2. There is insufficient evidence to establish with historical certainty what Jesus' early practice might have been as he departs from the company of John the Baptist. We are not limited, however, to propose a good hypothesis to adequately account for this situation.

THE BAPTISM OF JESUS

that "One mightier than I is coming after me. I am not worthy to stoop and loosen the thongs of his sandals" (Mark 1:7).[68] John expected that this *mightier one* would usher in God's judgment. This is supported by Mark, Q, John, and Acts and thus we can presume it is historically established.[69] That John is the forerunner to this *mightier one* is clearly intended in these passages.[70] John the Baptist is accurately described as a forerunner (precursor) of the *mightier one* to come and he understood himself as such.

If John understood himself as the forerunner of "the *mightier one* who is to come," did he understand Jesus as the one to follow? The Gospels of Mark and Luke do not describe John the Baptist as identifying Jesus as the *mightier one*. They are silent on who he is. On the other hand, Matthew and John indicate that John did know that Jesus was the *mightier one*.[71] This raises a question about the extent of John the Baptist's knowledge.

Can we resolve this difficulty? While in prison, John sends emissaries to Jesus to ask him "Are you the one who is to come?" (Matt 11:3// Luke 7:20).[72] It seems apparent that John did not know that Jesus was the *mightier one*. By his response, Jesus indicates to John's emissaries that he is indeed the one who was to come. When Jesus says, "Blessed is the one who takes no offense at me" he is addressing John without naming him (Luke 7:23). Meier believes that Jesus meant that John needed to understand that he is the Messiah (the one who was to come) and that he should accept this reality. This Q source casts doubt on John's recognition of Jesus as the *mightier one*. It is historically certain that John understood himself as the forerunner and expected the mightier one to come after him. It seems highly probable that he did not know that Jesus was the expected one.

---

68. The Greek word used in the Gospel is *iskurote*. It means stronger, mightier, more powerful.

69. See Mark 1:7; Matt 3:11//Luke 3:16, John 1:26-27; 3:28 and Acts 13:25. Acts 13:16-43 records Paul's address to a synagogue in Antioch of Pisidia in which John's place in salvation history is described.

70. Meier, *Marginal Jew*, 2:40.

71. Matt 3:11, 13-15; John 1:29-34, 3:30.

72. This is an important text. Jesus' response to the disciples is that he understands himself as the eschatological prophet. This will be examined at length in chapter 5. This Q source is Matt 11:2-19//Luke 7:18-35.

John the Baptist is clearly not an agent for the imminent judgment of God. He is the forerunner, a precursor of the one who is to come.[73] What this *mightier one* actually does is yet to be discovered. Everything about John identifies him with the Old Testament prophetic tradition. He is deeply rooted in the faith of Israel. John is a transitional figure, a bridge, between the Old Testament and the New. This is important. John is the end of the Old Testament prophets. He is the forerunner of the one who is to come.

The Temptations of Jesus

The baptism, theophany and temptations of Jesus are intimately joined in the Synoptics. Why then are we not examining the temptations with the Baptism? For one thing, the temptations of Jesus present us with problems. Meier does not believe that this is proper material for his research because there are no witnesses who can verify the event(s).[74] The temptation narrative, however, is an independent tradition.[75] Furthermore, the temptations may have occurred at times and in places distinct from Jesus' baptism.

The descriptions of the temptation of Jesus are highly stylized and unrealistic.[76] These narratives are entirely absent from the Gospel of John because they would not fit his high Christology. In the Synoptic tradition the temptation narrative does not belong to the general pattern of the Gospel. It is most certainly an independent tradition.[77]

---

73. This is found in Mark 1:7b; Matt 3:11; Luke 3:16; and John 1:20.

74. For this reason, Meier doesn't accept the temptation narrative as proper material for his study. See Meier, *Marginal Jew*, 2:272n1. This is not the sort of narrative he wants to consider because it does not provide sufficient material to deal with from an historical-critical method. Jesus would necessarily have been the source for his temptations if they are historical. My position is that they were indeed real, and this agrees with a long-standing tradition and the results of the historical critical method.

75. Jeremias, *New Testament Theology*, 74.

76. A number of literary genres have been suggested for these narratives. Among them are history, parable, and myth. They are described as legendary by a few scholars. A legend is a story coming down from the past and regarded as historical although not verifiable. It is often thought to have a basis in history. This narrative could have been a story or theologoumenon as some propose. It is quite possible that they are autobiographical but expressed symbolically. Note that there is another temptation that occurred in the garden before Jesus' crucifixion. The temptations are described as occurring at the beginning of Jesus' ministry and another at the end. They are significant.

77. Meier, *Marginal Jew*, 2:271n1. Jeremias, *New Testament Theology*, 71.

They are situated after Jesus' baptism but before he begins his public ministry.[78] They differ among themselves. Mark is extremely brief, no more than two verses. His version is a simple declaration that Jesus was led into the desert where he was tempted. Luke and Matthew (the Q version), though considerably longer than Mark, differ from one another on many details. Furthermore, no eyewitnesses are mentioned in the narratives who could verify the event.

The temptation narrative raises several significant questions. What was the nature of these temptations? Are they real or only symbolic? Where and when did the temptations take place if they are historical? The scenes do not at all appear historical. Tradition has always treated the temptation of Jesus in the desert as real. The fathers of the church and later theologians understood the Scriptures in a more literal way.[79] In his treatise on the temptations of Christ, Aquinas quotes numerous fathers of the church.[80] For his own position Aquinas appeals to the witness and authority of Scripture. But even a careful reading of the Scriptures would not provide a way to corroborate the reality of the temptations. The narrative itself makes us suspicious that they are to be understood as symbolic and theological. They appear much more literary than historical in nature. Does the literary description, however, mean that Jesus did not experience temptations?

The Reality of the Temptations

To provide clarity on this subject we need to properly understand the biblical meaning of *temptation*. The Greek word employed in the New Testament is *peirazo* (a verb). The meaning is to tempt or to test. It does not refer to an ethical or moral temptation. It addresses that which is deepest in us. It is a challenge.[81]

Are the temptations of Jesus real, actual? Many theologians and biblical scholars affirm them as real.[82] The historicity of the narratives in

---

78. The sources for this narrative are from Mark 1:12–13 and from Q (Matt 4:1–11, Luke 4:1–13). Meier has excellent remarks about the position of both the baptism and the temptations in the Scriptures. Meier, *Marginal Jew*, 2:101, 272n1.

79. Among this list we can include Leo the Great, Gregory the Great, Ambrose, Augustine, Chrysostom, Hilary, Bede, and many others.

80. Aquinas, *Summa Theologiae*, III, q. 41, aa. 1–4.

81. See Jeremias, *New Testament Theology*, 149.

82. Meier is of the opinion that this is a difficult task although he does seem to

question is supported by the historical-critical method. They are found in the Marcan and Q narratives.[83] There are multiple attestations of this narrative, which satisfy the first rule of the historical critical method. Joseph Fitzmyer adds two references from the Epistle to the Hebrews (Heb 2:18; 4:15).[84] He says, "Together with the gospel scenes, these verses assure the reality of temptations in the life of Jesus of Nazareth."[85] Because there are no witnesses to this event we can presume that, if the temptations are real, Jesus himself is the source.[86] This makes the temptations totally unlike the rest of the Gospel narratives which are all public. It would have been his personal experience which he related to the disciples.[87] There does not seem any good motive as to why the community would invent such stories.[88] Thus, the principle of discontinuity provides one more argument as to their historicity. The narrative describes a personal experience of Jesus. The temptations are an authentic experience of Jesus, but the description is imaginative and literary.

Nature of the Temptations

The temptations of Jesus can present a challenge to properly grasp their meaning. Meier is willing to admit their historicity as a possibility but because of the paucity of evidence he is doubtful that much more can be determined. Though Jesus experienced temptations, the sources are insufficient to establish anything further. It seems clear, however, that the temptations are extremely significant in the ministry of Jesus. Were these temptations actually a spiritual struggle that Jesus experienced, described as a battle between Jesus and the devil? Or were they a symbolic expression of the conflict between the devil and God to take place at the prophesied end time?[89] What can we gather from the Scriptures regarding

---

admit their historicity. Meier, *Marginal Jew*, 2:271n1.

83. Meier, *Marginal Jew*, 2:271n1. The Marcan narrative is Mark 1:12–13; the Q narrative is Matt 4:1–11//Luke 4:1–13.

84. These references are quite generic. They simply affirm that Jesus was tempted.

85. Fitzmyer, *Christological Catechism*, 43.

86. Jeremias, *New Testament Theology*, 74.

87. This favors treating the temptations, at their core, as coming from Jesus as autobiographical.

88. Meier, *Marginal Jew*, 2:271n1. Jeremias, *New Testament Theology*, 74. It would seem that the criterion of embarrassment would also apply.

89. Although the biblical story would support such an understanding, it would

the historicity and nature of the temptations of the historical Jesus? It has been suggested that Jesus' temptations were real and that they concerned his free deliberation to determine how to conduct his mission. They were "an inner spiritual struggle in preparation for his public ministry."[90] It was about the true understanding of Son of God, Messiah.[91] Jesus is portrayed as "one tempted to abandon his role as one faithful to his Father."[92] We do know that after this event, Jesus changed his mission from baptizer to that of itinerant preacher. The challenge was how he was to fulfill his mission. Jon Sobrino has suggested that Jesus' temptations concerned the type of power he was to use in his mission.[93] It concerned Jesus understanding of both his messiahship and the presence of the power of God against the anti-kingdom.[94] Jeremias proposed something similar. He proposed that Jesus was tempted to become a political leader.[95] It represented the conflict between Satan and the dawning of the kingdom.[96]

The Temptations: When and Where?

When and where did Jesus' temptations occur? The Synoptic Gospels situate them immediately after the baptism and just before the beginning of Jesus' Galilean ministry. No actual place other than the desert is ascribed but this may be entirely symbolic.[97] That these narratives are

---

seem to contradict the notion that this experience actually goes back to the Jesus of history. It would be a general description of the conflict between the kingdom of God and the opposing forces.

90. Meier, *Marginal Jew*, 2:272n1.

91. Meier, *Marginal Jew*, 2:271n1. Jesus is depicted in the identical way in his ultimate temptation in the Garden of Gethsemane (Mark 14:12–42//Matt 26:36–46//Luke 22:39–46). The Gospel of John places Jesus in a garden when he is arrested but, keeping with his high Christology, no agony or temptation is recorded. The fact that Jesus prayed and experienced an agony indicates a time of crisis, a time of interior challenge.

92. Fitzmyer, *Christological Catechism*, 45.

93. Sobrino, *Jesus the Liberator*, 149.

94. Meier understands the temptations in the wilderness in terms of "a symbolic representation of the apocalyptic struggle between God and the devil which was prophesied for the last days and which—according to Christian faith—became a reality in the ministry (especially of the exorcisms) of Jesus, culminating in his cross and resurrection." Meier, *Marginal Jew*, 2:272n1.

95. Jeremias, *New Testament Theology*, 71.

96. Jeremias, *New Testament Theology*, 74. This seems evident given Jesus' exorcisms during his ministry.

97. This could well be related to the temptation of the Israelites in the desert where

interpolations into the larger text leads us to suspect the temptations may have occurred at a different time and place than described. There may have been more than one episode.[98]

We are able to assign several possibilities for the temptations. First, Jesus experienced the temptations immediately after his baptism. This could have been reflective of an interior struggle with his decision to follow God's will as a disciple of John. Or it may have occurred immediately after the imprisonment of John the Baptist. This could very well have been a time of crisis for Jesus. Jesus chose to continue preaching the kingdom, no longer as a baptizer, but as an itinerant preacher.[99] Both Matt 4:12 and Mark 1:14 indicate that the public life of Jesus begins only after John was imprisoned.[100] Jesus may have been in John's company when he was arrested. This would have called for a decision on Jesus' part as to his own ministry.

The Galilean crisis is another logical possibility for Jesus' temptation. Edward Schillebeeckx suggests this as a time of testing or temptation for Jesus. This is an intriguing possibility. He sees a disjunction between Jesus' mission in Galilee and his eventual journey to Jerusalem. This journey is fairly well delineated in the Synoptic Gospels.[101] It could also have occurred during his ministry. Schillebeeckx believes that Jesus perceived his failure to inaugurate the kingdom in his ministry in Galilee and proceeded on to Jerusalem to bring matters to a conclusion. The temptation would have been the conflict involved in making this decision. Sobrino proposed a hypothesis close to Schillebeeckx's. He believed that Jesus had been rejected by the leaders and even by the crowds that had followed him. Jesus appears to have withdrawn from the crowds, according to Sobrino, and he began to focus

---

they wandered for forty years. The true Son of God is obedient even when tempted; the Israelites failed in this regard. John's baptism occurs in the desert, the wilderness.

98. Luke ends the temptation narrative with "when the devil had finished every temptation, he departed from him [Jesus] for a time" (Luke 4:13). See also Luke 22:3–6, 28, 31–34, 39–46.

99. The Synoptic Gospels are unanimous in placing the temptations immediately after the baptism and before the imprisonment of John the Baptist.

100. Luke is silent on the imprisonment of John, but he does indicate that Jesus left for Galilee after the temptation (Luke 4:14).

101. The chronology of the Gospel of John does not fit with this explanation. He describes Jesus as visiting Jerusalem on several (three or four) occasions. Dodd sharply delineates the ministry of Jesus between Galilee and Jerusalem. See his excellent work *The Founder of Christianity*, chapters 7 and 8.

on instructing his disciples. The rejection of his ministry by the Jewish leaders and the misunderstanding of his disciples is a possible cause of his temptation.[102] He points to the harsh rebuke to Peter because he failed to understand the nature of his messiahship during this time (Mark 8:27–33).[103] It appears that the temptations were multiple and occurred over a period of time and in history.[104]

It was suggested above that the baptism of Jesus was a show of solidarity with humanity. The temptations also affirm Jesus' solidarity with humankind. Except for sin, Jesus is like us in all things even in his susceptibility to temptation. And it suggests that Jesus, like all of us, had a growing consciousness. This is a considerable deviation from previous Christology. The older view, while having much to commend it, seems far different from our contemporary manner of imagining Jesus' situation. Nevertheless, even an older Christology admitted the reality of the temptations. Jesus was described as not only sinless but also impeccable, that is, not capable of sin.[105] His sinlessness would be proposed on dogmatic grounds: Jesus is true man, Jesus is true God.[106] Aquinas proposes that the temptation of Jesus would be about the means to an end and not about the end or purpose of something perceived as sinful. This corresponds with the more contemporary explanation that the temptations were subjective; they had to do with the change in the mode of his mission or the way he was to be God's Messiah. As human, Jesus would have had to figure out how he was to conduct his mission.

---

102. See Sobrino, *Jesus the Liberator*, 148–52.

103. The parallels to Mark 8:27–33 are Matt 16:13–20//Luke 9:18–26. Neither has recorded this rebuke.

104. The passion of the Lord should not be overlooked. It is the greatest of Jesus' tests which required his fidelity and obedience to his Father in the face of death.

105. Macquarrie would argue against the Augustinian notion that Christ could not sin. He says, "This again would appear to infringe his true humanity." Macquarrie, *Jesus Christ in Modern Thought*, 397. He does affirm, with the New Testament, that Jesus in fact did not sin. But that he could not be tempted or that he could not sin would "compromise his genuine humanity."

106. The Council of Chalcedon (AD 451) declared Jesus Christ to be true man and true God. That has been the governing dogma for all Christology since. Theologians proposed that Jesus Christ was a true, integral man. He possessed all the properties that every human has. Furthermore, they also proposed that he was a perfect man. This later theological proposal led to the theological opinion that Christ possessed the beatific vision during his lifetime. That proposal is no longer popular among contemporary theologians. It should be kept in mind that *Gaudium et Spes*, no. 22 and no. 45, describes Jesus as the perfect man.

John Macquarrie makes the challenging suggestion that "sin is not of the essence of humanity, it has no place in that 'archetypal' man conceived in the mind of God when he resolved to create a finite being in his image and likeness."[107] In speaking of the grace of Christ, Aquinas says something remarkably similar. "Sin forms no part of human nature, a nature which has God for its cause; rather it is contrary to nature."[108] Sin is understood as a defect of our human nature. It takes something away from it. That is why Jesus and Mary, though considered sinless, can be models for us to be imitated. Jesus and Mary are the goal for humans to achieve and not an unattainable example.

The temptation narratives depict Jesus as faithful and obedient to the Father.[109] The examination of the scriptural data supports this. Fitzmyer, who made the claim that the temptations were actual also made the claim that the meaning is more important than the historicity even though they are grounded in reality.[110] This is his rejection of a naive literalism.

Having examined Jesus' temptations at length we can conclude several important notions. The temptations were a true, actual, inner spiritual struggle of Jesus. They prepared him for his ministry as an itinerant prophet.[111] They are described as a struggle for a true understanding of his ministry; of his role as Messiah. That Jesus overcame the temptation is an act of fidelity or obedience to the Father.[112]

The Galilean Ministry: Jesus the Itinerant Preacher

If Jesus was a disciple of John the Baptist, it is clear that he did not remain so. Both history and faith tell us that his role in salvation history far

---

107. Macquarrie, *Jesus Christ in Modern Thought*, 129. The entire chapter 6 is worth reading for a deeper understanding of this subject.

108. Aquinas, *Summa Theologiae*, III, q. 15, a. 1.

109. This occurs again in Gethsemane. The obedience to the Father is the principal consideration in both events.

110. Fitzmyer, *Gospel According to Luke*, 2:510. This was quoted with approval by Meier, *Marginal Jew*, 2:272.

111. Meier, *Marginal Jew*, 2:272.

112. The Synoptic Gospels describe Jesus' agony in the garden as a temptation against his acceptance of his Abba's will. "He [Jesus] said, '*Abba*, Father, all things are possible to you. Take this cup away from me but not what I will but what you will'" (Mark 14:36). This reflects Jesus' true humanity. The outcome is that Jesus is faithful and obedient to his Abba even unto death.

exceeded that of the baptist. What may seem strange to us at first is that Jesus the Messiah, the Son of God, the Savior of the world, should have had a mentor or a predecessor.[113] We should remind ourselves that the Catholic tradition has always recognized intermediaries in the history of salvation. We need only point to the devotion given to the Blessed Mother and other saints as well as to Old Testament figures. It seems just as salutary to see John in a special role relative to the Christ. This is not a diminishment of the Christ but rather recognition that the divine plan included the role of human participation in a unique way even to the manner in which Jesus was introduced to his mission.

From Baptizer to Itinerant Preacher

Recent commentators have suggested that there was an actual shift in Jesus' ministry from baptizer to itinerant preacher. Interestingly enough, the Synoptic Gospels give no indication that Jesus was ever anything other than an itinerant preacher. He sent his disciples out to preach as he did, moving from village to village.[114] Furthermore, the Synoptic Gospels provide no evidence that Jesus ever baptized.[115] This seems at odds with the fact that the primitive church rushed to undertake this practice understanding that it came from Jesus.[116] The absence of these details from the Synoptics may have been a way that the evangelists reinforced their faith commitment to Jesus and not to John.

---

113. All four Gospels describe John as a forerunner of the Messiah, one who is to prepare his way.

114. It is clear that the Twelve (and Seventy-Two) are described as doing exactly what Jesus did during his Galilean ministry. See Mark 6:7–13; Matt 10:5–15; Luke 9:9–16; 10:1–12.

115. The Gospel of John contains the only scriptural evidence that Jesus baptized. See John 3:22–24; 4:1–2.

116. Matt 28:16–20. It is somewhat surprising that Jesus enjoined the duty to baptize only when he, postresurrection, gave them the Great Commission (Matt 28:16–20) if this practice was not familiar to them. Oddly enough, this injunction is in neither Luke nor John. This is somewhat perplexing since it was a practice immediately adopted by the early Christians. One answer to this is that it was already an established custom during the public life of Jesus—though it is not recorded.

Change in Ministry: When and Why

Jesus accepted the role of John the Baptist in the history of salvation. In accepting John's baptism, we can presume that he accepted his eschatological view. Among the most prominent similarities between John and Jesus were that both were prophets; both gathered disciples to whom they gave their personal instructions and taught to pray; both baptized; and both were martyred. This synopsis is much of what we know about the preaching and praxis of John the Baptist. There is much we do not know because of the limited nature of our sources.

If there was indeed a change in Jesus' ministry, and there is good evidence that there was, we can only speculate upon when and why the change occurred. It seems likely that Jesus followed the praxis of John until John was imprisoned.[117] This was a logical time for the shift in Jesus' ministry. Mark tells us that, "After John had been arrested, Jesus came to Galilee, proclaiming the gospel of God" (Mark 1:13).[118] Several motives can be offered as to why this change was made. If Jesus followed John until his imprisonment it would seem to be prudent to make this change in ministry out of fear of Herod Antipas.[119] Remaining where he had been baptizing might have been perceived as a dangerous situation. It is just as likely that Jesus changed his manner of preaching because he saw that being an itinerant preacher would be more effective than remaining a baptizer. He would go out to meet Israel and not wait for Israel to come to him.

Conclusion and Resume

This chapter has grown much longer than was originally anticipated. That fact simply points to the importance of Jesus' baptism and temptations. They should be understood as Jesus' preparation for the Galilean ministry. It is a foundation for all that will be investigated in the

---

117. Both Mark 1:14 and Matt 4:12 indicate the Galilean ministry began after John had been arrested.

118. While the Gospel of Matthew supports this, the Gospels of Luke and John make no mention of this shift in ministry.

119. It seems almost certain that John was in prison (Fortress of Machaerus) during Jesus' itinerant ministry. While in prison John had heard of Jesus' works (Matt 11:2) which indicates that Jesus was already deeply involved in his itinerant ministry. The entire narrative concerning John's disciples can be found in Matt 11:2–6 and Luke 7:18–23.

following chapters. It may have come as a surprise to the reader that so much information could have been obtained from such a paucity of data. The importance of Jesus' baptism, his theophany, and temptations, cannot be stressed enough.

A Brief Schematic History

A brief summation of what has been established is called for. It seems clear that Jesus was, at least for a time, a disciple of John the Baptist. It is unlikely that John recognized Jesus as the *mightier one* whose coming he had predicted. Jesus appears to have baptized in the same general area as John, and he appears to have gained disciples. Peter and his brother Andrew appear among these former disciples of John. Upon John's imprisonment, Jesus seems to have gone to Galilee as an itinerant preacher. It is not clear that this was because John had been imprisoned or because Jesus had made his decision independently of this event. John was still alive and in prison when Jesus had come to understand that he was the eschatological prophet. Whatever John's influence, Jesus had arrived at a self-understanding and a vision of his mission. The kingdom became the central theme of his preaching. While this schematic history is speculative, it does justice to the data.

Jesus and His Human Experience: A Look Ahead

This focus on his baptism is intended to establish whatever is possible of the Jesus of history, his human history. Before we move on to a discussion of the public ministry of Jesus it is helpful to note that what has been proposed is in harmony with the Council of Chalcedon. The great christological council declared that Jesus was a true, integral man. He possessed all of the qualities of a human being. This serves as the point of departure for all Christology. The human experiences which were examined tell us that Jesus did not begin fully equipped for his mission. Jesus functioned in a human, rational manner. He was not gifted with any supernatural powers. Jesus was influenced by John's teaching and praxis.[120] He accepted his eschatology. But he shaped his mission as a charismatic, creative person. Jesus' mission was his personal vision. Jesus

---

120. Unfortunately, we have no detailed record of John's teaching.

was an itinerant preacher, a healer, or a miracle worker.[121] There is no indication that John ever performed miracles. Jesus rejected the asceticism of the baptist. His movement is characterized as joyful.[122] His ministry featured festive meals to which Jesus invited sinners, tax collectors and others on the edge of being religiously unclean to enjoy a meal. These meals looked proleptically to the eschatological banquet shared in the future kingdom. Jesus also taught as a poet. He taught in narratives, sayings, proverbs, parables, blessings, and woes. Most importantly, John's call for God's judgment was modified by Jesus and became a new mode of salvation. This is a picture of both how Jesus began his public life and how it developed throughout the Galilean ministry and beyond. The following chapters will explore Jesus' teaching.

Jesus and the Beginning of His Movement

Jesus' public ministry is often referred to as the Jesus Movement.[123] The reason for this is twofold: first, it differentiates his ministry from that of John the Baptist; and second, it differentiates it as being pre-Christology in a proper sense. Jesus did not use the christological, honorific titles for himself during his public life with the exception of the title Son of Man. Neither does he permit others to use them of him.[124] In that sense, Christology proper is not born until the primitive community affirms the christological titles of him in faith after the resurrection. These provide us with our full understanding of the person Jesus Christ.

Jesus' ministry was rooted in his Abba experience. It was based on his vision of God and his kingdom. We will have more to say about this later in chapter 4. This experience is a singular moment of grace for

---

121. Jesus is described as a prophet in the line of Elijah who was a miracle worker. There are no miracle workers among the later or literary prophets.

122. Matt 11:18–19//Luke 7:31–34. As one might have suspected, this brief narrative saying is from Q which lends some credibility to it. Thus, Jesus understood his own mission as joyful without criticizing John's particular style.

123. This is not to be confused with the rather superficial movement of the fifties and sixties. Reference is made here to the beginning of Jesus prophetic and public ministry. While of limited usage it does permit us to speak of the Jesus of history and the christological affirmations proper.

124. There are some who believe that the confession of Peter that Jesus was the Messiah (Christ) was an exception and consider this to be authentic. Peter's confession can be found in Mark 8:29; Matt 16:16; and Luke 9:20. If true, it would be an exception to the rule.

Jesus. Jesus experienced God in a unique way and both his consciousness of God and his self-understanding developed from this experience over time. It was out of this experience that Jesus became the prophetic preacher of the kingdom of God.

The chapters that follow explore the major themes that constitute Jesus' mission in Galilee and Jerusalem. They will focus on his central teaching and praxis.

4

The Kingdom of God: Preliminary Considerations

Introduction

It should be abundantly clear that the center of our study is Jesus of Nazareth, who in faith is identified as the Christ, the Son of God. That the object of our faith is admittedly a historical person who lived in a historical context should not be minimized. It is a central dogma of the church. It is singularly important that our study recover as much of this authentic history as possible in both the teaching and the praxis of Jesus of Nazareth. It will solidly anchor our faith affirmations and help us to read the Scriptures more intelligently. And it will clearly influence and improve our Christology.

Given the nature of our sources, it is impossible to establish a sequence of historical events in Jesus' ministry. No clear timeline of the life of Jesus can be constructed from the Scriptures.[1] Our task therefore, since no chronology of the life of Jesus is possible, is to focus our attention on the major themes in the life of Jesus. We began our quest with the baptism of Jesus. We will now take up his active ministry. The preaching of the kingdom of God will be the first theme we will address because

---

1. For most of Jesus' ministry it is impossible to develop a chronological timeline. The evangelists arranged their material according to their own literary designs or theological perceptions. See Meier, *Marginal Jew*, 2:131.

it is the central part of Jesus' preaching. The other major themes, the miracles, and parables will follow.

The Kingdom of God: The Central Theme of Jesus' Teaching[2]

It has become commonplace among theologians to affirm that Jesus did not preach himself as the Christ during his public life.[3] It was postresurrection Christianity after having experienced Jesus raised from the dead who preached him as the Christ, the Messiah. During his public ministry Jesus avoided christological titles.[4] The principal focus of his ministry was preaching the *kingdom of God*. Kingdom of heaven is a typical Matthean usage which replaces the expression kingdom of God. There is no difference whatsoever between the expressions.[5] In spite of its centrality in his preaching, Jesus never explicitly explains the meaning of the kingdom of God. We can assume, however, that it was intelligible to those to whom he preached.[6]

---

2. Should the church be identified with the kingdom of God? It is not normally identified as such; however, Raymond Brown comes close. He says that it is at least partially identified. See Brown, *Churches the Apostles Left Behind*, 51–53. The church will not be identified with the kingdom of God in this text.

3. The period during Jesus public ministry is often referred to as the Jesus Movement to distinguish it from the Christ movement (Christology) which followed the resurrection. The use of this expression has been criticized and with good reasons. Therefore, it will not be used here. See also chapter 3, 74n123.

4. Perhaps with one exception, the Son of Man, a christological title, was used by Jesus as a self-designation. There are some who also think that the title Christ may have been used in a very limited fashion. This seemed to occur at Peter's confession of Jesus as the Christ (Mark 8:29 parr.). The christological titles all come from the primitive church and not from Jesus' earthly life. It is the early church's identification of Jesus and not Jesus' self-designation.

5. It is clear that kingdom of God and kingdom of heaven express the same identical reality. See Dowell, *HarperCollins Bible Dictionary*, s.v. "Kingdom of God." The latter expression is normally but not exclusively used in Matthew's Gospel. It accounts for his sensitivity to his community, largely composed of converts from Judaism, in order to avoid the use of the name of God directly. The pericope from Mark which describes the beginning of Jesus ministry uses kingdom of God (Mark 1:15) while the same event is described by Matthew as kingdom of heaven (Matt 4:17). Compare the expressions found in the two versions of the Beatitudes. Matthew refers to kingdom of heaven (Matt 5:3) and Luke refers to kingdom of God (Luke 6:20).

6. As a charismatic preacher Jesus drew large crowds and we can presume that these crowds were made up largely of uneducated peasants. The meaning of Jesus' preaching must have been intelligible to them since we are told that it made a great impression

The kingdom of God was absolutely central to Jesus' preaching. Both his words and deeds point to this message in an explanatory way. The expression permeates the synoptic tradition. The expression kingdom of God or its equivalent kingdom of heaven occurs 122 times in the Gospels; and is found on the lips of Jesus ninety-two times. Meier counts the expression in the sayings of Jesus alone as numbering fifty-nine.[7] The parables are almost always told in reference to the kingdom; and the miracle tradition is associated with the presence of the kingdom. The same can be implied in Jesus' festive meals.

Not only was the kingdom of God central to Jesus' preaching but he also sent the Twelve, a special inner group, to preach the same message and to cast out demons, a notion closely associated with the imminent presence of the kingdom.[8] The mission of the Twelve and their return can be found in Mark 6:7–13, 30; Matt 10:6–15; and Luke 9:1–6, 10.[9] These pericopes are most informative. The Twelve were chosen to be prophetic symbols of the regathering of the twelve tribes of Israel, an idea closely associated with the kingdom.[10]

---

on the crowds. It is the task of theologians to recover its meaning for a contemporary audience in an examination of Jesus' words and deeds.

7. Meier, *Marginal Jew*, 2:238. Others may count the number of this expression differently, but the resulting difference is insignificant and does not change the judgment that Jesus' preaching of the kingdom is absolutely central to his mission. Of these sayings, Mark contains thirteen sayings with the expression kingdom of God, Q has thirteen, M has twenty-four, L has six, and John has two. My count of these numbers is fifty-eight, a small discrepancy from Meier's count.

8. The choosing of the Twelve and their sending is included in the list of "almost indisputable facts" associated with Jesus' life. As a point of interest: Mark always refers to this inner group as the Twelve; Matthew refers to them as the twelve disciples, twelve apostles, and the Twelve; and Luke refers to the Twelve but also refers to them as the apostles (Luke 9:10). Meier argues for the historicity of the Twelve as well as for their mission activity. See Meier, *Marginal Jew*, 3:147, 154–63.

Meier quotes from Manson's work *The Sayings of Jesus* as saying that "the mission of the disciples is one of the best-attested facts in the life of Jesus." Meier is not willing to go this far but he quotes Manson approvingly. See Meier, *Marginal Jew*, 3:185.

9. Besides the sending of the Twelve, Luke also describes a mission of the Seventy-Two (Luke 10:1–12; 17–20). According to the notes in the NABRE, the sending of the Seventy-Two is a similar account to the sending of the Twelve and is based on the Q source. Luke has reshaped the mission to fit his particular interest. The sending of the Seventy-Two is thought to be a creation of Luke based upon the narrative of the sending of the Twelve.

10. The mission of the Twelve will be taken up below. Implied in their activity is behavior that is consistent with the kingdom of God as a present reality.

THE KINGDOM OF GOD: PRELIMINARY CONSIDERATIONS

The Kingdom of God: Background/Basis/Foundation

The expression kingdom of God was rarely used prior to Jesus' mission. It is not found in the Hebrew Old Testament, the deuterocanonical literature, or the pseudepigrapha.[11] It is found only once in the intertestamental literature (Psalms of Solomon). It is rare in the Christian Scriptures. In the Acts of the Apostles there are six passages; in the authentic Pauline Letters there are seven passages.[12] This fact points to the (almost) unique usage of the expression by Jesus.[13] As has been mentioned earlier, the expression is found in Jesus' sayings and parables; and it is expressed in his miracles and festive meals.[14] The expression is close to being original with the historical Jesus but the content or meaning that it expresses would have preceded him.

We can presume that Jesus' audience was not terribly sophisticated. They were largely peasants. What would the expression kingdom of God have signified to them? Would they have understood an expression such as this if it were unique to Jesus? We do know that his message, the use of the expression kingdom of God, resonated with those who heard it. We can presume that their preunderstanding permitted them to understand and accept his message.

The expression kingdom of God, however, does not come to us in a vacuum. It would be more than useful to discover the antecedents to this expression in the religious environment of Jesus' time. The question is this: What was the general religious understanding of Jesus' audience that informed their conception of his use of the expression kingdom of God? It is well worth spending some time on this issue since it is the matrix from which Jesus preaches. Determining the underlying notions or concepts will help us to arrive at a better understanding of the expression and Jesus' use of it.

Religious insights do not fall "free and without alloy" from heaven. They are first experienced in lived historical events. Edward Schillebeeckx put it this way: "Revelation presupposes a meaningful human event, an

---

11. Deuterocanonical literature is sometimes referred to as apocrypha.

12. It seems clear that after Jesus' death and resurrection there was a shift in nomenclature: Jesus, in his person, replaced the expression kingdom of God. The preacher became the preached and christological titles were attributed to him.

13. See Meier, *Marginal Jew*, 2:243–270. Meier carefully examines the entire canon of literature which might possibly contain the expression.

14. This satisfies the criteria of multiple attestation and discontinuity. This assures us of its historical usage by Jesus.

event which is already relevant in human terms without direct reference to God, *etsi Deus non daretur*."[15] This grounding of salvation, a saving event in human experience, permits reflection on its significance and the discovery of appropriate language to express it meaningfully.

The salvation history of Israel is marked by several significant events within which its relationship with God developed. This experience was passed on to successive generations. These formative epochs, each marked with a significant event or events in the history of Israel, resulted in the religious development of the people of Israel. The foundational insights, antecedent to Jesus' mission, defined Israel and its salvation history in a significant way.

What will help us understand the religious antecedents in this tradition that shaped Jesus' teaching? A necessary propaedeutic to the entire religious tradition of Israel is that God is foundationally understood as the creator who rules all of his creation.[16] This notion is basic to all that follows. God is understood as transcendent; he is the wholly other, the creator of all things. The creation narrative tells us that God is in the world that he created. The creation story does not describe the creator as one who has no interest in his creation. This is no deist God, like the God described in Voltaire's *Candide*.[17] He is not distant from the world or its people, but is present in it and active on man's behalf. God alone is the source of salvation.

The exodus from Egypt is the first and principle salvific event in the history of Israel. It is understood as a saving event in which God became active in history by leading the Israelites to freedom (salvation). The exodus and the covenant which followed it are tightly bound together. Chronologically they are separated by only three months according to the literary account in Exod 19:1. But there is an even greater unification between these two inseparable events. In the principal formative action

15. Schillebeeckx, *On Christian Faith*, 11. The translation of the Latin is "even if God did not exist." It is found first in Grotius, *De jure belli ac pacis*, 1625.

16. It should be noted here that Gen 1–2 clearly affirms the notion that God is creator and sustainer of all things and that they are good. This idea is repeated in many psalms and the book of Job.

17. Candide and his companions have a discussion with a dervish, probably supposed to represent a Sufi Muslim dervish. This conversation takes place in book XXX of Voltaire's *Candide*. The dervish asks, "When His Highness [God] sends a ship to Egypt, does he worry about whether the mice in it are comfortable?" In Voltaire's description, the dervish gives a deist view of God. God has created the universe but takes no interest in it thereafter. It is similar to winding up a clock and then letting it run itself out. This is far removed from the view of God professed by both Judaism and Christianity.

THE KINGDOM OF GOD: PRELIMINARY CONSIDERATIONS

of the Old Testament, after he has saved the Israelites, God revealed his name to them and formed them as his people over whom he reigns.[18] He gives them rules to govern both the religious and social dimensions of their lives. In these events, God is understood as personal and intimate.[19] These symbolic expressions reveal salvation history to us as taking place within our human condition, in history. God reigns over the Israelites as an earthly king or ruler ought to.

Several other noteworthy events followed which contribute to the development of Israel's tradition. The establishment of the monarchy was one such significant development. God rules his people; the kings are understood more properly as his vicars. This relationship between God and his people does not change. The temple became the place from which God rules. The temple worship, reflected in the psalm tradition, frequently names God as king.

The prophetic tradition adds another dimension to this development. In its frequent failures to honor the covenant agreement, Israel was continually called to return to its former relationship with God. God is always prepared to forgive the Israelites for their infidelities. This is an Old Testament concept which is prominent, at least conceptually, in the preaching of the prophets. Failure to live up to the covenant is met with punishment but it is always followed with forgiveness. In Isaiah we hear God saying, "See, I am creating new heavens and a new earth; the former things shall not be remembered or come to mind. Instead, shout for joy and be glad forever in what I am creating" (Isa 65:17–18). In effect he describes the kingdom without using the word. And it is an earthly kingdom. At this time in history no thought of an afterlife had yet been expressed in the tradition.

The conceptual notion of God's kingdom developed from the period of the prophets to first century Israel. It is clear that there is but one God and he alone is the Savior.[20] The event of the Babylonian exile, reflected in the later wisdom literature, saw the emergence of a faithful Israel but one which still experienced alienation from God. Israel no

---

18. The event in which God first revealed himself and offered a covenant was with Abraham. Abraham is understood as the father of monotheism. This event preceded the Sinai covenant (Gen 15 and 17). The formation of a people was not to come until much later when God revealed his name to Moses. The exodus, however, is the principle saving event for Israel.

19. Later in the salvation history of Israel, God is variously described as a father, a mother, a husband, and many other intimate expressions.

20. Isa 43:10–13. This text is from a period just before the Babylonian captivity.

longer saw its collective punishment in terms of its failure to be faithful to the covenant. This situation brought about the notion of the restoration of Israel regardless of the rationale for its experience of alienation. God was understood as a merciful, forgiving king. When Israel is fully restored (prophetic restoration) it will extend to and incorporate gentiles. Isaiah speaks of the gathering of the nations at the end time (Isa 66:18–21). We will see that many of these ideas were foundational in Jesus' preaching of the kingdom.[21]

The final stage of Israel's development occurs with the desecration of the temple by Antiochus IV Epiphanes. It was during this period that the notion of an afterlife developed. Salvation became understood and expressed as both a present and a future reality.[22] The good would be rewarded, if not in this life, then in the next. In the period just prior to Jesus' public life, there is a widespread and collective understanding that some form of afterlife exists which those who are faithful to God will enjoy.

From this far too incomplete examination of Israel's history, we can arrive at the following understanding. The expression of the mythic story of God's reign is evident from the first page of the Scripture to its last. It seems clear that the underlying message is that God acts on behalf of humanity in history. He is the creator of all and reigns over all peoples. He is the one and only source of salvation. God ruled over his people in a covenantal relationship. He is a God who both demands and expects fidelity to his commands and he both punishes Israel's transgressions and forgives them as well. And even in their infidelity, God will restore Israel to a place of peace and justice. When this restoration takes place gentiles will be included.

These antecedents would have permeated Jesus' social, cultural, and religious environment. The people would have understood these religious ideas since they were embedded in the fabric of first century Israel. Meier says that "he [Jesus] may well have been the first to forge and regularly employ the fixed phrase 'the kingdom of God' to evoke the Old Testament mythic story."[23] Though the expression kingdom of God appears to be used almost exclusively by Jesus as if it were his

---

21. There are numerous references in the psalmody that refer to the nations in a positive way. As an example, see Ps 67. This is a recognition that, in spite of their privileged place, God is the God of all nations. Israel recognized this as such.

22. Meier, *Marginal Jew*, 2:247. This is expressed in Dan 12:1—3:13.

23. Meier, *Marginal Jew*, 2:244.

THE KINGDOM OF GOD: PRELIMINARY CONSIDERATIONS

creation, it carried with it meaning easily understood by those to whom he proclaimed this message. These ideas will prove beneficial to us as we proceed. The Old Testament supplied Jesus with language, symbols and the story of God's royal rule. Jesus used this material to express his understanding as the kingdom of God.[24]

Conclusion: Jesus and the Expression *Kingdom of God*

The expression kingdom of God as used by Jesus cannot in any way be separated from its first century context. The general notion of God as king is not original with Jesus. The Old Testament supplied Jesus with the language and symbols, as well as with the story of God's royal rule.[25] Jesus would have been familiar with this story. It was part of his social and cultural environment as well as his religious experience. However, Jesus' use of this expression kingdom of God was uniquely his own.[26] Jesus did not invent the conceptual background or antecedents to his understanding of the kingdom of God. The idea has a history deep in the consciousness of Israel. Thus, as a child of his own culture and religious practices, we can presume that Jesus preached to an audience who would have understood him within an accepted conception of the expression. Having said this, not everyone would have understood the notion of kingdom in exactly the same identical way. The use of the expression kingdom of God was unique to Jesus and indeed he shaped it to signify his message.[27]

---

24. Meier, *Marginal Jew*, 2:252.

25. Meier, *Marginal Jew*, 2:252.

26. It was not widely used by either Jews or Christians following Jesus' life and death. See Meier, *Marginal Jew*, 2:239.

27. We need to be cognizant of this important detail. God as king is attested to in numerous places in the Old Testament. It is especially prominent in the Psalms that liturgically celebrate the reign of God as king. It would have been a significant part of the liturgical celebration in the temple. Jesus employed these concepts when he describes the kingdom of God. However, it is worth noting that Jesus never refers to God as king. The proper address for God and the one he taught his disciples is that God is his and our Abba or Father.

5

How Jesus Understood The Kingdom of God

Introduction

JESUS' VISION OF THE kingdom did not come to him independent of the religious environment in which he lived. Neither was it independent of his personal religious experience.[1] The Jewish tradition as it was lived and experienced in his time provided Jesus with the story of God's kingly rule. Jesus would have been familiar with this biblical story. It contained both the language and the symbols which grounded his personal understanding of the kingdom.[2] As has been pointed out earlier, Jesus was a Jew totally immersed in the Jewish tradition. The story of Israel and its salvation history was a significant part of his religious and social environment. It was Jesus who framed this lived, religious experience into the expression *kingdom of God*. Its use is almost exclusive to him. He shaped the expression to communicate his own meaning, but it was not without significant inherited intelligibility. His understanding

---

1. We make this statement fully realizing that the concept could have been infused or that it was received in some way by grace. But even having said this, the meaning must have a preunderstanding or be intelligible in his social and religious context. This study, without denying or denigrating the explanation of any older theology, focuses on what is grounded in Jesus' experience as much as we can identify this in our sources and what can be historically verified.

2. Meier, *Marginal Jew*, 2:252.

of the kingdom is also rooted in his personal experience of God, sometimes referred to as his Abba experience.[3]

Jesus' Understanding of the Kingdom

The kingdom of God is central to Jesus' message. It was a lived reality for him, but he never defined, described, or explained it. Neither is the meaning found directly in the Scriptures. How then is it possible to arrive at its proper signification? Does Jesus say or do anything that permits us to grasp his understanding of the expression? The answer is an unequivocal yes. The content of Jesus' message, principally his teaching about the nature of the kingdom of God, can be attained only from an examination of his ministry as a whole: his words and deeds. These serve as a disclosure of the meaning of the kingdom of God.

The kingdom of God cannot be identified as an earthly, political kingdom as one might easily imagine from the literal understanding of the expression. God's kingdom is not restricted by any territorial boundary although we will come to argue that it has a relationship to this world. Neither is it limited to an otherworldly reality.

The kingdom of God is better understood as a reign or rule. The expression *reign* connotes an office more than a territory. It is an exercise of power or authority. At times, translators of the Scriptures have preferred the term reign to kingdom because reign avoids the mistake of understanding it as a place.[4] The kingdom of God is more accurately expressed as the activity or presence of God. It is wherever God's presence is experienced or wherever he is perceived as active in the lives of men and women. It is an act of God, in which his rule is clearly manifest. Thus, the kingdom of God is best understood in an active sense in which God's

---

3. More will be said of Jesus' Abba experience as we proceed. It is clear that Jesus had a special relationship with the Father whom he refers to as his Abba and he teaches his disciples to do the same. In the Gospel of John Jesus says, "I have told you [the disciples] everything I have heard from my Father" (John 15:15). There is also another important Q source reference (Matt 11:25–27//Luke 10:21–24) which indicates that the Father is the direct source of Jesus' proclamation. Adolph Harnack believed that this was one of the most significant references found in the Synoptic Gospels.

4. Contemporary translations of the Scriptures seem to have given up on reign as a substitute and returned to a more traditional and more literal translation of the Greek *basileus* as kingdom.

power becomes effective in the world of human experience.[5] This use is an improvement to the more passive notion of rule or reign.

The Kingdom of God: An Eschatological Expression[6]

In its original connotation the word eschaton referred to the last things: heaven, hell, and purgatory. Under various theological developments it came to refer to that which is ultimate, final, or definitive. The kingdom of God has taken on these attributes. Eschaton and eschatology are not biblical terms, but they do express a biblical concept that is found in both the Old and New Testaments. It is a way of addressing the definitive or ultimate destiny of humanity. It expresses God's decisive action in human history. Eschatology expects the end of the present age and the ushering in of a time of fulfillment.[7] It is a transformation of the current state of affairs. The end time is often referred to as the *Day of the Lord*. It is signified by expressions such as the restoration of Israel; an eschatological banquet; a transformation; and a new covenant. The language, as one can see, is inherently ambiguous. The question is, in what sense is the kingdom of God ultimate or definitive? How should we understand the eschatology of the kingdom? Is the kingdom of God a present reality, is it imminent, soon to take place, or is it a future reality? Is it something that belongs to this world or is it otherworldly? Answering these questions helps us to understand better the nature of the kingdom as proclaimed by Jesus Christ.[8] There are scriptural passages which support each of these views. We will consider each in turn to determine which is authentic to the historical Jesus and we will provide an explanation as to what these various expressions might mean for contemporary men and women.

---

5. It is the activity of God as king. See Perrin, *Jesus and the Language*, 1–2.

6. In this sense, eschatology refers to that which is final or ultimate. It is that which is most important. Sometimes the expressions apocalyptic and eschatology are understood as conceptually identical. In this study we understand them as distinct. It would prove useful to examine this terminology in any good biblical dictionary or commentary.

7. *The New Jerome Biblical Commentary* contains numerous references to eschatology and related concepts. See also Freedman et al., *Eerdmans Dictionary of the Bible*.

8. Jesus describes the kingdom of God from within the framework of eschatology. This is the reason for understanding him as an eschatological prophet. "A completely un-eschatological Jesus . . . is simply not the historical Jesus." Meier, *Marginal Jew*, 2:317. Meier repeats this notion often and in various places in his five volumes.

The Authentic Teaching of Jesus: The Kingdom as Future

Jesus preached the kingdom of God as both future transcendent and future-immanent. A cursory reading of the Scriptures would seem to indicate as much. But can it be established as the authentic teaching of Jesus? Meier believes that this is an essential part of Jesus' message.[9] His arguments are well worth reading and are persuasive.

The Kingdom as a Future/Future-Immanent Reality

Meier established a framework of texts which are authentic teachings of Jesus. They are separated from narratives or sayings that are more likely to have been derived from the evangelists or the early church.[10] The reason for this technique is because a simple reading of the Scriptures will not decide the question of historical authenticity.[11] Our intention is to discover the authentic teachings of Jesus that affirm the future or future-immanent character of the kingdom.

Meier suggested the following four blocks of Jesus' sayings which he believes are pivotal to establish his conclusion. He adds a fifth collection of sayings which involves the end time of the kingdom. These blocks of sayings are (1) the Lord's Prayer (Matt 6:19//Luke 11:2); (2) the Last Supper (Mark 14:25//); (3) reclining with Abraham in the kingdom (Matt 8:11–13//Luke 13:28–29); and (4) the Beatitudes in the Sermon on the Mount/Plain (Matt 5:3–12//Luke 6:20–23).[12] There are other sayings that could be appealed to but these chosen sayings "have both solid arguments in favor of their authenticity and an unambiguous reference to the final

---

9. Meier, *Marginal Jew*, 2:291. Why should so much time and effort be spent examining this material? Because it is so pivotal to our study. The kingdom is the central proclamation of Jesus.

10. This is not an attempt to deny the value of any part of Scripture. It is an attempt to firmly ground our conclusions. See the explanation given in chapter 2.

11. Some of these sayings might be called "false friends." They tell the truth, but they are not derived directly from the historical Jesus. As an example of this we can point to various sayings regarding the end time. The following sayings found in Matt 10:23; Mark 9:1; and Mark 13:30 declare that the end time is coming soon. Although they are attributed to Jesus, they are actually from the early church.

12. Meier, *Marginal Jew*, 2:291. I have modified Meier's exact description of these blocks of material. Meier comes to his conclusion on the basis of the criteria of multiple attestations of both sources and forms. These sayings are from all the major strands of the Gospel tradition (Mark, Q, M, L, and tangentially John).

coming of the kingdom on the last day."[13] Each group of sayings contains references to the future kingdom and all are important. Thus, knowing that these narratives are authentic, it is a simple task to conclude that the future coming of the kingdom is central to Jesus' teaching.

"Your Kingdom Come" (Matt 6:10//Luke 11:2)

The Lord's Prayer is an authentic teaching of Jesus. The first two petitions are significant for our discussion. Its first petition is "hallowed be your name" and it is no different from the popular form that we pray. Meier persuasively argues that its meaning is: may you (God) be present, and may you rule as king. The second petition is "your kingdom come." Jesus' use of the expression kingdom of God is another way of saying that God is ruling his people. This is in line with the prophetic tradition. God will come (Isa 35:4; 40:9–10) and he will reign as king (Isa 52:7).[14] It seems clear that Jesus, in the prayer he taught his disciples, understood a future kingdom. The other petitions support this notion as they prepare the disciples for the future.

Jesus' teaching that the kingdom was future-immanent, that it was about to happen, agrees with the prophetic utterances of the Old Testament prophets. These prophetic utterances were never about a distant future.[15] But they do present us with a difficulty. In what sense did the community understand this imminent coming of the kingdom? How did they imagine the end time, the time of the Lord? What shape was the presence of God ruling his people going to take?

Drinking Wine in the Kingdom of God (Mark 14:25 par.)

One of the features of Jesus' ministry accepted as historical is his festive meals. Jesus invited many individuals who were on the fringe of society to share in these meals: the tax collectors, sinners, and those who were religiously unclean.[16] This joyous meal symbolized the final feast in the

---

13. Meier, *Marginal Jew*, 2:353 n. 5.

14. There is considerable support for this position in Meier, *Marginal Jew*, 2:299.

15. An immanent coming would agree with the preaching of John the Baptist to whom Jesus was closely allied and with the expectations of his disciples and the peasants to whom he preached.

16. Although prostitutes are often supposed to be at the festive meals according to the popular mind, they are never placed there in the Gospels. They are referred to

kingdom. It was a proleptic pointing to a reversal of positions which the faithful would experience in the final banquet.

Most scholars accept Jesus' final meal with his disciples as historical. It was a continuation of his other shared meals. During this last meal Jesus proclaims, "Amen, I say to you, I shall not drink again the fruit of the vine until the day when I drink it new in the kingdom of God" (Mark 14:25). The expression "amen, I say to you" is a solemn, emphatic introduction to the saying. Jesus foresees his death and he clearly understood that this is the last meal he will share with his disciples on earth. He anticipates that he will enjoy that banquet in the heavenly kingdom. Jesus' saying is authentic, and it points to the future enjoyment of the kingdom.

Reclining at the Table in the Kingdom (Matt 8:11–12//Luke 13:28–29)

Matthew places this significant saying of Jesus in the context of the healing of the centurion's servant. It is an appropriate response to faith: "I say to you, many will come from the east and the west, and will recline with Abraham, Isaac, and Jacob at the banquet in the kingdom of heaven, but the children of the kingdom will be driven out into the outer darkness, where there will be wailing and grinding of teeth (Matt 8:11–12)."[17]

This prophetic oracle expresses the understanding of the historical Jesus that there is a future definitive coming of God's kingly rule.[18] Though Luke situates this narrative in an entirely different context than Matthew, it differs only in his addition to the reference of people coming from the "north and south." (Luke 13:29). In all other details they agree. It is clear that gentiles (those from east and west) will replace the children of the kingdom (the Israelites) in the eschatological or final banquet in the kingdom of heaven.[19] The future reference is obvious; the mention of the patriarchs gives this banquet some permanency. It also gives it a present understanding since the patriarchs already enjoy the kingdom.

---

only twice in the Gospels (Matt 21:31–32). In this reference prostitutes are mentioned along with tax collectors as "entering the kingdom of God before you [chief priests and elders]."

17. This exclusion and substitution might also be seen in relation to the parables of the evil tenants (Mark 12:1-11 parr.) and the great supper (Matt 22:1–10). These are discussed in chapter 10.

18. Meier, *Marginal Jew*, 2:314–16.

19. The festive meals so prominent in Jesus' ministry look proleptically to the heavenly banquet.

The kingdom of heaven/God as spoken of by Jesus in this instance is an otherworldly and transcendent reference.

The Beatitudes (Matt 5:3–12//Luke 6:20–23)

The beatitudes confirm a future kingdom. Jesus preached the beatitudes to oppressed people. The happiness promised them is the future salvation of a suffering group. If they are happy now it is only because of the imminence of the kingdom which in some manner was already experienced in Jesus' festive meals.

The core beatitudes address a reversal of position for the poor, the mourners, the hungry, and those who suffer persecution.[20] This is a situation in which outsiders become insiders. It is a reversal of their condition.[21] It seems clear that this occurs with the future coming of the kingdom.

What Conclusions Can We Draw?

The framework of Jesus' sayings discussed above has been established as authentic. These sayings were traced back to the historical Jesus with a high degree of probability. Jesus clearly preached the future coming of the kingdom. In itself this is remarkable both for our theological reflection and for the exercise of our faith. We know that preaching the kingdom of God was central to Jesus' mission. What meaning of the kingdom of God can we draw from these sayings of Jesus? Meier summarizes his position as follows and it is worth quoting at length: "Each of these pivotal sayings has been tested by various criteria and judged authentic. Furthermore, taken together they clearly indicate (1) that Jesus expected a future, definitive coming of God to rule as king; (2) that this hope was so central to his message that he bade his disciples make it a central petition of their own prayer; (3) that the coming kingdom would bring about the reversal of present unjust conditions of poverty, sorrow, and hunger; (4) that this final kingdom would bring about an even more astounding reversal: it would include at least some gentiles,

---

20. These Beatitudes were part of the blocks of material Meier examined in order to show that the kingdom of God was authentically taught by Jesus as future. These four core beatitudes are from Q. They are Matthew's first, second, fourth and ninth beatitudes. These are also found in Luke's list.

21. Many parables also speak of reversal of position.

HOW JESUS UNDERSTOOD THE KINGDOM OF GOD

not as conquered slaves but as honored guests who would share the eschatological banquet with the Israelite patriarchs (risen from the dead?); and (5) that, despite the possibility of his impending death, Jesus himself would experience a saving reversal: he would share in the final banquet, symbolized by the prophetic event of the Last Supper."[22]

In itself this is a remarkable list. The presence of the patriarchs at this future banquet implies the transcendence of life over death. Thus, the final banquet is transcendent or discontinuous with this present world.[23] It is the joyful sharing of faithful Israelites and gentiles with the patriarchs of old. This notion will have considerable significance following the resurrection of Jesus. It is understood in terms of eternal life which, if not explicitly expressed here, is certainly contained implicitly and conceptually. What we have concluded then is that an authentic teaching of Jesus is that the kingdom was a future reality both as immanent and as transcendent. This is a significant distinction.

Included in Meier's summary is the notion that the kingdom would bring about the reversal of present-day unjust conditions of poverty, sorrow, and hunger. Meier expresses this differently when he says that the eschatological kingdom that Jesus proclaimed would mean "the reversal of all unjust oppression and suffering."[24] This will prove invaluable when we discuss the kingdom from a theological perspective. The banquet proves to be a significant symbol in giving meaning to the kingdom. It means more than the consolation of those who experienced unjust conditions of poverty, sorrow and hunger. Positively it means the joyful bestowal of happiness (beatitude) by God.

The Authentic Teaching of Jesus: The Kingdom is Present

This section will deal with the kingdom of God as a present reality. This is an important consideration which has significant ramifications for Christianity in general. It has come to the fore in recent liberation and political theology. As a present reality, the kingdom points to God's presence and activity in the world here and now.[25] Present eschatology is understood in Jesus' words and deeds and reflects his personal self-understanding.

---

22. Meier, *Marginal Jew*, 2:337.
23. Meier, *Marginal Jew*, 2:337.
24. Meier, *Marginal Jew*, 2:349.
25. It is worth noting that *Gaudium et Spes* (*Pastoral Constitution on the Church in*

Meier follows the same procedure for this issue as he did for Jesus' preaching the future transcendent and future-immanent kingdom. He suggested the following blocks of material plus a collection of sayings which supports the kingdom of God as a present reality.[26] They are (1) emissaries from John the Baptist (Matt 11:2–19//Luke 7:18–28); (2) an exorcism (Matt 12:28//Luke 11:20); and (3) Jesus' saying that "the kingdom of God is in your midst" (Luke 17:21).[27] Meier appeals to a saying which expresses a beatitude for those witnessing the miracles (Matt 13:16–17// Luke 10:23–24) and a saying on the rejection of voluntary fasting (Mark 2:18-20 parr.) which imply the presence of the kingdom.[28] All of these sayings are certainly worthy of serious study. Two of them, however, are worth commenting on here at length. They are important for establishing that the kingdom as present is an authentic teaching of Jesus.

Emissaries from John the Baptist: Matt 11:2–19//Luke 7:18–28

One of the most important texts/events which support present eschatology is Jesus' discourse with the disciples of John the Baptist.[29] According to the narrative, these disciples searched out Jesus while John was in prison. John had heard that Jesus was doing the "works of the Messiah" (Matt 11:2). The question put to Jesus by John's disciples is, "Are you the one who is to come . . . ?" (Matt 11:3).[30] Jesus replies to John's disciples with these word: "Go and tell John what you hear and see: the blind regain their sight, the lame walk, lepers are cleansed, the deaf hear,

---

the *Modern World*), which is one of the more central documents of Vatican II addressing the place of humanity in the world, makes several mentions of the kingdom of God. See *Gaudium et Spes*, nos. 1, 39, 45, 72 and 93.

26. The present notion of the kingdom destroys the idea of apocalyptic that is often found in the New Testament. The apocalyptic genre in the New Testament should be understood as a literary type or device and not so much as a reality.

27. Meier finds the saying "the kingdom has drawn near" (Mark 1:15) as problematic. This saying is found at the beginning of Jesus public ministry. The NABRE translates this passage as "the kingdom of God is at hand." Matthew 3:2 reports the same message but it is found on the lips of John the Baptist prior to Jesus' Galilean ministry.

28. These can be found in Meier, *Marginal Jew*, 2:399, 404, 423, 430, 434.

29. This discussion was begun in chapter 3.

30. The Coming One is not a title for "the Messiah or an eschatological figure." Meier, *Marginal Jew*, 2:132. Fitzmyer says that "the One who is to come" is the title of an awaited figure from Mal 3:1. See Fitzmyer, *One Who Is to Come*, 2, 54. The intended meaning of the expression is vague.

HOW JESUS UNDERSTOOD THE KINGDOM OF GOD

the dead are raised, and the poor have the good news proclaimed to them. And blessed is the one who takes no offense at me (Matt 11:4–6// Luke 7:22–23)."[31] Jesus' response, based upon the prophetic expression of Isaiah, is a clear, accurate and authentic self-identification. In this collection of sayings Isaiah describes the activity of the eschatological prophet who will usher in God's kingdom.

Jesus' answer to John's disciples is more implied than direct.[32] Nevertheless, it is a clear indication of Jesus' personal self-understanding. That he identified himself and his mission with the sayings from Isaiah is extremely significant. There is no direct mention of the kingdom, but it is strongly implied. This response is authentic to the historical Jesus.[33] His activity describes God's rule as experienced in the present. God is at work in Jesus' words and deeds.

The message Jesus gives to John's disciples is repeated in the synagogue scene recorded earlier in Luke's Gospel.[34] In this episode, Jesus visits the synagogue in Nazareth and reads from the scroll of Isaiah: "The Spirit of the Lord is upon me, because he has anointed me to bring glad tidings to the poor. He has sent me to proclaim liberty to captives and recovery of sight to the blind, to let the oppressed go free, and to proclaim a year acceptable to the Lord"(Luke 4:18–19). This passage is virtually an exact quote from Isa 61:1–2. This is the same message given to John's disciples in Matt 11:2–19 and Luke 7:18–19. Jesus declares that "today this scripture passage is fulfilled in your hearing" (Luke 4:21). Jesus' declaration is an obvious reference to the present reality of the kingdom. There is a question as to whether the words attributed to Jesus in this passage are authentic. Meier has his doubts. He believes that Luke has actually redacted Mark's version of Jesus' visit to the synagogue in Nazareth

---

31. This response, an authentic saying of the historical Jesus, is an allusion to the oracles of Isaiah. They are: the dead are raised (26:19); the deaf hear and the blind see (29:18–19; 35:5–6, 42:18); the lame will walk (35:6); mourners are comforted (61:3); The poor will rejoice (29:19); And the "Good News is proclaimed to the poor" (61:1–2; 52:7). Isaiah 61 refers especially to the restoration of Israel. Jesus appeals to the passages from Isaiah in a literal, not a figurative, sense. See chapter 11 below for a further discussion on this matter.

32. It is a personal statement and though less direct than the saying from the exorcism which we will examine below, it carries much weight.

33. Meier, *Marginal Jew*, 2:401.

34. Luke 4:16–22. Luke has transposed the narrative of the rejection of Jesus from an incident found in Mark 6:1–6 into his (Luke's) telling of the beginning of Jesus' ministry.

(Mark 6:1–5).³⁵ Fitzmyer, however, believes that the verses from Isaiah are from the historical Jesus.³⁶ Meier concludes that in his judgment it is *non liquet*, that is, it is not apparent.

Nevertheless, in spite of the dispute between Meier and Fitzmyer on this point of authenticity, it is certainly implied that the kingdom is present in Jesus' ministry. Meier concludes that Jesus' ministry is, "the good news of God's kingly rule, already powerfully at work in Jesus' healings and exorcisms, as well as in his welcome and table fellowship extended to sinners and toll collectors."³⁷

Jesus modifies John's understanding of the kingdom.³⁸ The kingdom of God is not only imminent, but it is also a present reality. Jesus teaches that it is not simply God's judgment, but it occurs in joyousness and conviviality. It is the reversal of all the suffering and oppression experienced by many of the Israelites.

The passage celebrating the greatness of John the Baptist is immediately followed by a saying that the kingdom of Heaven suffers violence (Matt 11:12).³⁹ Meier interprets this as the prevention of membership or entrance into the kingdom. There can only be opposition if the kingdom has taken on a concrete, visible form in the words and deeds of Jesus here and now.⁴⁰ The same eschatological kingdom already described as immanent is also at least partially present.⁴¹

An Exorcism: The Finger of God (Matt 12:28//Luke 11:20).

We have extracted a considerable amount of information from the study of Jesus and the emissaries from John. Jesus strongly implied that the kingdom of God is present and that he has a role in initiating it in his person. Another saying which is even more direct in its affirmation of the present reality of the kingdom is contained in the narrative in

35. Meier, *Marginal Jew*, 2:494n177. See also 1:9–71.
36. Fitzmyer, *Gospel of Luke*, 1:5–27.
37. Meier, *Marginal Jew*, 2:132–33.
38. John preached repentance. His eschatology also differs from that preached by Jesus. See the references above. It seems clear that John the Baptist was no miracle worker. Jesus offered a new mode of salvation.
39. This is part of the authentic Jesus tradition.
40. Meier, *Marginal Jew*, 2:403.
41. Meier, *Marginal Jew*, 2:404.

HOW JESUS UNDERSTOOD THE KINGDOM OF GOD

Luke in which Jesus was driving out a demon from a demoniac who was mute.[42] He is described as blind and mute in Matthew's version. Jesus was accused of driving out the demon by the power of Beelzebul, the prince of demons.[43] This miracle story is a historical event in Jesus' ministry.[44] Jesus' response to his accusers is significant. He says, "But if it is by the finger of God that [I] drive out demons, then the kingdom of God has come upon you" (Luke 11:20).[45] The expression *has come upon you* clearly refers to the *present moment*.[46]

According to Meier, Jesus' reference to the finger of God coming upon them is the star witness for determining that the kingdom of God is present.[47] He also affirms that it is the most important witness.[48] Jesus' exorcisms established God's kingdom. The power of the demon (Satan) is subject to the power of God. This is supported by a very brief authentic parable taught by the historical Jesus that is interpretive of this exorcism. "How can anyone enter a strong man's house and steal his property, unless he first ties up the strong man? Then he can plunder his house" (Matt 12:29).[49] The strong man is understood allegorically as Satan.[50] The implication is that Jesus binds him and renders him helpless.[51]

---

42. The reference is to Matt 12:22–28//Luke 11:14–20. This exorcism is from the Q source.

43. There is another narrative which speaks about Beelzebul in Mark 3:24–27. Jesus is accused of driving out demons by the power of Beelzebul, but no miracle is recorded.

44. The common view is that this is an authentic saying of Jesus. It is coherent with Jesus' activity as an exorcist.

45. Matthew's version (Matt 12:28) has "Spirit of God" in place of Luke's "finger of God." The expression "finger of God" is found in Exod 8:15 (NABRE) and Exod 8:19 (NRSV). During the third plague, Pharaoh's magicians say, "This is the finger of God." The note in the NABRE refers to the staff of Aaron but this seems unlikely. That this refers to the power of God seems to fit the context better.

46. The preferred translation of Luke 11:20 is, "The kingdom is among you." This is consistent with other references from Luke. It supports the understanding that the kingdom is also a concrete reality. See Luke 17:21 which repeats Luke 11:20. "For behold, the kingdom of God is among you." See page 105 below.

47. Meier, *Marginal Jew*, 2:399.

48. Meier, *Marginal Jew*, 2:450.

49. The parallel is in Mark 3:27 and Luke 11:21–22. This is a Q (Matt 12:29//Luke 11–21) and Mark overlap.

50. Jesus is the stronger man who overcomes the strong man. The meaning of this parable is that "Jesus' victory over Satan [is] demonstrated in his exorcisms." Meier, *Marginal Jew*, 2:419. There is no reason to deny the authenticity of this parable. See Meier, *Marginal Jew*, 2:420.

51. See the notes for this saying from Matt 12:29 in the NABRE. This saying should

It seems clear from what has been said that the kingdom of God is a present reality, and it is so taught by the historical Jesus. It is also clear that this expresses the conflict between God and all things that oppose his kingdom. What is less clear but appears implied is that the end time is inbreaking. That would certainly agree with the Jewish expectation, and it is something that needs to be developed theologically. Another implication is that the kingdom is connected with the person of Jesus. The precise relationship concerning his agency is unclear except that it does not seem that it can be divorced from his preaching and miracles.[52]

We have noted that the kingdom of God was central to Jesus' preaching. From what we have examined, it seems clear that the kingdom of God as a present reality is part of the authentic teaching of the historical Jesus. He initiated the kingdom of God proleptically, that is to say, his words and deeds were more than a mere symbol of a future reality; they actually caused it to exist as present. His words and deeds were creative.

While historical-critical research can never achieve absolute certainty we can conclude that Jesus' sayings can produce a high degree of probability.[53] Jesus' use of the expression *kingdom of God* is special to him; his phraseology is almost unique. Our investigation leaves us with the conviction that Jesus did indeed proclaim that the kingdom of God was a transcendent future, an imminent-future and a present reality.

The Relationship between the Present and Future Kingdom

We began the discussion of the kingdom of God by pointing out what a careful reading of the Scriptures would indicate: it is not a place or state; it is a dynamic expression of an existing reality. Beyond this, an examination of the authentic sayings of the historical Jesus indicated that it expressed a complex eschatology; it is both a future and a present reality. It is both a concrete, existential reality as well as a spiritual one.

The sayings of Jesus speak of both an immanent-future and a present kingdom. This relationship is not explained; it is simply announced.[54] No explanation is given by Jesus as to what either means or how they

---

be compared with the saying in Matt 11:12. There is a certain parallelism in these two sayings.

52. A similar inference was made concerning Jesus' response to the emissaries of John.

53. Meier, *Marginal Jew*, 2:443.

54. Meier, *Marginal Jew*, 2:451.

are related. There have been several attempts to describe this relationship. Cullmann speaks of the kingdom of God as an "already but not yet."[55] This would seem to indicate that the present kingdom is only partially realized. This will have to be addressed theologically later.

Beyond this discussion we should be clear that, in describing the reign of God, Jesus of necessity spoke metaphorically.[56] The kingdom of God is not a spatial, static expression. It is a dynamic expression which implies a relationship; God ruling over his people as king. It is not merely an idea; it is more properly a symbol which evokes an entire range of meanings. It tells a story that exists in the Old Testament from the first verse to the last.[57] This was examined in the antecedents above. Our present discussion reveals how difficult it is to grasp fully the kingdom of God even though it does address something basic in our understanding. Its very nature creates a tension between the already and the not yet, between the concrete and the spiritual. The kingdom of God is a poetic way of speaking of these realities. Perrin states that fundamentally the kingdom of God "is a tensive symbol and that its meaning could never be exhausted, nor adequately expressed, by any one referent."[58] This is a paradox, something like a riddle. We will see below that this is similar to the parables which are also challenging. And like the parables, the kingdom as both present in the preaching and praxis of Jesus and the future coming of God's rule "aims at teasing the mind into active thought."[59]

Further Questions

So far, we have learned that the kingdom of God is both a present and a future reality. As future it is described as both future transcendent and future immanent. We have also discovered that it is both a heavenly and an earthly, concrete reality. The admission of this later point is important.

---

55. Cullmann, *Salvation in History*, 166–85. On page 172, Cullman speaks of the kingdom as "already fulfilled, not yet completed." Meier prefers this description of the kingdom to others such a dawning or impinging kingdom. Cullmann's description seems better in terms of designating the time factor.

56. This will be understood more clearly when we discuss Jesus' parables in chapter 10 and 11.

57. Meier, *Marginal Jew*, 2:241

58. Perrin, *Jesus and the Language*, 31. The word *tensive* has been fashioned by Norman Perrin to explain that there is a tension between the various expressions. The kingdom is of such a nature that it is difficult to describe or explain it in simple terms.

59. Dodd, *Parables of the Kingdom*, 5.

While the use of the expression *kingdom of God* appears almost unique in its use by Jesus, its content contains the entire historical story of Israel. Furthermore, it is a poetic expression described as a tensive symbol which provides no simple understanding. It is a conundrum for which there is no easy answer or explanation. To that end, there are three important questions we will need to examine.

First Question: What Was Jesus' Role in the Kingdom? What was his self-understanding?

In Jesus' authentic teaching, there is no explicit affirmation of his role as mediator of the kingdom. The primitive community, however, recognized him as such. There is also no mention of Jesus' death as atoning.[60] We will say more about this later since there are many references found in the epistles that indicate the church's understanding.

Such a paucity of statements of this nature from the Jesus of history gives us pause. What is the role of Jesus in the drama of the kingdom? Can we reach into the texts to discern anything of his understanding of his role in initiating the kingdom? Meier makes the interesting observation that "we noticed the pattern of an eschatological prophet who in one sense avoids making himself the explicit object of his preaching and yet implicitly places himself squarely within the eschatological drama as a key figure."[61] This is an important observation. Jesus never preached himself as the Christ. He never explicitly declared that he initiated the kingdom or that he had a leading role in making it active in the lives of his disciples. Jesus indicates that certain of his actions mediate a partial experience of the future kingdom. Meier tells us that, "Jesus' proclamation-plus-realization of the kingdom as present inevitably moves the spotlight onto himself."[62] When Jesus responded to the emissaries from John the Baptist it seemed a clear implication that the kingdom was present in his deeds.[63] That he taught his disciples to pray to his Abba implies a special personal role. We noted that his festive meals made a

---

60. Meier, *Marginal Jew*, 2:308.
61. Meier, *Marginal Jew*, 2:453.
62. Meier, *Marginal Jew*, 2:453.

63. It seems difficult to imagine that this event is not at least an implicit claim to be the agent of the inbreaking of the kingdom.

partial realization of the kingdom as present.[64] The particular action that described Jesus as having a significant role in the present kingdom is found in his exorcisms. They are a direct challenge to the anti-kingdom, to Satan and the other demons. While none of this is explicit, the role for Jesus ushering in the kingdom is strongly implicit. It is difficult if not impossible not to see him having the unique role in the initiation of the kingdom. Jesus acted out the kingdom in his preaching and praxis. The early church certainly understood him in this way.

There is one last point for our consideration. Meir has observed that "it is almost as though Jesus were intent on making a riddle of himself."[65] Crossan makes a similar observation concerning Jesus and the parables.[66] Recognizing Jesus as a riddle or a challenging metaphor suggests that Jesus, as a prophet of God, cannot be easily described or explained.

Second Question: When Was the Kingdom of God to Arrive?

Jesus preached the immanent coming of the kingdom, but he gave no timetable as to precisely when the kingdom would arrive. That he does not know the time appears authentic. "But of that day or hour, no one knows, neither the angels in heaven, nor the Son, but only the Father" (Mark 13:32). This indicates the state of mind of the historical Jesus. He proclaimed an imminent, definitive coming of the kingdom of God, but he specified no timetable.[67] Meier explains, "It is the historical Jesus who is the origin of the imminent-future eschatology in the Synoptics. The early church soon found itself pressed to come to terms with the problems occasioned by that eschatology as the years (and deaths of Christians) multiplied. Imminent-future eschatology has its origins in Jesus; attempts to set time limits for that eschatology have their origin in the early church."[68] Dodd has addressed the question concerning the

---

64. Some may want to interpret this action in a more symbolic manner but the reaction of those who experienced it seems to say that it was more than symbolic.

65. Meier, *Marginal Jew*, 2:454.

66. Crossan, *In Parables*, xiv. Crossan states, "Jesus proclaimed God in parables, but the primitive church proclaimed Jesus as the parable of God."

67. Meier, *Marginal Jew*, 2:348. There are various sayings on the time of the coming of the kingdom (Matt 10:23; Mark 9:1; Mark 13:30) which seem to indicate that it will happen soon. But no definite time is given.

68. Meier, *Marginal Jew*, 2:348.

coming of Christ and the kingdom in a most interesting way.[69] His point of departure is rooted in the incarnation. Christ coming into the world is definitive in this event. "When Christ came into the world 1950 years ago, something quite new entered history." Dodd continues, "What came to earth then was final and decisive for the whole meaning and purpose of human existence, and we shall meet it again when history has been wound up."[70] He enlarged on this statement a few pages later when he indicated that the next phase is the response to this definitive event. "He came; it was an essential part of His total impact on history; and our response will be an essential part of His impact on our present situation."[71] It is necessary to understand that the coming of Christ is an invitation to all men and women to participate in the kingdom. In this understanding, Christ comes daily. This is our historical experience. He continues to speak of the final coming of Christ when he says, "It [the coming] is anchored also in the timeless truth that He is Lord of history and will appear as such when all is over."[72] To briefly summarize Dodd's explanation, we note that it comes about in three distinct but connected phases. The first is the ultimate entrance of Christ into history in the incarnation. The second is his entrance into particular lives which accept or reject him. This continues throughout history. The last entrance into history is at the end time, when "all is over." This is a thoroughly intelligible explanation of the coming of Christ. It is a way of dealing with the Son of Man statements which have caused so much difficulty in properly understanding them. Dodd does not look for the Son of Man coming as described literally in the Gospels.[73] That particular coming is identified with the end time. We need to make one more point about the coming of the Son of Man. Dodd explains the problem as follows: "Sometimes, it seems, they [several groups of sayings] associate the coming of the Son of Man in glory, the kingdom of God, and the Last Judgment, with the historical ministry of Jesus Christ; sometimes they

---

69. See his *The Coming of Christ*. This brief booklet is the collection of four broadcast addresses during the season of Advent. His explanation of the theme of the coming of Christ is very convincing.

70. Dodd, *Coming of Christ*, 34.

71. Dodd, *Coming of Christ*, 37.

72. Dodd, *Coming of Christ*, 37–38.

73. It is clear that the expectation of Christ, the Son of Man, coming soon was quickly given up by the early church.

associate it with historical crises yet to come; and sometimes with that which lies beyond all history, in another world than this."[74]

Dodd responds to these difficulties with a remarkably simple but powerful solution. Jesus spoke as a poet. He should not be understood in a literal way. This is evident on every page of the Gospels.[75]

Third Question: Were the Gentiles to be Included?[76]

Jesus conducted his mission primarily to the house of Israel. There are several scriptural references that make this clear. When Jesus visited the regions of Tyre and Sidon, a Canaanite woman begged him for a cure for her daughter (Matt 15:21–28). Jesus rebuffed her with the remark, "I was sent only to the lost sheep of the house of Israel" (Matt 15:24).[77] Mark's version has details that differ from Matthew, but he implies the same message. "Let the children [Israel] be fed first" (Mark 7:27).[78] The sense of this verse is that Jesus' mission is to Israel although we must remind ourselves that this event took place in gentile territory. Jesus also limited the missionary work of the Twelve to Israel. Jesus tells the Twelve not to go into pagan territory but "go rather to the lost sheep of the house of Israel" (Matt 10:6). This statement is not so clear in Mark (6:7–13) and Luke (9:1–6) but the same message seems implied. There is little indication that Jesus ministered in a systematic way to gentiles.[79]

74. Dodd, *Coming of Christ*, 18.

75. Dodd, *Coming of Christ*, 18.

76. Much of this has been discussed above when the future eschatology of the kingdom was elaborated on.

77. The parallel pericope can be found in Mark 7:24–30. The verse from Matt 15:24 appears to be an addition to Mark. This pericope is not found in Luke. Nevertheless, Jesus does cure the woman's daughter. Jesus also cured the servant of the centurion, and The centurion is praised for his faith (Matt 8:10). This cure which appears to be for the benefit of a gentile occurred in Capernaum.

78. While this was certainly true early on in Jesus' ministry, we need to account for the scriptural passages that seem to have placed him in a foreign land. There are several references in the Gospels that Jesus did in fact go to pagan territory. For example, Mark 5:1–20 reports Jesus preaching and performing miracles in the territory of the Gerasenes. Matthew has a parallel miracle, but he refers to this place as the territory of the Gadarenes. Mark's version refers to a single man; Matthew's version refers to two. This is a parallel version and Gerasenes seems to be the preferred name for the territory. There is also the pericope in John which records Jesus' conversation with the Samaritan woman at the well (John 4:4–41). The historical nature of this may be challenged but Jesus is described as ministering to Samaritans in Samaria.

79. Meier, *Marginal Jew*, 2:374n98.

One exception is his cure of the centurion's servant (Matt 8:5–14//Luke 7:1–10).[80] Neither is there any indication of the gentile acceptance of Jesus in faith.[81] These sayings are enigmatic especially since the early Christian movement understood itself as universal in nature.[82] How then do the gentiles fit into Jesus' ministry?

The exclusion of gentiles seems odd if true especially given the later missionary activity of the early church. However, besides the injunction to go only to the house of Israel, there are clear indications from authentic sayings of Jesus that gentiles were to be included in the kingdom.[83] The saying in Matt 8:11–12//Luke 13:28–29 refers to those reclining at the banquet in the kingdom with Abraham, Isaac, and Jacob. The children of the kingdom (the Israelites) who do not accept Jesus' words will be excluded and will be replaced by gentiles (from the east and the west). Luke's version refers to people who "will come from the east and the west and from the north and the south and will recline at the table in the kingdom of God" (Luke 13:29).[84] What seems apparent in Jesus' teaching is that the twelve tribes would be reconstituted in the end time and the gentiles would be included as full participants.[85]

---

80. This is from the Q source. Is this historical? It appears that it is.

81. Meier, *Marginal Jew*, 2:315.

82. Hence Christians come to use of the term Catholic (universal). Ignatius of Antioch is a prominent first century figure who used the term to express the universality of Christianity. A casual reading of the Epistles of Paul and the Acts of the Apostles will indicate that the early church saw its mission not just to the Jews but most especially to the gentiles. The magi story in Luke's Gospel is a symbolic way of expressing the revelation of the Christ to the gentile world.

83. This is an Old Testament idea that is prominently found in Isaiah and the Psalms.

84. Interestingly enough, Ps 107 uses the same language. Verse 3 reads "those gathered from foreign lands, from east and west, from north and south." It is suggested that this refers to those returning from the Babylonian captivity. The four corners of the earth are difficult to understand in this regard. There seems to be a return from too many directions. Verse 21 contains a reference to humankind. Did the psalmist mean that those returning would not necessarily be Israelites?

85. Meier, *Marginal Jew*, 2:314. Further evidence that gentiles will be included in the kingdom can be found in two authentic parables which are placed at the end of Jesus' ministry. They are the parable of the evil tenants (Mark 12:1–22)//Matt 21:33–44//Luke 20:9–18) and the parable of the great supper (Matt 22:1–10//Luke 14:16–24).

As we shall see, the reversal of position was an authentic characteristic of Jesus' teaching.[86] Jesus' festive meals reflect this reversal of position.[87] It is the sinners and the unclean whose position is changed and who become insiders sharing in the banquet. We also read in Matthew, "Thus, the last will be first, and the first will be last" (Matt 20:16). This verse is an interpretive element to explain the parable of the workers in the vineyard.[88] We will have more to say about this important parable in chapters 10 and 11. It is clear from the examples given above that the concept of reversal of position is clearly taught in the New Testament.[89]

We have grounded ourselves in the authentic teaching of Jesus. But there are precious few references to Jesus sending his disciples into the world in the preresurrection period. I have found one but there may be others. In Mark's Gospel Jesus warns his disciples that they will be persecuted by the world. He instructed them that "the gospel must first be preached [before the end time] to all nations" (Mark 13:9-10). It is likely that this saying was a postresurrection apologetic and reflected the actual church situation. There are a number of postresurrection references that indicate the church's mission is to the world. Matthew records the Great Commission given to the eleven just before Jesus' ascension. Jesus commands that they are to "make disciples of all nations" (Matt 28:19). It seems clear that this command is intended to include all humankind.[90] The theme of the Acts of the Apostles is that the message is to

---

86. Luke concludes his saying of the admission of gentiles into the kingdom with "for behold, some are last who will be first, and some are first who will be last" (Luke 13:30).

87. Jesus' festive meals were a prominent part of his ministry, and they look proleptically to the final meal in the kingdom. Some authors use the expression *table fellowship* to describe these meals.

88. This interpretive verse is referred to as a *nimshal*. See chapter 11 for an explanation of the nimshal.

89. The parable of the workers in the vineyard (Matt 20:1-16) is peculiar to Matthew. Matt 20:16 is called a nimshal and is an interpretive element. This verse, in reverse form ("But that many that are first will be last, and [the] last will be first."), is found in Mark 10:31 and Matt 19:30. It is questioned whether these verses are composed by the evangelist or whether he received it as a part of his tradition. The point made here is that the concept of the reversal of one's situation is commonplace in the Gospels, and it is attributed to Jesus. This simply supports what will be presented as the authentic teaching of Jesus on this matter.

90. Jesus declared that the gospel of the kingdom will be preached to the whole world (Matt 24:14; 26:13). His postresurrection command indicates the same message (Matt 28:18-20). John 1:9 and Luke 2:32 indicate the universality of the message. The epistle to the Rom 1:6 also teaches that the gospel (of God) is intended not only for the

be preached "to the end of the earth" (Acts 1:8). This is a response to the question, "Lord, are you at this time going to restore the kingdom to Israel?" (Acts 1:6). The universality of the response implies that God is the God of all humankind. The implication of the postresurrection church is quite clear. It understood that the God of Jesus Christ is the God of all humanity, and it is his will that everyone should be saved.[91] Would the church have invented this universal role if they had not understood Jesus to have taught it? The authentic sayings discussed above provide the basis for a universal mission of the church.

Conclusion: How the Kingdom of God is Characterized

We are now in a position to articulate Jesus' authentic understanding of the kingdom of God. Having spent considerable time examining the eschatology characterized by the expression *kingdom of God* it is now a much easier task. In a certain sense the content or meaning of the kingdom is not complicated. In its simplest terms, it is God present and active in the lives of men and women.

The kingdom of God was the central theme of Jesus' ministry. His understanding of God's reign was drawn from his immersion in the faith of Israel and its Scriptures. Jesus' personal experience of God, however, provided Jesus with a full understanding or vision of the kingdom. The kingdom of God was Jesus' chosen expression for this personal experience.[92] It seems likely that the expression originated with him as a way in which he could express his vision which was manifest both in words (sayings, parables) and in deeds (miracles, table fellowship).

What makes the understanding of the kingdom challenging is that Jesus never explains its precise meaning. Speaking in poetic terms, Jesus used the language of metaphor or poetry. The expression kingdom of God has a tensive quality, that is, it cannot be reduced to categories of space and time. This way of explaining our understanding of the kingdom has the advantage of accounting for the numerous ways of expressing it as found in the Scriptures. It cannot be explained easily in simple, direct, univocal terms. It might well be compared to the parables of Jesus which

---

Jews but also the gentiles.

91. This is certainly the authentic teaching of the later church. The same doctrine is repeated in the documents of Vatican II.

92. Meier, *Marginal Jew*, 2:269.

require effort to understand. The kingdom, like the parables, demand that one must be involved to understand its message.[93]

The Kingdom of God Understood as God's Presence

The kingdom of God does not have boundaries. It is different from an earthly kingdom as we normally envision one. It is better understood as expressing wherever God reigns or rules, both on earth and in heaven. The heavenly reign is described metaphorically as a great banquet. It needs to be understood in a spiritual or otherworldly sense, as a union with the divine. It is a personal existence with God without the limitations of this earthly life and certainly without anything present that is evil. God's heavenly reign is the prime analogate for his reign on earth. As an earthly reality, it is best understood as God's presence among humans. Some have understood this presence as a spiritual, interior reality existing within the individual. Support for this position relies on Jesus' response to the question of the Pharisee concerning when the kingdom would come. Jesus' response is often translated as "for behold, the kingdom of God is within you" (Luke 17:21).[94] This is generally considered a poor translation of the original Greek. This saying would be better understood as "for behold, the kingdom of God is among you" (Luke 17:21).[95] Luke's other statements concerning the presence of God would suggest that *among* is the correct translation of the Greek. Thus, it is preferred to understand the kingdom of God as a physical entity and not as a purely spiritual, interior one. To put this in better understood terms, the kingdom of God speaks about the reality of God's presence in the world. God's presence, his kingdom, is both an otherworldly and a worldly reality. Theologically we will come to see the kingdom of God as an earthly reality where justice and peace exist.

---

93. This will be taken up below in chapter 10.

94. This translation is found in the New King James Version and the RSV Interlinear Greek-English New Testament. In this particular verse, the Greek preposition *entos* can be better translated as *among* rather than as *within*.

95. This is the translation found in the New American Bible Revised Edition, the New Revised Standard Version, and the New Jerusalem Bible. Meier translated the phrase as "in your midst." It seems that *among* is preferred to *within* by most contemporary translations.

The Kingdom of God and Eschatology

The expression kingdom of God is a poetic, metaphorical expression which requires effort to understand. Furthermore, the eschatology in which it is expressed provides a singular set of difficulties. Norman Perrin describes the kingdom of God as a tensive expression difficult to define. It is even difficult to adequately describe. Scripture contains three seemingly distinct ways of speaking of the kingdom: it is future (transcendent), it is immanent (in the near future), and it is present.

The kingdom is a future reality.[96] Jesus often spoke of a future kingdom. The Christian expectation is that it will be the final human condition when every tear is wiped away, every evil is conquered. All human desires will ultimately be fulfilled.

It is also described as imminent or about to come. In this description, it is not yet realized. This understanding is closely associated with the Son of Man statements. There is a sense in which the primitive church lived in the expectation of God's coming presence. It was suggested above that part of the confusion caused by these statements is that Jesus spoke poetically. Dodd suggested that this expression of a coming which precedes the final fulfillment of the kingdom should be understood as the individual's acceptance of the kingdom in faith. There is considerable support for this interpretation. The incarnation has already made this immanent coming of Christ unintelligible since he is already present. In any case, these expressions of the imminent coming of the kingdom are the most difficult to understand and explain. The reality is that we no longer wait for an imminent coming. We do not live our lives as if this world does not matter and is to end in an apocalyptic manner.[97]

The kingdom of God is also a present reality.[98] This is the full impact of Jesus' preaching. The kingdom has already come, imperfect as it is. In this sense a great mystery confronts us. We spoke above of the kingdom as the presence of God ruling among his people.[99] Our expectation is that God is already present and that his presence is a lived

---

96. This is often referred to as consequent eschatology.

97. It should be understood that, however we interpret the Son of Man statements, Jesus was not an apocalyptic preacher. The reason we reach this conclusion is because the fact that Jesus preached the kingdom as a present reality makes the apocalyptic understanding impossible. We need to treat these expressions as literary and not intended to be factual.

98. This is expressed as realized eschatology.

99. The final experience of the individual with God is the beatific vision.

experience. We understand the present kingdom as not yet complete. This is obvious from experience. In the words of Cullman, "it is already but not yet." Or we might say that it has been initiated but is not complete. It is best understood as a process.

Concluding Thoughts

We have spent considerable time exploring Jesus' understanding of the kingdom of God and how this might have been understood by both a pre and a postresurrection assembly. This undertaking was not without its difficulties, yet we can be confident that we have recovered a considerable amount of Jesus' authentic teaching. We are now left with the task of translating these findings to the actual situation of a contemporary audience. This will be taken up in the following chapter.

6

The Kingdom of God: A Theological Reflection

Introduction

WE ARE NOW IN a position to reflect theologically on the data we have collected, which contains the substance of our faith. Jesus derived his understanding of God as both reigning and as Savior from the existing tradition of Israel. These fundamental concepts were rooted in the Old Testament tradition. It is also clear that Jesus derived much of his understanding from his personal experience of God, his Abba. These antecedents to Jesus' preaching of the kingdom have been examined above. The teaching of the historical Jesus has also been examined and we have obtained a clear and accurate understanding of his authentic teaching about the kingdom of God. This material provides contemporary Christians with a basis upon which to reflect theologically on Jesus' teaching of the kingdom of God.

The Challenge of the Teaching of Jesus: the Kingdom

The kingdom of God was absolutely central to the preaching of Jesus. Everything else in his ministry was related to it. Jesus chose this expression from the Old Testament tradition to provide all who heard his preaching with his vision of the kingdom of God. Our first challenge in properly understanding the meaning of the kingdom of God is that

THE KINGDOM OF GOD: A THEOLOGICAL REFLECTION

Jesus never explained or defined what he meant by it. Instead, it is Jesus' preaching and praxis, his words and deeds, that inform as to the meaning of the kingdom. Therefore, we must discover in our sources what is implied in this very rich concept of the kingdom.

There is a second challenge to properly understand the meaning of the kingdom. The eschatology in which the kingdom was expressed can be confusing.[1] Jesus preached the kingdom in three ways: as a future reality, as a future-immanent reality and as a present reality. Preaching the kingdom in this fashion has created a tension in our understanding of it. Thus, the very expression that Jesus used presents us with an interpretive challenge. It is difficult to understand precisely how those who listened to Jesus would have understood him. If the kingdom was immanent, how soon would it come? If it was present, why would there be an expectation that it was immanent? If it was future, would it be future only? Some explanations for this tension were offered above in chapter 5. The primitive church often understood this to mean that the kingdom would come *soon*. Because of this difficulty in establishing its meaning, the kingdom of God was described above as a tensive symbol. Theological reflection attempts to explain or reduce this tension. It is the task of the theologian to tease out the meaning from these expressions.

The Kingdom and the Primitive Church Context

How did this early group of Christians hear and understand the preaching of the kingdom? During his lifetime, Jesus proclaimed the kingdom of God principally to the Jews. This took place in a Palestinian, Jewish environment. A significant development occurs very soon after Jesus' death and resurrection. The original context in which Jesus proclaimed the kingdom of God changed. There was a shift in the primitive postresurrection community from Palestinian Judaism to the entire Hellenistic world. In this new context the postresurrection community experienced three distinct developments and understanding these stages of development will help us in our understanding of the kingdom.

The first and perhaps most important development was the postresurrection understanding of Jesus as the Christ. The experience of Jesus, now raised from the dead, ushered in a very significant development

---

1. Eschatology is used here to mean the time that the kingdom is expected to become a reality. This concept is defined in chapter 5, 86n6.

concerning the person of Jesus, the eschatological prophet. During his earthly life Jesus did not use or permit the use of what we identify as christological titles for himself. His self-designations for the most part were Son of Man and prophet.[2] His followers would have understood him as such. This changed radically after his death and resurrection. The resurrection experience brought about a new, deeper understanding of the historical Jesus. He was now identified as the Christ (Messiah), Lord, Son of God, Savior, and numerous other titles because they more fully described the faith understanding of the rapidly growing community.[3] This brought about a notable shift in focus from the kingdom of God to the person of Jesus as the Christ. We saw above that Jesus identified himself as intimately connected with a new form of salvation: the kingdom of God. This identification appears to be part of Jesus' personal self-understanding. It did not take the primitive community long to understand that it was Jesus as the Christ who was central to their preaching. After the resurrection, the preacher became the preached.[4]

The second development occurred almost simultaneously with the first. The primitive, postresurrection community first preached in the context of Palestinian Judaism, the environment in which Jesus of Nazareth accomplished his mission. But this soon became a missionary effort that moved into the Hellenistic world. This development required what we today refer to as *inculturation*. There was the need to frame Jesus' message in language and expressions that would make it intelligible in a new cultural context. The Hellenistic context differed considerably from the place in which Jesus carried out his ministry. How would the understanding of a Greek or Roman differ from that of a Palestinian peasant? We can only imagine. But this may also account for the shift in language the early church experienced.

The third development was brought about by Jesus' preaching of the kingdom as an immanent reality; the early church fully expected him to return immanently.[5] This notion is contained in the very prayer that

---

2. There were a few other non-christological titles employed, such as rabbi, but they are insignificant for our purposes.

3. See Fitzmyer, *Christological Catechism*, 47. This is the fourth theme that Fitzmyer considers as representing the authentic teaching of Jesus.

4. The expression *kingdom of God* is found in both the Pauline Epistles and the Acts of the Apostles. A cursory examination of any concordance of the Bible would reveal the infrequency of the title Christ in the Gospels and the frequency of its use in the Acts of the Apostles and the Epistles.

5. This is expressed as Jesus' "eschatological discourse." The Synoptics place this

THE KINGDOM OF GOD: A THEOLOGICAL REFLECTION

Jesus taught his first disciples. "Your kingdom come" (Matt 6:10b//Luke 11:2b). With the passage of time, however, the expectation of his return appeared to be delayed. The community asked, "What are we to do while we wait?" The shift, then, was from an immanent expectation of the kingdom to the present reality of their earthly lives. The kingdom as a present reality thus became central to the life of the early Christian.

What should be clear in our present experience, as it became in the early church, is that we no longer await an immanent coming of either the kingdom or of Christ. The kingdom is clearly understood as a future, transcendent reality. However, the kingdom is also clearly a present reality, and this concept will now occupy the greater part of our attention.

The Recovery of the Kingdom

Because of the christological shift referred to above, it is safe to assume that there was a shift from preaching the kingdom to preaching the Christ. Many older Christians would be hard pressed to remember a homily devoted to the kingdom. That is no longer true. The fifteen hundredth anniversary of the Council of Chalcedon in 1951 ushered in a plethora of studies on Jesus which proved invaluable. There was a change in focus from who Jesus is to what Jesus did. This included not only the miracle tradition but also what he taught. Recent research on the historical Jesus has enriched us even more. A consequence of this later research was a much more profound understanding of the kingdom of God which was central to Jesus' authentic message.

The *kingdom of God* is an expression most recently recovered in contemporary discussions. As has been noted above, there was a new focus after Jesus' resurrection: the preacher of the kingdom, namely Jesus, became the preached. This explains why the kingdom of God moved into the background; the focus became the historical Jesus understood as the Christ, the Savior.[6] Since God was the provider of

---

prior to Jesus' immanent death. It speaks of an early end of the age. See Mark 13. Matthew 24 and Luke 21 depend on Mark but modify and add to his account according to their own perspective. The "eschatological discourse" is a witness to the expectation of Jesus' immanent return.

6. This might have been expedited by the move of the early Christians into the Hellenist world. The gentile community would not have been familiar with the Old Testament tradition which provided background to the notion of the kingdom of God.

salvation one can see how this understanding found its way into the agency of Jesus as the Christ.

We will examine Jesus' authentic teaching to see how it relates to our present experience. What does the kingdom mean to contemporary men and women? We are fully aware that there are editorial additions to the primitive preaching of Jesus found in the New Testament. But we also understand that these texts are authoritative. To achieve an even better understanding of the kingdom of God we will employ all of the findings we arrived at above regarding the authoritative teaching of the historical Jesus. This is a hermeneutic which was not available to theologians for much of the last century. We would dismiss it at our own peril.

The Foundation: Presuppositions Underlying the Notion of Kingdom of God

The foundation of our examination of the kingdom of God is the authentic teaching of Jesus as well as his authentic praxis. Jesus' mission, his preaching of the kingdom of God, occurred in a particular historical and religious environment. Both the territory in which he preached, and the duration of his preaching were limited. But we can presume that Jesus' mission was understood by the people to whom he proclaimed his message.

God's Reign is Active in the Lives of Men and Women

The expression *kingdom of God* implies God's lordship or reign. It is the manifestation of his presence and activity in the lives of men and women in history. Salvation does not occur in a vacuum. This notion is at the center of salvation history.[7] The people of Israel fully understood this concept and its consequences. Christians believe that Jesus Christ is the epitome or the fulfillment of this notion. Thus, we maintain that Jesus' understanding and teaching is in continuity with the Old Testament (the Tanakh). He drew his inspiration from the religious environment in which he lived. He did not create his vision of the kingdom out of whole cloth. It is rooted in the history and development of Israel and the developments that it represents. He willingly accepted this role.

---

7. See Schillebeeckx, *On Christian Faith*, 1–14. Schillebeeckx points out that salvation history is broader than the history of revelation.

And he stands in agreement, not only with the sacred texts of Israel (the Old Testament) but most especially in line with its prophetic tradition. It was the voice of the prophets of old that most clearly articulated God's presence to the nation and his activity on its behalf. As a prophet, Jesus stands in the line of the great prophets of Israel. If Jesus differs in any way from this perspective, it would be that he moved away from speaking in terms of the nation and spoke more in terms addressing the individual. But the idea that God is active in the lives of *individual* men and women is crucial to our understanding of the kingdom.

The Role of Jesus: The Agent of the Kingdom.

What role in the kingdom can be assigned to Jesus of Nazareth? He clearly teaches that the kingdom of God is a present reality. There is also a developmental link between Jesus' preaching and the early church's faith in him. After his death and resurrection, his followers recognized both him and his teaching as salvific. This raises a question: is there evidence in the life of Jesus that he was the one who would initiate the kingdom as present among us? Did his disciples, during his lifetime, recognize him as such?

Jesus made no explicit declarations that he was the one who would usher in the kingdom. His prediction of his death at the Last Supper portrayed him as one who would be vindicated by what he was about to undergo, but no claim was made that his actions were salvific. However, during his ministry Jesus acted in a way that *implied* he had a special role in the kingdom of God. His response to the emissaries from John as well as the entire miracle tradition seems to point to his dynamic role in the kingdom.[8] It is clear that whatever was implicit in Jesus' activity, the early church saw that his death and resurrection were salvific. It also seems clear, however, that Jesus' self-understanding, as well as his activity, points to his role as agent of the kingdom even if he did not explicate it.

The Fundamental Notion: What Is the Kingdom of God?

The Gospels record Jesus as having preached the kingdom of God as both a future event, a future-immanent event and as a present event. These three

---

8. Jesus' interaction with the emissaries from John was discussed at length in chapter 5, 92–94.

expressions denoting different eschatologies have created interpretive difficulties. Their harmonization seems almost impossible. We will attempt to resolve some of the difficulties by first considering the kingdom as a future reality. The other two modalities will then be considered.

The Prime Analogate: The Kingdom as Future

In general terms, the kingdom of God is a future event. This is clear from the authentic teaching of the historical Jesus. As a future event, the kingdom was described as the divine banquet, a joyous place where all the evils of the present life are absent.[9] The most significant expression of this understanding of the kingdom was acted out in his festive meals as a proleptic symbol. The beatitudes describe the kingdom as a place of happiness; a place where sorrow, hunger, and poverty are no longer present. It is the place of perfect good, living fully in the presence of God. This is the perfection of the kingdom as a transcendent reality.

Theology came to refer to this in less poetic, more formal, imagery as living fully in the presence of God.[10] It is understood as the face-to-face experience of God which theologians refer to as the beatific vision. The kingdom as future does not provide us with many serious challenges. Thus, the kingdom as a future event is the prime analogate for all other descriptions of the kingdom. The present kingdom must participate in this future kingdom in some significant way.

The Kingdom of God as Present

We have come to accept the kingdom as existing in the present. This occupies most of our reflection since we are no longer in anticipation of the immanent return of Jesus. The question has become this: What

---

9. *Banquet* is a very common motif in the Old Testament literature. The expectation of the messianic banquet is common in the prophetic literature. Isaiah 25:6–8 is an excellent example of this. In this passage the banquet is extended to all earthly nations. As has been indicated earlier, Jesus inherited and assimilated this tradition. In his preaching he used the metaphor *banquet* for the future kingdom. The parable of the great supper (Matt 22:1–10 //Luke 14:16–24) and the narrative of the Last Supper (Matt 26:27–29//Mark 14:23–25//Luke 22:17–18) are uses of this expression that can be traced to the authentic teaching of the Jesus of history. This metaphor as the heavenly banquet can also be found in the Q source (Matt 8:11//Luke 13:29). It is found again in Luke 22:29–30.

10. As transcendent it is referred to as eternal life.

are we referring to when we speak about the kingdom as existing in the present? Our answer, in general, is that it is how our civil and religious lives are organized in the presence of God. This is obviously different for first-century Palestinians and twenty-first century Americans. The earlier view is more holistic than our common conception. Our notion of the separation of church and state would be far removed from the understanding of a first century Galilean to whom this separation would have been unthinkable. Yet, in spite of the difference in past and present contexts, our conviction is that Jesus' preaching of the kingdom has profound meaning for the present.

The Kingdom of God Is an Offer of Salvation

The notion of salvation or liberation needs to be rescued from a superficial use prevalent among many present-day Christians. One often hears the question: "Have you been saved?" or the affirmation that "Jesus has saved me." The underlying presupposition is that this is an act of God that requires faith alone, or that it is a purely private matter. Nothing could be farther from the truth. The notion of salvation is rooted in human experience and is much more complicated than a simple act of faith, as necessary as that act of faith might be.

Schillebeeckx, reflecting the Catholic tradition, reminds us of the connection between our lived human experience and revelation, between reason and faith. This was discussed to some extent in our introduction. Before we understand what the concept of salvation or liberation means in revelation, we must understand its meaning in the secular world of our experience. The secular experience is the basis for understanding revelation. There is never a dichotomy between reason and revelation.

Salvation, as we understand it here, addresses human desires and aspirations seen in terms of our relationship with God. This is precisely what Jesus preached. He differed from John the Baptist inasmuch as Jesus' preaching of the kingdom includes an offer of salvation.[11] The kingdom of God is associated with the human hope for salvation.[12] It is seen as residing in those aspirations common to human nature: the universal human search for peace, freedom, and justice. It moves

---

11. John the Baptist's preaching of the kingdom was a call for repentance, not an offer of salvation.

12. Schillebeeckx, *Church with a Human Face*, 21.

against every form of alienation, abandonment, marginalization, and slavery of whatever sort.

Our understanding is that we cannot overcome many of these situations unaided, without help that comes from beyond our own personal resources. Our experience is that we often pray to be saved in our actual concrete needs. For example, we pray to be saved from personal illness, from the destruction of war, from drought and other natural disasters, and from many other evils that afflict our lives. We pray for help in making our personal decisions, for removing us from situations that impact our lives negatively, for the removal of burdens we believe are too great for us. This is an implicit admission that we are not fully in control of our destiny. We require God's help, and we are not ashamed to ask for it. In short, we look for salvation or liberation from many of the conditions of life which are beyond our control.

The Kingdom of God as Liberation from the Forces of Evil

As described above, the kingdom of God can be understood as liberation or salvation rooted in our common human experience. Liberation is most commonly understood as liberation or freedom from something. In this context, the kingdom is understood as the state in which there is liberation from all forces of evil. It is liberation from every sort of sin, whether personal or social.[13] This liberation is seen as freedom from whatever impinges upon us negatively. It can also be understood positively as the fulfillment of those deepest aspirations of human nature. It is freedom to accomplish the full possibilities of our human nature. These ideas can be illustrated in five distinctly different points.

First Point: The Kingdom is Liberation from Evil on a Personal Level.

This would appear to be the most commonplace understanding of liberation or salvation. Personal sin, of its nature, is perhaps the most apparent object from which we require liberation. It is a broken relationship, the

---

13. Personal sin is an impediment to living in the presence of God. By social sin we think of social structures that might be considered as sinful, which prevent the attainment of full humanity.

cause of our separation from God. It is not uncommon to speak of this separation as a loss or a need for healing.

It is also liberation from all of the conditions of life which are enslaving, alienating, and marginalizing. These can cover a wide range but in sum they are all those things that are in some sense dehumanizing. These are found in all of those conditions of life that marginalize us as full human beings.

Second Point: It is Liberation from Evil on a Collective or Social Level

The kingdom of God is the reversal of all unjust oppression and suffering.[14] For the faithful the reward is a share in the heavenly banquet. This was proleptically celebrated by Jesus in his festive meals. But as we have already seen, Jesus' actions, his exorcisms and healings, his ritual baptism, his choosing disciples and teaching them to pray, his leaving them with a meal to continue his presence on earth, all point to the fact that the kingdom, which was the reversal of all unjust oppression and suffering, was intended to be a present reality. At the same time, it is intended to be a partial experience of the future kingdom. The "already but not yet" expression has already been appealed to in this regard.[15] The relation between the present and the future-immanent kingdom is not a challenge for us. We do not wait in expectation for the coming of the kingdom. The question is this: To what degree is the present kingdom already a partial fulfillment of the fullness of salvation which is future and transcendent?

In recent theology, there is considerable focus on liberation from sinful social structures or situations. These are social structures which alienate and dehumanize. This language has become commonplace in recent papal documents. Social structures are often seen as oppressive in themselves. Slavery, economic conditions which work against our basic interests, and political systems which are repressive are examples of some of these structures or situations. There are many others which could be added to this list, but it is clear we are not personally responsible

---

14. Meier, *Marginal Jew*, 2:349. As was indicated above, the reversal of situations shows up in numerous places in the authentic teaching of Jesus. Jesus' festive meals were events in which the lost were found. See Meier, *Marginal Jew*, 2:303. Many parables express a theme of the reversal of positions. There are numerous sayings in which the first shall be last and vice versa.

15. Cullman, *Salvation in History*, 172.

for the social structures or situations that confront us as much as we are responsible for our personal sins. At least we are not responsible for social structures immediately and directly. This notion of liberation is a relatively recent insight which has caught the attention of many theologians. These structures impact society as a whole.

How did Jesus react to social institutions which were sinful? What was his teaching in this regard? Jesus did not directly attack the social institutions of his day.[16] Meier notes that, "Compared with the classical prophets of Israel, the historical Jesus is remarkably silent on many of the burning social and political issues of the day."[17] However, his teaching did have an impact on them and the consequences of his teaching on social structures soon became evident. The Romans whose rule was oppressive and those who governed Israel through the Sanhedrin understood only too clearly what was implied in his message.[18] The good news called into question the improper use of power and those responsible for maintaining the structures were quick to understand the consequences.[19] The religious rulers were guilty of teaching the law too narrowly and restrictively. As a result, it became a burden. Jesus criticized the scribes and Pharisees for preventing people from entering into the kingdom.[20] The Roman occupation was oppressive of its very nature. Such oppression, religious or political, is antithetical to the very nature of the kingdom of God.

Jesus' appeal to the marginalized, the socially and religiously outcast, his invitation for women to be liberated and participate in his mission, was in itself a criticism of the religious and social structures of his

---

16. Meier makes the comment that Jesus did not preach a change of the world. He was not a social reformer. The Old Testament prophets did indeed address the nation and its social injustices. If Jesus did the same, he did it indirectly. He certainly condemned the hypocritical. The kingdom was a mirror which reflected the defects of social structures. This entire discussion is worth further examination. Meier, *Marginal Jew*, 2:331.

17. Meier, *Marginal Jew*, 1:199.

18. See Matt 20:25–34//Luke 22:25—27.

19. This would certainly have been a motive for wanting Jesus out of the way. His teaching on the kingdom was a serious challenge to them.

20. Matt 23:13//Luke 11:52. The entire chapter 23 of Matthew is a denunciation of the scribes and Pharisees. Jesus' critique is of behavior not consistent with the present kingdom. Interestingly he calls upon his disciples to "do and observe all things whatsoever they tell you, but do not follow their example" (Matt 23:3). The numerous woes taught in Matt 23 identify Jesus with the practice of the Old Testament prophets. In general, however, his message appears to be addressed more to the individual than the nation.

day. Patriarchy was included in this criticism.[21] These political, social, and religious structures prevented full participation in human life. Jesus could well be considered countercultural. If not explicit, Jesus' teaching was an implicit condemnation of social structures which are considered sinful. And from these he offered liberation and salvation.

Third Point: The Relationship between Personal and Social Sin

Jesus' teaching goes much deeper than personal conversion. There is a public component which needs to be addressed.[22] Jesus criticized a purely formal, pharisaic form of worship devoid of religious authenticity and human content. He was extremely critical of those who turned religion and the Sabbath into a burden. Along these lines, he is consistent with the great line of Old Testament prophets.[23] The prophetic teaching required "steadfast love and not sacrifice" (Hos 6:6). God does not desire the death of the wicked but rather his conversion (Ezek 33:11). It required a rending of "your hearts and not your garments" (Joel 2:13). Isaiah calls for true fasting: "Is this not, rather, the fast that I choose: releasing those bound unjustly, untying the thongs of the yoke; Setting free the oppressed, breaking off every yoke? Is it not sharing your bread with the hungry, bringing the afflicted and the homeless into your house; Clothing the naked when you see them, and not turning your back on your own flesh?" (Isa 58:6–7) The entire chapter 58 of Isaiah is a call for metanoia which is associated with social justice, as opposed to works of the law. It appealed to the interior life, that which is deepest within us.[24] Schillebeeckx described Jesus'

---

21. Matt 23:8–12. This is a rejection of titles or positions that produce inequality or improper relationships. The teaching to "call no man teacher, father, master" establishes proper relationships between God and disciple, between disciple and disciple. This is often interpreted as a critique of patriarchy. The rejection of these titles by Matthew is a rejection of superiority and pride. Paul makes clear the equality of all Christians in Gal 3:28.

22. Past generations of Christians have dealt with this in terms of the corporal works of mercy.

23. This is also true of the psalm tradition. Psalm 51:12 calls for a "clean heart" and a "steadfast spirit." The psalmist calls for "a contrite spirit; a contrite, humbled heart" (Ps 51:18–19). This is not a rejection of sacrifice per se, but it is a call for a right disposition. There are numerous references in the psalms that call for a proper disposition, a contrite, humble heart.

24. Meier points out that the choice between sacrifice and a contrite heart was not absolute. It means that a contrite heart takes priority over external actions.

challenge to the Pharisees and their narrow interpretation of the law as "the humanizing liberation of religion."[25]

For the prophets, this demand was inseparable from the denunciations of social injustice and from the vigorous assertion that God is known only by doing justice.[26] "To neglect this aspect is to separate the call to personal conversion from its social, vital, and concrete context."[27] Jesus must be seen within this context and his preaching of the kingdom of God only makes sense within it.

Fourth Point: The Kingdom Is the Freedom to Become Fully Human

The kingdom of God is a liberation that permits us to become fully human. Just as sin is seen as a defect, so also is the failure to achieve our full human potential. It is the absence of something that belongs to us in our human nature. It can be understood as a liberation or freedom from those things that prevent us from fulfilling the goal or purpose of human life. In this sense, liberation is seen in its positive connotation; we are freed *for* something. We mention above that the kingdom can be understood positively as a fulfillment of those deepest aspirations of human nature. It is also freedom to become fully human.[28] That is the end or purpose of our earthly life. St. Irenaeus, an early church father, is often quoted in this respect: "For the glory of God is a living man."[29] The gist of this statement is that an individual fulfilled in his God-given capacities is what God intended. On a more contemporary level, the conciliar document *Gaudium et Spes* articulates the church's relation to the world in which it functions.[30] The church through the activity of its members enriches the world by bringing to it the richness of the kingdom. The lived Christian experience is the means by which the kingdom comes alive in the lives

---

25. Schillebeeckx, *Church with a Human Face*, 24.

26. This is especially true for the written prophets: Hosea, Amos, Isaiah and Micah.

27. Gutierrez, *Theology of Liberation*, 134.

28. Jesus is described as the perfect man who teaches us how to be fully human. See *Gaudium et Spes*, no. 22, in *Vatican Council II*.

29. Roberts et al., *Apostolic Fathers*, 490.

30. It is worth pointing out at this point that the teaching of the Catholic Church is that both the secular government and the church each possess its own autonomy. The one should not exercise authority over the other. The church sees itself as bringing it's teaching to secular life that enriches it and brings it to its fullness.

of men and women. This goes beyond the personal morality in which an attitude of justice, love, and mercy is often absent.

Fifth Point: In General, the Kingdom of God is in Conflict With Evil of Every Sort, Both Physical and Moral

Evil is classically defined as "the absence of good."[31] Therefore it is a defect. This is true both in the physical and in the moral order. This gives the kingdom a broader corporeal significance rather than merely a spiritual one. The spiritual and corporeal are distinct but they are not actually separable.

Evil, as such, has no right to exist, and we must do everything in our power to eliminate it from our own lives and from society as well. But this principle has been subject to great misunderstanding and has been applied in ways that are contrary to the Gospel. We need to add a caveat: the kingdom does not signal the destruction of God's enemies.[32] Forgiveness and mercy are primary themes. Liberation is not a reversal of fortune.[33] While on earth, we live with the ambiguities of evil. This is a facet of the "all ready but not yet" of the kingdom.

The ultimate evil for humans is death. The kingdom offers eternal life. This becomes the meaning of the Easter mysteries, which are based upon life. Salvation is liberation from death. Positively, salvation is life lived to its fullest here and the enjoyment of eternal life.

Salvation Is Historical

Salvation takes place in history, in the present. Jesus initiated the kingdom and men and women participate in making it a reality. Schillebeeckx

---

31. Thomas Aquinas gave some organization to the reflections of Augustine on this subject and added his understanding that evil is a privation or absence of some due good, that is, a good that should exist but is absent. See *Summa Theologiae*, I, q. 48, a. 1 and I, q. 49, a. 1.

32. As a scriptural example we need look to the parable of the net thrown into the sea (Matt 13:47–50) and the weeds among the wheat (Matt 13:24–30). In both instances the parables describe the kingdom on earth as coexisting with the anti-kingdom.

33. Matthew 5:45 and Luke 6:35 both express God's demand to love one's enemies. Jesus' teaching on love of enemies is authentic and unique to him.

tells us that "this kingdom takes concrete form in human action."[34] It is a concrete, real possibility for the believing Christian.

The kingdom of God includes both the personal and the social dimensions of human life. Our physical and social lives are a part of salvation. In this sense, we do not possess two lives: one spiritual, the other physical. Human salvation is not salvation from the world. It is not an escape, but it is living the human life to its fullness.[35] It is liberation from personal sin. It is also liberation from sinful structures which prevent us from achieving our full potential. Of its very nature the kingdom of God corresponds to our deepest personal longing. It addresses what is best in our human nature.[36]

The kingdom then is not merely otherworldly. This would seem obvious from what has been said above. In the past, salvation has often been over spiritualized. This understanding was the result of decontextualizing the kingdom, separating it from the situation in which Jesus preached it. The proper reaction to this is to see the offer of salvation in its historical dimensions. Salvation is something concrete, and it is experienced, at least partially, in the present. It is here and now but not yet complete or fulfilled; "already but not yet."[37]

Salvation was preached by Paul as a matter of faith or grace. The expression *kingdom of God* was not totally absent from his writings. But it is either referred to in passing or it affirms that good moral behavior is necessary in order to enter it.[38] The kingdom of God is identified with Jesus as the cause of our salvation. Grace is a gift from God by means of which we are united to him. The understanding of grace enlarges or amplifies what has been said about the kingdom. It has been described as God present and

---

34. Schillebeeckx, *Church with a Human Face*, 20.

35. It is interesting to note that in its final session, Vatican Council II published one of its greatest accomplishments in *Gaudium et Spes (Pastoral Constitution of the Church in the Modern World)*. It delineates the church's role in salvation placed squarely in history.

36. This lies at the root of Catholic social teaching.

37. This is the meaning of the statement of Cullman that "the tension between the decisive 'already fulfilled' and the 'not yet completed' between present and future." Cullmann, *Salvation in History*, 172. Cullmann discusses the tension between present and future in pages 166–85.

38. The expression *kingdom of God* is found in Paul's writings somewhat infrequently. It is found in the authentic Pauline corpus 7 times, in the entire corpus 14 times. It is never spoken of as imminent. It is referred to in passing or about moral behavior. It is found 8 times in Acts. But the expression *kingdom of God* (*basileia tou theou*) is found in the Synoptic Gospels 121 times.

THE KINGDOM OF GOD: A THEOLOGICAL REFLECTION

active in the lives of men and women. The doctrine of grace is a fuller theological explanation of how this occurs. Furthermore, the notion of grace, while saving the prerogative of God as the giver of salvation, includes the individual's participation in salvation. Humankind has its part to play in making the kingdom of God present in the world.[39]

A word of caution is needed at this point. Not all Christians accept the notion that the kingdom of God as preached by Jesus includes both a present and future eschatology. Very conservative Christians are prone to see the kingdom of God only in future or otherworldly terms. For them, the kingdom of heaven is understood literally, in univocal terms; it is ultimately heaven and heaven alone. The kingdom is perceived as purely spiritual or otherworldly. The consequence of this particular point of view reduces the significance normally given to the world, to social justice and to other similar themes. Heaven alone is the goal for these individuals. Not only does this fail to do justice to the teaching of Jesus, which has been explored above at great length, but it also fails to account for our stewardship of the earth.

When the world is considered an evil place, the notion of original sin dominates. The idea is that we are simply pilgrims passing through this very temporary home and no intrinsic value is given to the world. Jesus' view of the world, the view of the creation story (Gen 1:1–3), is that the world is good, and that God wills the salvation of all men and women. As has been suggested above, we are not simply pilgrims passing through without concern for the world we live in. Such a view would be very foreign to Israel. Isaiah reinforces the idea of the goodness of creation when he declares, "For thus says the LORD, the creator of the heavens, who is God, the designer and maker of the earth who established it, not creating it to be a waste, but designing it to be lived in: I am the LORD, and there is no other" (Isa 45:18). Jesus falls squarely within this tradition.

The Present Kingdom Requires an Ethical Component

Meier has made the point that Jesus did not proclaim the reform of the world.[40] He proclaimed the kingdom of God. While this statement is accurate, it requires further explanation. Jesus did not preach as a social

---

39. Schillebeeckx, *Church with a Human Face*, 20.
40. Meier, *Marginal Jew*, 2:331.

reformer. He taught as a prophet.[41] As such, Jesus pulled back the veil on social situations. He permits us to see injustices as fundamentally incompatible with God's presence.[42] His focus was on God and God's activity among men and women. He chose the expression *kingdom of God* to give us his vision. The kingdom of God includes a moral or ethical dimension.[43] Jesus' authentic teaching demands a response that fulfills this ethical dimension. This is to say that the bringing about the kingdom on earth requires human agency.[44] This notion is certainly implied in the Old Testament prophetic tradition which saw that the failure of the Israelites to remain faithful and fulfill the law damaged their relationship with God. Their proper ethical behavior, that is, obedience to the law and to God was necessary. It was demanded of them by their covenant. The Old Testament was a call for justice for the widow, the orphan and the alien, a general expression that called for good ethical behavior. This is part of the content of the Old Testament that Jesus the Jew inherited from Israel. The new covenant imposes even greater demands. The present kingdom implies an ethic, that is, a way of living in our earthly existence, in the presence of God.[45] What shape does the present kingdom obtain? And what is demanded of the one who accepts it? That is the challenge that confronts every believer.

All social applications of the teaching of Jesus are based upon the idea that God is active and present in the world. Social solidarity is a consequence of the above principles.[46] We are by nature social beings

---

41. One of the major functions of an Old Testament prophet is to establish proper relationships: between the king and the people; between the people among themselves; and between the people and God. This in itself demands the elimination or reformation of social structures that are oppressive or sinful.

42. Jesus' program is implicitly contained in Matthew's judgment of the nations (Matt 25:31–46). It is a concern for the hungry, the thirsty, the naked, the ill, and prisoners. To put this in contemporary terms: it is the poor, the neglected, the immigrant, and those who suffer oppression or persecution. It is those who suffer the ill effects of a nation that is counter to the kingdom of God.

43. Meier, *Marginal Jew*, 2:451.

44. This is not meant in any way to negate the proposition that salvation is from God and God alone. Perhaps it would be helpful to see this relationship between the Savior and the saved in terms of the analogy of grace or faith. See Schillebeeckx, *Church with a Human Face*, 30–31.

45. See the judgement of the nations (Matt 25:31–46) and the Sermon on the Mount (Matt 5:1–7:28). The theme of these two chapters in Matthew's Gospel is "higher righteousness" which is the manner in which Matthew describes Jesus' teaching.

46. This is the basis for applying Jesus' teaching to society and social situations. It addresses both personal and social sins.

THE KINGDOM OF GOD: A THEOLOGICAL REFLECTION

who share and are bound together by a common nature, and we are all united to the one God as our common goal. This is a fundamental Christian principle.

Accepting the social nature of humanity and its relationship to the revelation made by God, we conclude that religion, while a personal matter, is not a private matter. Faith considered as a private matter requires a private revelation. This position is a denial that God acts and has acted for the entire human race. It implicitly denies that he has formed a people as his own. The practice of the Christian community rejects the view that faith is a private matter. Liturgy, which is the principal way of honoring God, is of its very nature communal. It demands that we come together as a community. The Lord's Supper carries with it the notion of solidarity. Jesus himself prayed "That all may be one, Father, as you and I are one" (John 17:21). There are social applications which must be drawn from Jesus' teaching. The kingdom of God demands an ethics or an orthopraxis.

Conclusion: A Characterization of the Kingdom of God[47]

There is a good reason for the length of this discussion on the kingdom of God. It is the principal content of Jesus' preaching, and it is foundational for his entire mission. The kingdom of God is an offer of salvation.[48] At its very core it addresses the civic and religious dimensions of human life. It opposes all that is marginalizing, alienating, or evil. Opposition to the kingdom is frequently described as the anti-kingdom. It is whatever opposes the presence of God in the world. It encompasses all that degrades or impedes the presence of God in the lives of men and women. The following is a summary of characteristics of the kingdom.

Characteristics of the Kingdom

The kingdom of God cannot be adequately defined. But it is within our means to describe its characteristics. First and fundamentally, the

---

47. The expression is a foundational idea in all Abrahamic religions: Israel, Christianity, and Islam.

48. Jesus is unique in the Christian recognition of him as God's revelation. We note that he is not the exclusive manifestation of God's presence in the world. God is not limited in this regard.

kingdom is God's universal saving love for humankind.[49] The kingdom expresses a relationship of intimacy between humanity and God. It is initiated by God.[50] It is understood as God's presence, active and involved in the lives of men and women.

Second, the kingdom is universal; it is extended to all humans. While the ministry of Jesus was limited in time and geography, his message was not. There were separatist movements during Jesus' time (Essenes, Zealots) but Jesus' ministry as an itinerant preacher was far from being a separatist movement. It was extensive and inclusive. Though the mission of Jesus was directed first to the house of Israel, it has been shown that gentiles were to be included. Salvation is offered to both the Jews as well as the gentiles.[51] No one is excluded. Surprisingly, those who were ritually unclean were a significant part of Jesus' ministry. All are invited to share in the kingdom.

Third, the kingdom is characterized by what is now often referred to as a preferential concern for the poor. Jesus' preaching of the kingdom included the poor and marginalized. It moved against the institutions that created the situation of poverty and oppression for so many. It is significant that the first beatitude as recorded by both Matthew and Luke speak of the blessedness of the poor because of their place in the kingdom.

Fourth, the kingdom rejects a narrow pharisaical legalism. This is recognized especially in the Gospel of Matthew.[52] It is a critique of the failed teaching of the officials of Israel, of those who identified fidelity to the covenant with the narrow fulfillment of the law. Jesus claimed that there is a higher righteousness that has to be fulfilled. The central problem with the Pharisees was that their interpretation of the Sabbath and the laws in general were often an impediment to achieving fullness

---

49. See Chilton, *Pure Kingdom*, 100

50. We might also note that the kingdom and human life must be seen in its context or environment. Contemporary theology is just now catching up to this point. Even the prophet proclaims that "God made the world a placed to be lived in" (Isa 45:18). Ecological concern must be seen as a part of the kingdom. This has been wonderfully expressed in Pope Francis's encyclical letter *Laudato Si' (On Care for Our Common Home)*.

51. It is salvation offered to all. This marks a difference with John the Baptist whose message was limited to Israel. Paul writes, "It [the gospel] is the power of God for the salvation of everyone who believes: for Jew first, and then Greek" (Rom 1:16).

52. Since the Gospel of Matthew developed within a Jewish context, it is understandable that it should be more critical of the pharisaical tradition. The early Christian community would have been in conflict with the synagogue and the Pharisees. See Matt 23. The entire chapter is a denunciation of the practices of the scribes and Pharisees.

of life. Jesus moved against this narrowness. The laws were intended to support and help men and women in their religious and social growth, not hinder it.

Fifth, the kingdom rejects social structures that marginalize and alienate. Jesus' death was brought about because of social structures that did not serve their given purpose. They did violence both to good governing and good religious practices. They were a misuse of power which worked against God living with his people. This is an especially significant characterization of the kingdom for contemporary men and women.

Sixth, the kingdom is characterized as something joyous. Jesus adds a note of joy, of conviviality, to the understanding of the kingdom. The beatitudes reflect Jesus' description of the kingdom as a source of blessedness. Jesus was accused of being a drunkard and glutton (Matt 11:16–19//Luke 7:31–35). This passage is from the Q source and is accepted as historically authentic. While we find it difficult to imagine Jesus as a drunkard, there is something in his public behavior upon which to base the accusation. Jesus' life and teaching was a thing of joy, and this was obviously reflected in his festive meals, itself a proleptic view of the kingdom.

Seventh, the kingdom is always positive. This means that the kingdom is not defined in terms of being against something. Rather, the kingdom is the completion of God's creative act found in Gen 1–3. Its goal is the full development of the person living in the presence of God. Jesus' "woe to you" statements are to be understood as a rejection of those things that are impediments to the kingdom.[53]

Eighth, the kingdom is not completely in the present. The kingdom as we experience it is participation in the future, transcendent kingdom. As Cullman so usefully described it, the kingdom is "already but not yet." This expression describes the tension between the present and the future kingdom. There is also tension in the fact that there is much opposition to the kingdom. The Christian is called upon to fully accept the invitation to be a part of the kingdom and to resist all that is anti-kingdom.

---

53. The woes are found in Matt 23:1–39; Mark 12:38–39; Luke 11:37–52; and 13:34–35. Much of this material is from the Q source.

The Message of the Kingdom Demands a Response

The kingdom is initiated by God calling upon us to live in his presence. It is an offer or invitation of salvation which calls for a free response. It requires metanoia, a turning to God and repentance. This calls upon individuals to cease relying solely on their own personal capabilities and put their trust in God. It implies a way of life which demands an orthopraxis, a correct way of behaving, as well as orthodoxy, a correct way of believing. It implies a personal commitment to participate in making the kingdom a visible, lived reality.

The invitation to participate in the kingdom implies the notion of freedom. The kingdom is not forced upon us; it is a matter of grace. The first objective response is to reject all that is contrary to the kingdom. It requires personal action, a decision to stand in the presence of God. There are ethical considerations on how we are to live our lives.

The kingdom is celebrated, not simply as an individual entity, but rather as social. Jesus' choice of expression would demand it. The kingdom is neither purely spiritual nor merely personal. It is concrete and communal. If, however, the kingdom is understood as both future and present, as a more modern approach would understand it, the kingdom is to be initiated during our lifetime on earth and is an integral part of the Christian life.

Furthermore, the kingdom is not a reversal of roles. We do not take the place of those who were our oppressors. They too must participate in the kingdom. There are no servant–master relationships. All power trips are eliminated. Jesus' teaching is quite clear on this. "But whoever wishes to be great among you must be your servant, and whoever wishes to be first among you must be your slave; just as the Son of Man came not to be served but to serve, and to give his life a ransom for many" (Matt 20:24–28 par.). These relationships are egalitarian. For in Christ Jesus all are children of God through faith.[54]

---

54. Paul also articulates this notion. "For all of you who were baptized into Christ have clothed yourselves with Christ. There is neither Jew nor Greek, there is neither slave nor free person, there is not male and female; for you are all one in Christ Jesus" (Gal 3:28).

THE KINGDOM OF GOD: A THEOLOGICAL REFLECTION

The Kingdom of God and the World

What is the relationship between the kingdom of God and the secular world we inhabit? Is the kingdom opposed to or separate from secular enterprises? That is, does one stand over against the other, creating a permanent divide?[55] Both the religious and the secular sphere have their own autonomy. They are distinct but not separate. The truth is we do not have two lives, one spiritual and the other secular. The kingdom of God informs the very life we possess, giving it direction. The kingdom reflects how our civil life ought to be lived. Does our response call for political or social action? In our present context, it would seem to be called for. Did Jesus' earliest disciples change society? It would seem so in more ways than can be imagined. Did they change social structures? Their impact was probably indirect. The challenge for contemporary Christians is to be more proactive in living out the demands of the kingdom on earth.

What does the Kingdom of God as a Present Reality Look Like?

How does one perceive a world in which God is truly present? What would that world look like? How would our present political, social, and religious institutions function? What changes need to take place in order to adequately reflect God as present among us? Are these realistically within our reach?

In order to imagine God's presence among us, we need to examine Jesus' life. Jesus reflects God's kingdom, God's life among us. His activity ought to be an indicator concerning the kingdom's visual presence. Jesus acted out the kingdom in various ways. Schillebeeckx informs us that "Jesus is aware that he is acting as God acts."[56] Jesus' life reflects God's presence. He acts as God acts.[57] To use another metaphor, he is the window through which we see God acting on our behalf. God is in history in the person of Jesus Christ. His miracles indicated God's inbreaking and the conflict with the powers of evil. His festive meals were

---

55. It is true that Jesus did not directly preach the change of the world. To do so would have been anachronistic. If Israel was a theocracy, it is apparent that this religious/political structure is no longer in vogue.

56. Schillebeeckx, *Church with a Human Face*, 21. This is reflected in his miracles, parables,table fellowship (festive meals), and all other events in Jesus' ministry.

57. Schillebeeckx, *Church with a Human Face*, 21.

an enactment of the final banquet, but it also indicated something of a present reality. Jesus' choice of an inner group of Twelve would indicate the need for organization both in giving expression to its fulfillment as well as to indicate its present existence.

Jesus was recognized as countercultural during his own time. He moved against the status quo. He recognized how the social, religious, and political structures of his own time were the anti-kingdom.[58] The kingdom of God demands proper social relationships and proper social structures. If this was not preached explicitly by Jesus, it was certainly implicit. As Schillebeeckx has reminded us, "This kingdom takes concrete form in human action."[59]

To put this in a simpler manner, the kingdom of God expresses Jesus' view of God and the world. It is based on his Abba experience. The challenge for us is to translate the activity of Jesus into our own culture, in a contemporary situation. We need to extend the results of his mission to our present life. What is there in our own social situation that militates against the kingdom? And in what way can we become a leaven as the parable suggests? Another way of looking at this is to ask ourselves what our view of God and the world is. How does it compare to Jesus' view? These questions will be taken up in the next chapter. But it is obvious that those who have a personal attachment to the person of Jesus Christ are called to act as he would act and to give the kingdom a concrete form in the world.

---

58. This has been taken up in a most profitable manner in liberation theology. Among some of the significant works expressing this are Sobrino, *Jesus the Liberator*, Ellacuria and Sobrino, *Mysterium Liberationis*, and Gutierrez, *Theology of Liberation*.

59. Schillebeeckx, *Church with a Human Face*, 20.

7

Miracles: Preliminary Considerations

Introduction

AN EXAMINATION OF THE biblical data necessarily precedes theological reflection. In this section we will examine the extrabiblical miracle tradition, the biblical tradition outside the Gospels, and the biblical tradition associated with Jesus in the Gospels.[1] This chapter will determine the context in which Jesus performed his miracles as well as the general contours of their expression. The Scriptures will be subject to a careful, deep reading. We will also account for the first-century religious and social context. In the following chapter we will examine the miracle tradition by application of the historical-critical method. This will establish with historical certainty (or probability) that several of the miracles do go back to the Jesus of history. We will also attempt to determine Jesus' personal understanding of his miracles.

Extrabiblical Miracle Tradition

There is an extrabiblical miracle tradition that corresponds chronologically with the time of Jesus.[2] Although it is not our primary concern to

---

1. The Old Testament miracle tradition is of little interest to us in this study. Our interest is in establishing the fact that miracles were well accepted during the time of Jesus.

2. There was always a possibility of the evangelists borrowing from extrabiblical sources. That gives us sufficient motive to point this out.

examine the miracle tradition outside the New Testament, we should be aware that there was significant acceptance of miracles during the first century AD. In the gentile world miracles were commonly accepted. Among the more famous were the cures at Epidaurus, an ancient town in Argolis, in the southeast of Greece. The sanctuary of Asclepius, son of Apollo the god of medicine and healing, was prominent here. This sanctuary was the site of many apparent miraculous healings during the first century. The miraculous was universally accepted during this time and at this place.[3]

There were numerous references to rabbinical cures in the first century. Some of the more noted of these were Honi the Rainmaker and Hanan ha Nehba and Abba Hilkiah, grandsons of Honi.[4] Hanina ben Dosa, a man of deed, was a first-century holy man and miracle worker. He lived in Galilee and was roughly contemporaneous with Jesus. Several of the miracle stories brought about by his prayer reflect the miraculous deeds of Jesus.

Thus, we should be mindful that, as we discuss the miracle tradition attributed to Jesus, miracles were certainly not outside the belief world in which he lived. Jesus was not unique as a miracle worker.[5] The miraculous was a part of the environment of his time. Healings and other miracles were commonly accepted in both the Jewish and the gentile world.[6]

The Biblical Tradition Outside the Gospels (Epistles and Acts)

Miracles represent a special part of the activity of the primitive church. There is a miracle tradition that exists outside the four Gospels which can be found in the Acts of the Apostles and in the Pauline epistles. It

---

3. The Temple of Asclepius at Epidaurus was built in the early fourth century BC and flourished well into the second century AD. It is now a UNESCO World Heritage Center. The sanctuary and the theater also built at this time are one of the purest pieces of Greek architecture.

4. Honi the Rainmaker is more often referred to as Honi the Circle Maker. He lived during the first century BC. Honi was stoned to death around BC 63.

5. The Synoptic tradition is witness to another exorcist during Jesus' ministry (Mark 9:38–41 par.). He is brought to the attention of Jesus and the narrative describes Jesus as recognizing and welcoming him.

6. Meier often describes Jesus as being like Elijah the prophet. The association is made because Elijah was an Old Testament prophet who performed miracles. Elisha is also counted among this number.

MIRACLES: PRELIMINARY CONSIDERATIONS

indicates that the apostles and Paul knew of Jesus' miracles and they themselves are reported to have performed miracles.

The Petrine Kerygma

The Petrine kerygma in the Acts of the Apostles reports the miracles of Jesus. Jesus' "mighty deeds, wonders, and signs" are referred to in Peter's preaching (Acts 2:22). What is significant about this is that the kerygma is not attempting to make a symbolic statement about the meaning of the miracles of Jesus. It simply affirms the miracle tradition of Jesus as fact. Later in Acts there is a record of Peter preaching to the gentiles in the house of Cornelius. He reported that Jesus "went about doing good and healing all those oppressed by the devil, for God was with him" (Acts 10:38). Both references point to the miracle tradition of Jesus as something that actually happened. There is no indication that these refer to anything that should be understood symbolically.

Besides referring to the Jesus tradition, there are references to Peter performing miracles. This part of the tradition supports the activity of Jesus. Peter cured a man lame from birth (Acts 3:1–10). He cured Aeneas, a paralytic (Acts 9:32–35). And he raised Tabitha from the dead (Acts 9:36–42). It is worthy of note that Simon the magician stands as a witness to this miracle tradition. "When he saw the signs and mighty deeds that were occurring, he [Simon] was astounded" (Acts 8:13).

The Pauline Testimony Regarding Miracles

Paul speaks of his own miraculous activity in 2 Cor 12:11–12 and in Rom 15:18–19. He uses the same linguistic expression which was used later in the Gospels. Miracles or mighty deeds seem common to Paul's ministry. Besides his personal activity, Paul lists miracles with the other gifts which he enumerates in 1 Cor 12:9–10, 28. In Gal 3:5 he mentions the mighty deeds that have been worked in the community. These are described as if they were actual occurrences.

The Acts of the Apostles also records several narratives containing Paul's healing activity. Paul raised a man to life who had fallen from a window (Acts 20:9–11). He also healed a man crippled from birth

(Acts 14:8–10).[7] At another time Paul cured a man who had a fever and dysentery (Acts 28:8).

These miracles, taken together, indicate that the miraculous was a part of the environment during and after the time of Jesus. It also indicates that the miracle tradition is not unique to Jesus. These are important hermeneutical considerations to keep in mind when examining the miracle narratives.

The Gospel Tradition Which Refers to Jesus' Miracles

The evangelists as well as Peter and Paul intended to report on miracles as actual, historical, real occurrences. That much seems clear from reading the appropriate texts. The stories were told with the intention of reporting the mighty deeds of Jesus as well as their own. These were not intended simply to be edifying stories or symbolic, metaphorical depictions. They refer to a tradition that is understood as the hand of God acting in history in their midst. These witnesses to Jesus' mighty deeds support the historicity of the miracle tradition attributed to Jesus.[8]

Miracles Represent a Special Part of Jesus' Activity

Miracles are an integral part of the New Testament. Jesus associated his miracles with the inauguration of the kingdom of God and the kingdom was the principle focus of his preaching.[9] The disciples recognized this.

---

7. Contemporary translations of the Scriptures have struggled to use appropriate sensitive language to describe disabilities. The NRSV translates this passage as a man who "had been crippled from birth." The NABRE translates the passage as "a crippled man, lamed from birth." It is suggested to avoid expressions such as "a crippled man," "a disabled person," or "handicapped person." A better expression is "a person with a disability" stressing the person and not the disability. It is difficult, however, to see how this later expression would properly suit the miracle narrative.

8. We are examining how Jesus' miracles were received during his ministry in the first century. Ultimately, we have to ask how they would be understood in our own culture. The answer to this question must wait until we have examined the miracles of Jesus in their own context and culture. This will be addressed in chapter 9.

9. Meier, *Marginal Jew*, 2:837. A unity exists between Jesus' preaching the kingdom and his performing miracles. *Dei Verbum (The Dogmatic Constitution on Divine Revelation)* from Vatican Council II notes that "this economy of revelation is realized by deeds and words, which are intrinsically bound up with each other." See Flannery, *Dei Verbum*, no. 2. A specific miracle that points to the centrality of Jesus' miracles and his proclamation of the kingdom is his cure of a demoniac (Matt 12:22–28//Luke

They themselves were sent to usher in the kingdom and in so doing they also shared in Jesus' power.[10] Their missionary activity gives witness to the miracles Jesus' performed.

The Gospel narratives take for granted the miracles of Jesus. The difficulty which needs to be resolved is that the evidence passes through an oral tradition and undergoes considerable exegetical and theological development before it is committed to writing. It remains to be determined whether this tradition is from the early postresurrection church as is often argued, or whether it is founded in Jesus' ministry?

Miracles are found in the earliest layers of the narrative tradition of the Gospels. This includes the Q source, Mark, L, and M. A great deal of the Gospel of Mark is devoted to the miracles of Jesus. In the narrative section of Mark (chapters 1–10), 200 of 425 verses are related to the miracle tradition. Christ's own testimony concerning the miracle tradition is also found in the earliest layers of the Scriptures.

The evangelists refer to the general memory that Jesus performed miracles without referring to any specific miracle. Mark refers to the astonishment of the crowds. "He has done all things well. He makes the deaf hear and the dumb speak" (Mark 7:37). In another place Mark makes a general reference to Jesus' miracles. "And wherever he went, to village, or town, or farm, they laid down the sick in the open spaces, begging him to let them touch even the fringe of his cloak. And all who touched him were cured" (Mark 6:56). Matthew also refers to the miracles of Jesus in general terms. He says, "He went around all of Galilee, teaching in their synagogues, proclaiming the gospel of the kingdom, and curing every disease and illness among the people. His fame spread to all of Syria, and they brought to him all who were sick with various diseases and racked with pain, those who were possessed, lunatics, and paralytics, and he cured them" (Matt 4:23–24).[11]

11:14–20). Meier identifies this miracle as the star witness that indicates the kingdom of God is present.

10. See the Mission of the Twelve (Mark 3:14–15; Matt 10:1, 7–8; Luke 9:1). In every case Jesus gives the Twelve the power to cure diseases and cast out demons. These two categories will be examined in depth below. In his Gospel, Luke has included a Mission of the Seventy-Two (Luke 10:1). Jesus instructs the Seventy-Two to "cure the sick" (Luke 10:9). In each of these cases recorded in the Synoptic Gospels, Jesus appoints these men to assist him in proclaiming that the kingdom of God is at hand. The high Christology of John's Gospel precludes the missionary activity of Jesus' apostles/disciples. There is ample evidence in the Gospel of John concerning Jesus' miracles. They are referred to as signs.

11. There are numerous references that indicate Jesus attracted huge crowds by his

The general observation is that Jesus cured people of their illnesses and exorcised demons. These general observations are found throughout the Gospels and in their earliest levels of composition. This will be important when the historical-critical method is employed to this data in examining individual miracle narratives.[12]

Jesus is Never Portrayed as a Wonder-Worker[13]

Faith in a wonder-worker is not expressed in the Gospels but rather it is faith in God. The Gospels are written from the perspective of resurrection faith directed to the power of God. The Acts of the Apostles refers to Simon the Magician, which leads us to presume that wonder-workers existed in the first century.[14] Jesus was not one of them. This can be observed in his attitude toward his miraculous powers.

The Scriptures describe Jesus as being unwilling to perform miracles solely to exhibit his power. This can be verified in several incidences. The first is located in his temptation in the desert (Matt 4:1–11; Luke 4:1–13). It seems apparent that the temptation was to challenge Jesus' personal view of his messiahship. In an incident during his public ministry, the Pharisees ask Jesus for a sign, but his response is that none will be given except the sign of Jonah (Mark 8:11–13//Matt 12:38–42). In a similar fashion during his crucifixion Jesus is challenged to use his power to save himself. He does not respond to the jeers of the crowds, the chief priests, and the scribes (Mark 15:29–32//Matt 27:39–43//Luke 23:35–37). These incidences point to an improper use of power relative to Jesus' understanding of the kingdom, and he will do no such thing. It distinguishes him from wonder-workers and other types of miracle

---

miracles. See Mark 3:7–8//Matt 4:25//Luke 6:17–19; Matt 15:29–31.

12. Fuller argues for the generalized statements of Jesus' miracles as authentic historical memories. Specific miracle narratives, however, are dependent upon these memories. Fuller, *Interpreting the Miracles*, 35–36. This work has a very good list of Gospel miracles on pages 126–27.

13. Jesus is not portrayed as a wonder-worker in the Gospels. See Brown et al., "Aspects of New Testament Thought," in *NJBC*, 81:108. Morton Smith describes Jesus as a wonder-worker in his work entitled *Jesus the Magician*. But a wonder-worker did prodigious and marvelous things to attract attention. Jesus never did. Mark 7:31–35 is an example of Jesus leading a blind man away from the crowd before he is cured. The blind man of Bethsaida was also led outside the village before he is cured (Mark 8:22–26). The thesis that Jesus was a magician is questionable.

14. This was referenced above in the discussion of the Petrine tradition. See Acts 8:9–24.

workers. Jesus had a specific understanding of his miracles quite different from that of a wonder-worker.

As one might suspect, the miracle tradition cannot entirely escape similarities to the world of gentile or Jewish miracle workers. One of Jesus' miracles, the finding of the coin in the fish's mouth, is somewhat similar to a Hellenistic wonder-worker. However, in this case, the real intent of the narrative is symbolic or didactic. It is a pericope recast to look something like a miracle. As we shall see later, this is not accepted as an authentic part of the miracle tradition. The Gospel of Mark has two miracle stories in which Jesus uses spittle. In one of these Jesus puts spittle on the eyes of the blind man of Bethsaida (Mark 8:23) and in another Jesus puts spittle on the tongue of a deaf man who had a speech impediment (Mark 7:33).[15] It is recorded that both men were cured. There is a similar miracle recounted in John 9:6 in which spittle is used to make mud. It is then applied to the blind man's eyes. The fact that the use of spittle is similar to other miracles in the gentile world gives us pause to accept these as authentic. They could have been borrowed from the gentile tradition. Meier, however, appealing to the rules of discontinuity and embarrassment argues for their authenticity.[16]

New Testament Miracles in Their Context

The miracle tradition was often incorrectly understood as events that contravene the laws of nature. This understanding is still accepted by many. A careful examination of the tradition, however, gives us quite a different picture. In order to adequately understand the miracle tradition we need to account for the context or environment in which the miracle events and their narratives take place. The New Testament miracles were not understood or referred to with expressions indicating a discontinuity or breach with nature or the natural law.[17]

---

15. In the parallel in Matt 15:29–31 there is no mention made of Jesus touching the tongue.

16. Meier, *Marginal Jew*, 2:693, 697.

17. See Brown et al., "Aspects of New Testament Thought," in *NJBC*, 81:92–95. This article is an explanation of the biblical view of miracles which does not look upon the miraculous as a rupture of nature, nor does it view nature as a closed system of laws. Concerning the proper understanding of literary forms see Flannery, *Dei Verbum*, no. 12. The meaning intended by the sacred writer is required. What literary form did the author use; what did he intend to express? *Dei Verbum*, no. 12 tells us that "due attention must be paid both to the customary and characteristic patterns of perception,

In the present time there is a sharp distinction between nature and the activity of God; between the object of science (nature) and the object of theology (God). In biblical times no such distinction was made. Activity attributed to the power of God was not radically distinguished from the laws of nature. No distinction was made between God as the source or cause of the world and the working of nature. Natural phenomena were often described as a sign from God or his activity in the world.

The Cultural Environment of the New Testament

The biblical approach to the miraculous must be understood in its own context.[18] The Bible is prescientific in its view of the world. It does not understand nature as a closed system of laws. First-century civilization had a considerably different view of nature from our current twenty-first-century view. They readily accepted the hand of God active in both ordinary and extraordinary events. The ordinary working of nature was often attributed directly to God. This point of view often did not consider secondary causality. For example, storms, famine, and plagues were considered in terms of God's activity and not as typical phenomena of nature.[19]

There is no sharp distinction made between healing and nature in the first century. Both are expected in this older world view. In the New Testament context they are related to the inbreaking of the kingdom and understood as contrary to the powers of Satan. The cultural environment provided the matrix in which the miracle story is told.

This ought not surprise us. Even in our own culture we often attribute two different views to the same event: a secular or historical one and a religious one. In common conversation we often see nature and God working together without contradiction. Consider the phenomenon of wind. We assign a meteorological explanation to it, explaining it in terms of variables which can easily be measured. The wind, or other

---

speech and narrative which prevailed at the age of the sacred writer." Fuller also addresses this issue. See Fuller, *Interpreting the Miracles*, 8.

18. The critical explanation or interpretation of a scriptural text is called exegesis. Interpretation of a scriptural text by reading one's own ideas into it is called eisegesis. Exegesis, not eisegesis, is our goal.

19. This is often experienced at the present time. There are those who considered Katrina, a devastating hurricane that hit the eastern seaboard of the United States August 29–31, 2005, as a punishment from God. Similarly, Pat Robertson claimed that Ariel Sharon's heart attack was a punishment because he had not upheld Israel's territory sufficiently.

weather phenomena, is often attributed to God's power.[20] Even though we understand the meteorological laws associated with rainfall, yet we pray for rain in time of drought. We would more than likely identify this with second and first causes, with nature and with God. The ancient mind made no such distinction.

The Bible sees actions that are within the realm of nature or history as miraculous. Several events narrated in the Scriptures, such as the plagues which preceded the Exodus or the destruction of the walls of Jericho, are described as occurring because of divine intervention.[21] But while we read the Scripture in this manner, we also understand that there are natural, historical, and social reasons for the events.

Historical forces were often considered miraculous. A miracle is often a historical event seen through the eyes of faith. *The New Jerome Biblical Commentary* informs us that "the biblical notion of the miraculous includes acts that are explicable on the level of human interaction as well as those that are not."[22] Armed with this understanding we should be able to approach the tradition with greater objectivity.

We Should Not Impose a 20th Century Scientific Model Upon the First-Century Culture

The Scriptures do not deal with nature scientifically; they look to nature from the perspective of faith, or they look to nature theologically. There is strong agreement among scholars that the New Testament miracles are extraordinary events that find no explanation in the ordinary world of time and space. The miraculous is perceived as an extraordinary event which is often unexpected. It provokes amazement and calls attention to itself. We might also note that this is no different than the approach the church takes when it looks to more modern-day miracles. The cures that occur in various Marian shrines, such as Lourdes, Fatima, or Medjugorje are documented so as to exclude such things as hysteria or psychological causes. They are sudden and inexplicable, but they are not seen as a breach of the laws of nature. A similar observation should be made regarding the miracles required for the canonization of

20. Kasper, *Jesus the Christ*, 92.

21. Some scholars have argued that the geological evidence indicates that the walls of Jericho were not actually standing when Joshua and the Israelites passed by the city. The walls had been destroyed decades earlier.

22. Brown et al., "Aspects of New Testament Thought," in *NJBC*, 81:93.

saints. Miracles are not examined in an effort to discover a rupture of nature. They ought to be understood as the hand of God, a sign as to the sanctity of the person under examination.

Conclusion and Resume

It is evident that an understanding of the context of any issue is important. The context is itself an interpretive factor. By a careful, deep reading of the Scriptures that accounts for the first century social and religious context we were able to situate the miracle tradition associated with the Jesus of history. In the first century, miracles were widely accepted both in the gentile and Jewish worlds. A well-founded rabbinical tradition of miracle workers existed in the first century. It should come as no surprise that a miracle tradition is found in the New Testament. Peter and Paul and other disciples apparently performed miracles. These miracles were intended to be seen as actual events and not simply as symbolic in nature. In the Gospels, Jesus was described as a miracle worker and his *signs* or *mighty deeds* were a significant part of this tradition. We were further able to determine that Jesus was not described as a wonder-worker and his miracles were not seen as ruptures of nature. They were understood as being associated with his person and his mission. From this reading it is clear that the miracles must be judged in their own context and not according to a twentieth-century understanding.

There are a number of significant questions regarding the miracle tradition of Jesus that have either already been asked or will be asked and addressed in the following chapters. Are miracles creations of the early church, the product of Christian faith? Are these miracles literary borrowings from Judaism or the Hellenic world? Are these actual miracle stories based on genuine specific memories, that is, do they reflect actual experiences in Jesus' ministry? Or are they simply narratives derived from the evangelists based on general memory?[23] We will begin looking for answers by determining whether the miracles of Jesus can be grounded in history. Can they be traced to his personal activity rather than the creativity of the primitive community? Are the miracles

---

23. See Fuller, *Interpreting the Miracles*, 35–36. Fuller argues for the generalized statements of Jesus' miracles as authentic historical memories. Specific miracle narratives, however, are dependent upon these memories. This work has a very good list of Gospel miracles on pages 126–27. This is an excellent text for the beginner.

MIRACLES: PRELIMINARY CONSIDERATIONS

attributable to Jesus, that is, are the *mighty deeds* and *signs* recorded in the Scriptures things Jesus actually did?

We are now in a position to address the specific miracles attributed to Jesus in his ministry. In anticipation of the following chapter, we can affirm that Jesus performed miracles and understood himself as a miracle worker. Meier tells us that Jesus was "a 1st-century Palestinian Jew who performed startling actions that both he and at least some of his audience judged to be miraculous deeds of power."[24] This conclusion and the specific miracles which appear in the Scriptures as being historical will be examined below. The rules for examining these miracles to determine if they are authentic, that is, that they go back to the Jesus of history will be employed. Among the several sources that have been employed, two deserve particular attention. Reginald Fuller is an early and excellent source for exploring the historical method and its rules. Even though we shall see that he is incapable of identifying any specific miracle narrative dependent on a specific memory, he is a good read for the beginner. A more recent source is John Meier who followed Fuller by almost thirty years.[25] We will depend more heavily on Meier and his conclusion while incorporating Fuller and other scholars as supportive of our effort. It was pointed out earlier that the rules are explained in chapter 2.

---

24. Meier, *Marginal Jew*, 2:837.

25. Meier, *Marginal Jew*, 2:619–31. This study is heavily depended upon the research of John Meier. However, we do not neglect the research of other important scholars.

8

Jesus as a Worker of Miracles

Introduction

THE NUMBER OF SPECIFIC miracles found in the New Testament depends in large part on how they are classified. This varies from author to author. John Meier counts thirty-two separate, specific miracles.[1] *The New Jerome Biblical Commentary* lists thirty-five. *Eerdmans Dictionary of the Bible* also lists thirty-five. Fuller's list includes thirty-three separate miracles and twelve general healings attributed to Jesus.[2] This disparity is due largely to the judgment that some supposed miracle stories are not miracles at all but belong to another literary genre. Some

---

1. This part of our investigation is heavily dependent upon the work of Meier, *A Marginal Jew*. As has been mentioned earlier, this work is excellent. Fuller, *Interpreting the Miracles*, though a much earlier study than that of John Meier, is also frequently referred to. This work is an excellent point of departure for the beginner. Fuller provides very useful lists of Gospel miracles and Gospel sayings referring to miracles on pages 126–27. Both Meier and Fuller are supplemented by the works of numerous other scholars.

2. Fuller's list describes the feeding of the five thousand and the feeding of the four thousand as two separate miracle narratives. Other scholars treat them as a doublet, a single miracle narrative. Luke 8:2 is absent from his list but it is included by Meier in his. Fuller adds John 2:23-25 to his list but no miracle is referred to in this narrative. Fuller also adds a list of ten "Sayings Referring to Miracles." I have discovered another list of miracles that numbered thirty-seven but two of these were general healings. Another list numbered thirty-four distinct miracle narratives, but the list included the resurrection of Jesus and did not include the miracle story of Jesus walking on the water and the narrative of the temple tax in the fish's mouth. All of this indicates the care needed in examining the miracle tradition.

are literary parallels or variants.³ There is no dispute, however, that Jesus' miracles can be divided into four distinct categories: exorcisms, healings, raisings from the dead, and so-called nature miracles.⁴ The following exposition corresponds with these four general categories. This will be followed by an examination of other narratives that are often identified as miracles but in fact are not.

The Miracle Tradition

In this section we will look for the miracle narratives that are likely historical, that is, events understood as miraculous by their observers which can be established as going back to the historical Jesus and provide the basis for the narratives.⁵ We are concerned with actual historical events and not literary accounts. Does the narrative depend upon a specific memory or is it based upon some general memory? As was the case in our examination of the kingdom of God we will appeal to the historical-critical method. It is Meier's opinion that the most important criterion in examining the miracle tradition is the criterion of multiple attestations although he does appeal to other criteria.⁶ We will see this criterion's usefulness when we examine the so-called nature miracles. The principle of multiple attestations simply stated is that the event must be found in more than one literary source (Mark, Q, M, L, and John). It must also be found in several literary forms. This would ensure that the narrative comes from several independent traditions.

We will first briefly examine the evidence for exorcisms, healings, and raisings from the dead. More time will be spent discussing the so-called nature miracles because of the rationale for rejecting most of them as historical events.

---

3. Meier, *Marginal Jew*, 2:218.

4. The reason for identifying nature miracles as so-called nature miracles will be explained below.

5. The miracle narratives should not be envisioned as brief video recordings of an historical event. The original tradition has been subjected to considerable literary and theological editing. A number of these narratives, however, can be shown to depend upon an historical event.

6. Meier, *Marginal Jew*, 2:619, 630. Meier applies the criteria to the miracle tradition of the Gospels taken as a whole on pages 619–31.

The Exorcisms

There are seven distinct exorcisms reported in the Gospels.[7] The result of the application of the historical-critical method to the miracle tradition concludes that the evidence in the New Testament that Jesus was an exorcist is overwhelming. Jesus' activity as an exorcist is found in the earliest strata of the Synoptic Gospels. His exorcisms are multiply attested, that is, they are found in several different sources and forms (Mark, Q, M and L). They are attested to by Jesus' opponents who do not deny their existence but rather give them an unflattering interpretation (Matt 9:34//Luke 11:15).[8] The conclusion: exorcisms in fact go back to the person of Jesus and are not an invention of later Christians. Jesus was a first-century exorcist.[9]

We have already discussed an extremely important miracle narrative which provides insight into Jesus' self-understanding.[10] After casting out a demon from a mute person, Jesus addresses the crowds. "But if it is by the finger of God that [I] drive out demons, then the kingdom of God has come upon you" (Luke 11:20; brackets in the original). There is wide acceptance among scholars that this is an authentic saying of Jesus.[11] That Jesus performed exorcisms is historically certain. That he understood himself as an exorcist and considered it as a significant part of his ministry is also historically authentic.

The question that follows is whether the narratives of Jesus' exorcisms are from a specific or only a general memory. Can we identify any narrative of an exorcism that represents a historical event in the ministry of Jesus? Based on his application of the historical-critical method, Meier concludes there are two narratives that are likely based upon some historical memory: the possessed boy (Mark 9:14–29 parr.) and the reference to Mary Magdalene (Luke 8:2). There is sufficient evidence in these

---

7. The distinct exorcisms are the demoniac in the Capernaum synagogue (Mark 1:23-28//Luke 4:33-37; the Gerasene demoniac (Mark 5:1-20); the possessed boy (Mark 9:14-29//); the mute and deaf demoniac (Matt 12:22-23//Luke 11:14); the mute demoniac (Matt 9:32-33); the Syrophoenician woman (Mark 7:24-36//Matt 15:21-28); and a reference to Mary Magdalene (Luke 8:2). The list of these exorcisms and their examination can be found in Meier, *Marginal Jew*, 2:646-61. Fuller's list does not include Luke 8:2, a reference to Mary Magdalene "from whom seven demons had gone out."

8. The remainder of this narrative is important. See Luke 11:19-20. This has already been established as an important, authentic pericope.

9. Meier, *Marginal Jew*, 2:406, 648.

10. See above chapter 5, 9–12.

11. Meier, *Marginal Jew*, 2:406.

two narratives to indicate that they go back to some event in the ministry of Jesus. Concerning the other exorcisms, however, none of the references provide us with sufficient information to declare them as historically authentic, that is, historical events which gave rise to the narrative.[12] Even the authentic pericope from Luke 11:20 mentioned above does not provide us with sufficient information to declare that the exorcism recorded in the narrative is based upon some historical event.[13]

The Healing Miracles

There are fifteen particular cases of cures or healings in the Gospels. Added to this list is the oft quoted Q source (Matt 11:2–6//Luke 7:18–23).[14] This historically authentic source enumerates the blind, the lame, lepers, the deaf and the dead. That Jesus was a healer has a solid historical basis. It has multiple attestations of source and forms. It is found in Mark, Q, L, and John.[15] The evidence in the Gospels that Jesus healed and that he understood that this charism was a significant part of his mission is very strong.

We discovered above that establishing the historicity of Jesus' particular exorcisms proved elusive. We are on more solid ground for the healing miracles. Several of the healing narratives can be established as historical. It seems likely that there is a historical core, a specific memory, upon which the narrative is based.[16] They satisfy the rules for establishing their historicity. They can be traced to Jesus in his ministry. Among the healing miracles there are seven narratives that have a good possibility of going back to some event in the life of Jesus. Meier tells us that the

---

12. Meier points to the possessed boy (Mark 9:14–29 parr.) and the reference to Mary Magdalene (Luke 8:2) as possibly going "back to historical events in Jesus' ministry." He has his doubts about the other distinct exorcisms. See Meier, *Marginal Jew*, 2:661.

13. The curing of the demoniac serves as an introduction to the Beelzebul controversy, an important narrative, but it is not listed with the miracle narratives.

14. For a list of healing miracles see Meier, *Marginal Jew*, 2:678-727. Besides these particular instances there are numerous general sayings of healings in the Gospels. Examples of general sayings are Mark 1:32-34; 3:10-12; and 6:55-56. Other references could be added to this list. See the "Sayings Referring to Miracles" in Fuller, *Interpreting the Miracles*, 127. Note that the very first reference to the Beelzebul controversy in Fuller's list is incorrect. It should read Mark 3:22–27 and not Mark 3:30–33.

15. Meier, *Marginal Jew*, 2:678.

16. Meier, *Marginal Jew*, 2:726.

basic history of the miracle stories of blind Bartimaeus (Mark 10:46–52 parr.) and the blind man of Bethsaida (Mark 8:22–26) are quite strong; the miracle story for the man born blind (John 9:1–41) is also strong.[17] To this list, Meier included several healings of the paralyzed and crippled.[18] It includes the paralyzed man who was let down through the roof (Mark 2:1–12 parr.) and the man cured at the pool of Bethesda (John 5:1–9).[19] He argues for the addition of the deaf mute (Mark 7:31–37) to the list although he realizes that many others would not find the evidence very clear.[20] Meier also argues for the addition of the healing of the servant or son of a royal official/centurion (Matt 8:5–13//Luke 7:1–10; John 4:46–54). The Q version and John's version are thought to be alternate forms of the same primitive tradition. This reflects an event that goes back to the ministry of the Jesus of history.

There are other healing narratives for which the evidence does not allow us to establish their historicity. The results of the arguments are unclear. Most of the cures of lepers fall into this category.[21] There are many other cures for which we simply must concede a lack of any degree of historicity.

The Raisings from the Dead

The greatest challenge to contemporary belief in the miracle tradition would more than likely come from the raisings from the dead. A careful examination of these particular miracles has proven extremely beneficial.

The Gospels contain numerous references to raising the dead to life in a general sense. This has been mentioned in Jesus' response to John's disciples (Matt 11:6//Luke 7:22). The response is based upon the fulfillment of messianic prophecies.[22] Is it possible for us to understand

---

17. Meier, *Marginal Jew*, 2:698.

18. Meier, *Marginal Jew*, 2:726–27. Meier's list includes the three miraculous cures of blind men; however, he has already argued for their historicity. See Meier, *Marginal Jew*, 2:698. His complete list is in *Marginal Jew*, 2:726–27.

19. Meier identifies this man as a paralytic but there is no such identification in the pericope. See Meier, *Marginal Jew*, 2:726.

20. Meier, *Marginal Jew*, 2:714. Compare with 2:726.

21. It seems well established however, that Jesus cured lepers. Meier, *Marginal Jew*, 2:706.

22. The response is taken from Isa 26:19; 29:18–19; 35:5–6; and 61:1.

these references in a metaphorical or figurative sense?[23] Could this mean that there are those who are blind and deaf to the good news being preached? In fact, there are places in the New Testament where the expressions *seeing* and *hearing* are used in this manner. The passages bracketed in Mark 8:31—10:52 employ the theme of blindness in a symbolic sense. It refers to the disciples' failure to understand in terms of seeing or hearing. However, that the references from Matt 11:5-6 are meant in a metaphorical or symbolic sense doesn't seem likely.[24] The context doesn't permit this understanding. More to the point, this passage (Matt 11:5-6) differentiates Jesus from John the Baptist. It is not a comment addressed to the crowd or to Jesus' disciples. The passage is related directly to John, and is an expression of Jesus' mission.

More importantly for our consideration, the Gospel contains three instances of raising the dead to life in a literal sense.[25] These are the raising of the son of the widow of Nain (Luke 7:11-17), the raising of the daughter of Jairus (Mark 5:22-43 parr.), and the raising of Lazarus (John 11:1-44). The question is this: Do these events go back to some event in Jesus' ministry recognized as miraculous or are they creations of the early church? An examination of the texts reveals multiple attestations of sources (M, Q, L, and John); there appears to be multiple attestations of forms; and there does not appear to be any borrowing from other sources. We conclude, therefore, that these events are attributable to Jesus himself.

What does all of this establish? As brief as this summary is, most importantly it establishes that the early church did not invent the picture of Jesus raising the dead to life. We can conclude that the events go back to the public life of the Jesus of history. It still remains for us to determine what these events were, given the fact that the historical-critical method has established their historicity prescinding from any faith consideration. Did these narratives report an actual raising a dead person back to normal life or was it something else?

---

23. Consider Matt 8:22 and parallels. "Let the dead bury the dead." This response is to prospective followers. Is this used figuratively or in a literal sense?

24. Meier, *Marginal Jew*, 2:835. This Q source was treated at length in chapter 5, 92–94.

25. There are references in the Acts of the Apostles in which Peter raised Tabitha from the dead (Acts 9:36-42) and Paul raised a young man named Eutychus to life (Acts 20:7-12).

In sum we can conclude that Jesus was a first-century exorcist and healer. He was perceived to have raised several individuals from the dead. We are able to conclude that Jesus recognized that he possessed these charisms; that he was a miracle worker. He understood that these signs, these mighty works of God, ushered in the kingdom of God.

The So-Called Nature Miracles

The discussion of the nature miracles is separated from the exorcisms, healings, and raisings from the dead. This category of miracles was not accepted as historical by many on the grounds that the modern mind could not believe them as historical. The reason for referring to nature miracles as so-called nature miracles will become clear as we proceed. Surprisingly, the skeptical rejection of this category of miracles as historical has been found to be accurate in most cases but for the wrong reasons. However, rather than reject the so-called nature miracles on the basis of an a priori judgment, they will be carefully examined from a historical-critical perspective. We will indicate why these specific so-called nature miracles, with the exception of the feeding of the multitude, fail as historically founded.

The So-Called Nature Miracles Examined

There are seven particular cases of nature miracles.[26] Five of these listed here are considered to be proper miracle stories in their form. Two others have the form of miracle stories but are better read as didactic events. The five genuine miracle stories are Jesus changing water into wine (John 2:1–11), feeding the crowds in the desert (Mark 6:32–44//Matt 14:13–21//Luke 9:9b–17//John 6:1–15), Jesus walking on the water (Mark 6:45–52//Matt 14:22–23; John 6:16–21), the stilling the storm (Mark 4:35–41//Matt 8:23–27//Luke 8:22–25), and cursing the fig tree (Mark 11:12–14, 20–21//Matt 21:18–20). The two stories that are didactic will be examined below as non-miracles. They are Peter's catching of fish (Luke 5:1–11; John 21:1–4) and the coin in the fish's mouth (Matt 17:24–27). There is one other miracle story which is not a so-called nature miracle but a cure story. We will treat it last as some

---

26. See Brown et al., "Aspects of New Testament Thought," in *NJBC*, 81:101 for the list.

consider it a miracle, while others do not. This is the cure of Peter's mother-in-law (Mark 1:29–31 parr.). The challenge is to determine whether this narrates a true miracle.

Because nature miracles have posed a problem in as much as they cast doubt upon the miracle tradition in general, special attention needs to be paid to them. The following categories follow John Meier's division. We will take them up in turn.

Changing Water into Wine at Cana (John 2:1–11)

This miracle story is found only once in the New Testament, in the Gospel of John. Therefore, multiple attestations are not possible. Having admitted as much, it is difficult to distinguish tradition from the evangelist's redactions. There are also christological issues with the pericope which would call its historicity into question.[27] The christological issues indicate that this is a postresurrection narrative and not historical. The general conclusion is that this miracle is not accepted as historical.

Feeding the Multitude (Mark 6:34–44; Mark 8:1–9)

In Mark 6:34–44, Jesus feeds five thousand and in Mark 8:1–9 Jesus feeds four thousand.[28] This episode is considered a doublet, that is, a particular story told several times, and which differs in some details.[29] This pericope is also found twice in Matt, 14:13–21 and 15:32–38. It is found once each in Luke 9:10–17 and John 6:1–13.

Unlike the wedding feast at Cana, there is strong multiple attestation of sources for the feeding of the multitude. It appears in all four Gospels, the only miracle story to do so. It is also found in the earliest strata of writing. Furthermore, there is coherence with Jesus' ministry;

---

27. This first sign of John as well as the other six are understood as Jesus revealed in his glory. He is understood as the Christ and not simply as Jesus of Nazareth. See Brown, *Gospel According to John*, 1:97–110. See also Perkins, "Gospel According to John," in *NJBC*, 61:40.

28. The traditional place where this event is said to have occurred is Tabgha on the northwestern shore of the Sea of Galilee.

29. Fuller proposes that these references are different versions of the same event. They "grew out of a genuine memory." Fuller, *Interpreting the Miracles*, 57. What actually happened "can no longer be recovered." Fuller, *Interpreting the Miracles*, 37.

with his parables and sayings of the kingdom as a banquet; and with his own festive meals.

We conclude that the feeding of the multitude was a memorable communal meal of bread and fish that was celebrated by Jesus, his disciples, and a large crowd by the Sea of Galilee. This communal meal had eschatological overtones. For reasons enumerated above this miracle story is judged to be historical. It should be noted that exegetes are somewhat careful about saying that an actual multiplication of loaves and fish took place. Their conclusion seems to be that the event took place and was reported in the fashion we now have in the Gospels. In whatever manner one explains this miracle narrative, it is historically certain that the event goes back to the Jesus of history.

Jesus Walks on the Water (Mark 6:45–52 parr.)

There is one epiphany miracle, Jesus walks on the water (Mark 6:45–52//Matt 14:22–33//John 6:15–21). This particular miracle story is of great interest in the sense that it has been dismissed by skeptics a priori by suggesting that Jesus found stones near the surface of the water which made it appear that he was walking on the water or that he was actually walking on the shore. The text of John can be subject to such a reading. Evidently it presumes that the disciples were rather gullible or deceived. The problem with this explanation is that it does not account for or do justice to the literary genre.

With the help of the historical-critical method, we can conclude that there are actually multiple attestations of sources found in Mark and John. This satisfies at least one of our rules of criticism. However, there is no multiple attestation of form.[30] It fails the test of historicity in this regard. Furthermore, there is discontinuity with Jesus' other miracles. One of the difficulties with so-called nature miracles in general is that they are witnessed only by Jesus' disciples; they are not public events.

This miracle story, Jesus walking on the water, has all the characteristics of a postresurrection narrative. During the storm, Jesus calms the fears of his disciples. "Take courage, it is I, do not be afraid" (Mark 6:50 parr.). Jesus' self-identity, "it is I," is a clue to the high Christology recognized by the early community. In the Greek New Testament this

---

30. The Gospels are composed of many smaller units or pericopes which circulated prior to their formation. Form describes the form or pattern of these stories (pericopes). Forms are the subject matter of form-criticism.

self-identity is the Greek expression *ego eimi* and it is literally translated as "I am." The note in the NABRE tells us that "this may reflect the divine revelatory formula of Exodus 3:14."[31] Yahweh reveals himself to Moses and gives him his mission. "God replied, 'I am who am.' Then he added, 'This is what you shall tell the Israelites: I AM has sent me [Moses] to you [the Israelites]'" (Exod 3:14).[32] Yahweh (I AM) sends Moses to the Israelites giving them his name.

The Christology of the *ego eimi* situates the miracle as a narrative from the early church. The miracle story indicates continuity with the situation of the church which is undergoing persecution (the storm). The church is expressing its faith in Christ who is now understood as the Son of God (an identity with the Father) and that this same Jesus will bring salvation to a community laden by persecution and difficulties. The story is a post-Easter creation.

Jesus Stilling of the Storm (Mark 4:35–41 parr.)

There is only one rescue miracle, (Mark 4:35–41//Matt 8:18–23//Luke 8:22–25). In this event, Jesus exhibits his saving power. What can the historical-critical method tell us about the miracle in which Jesus calms even the elements of nature? Consider the following points.

Mark alone is the source of this miracle story thus there is no multiple attestation. It is impossible to distinguish tradition from redaction. Furthermore, this miracle is discontinuous from the Jesus tradition. There are no other saving miracles. It is apparent that it is in continuity with the early church miracle tradition. It points to primitive form of "narrative high Christology."[33] Therefore, this miracle is more than likely a product of the postresurrection church.

Fuller believes that the two miracle stories, the walking on the water and the stilling of the storm, both rest on the same historical memory. Fuller does not believe the miracles were created out of whole cloth by

---

31. This revelatory formula is also reflected in Isa 41:4, 10, 13; 43:1-3, 10, 13.

32. In its translation of the Gospel of John, the NABRE has adopted the convention of capitalizing the *ego eimi* (I AM) wherever it refers to Jesus as divine. See John 8:24, 28, 58; 13:19; and 18:5–8.

33. High Christology refers to affirmations that include a reference to the divinity of Christ. Harrington, "Gospel According to Mark," in *NJBC*, 41:34 informs us that "the disciples' question at the end [of Mark 4:35-41] ('who is this . . . ?') expresses the Marcan emphasis on Jesus' identity and constitutes an implicit christological claim regarding the divine character of Jesus, for Jesus does what God does."

the early church but rather that some historical event in the life of Jesus, some general memory, suggested these narratives.[34] Nevertheless, there is no credible way to establish the historicity of either.

Jesus Curses the Fig Tree (Mark 11:12–14, 20–21//Matt 21:18–20.)

There is one curse miracle recorded in the Gospels. Jesus curses a fig tree. Mark's version is a two-part story with the cleansing of the temple interpolated between these parts. Matthew conflates Mark's narrative, and the withering of the fig tree takes place immediately following the curse. Luke has a parable (Luke 13:6–9) and a lesson (Luke 21:29–33) concerning the fig tree but no miracle.

This particular miracle story is of particular interest because it not only fails the test of the historical critical method but there are literary characteristics that help us understand something of the dynamic that occurs in positing this form of miracle.

This miracle does not appear to be historical for several reasons. First, there is a singular attestation. Second, there is a lack of coherence. This is not how Jesus behaved. We have no other incident in the Gospels indicating that Jesus cursed anything in such a manner. Furthermore, the expectation of figs was totally unrealistic. The first figs of the season are in June. Mark, however, situated this event during the last week of Jesus' life, after his final entry into the Jerusalem. If our dating of the death of Jesus is correct this would have placed the incident prior to June by several months.[35] Mark himself tells us that this was not the time for figs (Mark 11:13).

The conclusion is that this is an interpretation created by a pre-Marcan source. It is a *theologoumenon*, that is, a theological idea which interprets the cleansing of the temple. This can be seen from the literary description below. A careful literary examination of this miracle story reveals the following. Mark records this story as a frame and this literary device is particular to Mark.[36]

A^1 Mark 11:12–14. Fig tree is cursed.

B Mark 11:15–19. Cleansing of the temple.

A^2 Mark 11:20–21. Fig tree is withered.

---

34. Fuller, *Interpreting the Miracles*, 38.
35. Meier places the death of Jesus on April 7, AD 30. Meier, *Marginal Jew*, 1:402.
36. See Borg and Crossan, *Last Week*, 32–34.

The cursing of the fig tree interprets the cleansing of the temple. A careful reading of Mark 11:12–14 indicates an impossible situation. No figs should have been expected to be found since it was not the season. Therefore, the pericope is best interpreted symbolically. As we shall see, the cleansing of the temple, while an historical prophetic act, must also be interpreted symbolically. It signifies the end of temple worship. The cursing of the fig tree is a story that symbolically reinforces this idea.

It should be noted that this particular literary structure is found in five other places in Mark.[37] It is known as *intercalation*. It is a device that Mark found useful in expressing a particular theological point. Given the information derived from the historical critical method and the literary examination, we should have no difficulty in recognizing this event for what it truly is: a theologoumenon.

Concerning the So-Called "Nature Miracle"

Fuller proposed that nature miracles are not a separate category for the New Testament writer. However, the disciples are the only ones who witnessed them. And they are not considered a feature of Jesus' public ministry.

Meier concludes that with the one exception, the feeding of the multitude, nature miracles simply do not pass the test of historicity. There is theological coloring in all of them. The nature miracles are rare, that is, they are less common than the others and they are not found in the earliest strata of the New Testament development. They are absent from Q. They are also absent in the sayings of Jesus. They are absent from Mark's summaries. And, as has already been mentioned, only the disciples witness them. Furthermore, they seem to have entered the tradition late, after the healings and exorcisms. This casts doubt on them as having occurred as written. There may be some historical basis for them because the tradition is not created out of whole cloth. Thus, they deserve to be referred to as so-called nature miracles because they are most likely literary creations.

---

37. Framing occurs six times in Mark. They can be found in Mark 3:20–35; 5:21–43; 6:7–30; 11:12–21; 14:1–11; and 14:53–72.

Non-Miracle

The temple tax (Matt 17:24–27) and miraculous catch of fish (Luke 5:1–11//John 21:1–14) are often listed in the miracle tradition; however, they actually do not possess the form of a miracle story. They are better left off the list of miracles entirely.

Miraculous Catch of Fish (Luke 5:1–11//John 21:1–14)

There are two pericopes which refer to a miraculous catch of fish, the one in John 21:1–14 and the other in Luke 5:1–11. Luke's version of this miraculous catch appears to be a postresurrection appearance which has been retrojected into the earthly life of Jesus as a call story. After the catch Peter and his companions immediately leave their nets and follow Jesus.

Fuller believes, and it seems Meier agrees, that the catch of fish in John 21:1–14 was originally a resurrection appearance.[38] It was recast in Luke. Its purpose was didactic, such that Jesus said, "Do not be afraid; from now on you will be catching men" (Luke 5:10). Mark and Matthew's parallel call stories ends with Jesus saying, "I (Jesus) will make you fishers of men" (Mark 1:17//Matt 4:19). Neither Mark nor Matthew joined this call story with any miraculous catch of fish. The disciples are simply "casting a net into the sea" (Mark 1:16//Matt 4:18). The Miraculous catch of fish is Luke's interpolation into a call story. It is not historical.

The Temple Tax (Matt 17:24–27)

This episode presents Jesus as sending Peter to catch a fish in whose mouth would be found a coin of sufficient value to pay the temple tax for both Jesus and Peter. This is not thought to be an actual miracle. It is a creation of Matthew.[39] Its purpose is *didactic*. The category is *sui generis*, of its own kind. It is possible that it is based on an early Christian dispute with the Jewish authorities.[40] This would not have gone back to the disputes of the historical Jesus with his adversaries. Interestingly enough, there is a fish, native to the Sea of Galilee, which is popularly known as Saint Peter's fish

---

38. Fuller, *Interpreting the Miracles*, 37. See Meier, *Marginal Jew*, 2:904.
39. Meier, *Marginal Jew*, 2:881.
40. Meier, *Marginal Jew*, 2:883.

(*Sarotherodon galilaeus*). It belongs to the genus *Tilapia*. The fish is known to pick up small stones or bottle caps in its mouth.

Peter's Mother-in-Law and Her Fever[41]

This pericope does not have the form of a miracle story. Though it is very concrete it is only three verses long. Even so, some exegetes treat it as a miracle. Kasper argues that the lack of tendentiousness is support for it as a miracle.[42] Fuller believes that this is a true reminiscence of Peter.[43] Meier argues that because it records considerable specificity (names of individuals, the place) it might be a genuine memory.[44] But it would seem that, if it is a miracle, it does not have the force of healing that other events do. Meier argues that the evidence does not permit identifying this narrative as a genuine miracle.[45] This would be the best solution given the rules of the historical-critical method.

Conclusion and Resume: Jesus' Self-Understanding and the Miracle Tradition in the Gospels

During the last several centuries there have been considerable challenges to the historicity of the miracle tradition as recorded in the New Testament. Contemporary experience, it is argued, differs considerably from the biblical description of the miraculous. We neither experience them nor do we expect them. The modern mind simply cannot accept them.[46]

In chapter 7 we turned our attention to the data as it is found in the Scriptures. The conviction expressed above is that the Scriptures (or any ancient document) must be read within its own context. A twenty-first century understanding cannot be imposed upon a text from an earlier age. The earlier document must be read within its own

---

41. Mark 1:29-31//Matt 8:14-15//Luke 4:38-41.
42. Kasper, *Jesus the Christ*, 91.
43. Fuller, *Interpreting the Miracles*, 49.
44. Meier, *Marginal Jew*, 2:707-8.

45. The argument is that there is only one source and therefore it is not clear (*non liquet*) that it is historical. Meier suggests that he could be persuaded of its historicity. See Meier, *Marginal Jew*, 2:707.

46. This is not the way many people understand it. Consider the many shrines such as Fatima, Lourdes, Medjugorje, and the shrine of our Lady of Guadalupe. The miraculous is not as absent from our culture as many would presume.

social and religious context, from its own world view. The data from the Scriptures was considered in this light. What was discovered was that the miracle tradition in general was widely accepted in the first century. This was true from gentile, Jewish, and Christian perspectives. This context did not share our scientific world view and this difference was accounted for. This is clear from an examination of the language in which miracles were expressed. It also became clear that New Testament witnesses rejected the notion that miracles were a disruption of the laws of nature. They were expressed as the power of God or as a sign from God. They were generally a call to faith. This is how the first disciples understood the miracle tradition.

Part of our examination focused on specific miracles. Meier's work was heavily depended on and served as a basis for this examination.[47] It is interesting to note that many of the conclusions of the skeptics are now actually accepted as accurate. What is not accepted is the a priori judgment that miracles simply cannot exist. Rejecting the historicity of the miracles because they were borrowed from gentile or Jewish sources or that they were creations of the primitive community are legitimate rules for the historical-critical method. The conclusion we reach is that a solid deposit of miracles can be traced back to the Jesus of history. This includes exorcisms, healings, and raisings from the dead. Our conclusion actually agrees with better supported conclusions of earlier theologians and biblical scholars. It does not establish what actually happened. It does establish that some of these miracles go back to a specific event in Jesus' activity. The nature of Jesus' miracles will be addressed in chapter 9. A considerable amount of time was spent on the so-called nature miracles and for good reasons. One of these miracle narratives, the multiplication of the loaves, was actually well established as being historical. The other so-called nature miracles were rejected as historical because they lacked multiple attestation, or they reflected a postresurrection Christology. They were literary creations of the postresurrection church. This does not diminish their importance but rather gives them a new distinction. They are expressions of the faith of the early church. They also express the Christian faith in general.

The examination above also gave us further important information. It established that a solid deposit of miracles goes back to the Jesus of history. They are all, for the most part, related to his preaching the kingdom

---

47. Other authors were consulted but volume 2, chapters 17–23 in Meier's *A Marginal Jew* proved to be the most extensive treatment.

of God and therefore reflect his authentic self-understanding. We can point to several miracles already established as historical to support this. In his exorcism of the man blind and mute Jesus responds to his detractors by saying, "But if it is by the finger of God that [I] drive out demons, then the kingdom of God has come upon you" (Luke 11:20; brackets in the original). Meier refers to this saying as the star witness that Jesus has declared the kingdom as present. In another authentic saying of Jesus, we hear him saying to his disciples, "But blessed are your eyes, because they see, and your ears, because they hear" (Matt 13:16//Luke 10:23). Jesus is referring to his mighty deeds. This is a clear indication of his self-understanding. Again, we discover in Jesus' response to the disciples of John the Baptist that he both affirmed that he has performed miracles and he gives us a rationale (Matt 11:4//Luke 7:22). The kingdom of God is a present reality. In all of these narratives Jesus understands himself as the one who is to usher in the kingdom.

Our examination of the miracle tradition has proven both interesting and profitable. It has firmly established that a large body of miracles can be traced back to the Jesus of history. We have learned something significant about Jesus' self-understanding. We have also learned how these miracles fit into Jesus' ministry, his preaching of the kingdom of God. It remains for us to examine them theologically to see if we cannot deepen our present understanding.

9

A Critical Appraisal of the Miracle Tradition

Introduction

THE DATA PERTAINING TO the miracle tradition has been examined at length. We saw that Jesus understood himself as a miracle worker, a healer, and an exorcist. It was also concluded that the miracle stories cannot be established as exact historical representations of Jesus' miracles. This is largely because of the transmission and editing of the stories. They are shaped by the evangelist's literary artistry and theological perspective. However, it was concluded that for many of the miracle stories in the Gospels some extraordinary event behind the story can be traced back to Jesus in his historical context. The historical-critical method made no claim for the exact nature of the events that occurred. It simply secured for us the conviction that many of the events expressed in the Scriptures were a historical part of Jesus' ministry. As secure as we might be in these conclusions, we are mindful that the affirmation "this event is a miracle" is a statement of faith and not of historical or exegetical proof. In other words, though we have established that an event (miracle) can be traced to Jesus' historical mission, it does not answer the question about its nature.

We now have a new task before us. We need to determine what kind of theological conclusions can be drawn from this investigation. An examination of the first-century context or environment in which these miraculous events occurred has already been done. We will now examine the linguistic context, the expressions the evangelists used to express the miraculous in an effort to discover how the miracle tradition was understood by the early church. This prevents us from imposing a twenty-first century impression upon the Gospel narratives. This will be followed by an attempt to articulate both their meaning and their purpose. Finally, we will then be in a position to determine more precisely the nature of Jesus' miracles, that is, to interpret for our contemporaries the significance of Jesus' exorcisms, his healings, and his raisings from the dead.

Biblical/Literary Expressions of the Miraculous

A clue as to the nature of the miraculous can be discovered by determining what the evangelists were attempting to express by the language they chose. We will examine the expressions which were used both in the Old and New Testament environments for an indication as to their intended meaning. This will be followed by a discussion of the context in which the miracle tradition occurred.

Extrabiblical Expressions for Miracle or the Miraculous

The common words used to express the miraculous in the ancient Greek world were *teras* and *thauma*. *Teras* is translated as sign, wonder, omen, or marvel; *thauma* is translated as wonder, portent, marvel, and miracle.[1] *Thauma* is the normal word for miracles in the ancient Greek-speaking world. The terms *thauma* and *teras* as used in the ancient Greek world signify acts discontinuous with nature. The notion of wonder-worker or magician was common during the first century.[2] It referred to someone who did spectacular events and the terms *teras* and *thauma* were used to describe their exploits. To consider Jesus a magician is a failure to understand his mission, as a reading of the New Testament accounts would verify.[3] Jesus was no wonder-worker and the language of the Gospels clearly

---

1. For a more developed understanding of these words check *A Greek-English Lexicon of the New Testament and Other Early Christian Literature*.

2. References to magicians are found in Acts 8:9–25 and 13:4–12.

3. In this regard see Smith, *Jesus the Magician*, and Horsley, *Jesus and Magic*. This present study does not accept the conclusions of either Smith or Horsley.

indicates this. As will be pointed out below, the Gospels never consider the miracles of Jesus as marvels or prodigious events.

Both of these Greek terms are used in the Septuagint, the Greek version of the Hebrew Old Testament. In the Greek New Testament, however, the word *thauma* is never used. *Teras* is frequently used in the Acts of the Apostles. It is also found in the Pauline Epistles and the Epistle to the Hebrews.[4] There was no hesitation in speaking of "signs and wonders" (Acts 4:30; 5:12) or "wonders and signs" (Acts 2:19; 2:43; 6:8) or "mighty deeds, wonders, and signs" (Acts 2:22).[5] However, all of these examples are postresurrection and used in a general sense. More to the point, *teras* is used only twice in the Gospels. It was used once in the Synoptic Gospels. "False messiahs and false prophets will arise, and they will perform signs [*semeia*] and wonders [*terata*] so great as to deceive, if that were possible, even the elect" (Matt 24:24//Mark 13:22). It is used once in the Gospel of John in a rather negative sense. "Unless you people see signs and wonders [*terata*], you will not believe" (John 4:48). It is never used to refer to Jesus' miracles. The absence or limited use of *thauma* and *teras* to describe Jesus' miracles is a very strong indication that the miracles of Jesus were understood quite differently from the extrabiblical understanding. It is of some interest to note that the Latin word that expresses miracle is *miraculum*. Surprisingly, this term is not found in the Latin Vulgate which was translated from the Hebrew and Greek Bibles.[6] More will be said about the vocabulary used in the Gospels to express the miraculous below.

Old Testament (Hebrew) Expressions for Miracle

The Hebrew expressions for miracle are *mopeth* and *oth*.[7] Both of these terms are the common way of expressing miracle in the Hebrew Bible.

---

4. A few examples of *teras* in Acts are 2:19; 2:43; 4:30; 5:12; and 6:8. There are others. In these examples there is a conjunction of *semeia kai teratas* (signs and wonders). Teras is also found in Rom 15:19; 2 Cor 12:12; 2 Thess 2:9; and Heb 2:4.

5. There are many other similar references.

6. In AD 382 Pope Damasus I commissioned Jerome (AD 340–420) to translate and correct the Old Latin (*Vetus Latina*) Gospels. He extended his translating to include most of the books of the Greek and Hebrew Scriptures. He completed his work in AD 405. This translation, known as the Vulgate version of the Bible (*Biblia Sacra Vulgata*), became the official version of the Bible for the Roman Catholic Church at the Council of Trent, AD 1546.

7. For a brief explanation of the terms used in both the Old and the New Testament,

They are often used together as synonyms.[8] *Mopeth* signifies the notion of a symbolic act. This is the Old Testament (Hebrew) expression for wonder (miracle).[9] It is translated as *teras* in the Septuagint.[10] The Hebrew word *oth* signifies sign.[11] It is used to refer to the plagues associated with the exodus. In the Septuagint it is translated as *thauma* (miracle). The conclusion drawn from this linguistic use is that the original expression found in the Hebrew Bible (Hebrew Old Testament) signifies something quite different from the Greek expressions used to translate them in the Septuagint. *Thauma* and *teras* are closer to the common usage referring to miracles as marvels, wonders, or something outstanding or prodigious. The Hebrew Scriptures understand miracles as signs or symbolic acts. This is much closer to the expressions in the New Testament Gospels that refer to miracles.

New Testament Expression for Miracle

The New Testament Gospels use three Greek terms to express miracle: *dunamis, semeion, and ergon. Dunamis* generally expresses the idea of mighty act or act of power. *Semeion* indicates a sign. *Ergon* expresses the idea of a work. These terms are found in the following usages.

In the Synoptic Gospels *dunamis* is the common, normal word used to refer to Jesus' miracles. It expresses something close to the idea of mighty acts, acts of power. It suggests an act of God.[12] *Semeion* indicates a sign. This is never used in the Synoptic Gospels to refer to Jesus' miracles. It is used once in a negative sense. The Pharisees asked for a sign (*semeion*) from heaven. Jesus would not give a sign to legitimate his ministry (Mark 8:11–13). *Ergon*, which signifies work, appears only once

---

see "Miracles, Signs, Wonders" in Butler, *Holman Bible Dictionary*.

8. *The Holman Bible Dictionary* lists Exod 7:3; 7:9; Deut 4:34; 6:22; Ps 105:27; Isa 8:18; and many other references using these words. See "Miracles, Signs, Wonders" in Butler, *Holman Bible Dictionary*.

9. See Exod 11:10.

10. The necessary change to Greek vocabulary does not do justice to the Hebrew signification. This is always a danger in any translation but more so here.

11. See Exod 3:12; 4:8; 4:9; 7:3; 8:19; and 10:1. This later reference is very illuminating. "Then the LORD said to Moses, 'Go to Pharaoh, for I have made him and his servants obstinate in order that I may perform these signs of mine among them'" (Exod 10:1). This is an excellent example of the Old Testament understanding of miracle.

12. This term is also used by Paul in his Epistles. This use predates the Synoptic Gospels by a decade. See 1 Cor 12:10; 2 Cor 12:12; and Gal 3:5.

in the Synoptic Gospels. It is found in Matt 11:2. In this verse, John the Baptist had heard of Jesus' works (*erga*). This same episode found in Luke makes no mention of John hearing of Jesus' works.

In the Gospel of John, the word *semeion* signifies sign (significant deeds). The word is very Johannine. The first part of John's Gospel is referred to as the Book of Signs. The acts of Jesus in the Gospel of John are expressed as *semeia* or signs. John uses the expression in the Old Testament sense as pointing to God.[13] There is a shift from the messianic identity of Jesus as expressed in the Synoptics to a higher Christology in John. *Sign* points out the christological significance of Jesus' deeds. John also speaks of *ta erga tou Christou*, that is, the works of Christ. He uses the expression often.[14]

Thus, we observe that the New Testament expressions *semeion*, *dynamis*, and *ergon* are frequently used to express the miracle tradition. The use of other words is rare. Those words that indicate wonderworker, and that are used often by pagan authors, are not often found. *Teras* is never used in the Synoptic Gospels. *Thauma* is never used in the New Testament.

We have spent considerable time and effort exploring the Greek and Hebrew linguistic expressions that describe the miraculous in the ancient Greek world and the Old and the New Testaments. Our rationale was to determine as closely as possible the understanding of the evangelists in reporting Jesus' miracles. The language of the New Testament indicates or intends to tell us that the miracles of Jesus are signs or works and power of God. The expressions are conceptually identical (similar) to the linguistic usage in the Hebrew Old Testament. The New Testament Gospel expressions are quite different from the ancient Greek world. This is an important distinction in properly understanding the miracle tradition.

The Meaning or Significance of the Miracle Tradition

We are now in a better position to understand the miracle tradition of Jesus. We have already established that Jesus was a miracle worker and that there were both general and specific memories of his *mighty*

---

13. The term is not used like this in the Synoptic Gospels.
14. The term can be found in John 5:20; 5:36; 7:3; 10:36; 14:11–12; and 15:24.

deeds.[15] We know that they were not understood as ruptures of nature. The first-century Israelites did not sharply distinguish acts of nature and acts of God. We are now in a position to articulate the significance of the miracles. What meaning did Jesus give them and how did his disciples understand them? There are three points worth noting.

Miracles: Jesus is the Eschatological Prophet[16]

The miracles of the New Testament are often understood as a fulfillment of the Old Testament. This is especially clear in Matthew's Gospel. One very important example occurs when the disciples of John the Baptist are sent as emissaries to Jesus to learn his identity (Matt 11:5–6//Luke 7:22–23).[17] They ask Jesus, "Are you the one who is to come?"[18] John and his emissaries anticipated a prophet who would usher in the kingdom. In chapter 3, we referred to John as a forerunner of what we have identified as the eschatological prophet. Jesus responds to the question, "Go and tell John what you hear and see: the blind regain their sight, the lame walk, lepers are cleansed, the deaf hear, the dead are raised, and the poor have the good news proclaimed to them. And blessed is the one who takes no offense at me" (Matt 11:4–6).[19]

This response, an authentic saying of the historical Jesus, is an allusion to the oracles of Isaiah.[20] Jesus uses these oracles drawn from

15. In his magisterial work *Jesus: An Experiment in Christology*, 79, Schillebeeckx writes that, "the primary question [about miracle-stories] should not be: Did Jesus actually perform miracles? but: What is it they signify?" Fuller says much the same thing. See *Interpreting the Miracles*, 112. They propose that the search for the historical follows the search for the significance. It is clear that we did not follow this order. The early disciples experienced Jesus before they believed in him; before they understood his significance. Our conviction is that the historical-critical method has provided us with the tools to discover what is foundational for Jesus' significance, for faith in him.

16. This was developed earlier. Because of the importance of this Q source (Matt 11:5–6//Luke 7:22–23) it will be examined again for further clarity.

17. This pericope is from the Q source. It has been dealt with extensively in chapter 5. While in prison, John had heard of the works (*erga*) of Jesus (Matt 11:2).

18. For a brilliant history of this concept see Fitzmyer, *One Who Is to Come*. While the Gospels refer to Jesus as the Christ, the title was not used during his public life. See Fitzmyer's comments in *One Who is to Come*, 139. Fuller speaks of the identity of Jesus as Messiah as coming from the early church. It is how they recognized him.

19. Luke has reshaped this saying and placed it at the beginning of Jesus' ministry in Capernaum. The saying in Luke 4:18 is a very close replication of Isa 61:1–2.

20. This reading of Matthew is identical to Luke's version. The note in the NABRE for Matthew's passage lists the references to Isaiah. They can all be verified by the use

Isaiah to refer to his mission. The time of salvation, the end-time reign of God, is manifest by deeds (miracles) like these which are now being done by Jesus. Jesus' response to the emissaries clearly implies that he is the eschatological prophet.

The Q passage (Matt 11:5–6//Luke 7:22–23) identifies Jesus as the eschatological prophet and this identification is pre-Easter. Therefore, this is neither a retrojection or an invention of the early church.[21] During his lifetime, Jesus understood himself as the eschatological prophet and his works/deeds identify him as such. This is Jesus' self-identification which is associated with his miracles.

Miracles are Kerygmatic in Nature

Jesus proclaimed the kingdom of God by his words. Analogously he also proclaimed it by his deeds. The miracles are kerygmatic of their very nature; they are a proclamation. As kerygmatic, they point to several significant realities.

The first of these is that the miracles announce the arrival of the kingdom of God. In the oft quoted Q source (Luke 11:14–20//Matt 12:22–28) Jesus interprets his miracle, a pericope we have already discovered to be an authentic teaching of the Jesus of history. Luke describes Jesus as saying, "But if it is by the finger of God that [I] drive out demons, then the kingdom of God has come upon you" (Luke 11:20; brackets in the original).[22] Matthew replaces the expression "finger of God" with "Spirit of God" in his recounting this miracle narrative, but the meaning is identical to Luke's (Matt 12:28). Jesus' miracles are a declaration that the kingdom of God is present.

There is a second significance to Jesus' miracles which is related conceptually to the first. Jesus' miracles express the conflict between God and Beelzebul (Satan or the evil one).[23] The references in the Synoptic

---

of a concordance.

21. Consider the theory that Jesus' raising the three persons from the dead was a creation of the church because this was its affirmation that he was the Eschatological Prophet. But this is impossible because Jesus' miracles indicated that he was the Eschatological Prophet in his earthly life, and not as a postresurrection title.

22. It has been pointed out numerous times above that this is an authentic statement of Jesus. He understands the relation between miracle and message.

23. This conflict was first expressed in Jesus' temptations, at the very beginning of his ministry. It was a choice on how he was to conduct his mission.

Gospels to Jesus' conflict with demons or unclean (evil) spirts are numerous.[24] It is recorded in Mark's Gospel as Jesus' first miracle (Mark 1:21–27). The demonic (unclean spirit) cried out, "What have you to do with us, Jesus of Nazareth? Have you come to destroy us? I know who you are—the Holy One of God!" (Mark 1:24). This set the stage for the conflict that follows. Jesus is accused of being possessed himself and casting out demons by Beelzebul, the prince of demons (Mark 3:22; Matt 9:32–34; Luke 11:14–15//Matt 12:21).[25] This clearly describes the conflict between God and whatever opposes his kingdom.

The acts of power, these signs, came either from God or from Beelzebul (the evil one). Jesus' activity was open to a dual interpretation as the Gospel indicates. This is rooted in history. Schillebeeckx calls this an important datum in the miracle tradition.[26] Jesus' contemporaries, those who believed in him, would have seen this as Jesus acting with the power of God. The miracles do something that words alone could not do. There is a necessary connection between event and kerygma. The miracles are meaningless unless they point to a message. They make possible the recognition that Jesus initiates the kingdom of God and opposes the evil that is against it.

Jesus' defeat of evil must be seen in a context larger than in isolated exorcisms or healings. They are works of salvation. Mark hints at this after Jesus has healed a deaf man. Those who witnessed the event declare that "He has done all things well. He makes the deaf hear and [the] mute speak" (Mark 7:37b; brackets in the original). Doing all things well seems to imply more than the specific miracles. In the Acts of the Apostles, Peter declares in his speech that "he [Jesus] went about doing good and healing all those oppressed by the devil, for God was with him" (Acts 10:38). I am inclined to understand the expression "doing good" associated with the miracle tradition as referring to the liberation from all of those things in life that inflict pain, suffering or alienation. This is the result of the kingdom in our midst.

---

24. *Demon* or *demons* is used over forty times. *Evil* or *unclean spirit* is used over twelve times. They are used synonymously.

25. The name Beelzebul is used in five places in the Synoptics. He is referred to as the prince of demons.

26. Schillebeeckx, *Jesus*, 183.

The Purpose of Miracles

Jesus' miracles have two purposes: they announce the presence of the kingdom of God; and they make faith and discipleship possible.

Principal Purpose: Miracles Usher in the Kingdom of God

We have already shown that Jesus' deeds, his festive meals, and miracles, were a proleptic view of the kingdom of God. While Jesus' festive meals symbolized God's kingdom, Jesus' miracles went further. They were symbolic of faith, but they manifested the reality of the conflict with the evil one. They also indicated God's presence, hence his reign. The kingdom is indicative of the presence of God in the lives of men and women here and now. It is expressive of his goodness and the defeat of evil of whatever sort. Jesus' miracles accomplished this.

Jesus is recognized as the agent of salvation for God. "What Jesus' miracles are ultimately saying is that in Jesus God was carrying out his plan, and that God acted through him for the salvation of mankind and the world."[27] Miracles are not merely symbolic, as Rudolph Bultmann has suggested. It seems clear that this is not the case if the miracles have a historical grounding. Jesus' own understanding was that the miracles announced the presence of God in a special and unique way. Hence, we read of Jesus' personal understanding of his miracles. "But if it is by the finger of God that [I] drive out demons, then the kingdom of God has come upon you" (Luke 11:20; brackets in the original).[28]

A Second Purpose: Faith

Jesus miracles are not proofs either for his person or his mission. They are signs of a divine reality. Jesus refused to legitimize either his vocation or his message by signs. This is abundantly clear in the temptations in the desert (Matt 4:1–11//Luke 4:1–13). Later in his ministry, when the Pharisees ask for a sign, Jesus refused to work one (Mark 8:11–12// Matt 12:38–42//Luke 11:29–32). Jesus was not a wonder-worker nor

---

27. Kasper, *Jesus the Christ*, 98.

28. It was mentioned above that Meier refers to this miracle as the "star witness" to the presence of the kingdom of God.

A CRITICAL APPRAISAL OF THE MIRACLE TRADITION

were his miracles demonstrations of his divine sonship. Rather, they are a clear sign of the presence or power of God.

Faith is necessary to affirm that miracles are from God.[29] Their purpose is to elicit faith but not to demand or compel it. If there is no faith, then there is no miracle. We need only examine the pericopes that refer to Jesus' visit to Nazareth, his home. He could do no miracle there because of their lack of faith (Mark 6:5–6; Matt 13:58). Jesus failed to impress his relatives at Nazareth.

Miracles are often a preamble to faith. They lead to faith and discipleship. Their purpose is to awaken a human attitude of wonder. Jesus announced to the woman with a hemorrhage whom he had cured, "Your faith has saved you" (Mark 5:34//Matt 9:22//Luke 8:42). Jesus said much the same thing in the cure of Blind Bartimaeus (Mark: 10:52) and to a leper whom he had healed (Luke 17:19).[30] It is not a passive act on the part of the one who was the beneficiary of Jesus' miracle, but it occurred to someone actively seeking God's help.

Miracles are signs of faith already possessed. Even the Pharisees and others witnessed the miracles. The event was observable by all. But not all expressed faith in them and in Jesus. Fuller sums up the matter in this way: "To sum up, we may say that for Jesus his exorcism and healings, while not unique in themselves, are unique in their relation to his message of the dawning Reign of God. They constitute a challenge to faith—faith in the redemptive action of God that is breaking through in his person, his words and deeds. But they are not proofs. They summon men to a decision. Those who witness Jesus' exorcisms and healings are perfectly free to decide negatively, to decide that they are done by Beelzebul, the prince of the devils. But they may also decide that they are miracles, wrought by the spirit and finger of God."[31]

---

29. Numerous miracles indicate a faith component. Examples for this are the lowering of the paralytic through the roof (Mark 2:1–12); Jairus's daughter (Mark 5:21–24, 35–43); women with hemorrhages (Mark 5:25–35); Syrophoenician women (Mark 7:24–30); boy possessed (Mark 9:14–29); and the healing of Bartimaeus (Mark 10:40–52).

30. This is a cure of a non-Jew, a Samaritan. It is found only in L.

31. Fuller, *Interpreting the Miracles*, 44–45.

The Nature of Miracles: Several Theological Opinions

We have examined the data regarding the miracle tradition of Jesus at some length. We have concluded that Jesus self-identified as a miracle worker, an exorcist, and a healer. Many of his contemporaries also understood him as such. We discovered that many of the miracle narratives were not inventions of the early church but belonged to Jesus' ministry. We concluded that behind many of the miracle narratives stood a historical event which was recognized by Jesus' disciples as coming from the hand of God. We concluded that the miracles were not to prove Jesus' divinity or the origin of his ministry, but rather to identify him as the eschatological prophet and that they ushered in the kingdom of God.

The remaining question is: What was the nature of these miracles? Were exorcisms in fact the expulsion of demons? Did Jesus actually heal? Did he raise people from the dead? The results of the historical-critical method now demand a theological investigation.[32]

There is a Core of Miracles Which are Historical

There is a growing consensus among theologians and biblical scholars that there is a core of miracles attributed to Jesus that must be accepted as historical. We will examine the conclusions of several.

Fuller wrote his work *Interpreting the Miracles* in 1963 at the beginning of the present phase of the historical-critical method. He concluded that Jesus performed miracles and based his conclusion on the authentic words of Jesus. He appealed to two Q pericopes, the one in which Jesus claims to cast out demons by the finger of God (Matt 12:27//Luke 11:19) and another in which Jesus responds to the emissaries from John (Matt 11:4–6//Luke 7:22).[33] He admitted that Jesus truly performed exorcisms, healed and raised people from the dead, but was hesitant in admitting that any of the miracle narratives contained a specific memory of a cure. He was willing to admit that the narrative of the feeding of the multitude was based on a specific memory as well as

---

32. Meier is the basis for our establishment of the miracle tradition. He does not offer an interpretation of these miracles. His method is to show that a sizeable number of the reported miracles do go back to Jesus, and these must be seen in terms of one's faith. As a biblical scholar, he would leave the theological explanation to others. That is what we will take up now.

33. If you have read this far you will recognize how often we appealed to these two authentic teachings of Jesus.

the narrative of the healing of Peter's mother-in-law and the curing of Bartimaeus, but this is the extent of his list. He says that "we can never be certain of the authenticity of any actual story in the Gospels. While a few of them may rest upon a specific memory, most of them have probably been shaped out of generalized memories."[34]

Hans Küng, a systematic theologian, wrote ten years after Fuller. He describes his own methodology as a literary-historical analysis. From his analysis Küng concluded that there is no need to accept all miracle stories as historical, certainly not those that are legendary.[35] He suggests that the Gerasene (Gadarene) demoniac (Matt 8:28–34//Mark 5:1–20//Luke 8:26–39) might actually be a folk tale.[36] But he concludes that there is a core of miracles that are defensible as historical. "There must have been *cures of varied types of sickness* which were amazing at least to people of that time."[37] He understood that cures of the possessed were people who experienced mental or psychosomatic illness or who were epileptic.[38] He is skeptical, however, that we can reach the real event underlying these cures.[39] Although Küng must be complimented on his effort, he lacked the benefit of the historical-critical method.

Walter Kasper, a contemporary of Küng, also focused on the historical quest for Jesus Christ.[40] His study of the miracle tradition is necessarily a part of this search. In his book *Jesus the Christ*, Kasper articulates his opinion about the miracle tradition.[41] "There can scarcely be a single serious exegete who does not believe in a basic stock of historically certain miracles of Jesus."[42] He continues, "Even a critical historical consideration of the gospel miracle tradition leads to the conclusion that a historical core of the miracle tradition cannot be disputed."[43] His methodology can be summarized very briefly. First, if there is not a core of historically

---

34. Fuller, *Interpreting the Miracles*, 39.
35. See Küng, *On Being a Christian*, 229.
36. Küng, *On Being a Christian*, 233.
37. Küng, *On Being a Christian*, 229.
38. Küng, *On Being a Christian*, 230.
39. Küng, *On Being a Christian*, 229.
40. Kasper's use of literary criticism is much like Küng's.
41. Kasper, *Jesus the Christ*. Kasper formerly taught in the Catholic faculty at the University of Tübingen and is now a cardinal. This would lend some authority to his orthodoxy.
42. Kasper, *Jesus the Christ*, 90.
43. Kasper, *Jesus the Christ*, 91.

certain miracles, the miracle tradition would be inexplicable. Second, we should accept as historical whatever is in the tradition that cannot be explained as borrowed from Jewish or Hellenistic literature.[44] He enumerates the Sabbath healings as discontinuous with Judaism therefore they are more than likely historical. Kasper concludes that the Capernaum demoniac (Mark 1:23–28) and the crippled woman (Luke 13:10–17) are historical miracles. He also accepts the Q saying (Luke 11:20//Matt 12:28) in which Jesus drives out demons by the finger of God as authentic.[45] Third, those miracles that lack tendentiousness must be original. Among this he numbers the cure of Simon's mother-in-law (Mark 1:29–31) and the reproaches to unrepentant towns (Matt 11:20–22).[46] He rejected what he calls the so-called nature miracles. His further effort is devoted to an explanation of the miracles theologically.

In his excellent work entitled *Jesus: An Experiment in Christology*, Edward Schillebeeckx laid out his methodology for discovering the Jesus of history in great detail.[47] This work was originally published in 1974, the same year that Küng and Kasper published theirs. He is an extremely important authority for our investigation since he was the first Catholic systematic theologian who understood the need to be grounded in the contemporary biblical exegetical method. Before he began his study of Christology, he immersed himself for several years in the formal study of the Scriptures.[48] He spent considerable time and effort in articulating his criteria.[49] He believed that historical criticism "is essential for the access of faith to the authentic gospel."[50]

Schillebeeckx' approach seems to be more profound than many of his contemporaries. He begins by determining the meaning of the miraculous found in the Scriptures. What, he asks, were the evangelists getting at with the miracle tradition? Only then can the miracles be

---

44. Kasper accepts the criteria that are used to establish the historical Jesus. He only enumerates the criterion of discontinuity (borrowing from Hellenistic or Jewish sources).

45. It should be noted that the exorcism in this pericope is simply an introduction to the narrative. The narrative, however, is historically authentic and extremely important to our discussion.

46. Kasper, *Jesus the Christ*, 90–91.

47. See "Part One: Questions of Method, Hermeneutics and Criteria" in Schillebeeckx, *Jesus*, 43–104.

48. See Schillebeeckx, *Jesus*, 36–37.

49. See Schillebeeckx, *Jesus*, 43–104.

50. See Schillebeeckx, *Jesus*, 75. He fully articulates his criteria on pages 92–100.

A CRITICAL APPRAISAL OF THE MIRACLE TRADITION

addressed in their own context.[51] He then searches for the historical—the theologian at work. He concludes, however, that the miracle tradition is meaningless unless there was a basis in fact for it. This agrees with the other theologians mentioned above. Schillebeeckx pointed out that Jesus' miracles engendered two differing interpretations for the same event. They were either from God or they were from the devil. Schillebeeckx proposes that this is the chief datum in the miracle question, and it provides the point-of-departure. He discovers the meaning in two Q miracles, Jesus and Beelzebul (Luke 11:14–23//Matt 12:22–30) and the healing of the centurion's servant (Luke 7:1–10//Matt 8:5–13). Schillebeeckx accepts both miracle narratives as historical. He understands their meaning as God's reign is present and Jesus is the eschatological prophet who initiates it. He proposes another Q source, the emissaries from John the Baptist (Matt 11:2–5//Luke 7:18–23). Schillebeeckx does not accept this narrative as historically authentic, but he accepts its message as explaining the community understanding: Jesus is the eschatological prophet. Jesus' mighty acts have kerygmatic implications. There must be an underlying event of which there was reminiscence, otherwise, it is meaningless. He affirms a growing conviction among scholars that Jesus conducted historical cures and exorcisms.[52] Although his major interest is in giving a theological understanding to the miracle tradition in general, he does give his judgment on several particular narratives. The story of the temple tax (Matt 17:24–27) is a parable based on fable. The cure of Peter's mother-in-law (Mark 1:29–31 parr.) is based upon an historical reminiscence. The cursing of the fig tree (Mark 11:12–14, 20–21//Matt 21:18–20) is rejected as historical. It is a prophecy in action. Jesus' stilling the storm (Mark 4:35–41//Matt 8:23–27//Luke 8:22–25) is a post-Easter story and therefore not historically authentic. Besides this historical search, Schillebeeckx spends a good deal of time concerned with miracles as both requiring faith and calling for faith.

The time spent on these four individuals provides us with a picture different from what we have concluded so far. Fuller wrote during the early part of last phase of the development of the historical-critical method. He established that several the miracles of Jesus were historical. The other three theologians wrote their works shortly after Fuller.

---

51. We actually reversed his order. The search for the historical preceded the meaning. The justification for this is that the present search for the historical is better established than it was during Schillebeeckx' research.

52. Schillebeeckx, *Jesus*, 189.

They were primarily interested in establishing the historical Jesus, but the miracle tradition was part of this search. It should be clear that the material we have examined thus far would have served all three of our theologians well. It justifies our reliance so heavily upon Meier. While he may not be the last word, Meier is an excellent point-of-departure for the beginner. It is unfortunate that the scholars referred to above did not have *A Marginal Jew* in front of them when they reflected upon Jesus in general and the miracle tradition in particular. They anticipated Meier in his program of discovering "what, within the Gospels and other sources available, really goes back to the historical Jesus."[53]

Meier wrote more recently than the theologians mentioned above. He began publishing his monumental five volume work *A Marginal Jew: Rethinking the Historical Jesus* in 1991, seventeen years after the other theologians mentioned above.[54] Meier, a biblical exegete and not a systematic theologian, has become the classic study for research on the Jesus of history. Meier has been much more successful, on historical-critical grounds, in establishing the basis for the miracle tradition than those excellent theologians mentioned above.

Meier is the basis for our establishment of the miracle tradition. He does not offer an interpretation of these miracles. His method is to show that a sizeable number of the reported scriptural miracles do go back to Jesus, and these must be seen in terms of one's faith. As a biblical scholar, he would leave the theological explanation to others. That is what we will examine now.[55]

The Theological Conclusion Regarding the Miracles

We have arrived at the most important part of our study. Having determined that there is a significant core of Jesus' miracles that are historically authentic we need to ask the next question: What is the nature of these miracles? What actually happened? Faith is required for us to accept that these events, identified as miracles, are the result of an act of God. A true miracle requires faith that God has directly acted to heal a particular

---

53. Meier, *Marginal Jew*, 1:10.

54. The other four volumes were published successively in 1994, 2001, 2009, and 2016.

55. At the beginning of his magnum opus, Meier tells us he "would be delighted if systematic theologians would pick up where this book leaves off and pursue the line of thought further." Meier, *Marginal Jew*, 1:6.

individual.⁵⁶ It also requires theological reflection to develop an understanding as to what the nature of the miracles might be.

There is considerable agreement concerning Jesus' healings among theologians in general and among those we have relied upon for our examination. Walter Kasper proposed that the curing of diseases is miraculous. Hans Küng concludes likewise. There must have been cures of various illnesses. Schillebeeckx' conclusion is close to both Kasper and Küng. Fuller believes that many of the miracles reported as healings were actually exorcisms, but it is not clear why he thinks this. Nor have I discovered what he believes the true nature of the exorcism is.⁵⁷ Thus, a common opinion is that Jesus did indeed cure. He was a healer in the literal sense. This agrees with his self-understanding. But as we discovered, the actual historical event that prompted the narrative is difficult to determine. Were the lepers cured of their skin disease? Did the blind receive actual, physical sight? Any attempt to answer such questions can only lead us into speculation. However, something happened which was recognized by many observers as some good coming from the hand of God.

Concerning the exorcisms of Jesus there is also widespread agreement, although each theologian has his own perspective. Kasper concludes that the cures of those possessed are miraculous, but he understands these as more properly symptoms of diseases which were understood as signs of possession during Jesus' time. Küng's position is similar to Kasper's. Cures of the possessed must have occurred; however, these are actually healings of the mentally ill or those who were epileptics. Schillebeeckx' position needs to be examined since it is not clear whether he has proposed a definite interpretation on this point. But he believed that the conflict over the exorcisms is a primary datum. It is recognized as either the hand of God or the work of the devil. Fuller is a strong believer that Jesus was an exorcist. What this means in any concrete sense we have yet to discover. Meier has joined his judgment with this group of theologians. In describing the miracle of the possessed boy (Mark 9:14–29//) he says that "the boy seems to have suffered from some form of epilepsy."⁵⁸ He continued by pointing out that instances of possession might not only be cases of epilepsy but might also be understood as "various types of

---

56. Meier, *Marginal Jew*, 2:647.

57. Fuller, an Anglican biblical scholar, holds a more conservative view than these Catholic scholars.

58. Meier, *Marginal Jew*, 2:655. See the discussion on page 647.

mental or psychosomatic mental illness."⁵⁹ He has made this judgment earlier in his work: "Jesus no doubt saw them [exorcisms] as part of his overall ministry of healing and liberating the people of Israel from the illnesses and other physical and spiritual evils that beset them. Granted the primitive state of medical knowledge in the 1st-century Mediterranean world, mental illness, psychosomatic diseases and such afflictions as epilepsy were often attributed to demonic possess."⁶⁰

Thus, there seems to be a number of theologians who would explain exorcisms in terms of actual physical or mental illnesses. The general idea is that, during the time of Jesus, the epileptic or the one who was mentally ill could be understood as possessed. Thus, exorcisms during Jesus' time are factual but in a modern sense they are healings. The people of the first century identified diseases such as epilepsy and mental illness as possessions.⁶¹ It is interesting that Walter Kasper, now a cardinal, received approbation for his work in which he put forward this particular understanding of exorcisms from Cardinal Karol Wojtyla.⁶² This leads us to believe that it is an acceptable interpretation of exorcisms in the Catholic Church.

There is another modern way of considering the psychological and sociological context of first-century Palestinians. What are the dimensions of psychological and social illness?⁶³ These are important considerations. They treat the impact of oppression on people in terms of mental health but see it expressed in terms of demonic possession. It has been documented that oppressive social and political situations can cause mental illness. Several scholars have concluded that the oppression of the Roman occupation of Israel caused these kinds of mental conditions in some of the inhabitants and these were perceived as possessions

---

59. Meier, *Marginal Jew*, 2:661.

60. Meier, *Marginal Jew*, 2:407. Fuller seems to agree with this assessment.

61. This is what is called protological thinking.

62. Cardinal Kasper republished *Jesus the Christ* unchanged from the original in 2018 as volume 3 in the Collected Works of Walter Kasper. In the notes to the introduction to the new edition, Kasper writes that "I was particularly pleased that Cardinal Karol Wojtyla (later John Paul II) used *Jesus the Christ* in his spiritual exercise lectures to the Roman Curia in Lent 1976" (xxiii). This approbation of Cardinal Wojtyla (John Paul II) surely should serve as an *imprimatur* or a *nihil obstat* on Kasper's Christology.

63. See Brown et al., "Aspects of New Testament Thought," in *NJBC*, 81:110. This is a very important and informative section. It suggests that "phenomenon such as demon possession and exorcism can have social and political meaning as well as an explicitly religious one." It references the Gerasene demoniac (Mark 5:1–10). This entire subject calls for further study. See Hollenback, "Jesus, Demoniacs, and Public Authorities."

by demons.[64] It is of no little interest that Jesus' healing of the Gerasene demoniac supports this. Jesus asked the unclean spirit for his name, and he replied, "Legion is my name. There are many of us" (Mark 5:9).[65] It is easy to identify this Legion with the Roman legions who were extremely oppressive. One can easily see how the Gerasene demoniac could have been suffering mental illness brought about by the Roman occupation. There is modern evidence to support this hypothesis.

There is no clear position concerning Jesus' raising people from the dead. None of our chosen theologians, Kasper, Küng, Schillebeeckx, or Fuller, addressed these events directly. The fact that they do not discuss this leaves us with a puzzle. The historical-critical method has convinced us that these events, the raising from the dead, actually go back to Jesus' historical ministry and activity. They are not a symbolic expression of an eschatological idea. Nor are they drawn from a general memory. Thus, the question would be this: Were these individuals actually dead? Or were they in a physical state such as a coma that led people to think that they were dead? The one thing that we can say for certain is that Jesus seems to have understood himself as having raised the dead to life. Faith alone can settle this issue for us.

Concerning the so-called nature miracles, we have offered a better solution to their existence or nonexistence than those who rejected them from an a priori position. We have already examined the nature miracles from the perspective of Meier. Kasper rejects nature miracles as historical. For example, the calming of the storm and the curing of the man with a withered arm are rejected by him as miraculous, but his explanation is deficient as to why this is so. This seems to be an a priori determination. Küng claims that nature miracles must have been occasioned by some event, even if not actually miraculous. He believes that the calming of the storm, a nature miracle, was not historical but was based upon an event in the life of Jesus. Schillebeeckx has no opinion recorded that I have found. Fuller accepts nature miracles as real but observes that no distinction was made between nature and ordinary life during the time of Jesus. This position seems to be a minority opinion. He is at odds with the other theologians quoted here. He is certainly at odds with the opinion

---

64. This is a very worthwhile direction for investigation. At the present time, it awaits further research.

65. Luke 8:26-33 differs only in a few details but is substantially in agreement with Mark 5:1-20. Matt 8:28-34 shortens this pericope and changes the place where this encounter takes place to Gadara. In this version Jesus does not ask the demon's name.

of Meier. Meier gives us a better solution regarding the historicity of the so-called nature miracles. His position is arrived at by a rigorous application of the historical-critical method. For the most part, so-called nature miracles fail the historical-critical test. Most appear to be postresurrection narratives retrojected back into the life of Jesus.

Conclusion and Resume

The miracle tradition is one of the most interesting and fruitful areas of theological and biblical investigation in recent years. The historical-critical method has provided us with results that may at first seem surprising. It concludes that there is a significant body of miracles that in fact can be traced to the historical Jesus. This is a wonderful, academic counter to those who are skeptical of the tradition.

Secondly, we have a rational understanding of the so-called nature miracles attributed to Jesus' ministry. In general, they are not historical, with one exception, but they are important from a theological perspective. They are ecclesial expressions of the faith of the primitive community and still accepted by the faithful today.

Third, there is considerable room for speculation as to the nature of the miracles performed by Jesus. Exorcisms are generally interpreted as healings of diseases or mental illness which were understood in Jesus' time as possessions. This is a sensible reading of the miracle tradition in its own context.

Finally, Jesus self-understood his miracles as ushering in the kingdom of God. He was not a wonder-worker, that is, his miracles were not demonstrations of power. Nor were they proofs of his divinity. They were instrumental in leading the disciples to profess in faith that he was indeed the eschatological prophet ushering in the kingdom of God. This gives us a better understanding of how the miracle tradition ought to be understood.

10

The Parables: Preliminary Considerations

Introduction: The Parables[1]

To this point in our study, we have explored Jesus' proclamation of the kingdom of God which was central to his mission and message. We discovered that his miracles were events pointing to the reality of the kingdom. The preaching of the kingdom as well as the miracle tradition that supported it are authentic to the Jesus of history, that is, they can be traced back to him during his mission.[2] Furthermore, we saw that Jesus understood himself as having a special role in ushering in the kingdom. We are now in a position to examine Jesus' parables, which were a significant part of his teaching.[3] Jesus' preaching of the kingdom and his miracles will provide a framework for us to better understand the meaning of his parables. This chapter will examine Jesus' parables both as to their content as well as to their method. This will be followed

---

1. There has been considerable research done on the parables. My earlier research on the parables has been greatly enhanced by Meier, *Marginal Jew*, vol. 5.

2. Jesus' preaching of the kingdom and his deeds (miracles) more than adequately satisfied the historical-critical criteria. The same criteria will be employed to the parables in an attempt to determine their authenticity. We will also pay attention to literary considerations.

3. The discussion of parables was postponed until the kingdom was discussed because knowledge of the kingdom would help us understand the parables better.

by an exploration of the biblical evidence both theologically and historically in chapter 11.

The Significance and Importance of the Parables.

Jesus employed numerous literary devices in his teaching. The parables, however, hold a singular place in his ministry. They are a special mode of expression popular among both preachers and Christians alike. Almost everyone can quote one or more of Jesus' parables. John Dominic Crossan has described the importance of the parables as follows. "There is, of course, more to Jesus' life than the parables which express its ontological ground. He was not crucified for parables but for ways of acting which resulted from the experience of God presented in parables."[4]

Meier argued that Jesus told parables within the prophetic tradition of Israel.[5] These parables foreshadowed the coming of the kingdom as a challenge to the authorities. Jesus was not put to death directly as a narrator of parables, but they were a remote cause of it. It seems clear that several of Jesus' prophetic acts, his triumphant entrance into Jerusalem, his prediction of the destruction of the temple, his driving the money changers from the temple, were the immediate causes for the authorities to put him to death. These events proved to be the collective straw that broke the camels' back. But the parables played a significant role in Jesus' fate. The Jewish and Roman authorities understood the kingdom about which Jesus preached, both in his sayings, his narratives, and in his parables, to be a challenge to their power which provided a sufficient motive for them to eliminate him. Jesus was not put to death for telling parables but, as Crossan and Meier suggested, he was crucified for the consequences of their content.

Locating the Parables

When we refer to parables in this study, we are referring to narrative parables. A narrative parable is a self-contained story complete in itself. It has a beginning, middle, and an end. This will be further elaborated

---

4. Crossan, *In Parables*, 32.

5. Meier, *Marginal Jew*, 5:37, 40. As we shall discover below, the parable tradition of Jesus comes from the prophetic tradition of Israel and not the wisdom tradition.

THE PARABLES: PRELIMINARY CONSIDERATIONS

on in chapter 11. Not every parable has the form or structure of a narrative parable.[6]

The parables were not the only literary genre Jesus employed in his preaching, but were a significant part of his preaching. Interestingly enough, they are not found in the Gospel of John. They are found exclusively in the Synoptic Gospels.[7] The parables of Jesus express his experience of God and hence his vision of the kingdom. This vision demands an appropriate way of acting, an orthopraxis, in order to bring about the kingdom as a present, lived reality.[8]

As we pursue our examination of the parables it is useful to keep several things in mind. We need to distinguish the Synoptic Jesus from the historical Jesus.[9] As is clear from our previous discussions the Synoptic Jesus or the Jesus of the New Testament is related to but not coterminous with the historical Jesus. The one we identify and believe in by faith; the other we can identify by means of the historical-critical method. In like manner we need to distinguish the Synoptic narrative parables from the parables of the historical Jesus. While this distinction might at first seem odd, we can anticipate that there are more narrative parables in the Gospels than can be traced to the historical Jesus. As we shall see, many of the parables are either elaborations of Jesus' original parables or they are creations of the early church.[10] This will be examined and clarified below.[11]

---

6. For a few examples of nonnarrative parables, see Matt, 13:31–33, 44–48.

7. The parables are unique to Jesus in the New Testament literature. He is the only one recorded as teaching in parables.

8. We have already discussed a considerable portion of Jesus' mission and ministry. Our knowledge of the kingdom and the miracle tradition will be instrumental in assisting us in understanding Jesus' parables.

9. Meier makes a useful distinction by referring to the historical Jesus and the Synoptic Jesus. All the parables of the New Testament are attributed to the Synoptic Jesus, that is, they are all recorded in the Synoptic Gospels as coming from the mouth of Jesus. As we shall see, not all of the parables (only a few) can be established as authentic to Jesus.

10. The reason for this judgment becomes more apparent when we realize that the audience to whom Jesus preached was quite different from the audience to whom the early church preached. This helps us distinguish material which is authentic to Jesus from the proclaimed material of the early church.

11. We need to be aware that not all parables can be traced to the historical Jesus. Meier was able to determine that only four parables can be assigned this designation. Some of the parables come from the early Christians, and at least one seems to be the creation of the evangelist Luke. More will be said about this in chapter 11.

Jesus' Teaching Method or Style: In Parables

Is there anything distinctive in Jesus' teaching that differentiates him from his contemporaries? Leaving aside for the moment the content of Jesus' teaching, the question becomes, was there anything about his teaching that belonged to him uniquely as to his method or style? He was deeply immersed in the Old Testament tradition. Much of his teaching was not dramatically different from its central tenants. Jesus employed numerous types of literary devices to communicate with the crowds that followed him. Among them were his narratives, sayings, apothegms or proverbs, the amen statements, the beatitudes, as well as other literary genre.[12] Jesus spoke in terms that everyone could understand. The images he employed in the parables were commonplace, chosen to appeal to the crowds.

Jesus as Teacher: What Is Characteristic?

What kind of a teacher was Jesus? A cursory reading of the Gospels indicates that he was a very attractive, charismatic person; someone who could draw large crowds and attract disciples. That much appears clear. But what is characteristic of his teaching or his teaching method?

There is no one singular description of Jesus as teacher. The New Testament view is complex. As a devout Jew, Jesus was deeply attracted to the law both intellectually and devotionally. The Gospels frequently describe Jesus as teaching about the law.[13] This is a Jesus who assimilated the law and who engaged in debate with his religious contemporaries. Meier is fond of referring to him as the halakic Jesus.[14] Jesus interpreted the law much like a scribe or rabbi. He seems to have employed the standard teaching technique of the rabbis in his disputes with them. But his parables are quite distinct from this form of teaching.

---

12. It should be noted that there are many more beatitudes than the eight enumerated in Matthew and the corresponding four in Luke. An excellent example can be found Luke 10:23–24. There are numerous others in the Gospels. Beatitude is a literary genre. It should also be noted that Jesus use of amen is not said as an agreement to something someone did or said but it is used as an emphatic to what he is about to say. Many of these amen statements are thought to be authentic Jesus' sayings.

13. It appears that Jesus had no great interest in purity laws, but he did teach about divorce and the taking of oaths.

14. Meier, *Marginal Jew*, 4:1. Meier repeats this in several other places.

THE PARABLES: PRELIMINARY CONSIDERATIONS

Is Jesus a wisdom teacher? There are some who believe that he is.[15] Others think he is not.[16] Jesus was a first-century teacher of the law deeply engaged in the halakic debates of his day.[17] Meier adds, "He [Jesus] was, after all, not only an eschatological prophet but also a teacher of wisdom."[18] Meier affirms that "law and wisdom were notable dimensions of his (Jesus') public ministry—which is hardly surprising, since the two were closely intertwined in the religious thought of late Second Temple Judaism."[19] However, Jesus was not a typical sage in the mold of the Old Testament. He did not give practical advice on how to conduct one's life. It would be difficult to equate Jesus with someone like Qoheleth or Ben Sirach.[20] He did not teach like the wise man described in the book of Proverbs although he did occasionally use proverbs in his teaching.[21]

Wisdom is not totally absent from Jesus' teaching. An example of wisdom in his teaching can be found in Matt 18:15–20. This pericope concerns the correction of another. In Matthew's telling, it is most likely the settling of disputes within his community. Jesus expresses a way of properly settling disputes which corresponds nicely with

---

15. *The HarperCollins Bible Dictionary* describes the Jesus of the Synoptic Gospels as a wisdom teacher, a rabbi. See the entry "Jesus Christ," 458–68. See also the entry "Wisdom," 1106–107. As an example of Jesus as a wisdom teacher it quotes Matt 6:19—7:27. The position is that these sayings of Jesus were cast in the aphoristic style of the sages. An aphorism is a concise statement of a principle or truth. It is not clear by any means that a rabbi functioned as a sage. *Eerdmans Dictionary of the Bible* makes no reference to Jesus as a teacher of wisdom.

16. Kummel, *Introduction to the New Testament*, 72. Kummel believes that it cannot be demonstrated that Jesus was a wisdom teacher.

17. Meier refers to the debates of Jesus with the rabbis as halakic teaching. Meier, *Marginal Jew*, 4:8. It refers to the discussion or interpretation of the Mosaic law. Halakic is his spelling which I will follow but the word is more often than not spelled halakhic and sometimes halachic. Halakha is the Jewish religious law derived from the written and oral tradition. More will be said about this in the chapters below.

18. Meier, *Marginal Jew*, 5:557.

19. Meier, *Marginal Jew*, 5:40.

20. The former is the author of the book of Ecclesiastes; the latter is the author of the book of Sirach also known as Ecclesiasticus.

21. See Luke 9:57–62. The first two proverbs are from the Q source lending some weight that these could be proverbs taught by the historical Jesus. In any case it is doubtful that proverbs have their origin in Jesus' teaching. There are a significant number of proverbs in the Synoptic literature; most of these appear to be in Matthew. Jesus appears to defend his ministry with a proverb when he declares, "Amen I say to you, no prophet is accepted in his own native place" (Luke 4:24). In this instance he is responding to his detractors with a proverb. Consider also the three sayings in Luke 9:57–62, which appear to be reshaped proverbs.

wisdom teaching. But by-and-large Jesus does not teach like a sage or wise man. The sage taught in the schools or at home. Jesus was an itinerant preacher. He is much more easily identifiable with the prophetic tradition than the wisdom tradition.[22] But he did include some wisdom themes in his teaching.[23]

Jesus was a prophet-preacher. He understood himself as a prophet and accepted the title (Luke 4:24//Matt 13:57).[24] He spoke like a prophet. He issued warnings and woes (Matt 23:1–33; Luke 6:24–26).[25] Both Matthew and Luke present Jesus as addressing the people as "this generation" implying that they were offensive to God. He understood that the fate of the prophets was to be killed and it was likely to be his fate (Matt 23:37// Luke 13:34). He anticipated his death (Mark 8:31–33; 9:30–32; 10:32–34 parr.). All of this points to Jesus' understanding of himself as a prophet and he used the manner of speech common to prophets.[26]

The picture of Jesus as teacher is multifaceted. Parables were a particularly specific literary genre in his teaching. They are central to his method in proclaiming the kingdom. That gives them their particular significance. When Jesus taught in parables he also taught as a poet.[27] He used poetic, metaphorical ways of expressing his message. This chapter will focus on this manner of teaching because, as we shall see, he possessed a very singular, even unique, method using parables in his teaching.

---

22. Meier proposes that his teaching of the parables was from the prophetic tradition and not from the wisdom tradition. Jesus was much more the prophet than the sage. He says, "In short, Jesus the teller of parables is not Jesus the sage but Jesus the prophet." Meier, *Marginal Jew*, 5:365. The entire "Conclusion to Volume Five" is worth reading. Meier, *Marginal Jew*, 5:363–75.

23. Examples of Jesus' wisdom can be found in the Q source as well as his commands of love. Jesus does use wisdom in the parables, but he doesn't teach as a wisdom teacher might.

24. Jesus identifies himself as a prophet in his hometown of Nazareth when he was rejected (Luke 4: 22–24). His association with John the Baptist would seem to make Jesus' personal identity as a prophet indisputable.

25. Woes are prominent in the written prophets. Jesus continues this tradition. Mark records only two woes but Matthew and Luke contain twenty-eight. Matthew devotes his entire chapter 23 to woes. There are no woes recorded in John.

26. It is clear from the references given that the disciples understood Jesus as a prophet. There is sufficient scriptural evidence to support that this was also Jesus' self-understanding.

27. Crossan, *In Parables*, 20. Meier, *Marginal Jew*, vol. 5 also refers to Jesus as teaching as a poet but with some qualifications. Dodd, Parables of the Kingdom, 195, implies that Jesus taught as a poet.

THE PARABLES: PRELIMINARY CONSIDERATIONS

The Centrality of the Parables in the New Testament

Are the parables central to Jesus' teaching as a method much as the kingdom was as to its content? They are certainly described in that fashion in the New Testament. Narrative parables are supported by every Synoptic source. This includes Mark, Q, M, and L.[28] The parables are a major feature of Jesus' teaching. They are not simply one of many ways, but they are a significant and integral part of his teaching. Jesus explained his vision of God and the kingdom in parables. New Testament evidence in the Synoptic Gospels points to their centrality.

There are parallel passages in Matthew and Mark concerning Jesus' teaching in parables that deserve comment. Matthew tells us that "all these things Jesus spoke to the crowds in parables. He spoke to them only in parables" (Matt 13:34//Mark 4:34).[29] This seems to indicate that Jesus taught the crowds exclusively in parables. This presents a difficulty which requires some explanation. Matthew 13:10–15 indicates that the purpose of the parables was to prevent the hearers from understanding; to conceal the meaning from the crowds. Jesus explained the parables to his disciples privately (Matt 13:36). But on reflection this presents more difficulties than it answers. Did Jesus not want the crowds to understand his teaching of the kingdom, which he taught in large measure through the parables? This seems unlikely. It is more likely that Matt 13:10–15 is an editorial comment introduced by the evangelist to explain why the crowds did not understand or accept the message of the parables while the disciples did.[30] In fact, Jesus' purpose in teaching in parables was precisely so that the crowds would understand his teaching on the kingdom. It seems more likely that the reference to the crowds' failure to hear, that is, to understand the meaning of the parables actually refers to their rejection of the message contained therein.

---

28. Meier, *Marginal Jew*, 5:190. The parable tradition is similar to the preaching of the kingdom of God and the miracle tradition. In these cases, there is considerable multiple attestation to establish their authenticity. As we shall see, the same cannot be said for specific parables. The Synoptic Gospel support that Jesus actually taught in parables is overwhelming. Support that Jesus taught specific parables, however, is limited. The identification of which specific parables can be traced to the historical Jesus is more difficult than to establish the fact that he taught in parables, and this will be discussed in chapter 11. The designation of Mark, Q, M, and L as sources was discussed in chapter 1.

29. See also Mark 4:10–11.

30. Both the obtuseness of the crowds and the faith of the disciples must be seen in human responsibility and God's grace.

The Number and Distribution of the Parables in the Synoptic Gospels

The entire corpus of parables is found in the Synoptic Gospels. There are no parables in the Gospel of John or other writings of the New Testament.[31] How many parables are recorded in the Synoptic Gospels and how are they distributed? It should not surprise us that scholars variously count the number of parables. This is largely due to the manner in which the parables are defined or described.[32] According to Pheme Perkins, the total number of distinct parables in the Synoptic Gospels is forty-two.[33] Dodd identifies forty-four narrative parables.[34] Jeremias spoke of forty-one parables.[35] Crossan lists thirty-seven parables.[36] Meier lists thirty-four parables. This should lead us to understand that it is difficult to determine what counts as a parable because of the differing ways of understanding figurative language.[37]

Much more important than establishing the number of parables is the determination of their particular relationship to Jesus and his preaching. There can be little doubt that the Jesus of history taught in parables. The challenge will be to determine which parables can credibly be established as authentic to the historical Jesus. This will be discussed in chapter 11.

---

31. Brown refers to the narrative in John 10:1–18 as "shepherd parables." They are not included here because they do not satisfy our definition. See Brown, *Gospel and Epistles of John*, 58.

32. We will more formally define the parables below but for now we shall list the number of parables according to several scholars. The inconsistency in numbering the parables was noted as occurring in the miracle tradition as well.

33. Perkins, *Hearing the Parables of Jesus*. Perkins has a "Parable Index" on pages 218–20. Meier's list of parables can be found in Meier, *Marginal Jew*, 5:192–97. Thus, different scholars give differing enumerations. At an earlier age Adolph Jülicher enumerated fifty-three parables. See Meier, *Marginal Jew*, 5:35 for a list of various scholars and their enumeration of the parables. The numbers recorded in the *NJBC* is quite different from that recorded here. The difference in enumerating them differently is of little consequence in our effort to discover the nature of Jesus' parables. Interestingly, Stern, *Parables in Midrash*, 197–200, lists eleven or twelve narrative parables, but it is not clear that he intended to give an exhaustive list.

34. See Dodd, *Parables of the Kingdom*, 173.

35. Jeremias, *Parables of Jesus*. Jeremias provides an "Index of Synoptic Parables" at the end of his work.

36. Crossan, *In Parables*, 138–39

37. See the discussion in Meier, *Marginal Jew*, 5:34.

THE PARABLES: PRELIMINARY CONSIDERATIONS

Transmission of the Parables

We are conscious of considerable redaction in the parable tradition. There is a marked change from Jesus' preaching the parables and in the retelling of these parables in the Christian community in the decades that followed. We can presume that changes took place in the parables from their original form because the original context changed. Jesus' audience included the curious, the skeptical, the hostile, the authorities, the hopeful as well as his disciples. The early Christians and ultimately the evangelists discovered themselves in a context considerably different from that of Jesus. They retold the parables to those who had already accepted Jesus' message. Thus, the early Christians attempted to interpret the meaning of the kingdom for their situation or context. Though Jesus left the parables open ended, leaving it for his audience to discover the meaning, as we shall see, the primitive church often included an interpretation which addressed its particular situation.[38]

Many parables have been reinterpreted or redacted to address a particular need in the community. Such a development is to be expected. The question is this: in what way did the preachers and missionaries shape the original parables of Jesus to suit their needs? Redactors sometimes added sayings to the original parable to universalize them.[39] An examination of parallel versions of the parables makes this eminently clear. A suitable example is the parable of the lost sheep found in both Matt 18:12–14 and Luke 15:3–7. Because this is from the Q source, we can presume that it is the same parable. Each evangelist, however, has his particular point of view and each interprets the same original parable in a slightly different manner. Matthew concludes his version of the parable of lost sheep with "in just the same way, it is not the will of your heavenly Father that one of these little ones be lost" (Matt 18:14). Luke concludes his version with "I tell you, in just the same way there will be more joy in heaven over one sinner who repents than over ninety-nine

---

38. Though Jesus' narrative parables were complete in themselves, they may have been accompanied by explanatory statements, a nimshal, which may have come from Jesus himself. This will be discussed at length in chapter 11.

39. Perkins, *Hearing the Parables of Jesus*, 30. There are numerous pericopes which indicate editing or addition. Luke 23:39–43 is the only Gospel to record Jesus' conversation with the good thief, an obvious editorial addition. In the pericopes indicating Peter's confession of Jesus as Christ (Mark 8:27–30//Matt 16:13–20//Luke 9:18–21) Matthew adds "the Son of the living God" to the statement recorded in Mark indicating his personal Christology. There are numerous examples of this sort of editing.

righteous people who have no need of repentance" (Luke 15:7). Matthew focuses on the concern of the Father for the lost sheep; Luke focuses on the community and its joy because one of the sheep has returned to the community. Both evangelists are retelling the same original parable, but each gives a different interpretation. It is easy to see how the early community found both of these interpretations satisfying. It is also easy to see that in each case there is an addition to the original parable.[40] The new context made this addition possible.[41] What has been said of this parable can easily be established for others.

The Parables: The Scriptural Background

A pivotal moment in the study of the parables of Jesus came with the work of Adolph Jülicher at the end of the nineteenth century.[42] His contribution was to distinguish parable from allegory. He rejected the elaborate allegorizing of the parables by the fathers of the church and medieval theologians. According to Jülicher, Jesus never used allegory. Later research has somewhat modified Jülicher's position. Scholars who succeeded him made their own important contributions to this research.[43] In addition to this important scholarship, another great help in understanding the parables is the recent focus on the Jewishness of Jesus. Jesus was a person of his time, and he was steeped in the Jewish religion and culture. It should come as no surprise that we would gain a deeper understanding of Jesus' parables by situating him in his religious and social context. Much of Jesus' teaching has its antecedents in the Old Testament. We saw this in our examination of the kingdom. This is no less true for the parables. We will briefly examine some of the prehistory of Jesus' parables in order to gain a better understanding of them.

---

40. This addition or explanation may well be what will ultimately be called a nimshal. This will be explained below.

41. It seems clear that these explanations did not come from Jesus since they are so different. The only conclusion is that they are the additions of the evangelists. We shall discuss the possible additions of Jesus, the nimshal, below.

42. Jülicher, *Die Gleichnisreden Jesu.*

43. The list would be too long, but we can mention several: C. H. Dodd and Joachim Jeremias are notable contributors. Raymond Brown should be added to this list.

The Old Testament Understanding or Use of the Term Parable (Mashal and Parabolé)

Are there antecedents to Jesus' parables to be found in the Old Testament? The most prominent candidate for this honor is the literary expression referred to as a mashal.[44] Mashal is a many-faceted literary genre whose meanings or uses include proverbs, riddles, similitudes, allegories, aphorisms, and what we shall refer to as narrative parables. A cursory examination of the Old Testament would reveal the extent of its meaning. The word *mashal* is used to refer to proverbs (Ezek 18:2–3; 1 Sam 24:13–14; Prov 1:1, 6), riddles and enigmas (Ps 78:2; Ezek 17:2), taunt-songs (Isa 14:34; Hab 2:6), and prophetic oracles and allegories (Ezek 15:1–8; 24:2–5).[45] Besides these literary genres which can be found under the umbrella of the term *mashal*, we also include what we have called narrative parables. The song of the vineyard (Isa 5:1–5) and Nathan's parable with which he confronted David (2 Sam 12:1–6) are examples of narrative parables. Meier adds five other cases of narrative parables from the Old Testament to this list.[46] It is clear that there are antecedents in the Old Testament to the narrative parables found in the Synoptic Gospels. Narrative parables in the literary prophets are often found with allegorical elements.[47] This will be significant in the understanding of the New Testament parables.

The Hebrew word *mashal* is translated as *parabolé* in the Septuagint, the Greek translation of the Old Testament, and it is translated as *parabola* in the Latin Vulgate. It is easy to see the derivation of the English word parable. The use of this term *parable* for the more extensive usage of mashal has caused considerable confusion. The use of the term *parable* for what we refer to as Jesus' parables is much more restricted than the Old Testament expression *mashal*. Nevertheless, as has been indicated above, there are antecedents in the Old Testament to the parables in the New Testament. It is clear that one of the uses of

---

44. Meshalim is the plural form of mashal.

45. See Brown et al., "Aspects of New Testament Thought," in *NJBC*, 81:60. The *NJBC* gives another list other than that given here. See also "Proverb," in Freedman et al., *Eerdmans Dictionary of the Bible*, 1089, and Meier, *Marginal Jew*, 2:146, 4:281, 5:35–36.

46. Meier lists five clear cases of narrative parable in the Old Testament. They are Judg 9:7–15; 2 Sam 12:1–4; 2 Kgs 14:19; Isa 5:1–6; and Ezek 17:3–10. There are also many borderline cases. See Meier, *Marginal Jew*, 5:63n16.

47. Meier, *Marginal Jew*, 5:64n20.

mashal includes what is referred to in the New Testament as narrative parable. Jesus falls within this tradition.

It was mentioned above that the Old Testament narrative found in 2 Sam 12:1–12 was a parable.[48] It is worthwhile to examine this more closely because of its peculiar structure. In this episode, Nathan told David a parable (mashal) about a powerful man who had stolen the lamb of a poor man. It referred to King David taking Bathsheba, the wife of Uriah. David got the point of the story as soon as he understood that Nathan was talking about him as the rich man. Uriah was understood as the poor man; Bathsheba was understood as the lamb. Although this appears to have the form of an allegory, the New American Bible and the New Revised Standard Version of the Bible describe this mashal as a parable.[49] Meier considers 2 Sam 12:1–12 as the most famous parable of the Old Testament. The parable or mashal (2 Sam 12:1–6) is explained allegorically in 2 Sam 12:7–12. What makes this a parable and not an allegory is because it is not the point-by-point comparison that is the intent of the story; it is the entire story. Nathan indicates as much when he said, "Tell me how you judge this case" (2 Sam 12:1). The opening sentence serves as an explanation to the meaning of the parable. This narrative *mashal* is the type of parabolic speech most peculiar in the Synoptic parables in the New Testament. The allegorical method, as we shall see below, is not the method used by Jesus in his parables. Nathan provides an interpretation of his parable (2 Sam 12:7–12). This explanation will come to be known as a nimshal of which we will have more to say in chapter 11. It is not the point-by-point understanding of the parable that is the intent of Nathan but the accusation that David is the man who committed a crime and that the house of David will pay for his sin.

Thus, we can see that the narrative parable is not unique to Jesus. There are, as has been indicated, antecedents in the Old Testament prophetic literature. We do not find this type of narrative parallel in the wisdom literature. Jesus is consistent with the prophetic tradition in his use of narrative parables.

48. The New American Bible Revised Edition and the New Revised Standard Version describe this as a parable. Meier also indicates that this is a parable with allegorical elements. See Meier, *Marginal Jew*, 5:37, 64n20. On the face of it one might have no small difficulty in seeing that this is not an allegory. More study is required. See Dodd, *Parables of the Kingdom*, 11.

49. The New Jerusalem Bible makes no such identification. It may well be that the other translations of the Bible used the term parable simply because that is a common usage in the Septuagint.

The Parables in the New Testament

Much of this has been discussed above but in order to add a word of clarity we will make the following remarks. The word parable (*parabolé*) occurs in the Synoptic Gospels forty-eight times and almost all of these refer to narrative parables.[50] There are a few parables that are not considered narratives, but these are of no concern to our examination. We indicated above that various New Testament scholars listed the number of actual parables as between thirty-seven and forty-four. It was not an exhaustive list. Meier listed the actual individual parables as thirty-four.[51] In this study, when we speak of parables in the New Testament, we are referring to narrative parables.

A true narrative parable "is a metaphor or simile stretched out into a whole narrative into which the audience can be drawn, a narrative with a beginning, middle, and end (at least in miniature)."[52] We will examine this more thoroughly below, but this is an excellent working definition. A parable as we understand it is a comparison, a metaphor or a simile, that has been stretched into a story. They are ways of expressing a truth that is not immediately obvious and it is intended that the audience ultimately understands them. A metaphor or simile is a form of figurative language in which we compare two things. One element of the metaphor is made to stand for or express some truth about something else. It is a view of reality expressed poetically. We are speaking of similarity or identity and differences between the reality we speak of and the expression we use for it.[53]

The New Jerome Biblical Commentary describes the manner of the parables' expression. "As metaphors, the parables of Jesus use concrete and familiar images which touch people in their everyday lives, but which point to a reality (God's reign or Kingdom) that transcends

---

50. Meier, *Marginal Jew*, 5:62n15.

51. Meier lists thirty-four parables according to their source (Mark, Q, M, and L). Several may be doubted as actual narrative parables. Meier, *Marginal Jew*, 5:191–97.

52. Meier, *Marginal Jew*, 5:61n14. Meier also considers fables as falling within the scope of the descriptive definition. See Meier, *Marginal Jew*, 5:63n16.

53. The comparison is by means of an analogy. It is useful to appeal to Thomistic epistemology for a better understanding. Words are the way we express concepts and concepts are about reality. The parable is a way of expressing a reality or truth. There are many expressions of truth other than simple historical narrative. The parable is one of these expressions.

definition or literal description."⁵⁴ For the most part, the images Jesus employed in the telling of the parables are commonplace; they are sheep, shepherd, coin, net, wheat, tares, treasure, workers, sowers, sons, kings or rulers, and many other similar concrete expressions. These images would in general fall within the experience or understanding of even the least educated peasant.

The Method of Jesus and the Rabbis Compared

The use of the narrative parable in the New Testament was unique to the Jesus of history. There are no narrative parables found in the New Testament literature except those attributed to Jesus. Did Jesus' contemporaries employ parables in their teaching and if so, how did they use them? It is useful to compare the methods of the rabbis and that of Jesus for clarification. This will give us a deeper appreciation of the narrative parables so common in the Synoptic Gospels.

We spoke above of the use of the mashal in the Old Testament. This tradition continued after the canonical Scriptures were written.⁵⁵ Originally Jewish scholarship was oral. This changed with the destruction of Jerusalem and the temple in AD 70. Midrash was a written commentary on the Hebrew Scripture. It had its origin in the second century although much of its content is older. It reached its final form in the fourth century AD. The Talmud is the record and commentary on the oral tradition. Its origin was in the second century but found its written expression in the third or fourth century AD. During this period of written commentaries, the method of the rabbis was exegetical.⁵⁶ Their use of mashal (parable) was a method of expounding Scripture. Feldman's point is that the law was interpreted, that is, the exegesis of the law was accomplished by means of metaphors and similes as well as parables. We understand this use of parable to be coterminous with the notion of mashal. It is difficult to know whether this was the actual method used by rabbis contemporaneous with Jesus, but it seems highly likely. The famous rabbi Hillel, who died in Jerusalem circa AD 10, was a great influence in the formation of the Talmud and Mishnah. He gave a long list of examples which were

---

54. Brown et al., "Aspects of New Testament Thought," in *NJBC*, 81:68.
55. Stern, *Parables in Midrash*, 190.
56. Feldman, *Parables and Similes*, 2.

employed to explain a text.⁵⁷ He refers to these examples as parables but in fact they include similes, metaphors, allegories, and parables. This use has its origin at a date earlier than the Midrash and Talmud.⁵⁸ It indicates that this particular method of exegesis which was employed by the rabbis was more than likely coterminous with the public ministry of Jesus. We can presume that Jesus would have been aware of this method of exegesis since he had frequent contact and disputes with the rabbis. David Stern affirms that Jesus stands in the tradition of the mashal. But in examining Jesus' parable of the wicked tenants (Meier identifies this parable as the evil tenants of the vineyard) Stern says that "Jesus was not an exegete of the same sort as the later Rabbis."⁵⁹ We know that Jesus' contemporaries would have been familiar with the Old Testament and its meshalim as was Jesus. And we know that they did engage him in the interpretation of the law. We have little information on how they employed figurative language, but it appears that they used figurative language to exegete texts. Later on, there are collections or anthologies of rabbinic interpretation or exegesis of texts.⁶⁰

This examination is important to understand the parables of Jesus. It is clear that the rabbis used figurative language for didactic and pedagogic reasons.⁶¹ Its purpose was to interpret or exemplify a problem of life, a moral lesson, or interpret a text in Scripture in a very precise and specific fashion. Every good teacher wants to illustrate information; to clarify a point; to aid in teaching; to exegete a text. This is apparently what the rabbis did.

Jesus was not an exegete in the same sense as the later rabbis.⁶² The method employed by Jesus was quite different from that of the rabbis as

---

57. Feldman, *Parables and Similes*, 22–23.

58. Feldman, *Parables and Similes*, 19.

59. Stern, *Parables in Midrash*, 197.

60. Stern, *Parables in Midrash*, 152. The Talmud consisted of running commentaries on Scripture (the Old Testament). It consisted of exegetical opinion. This began before the Common Era according to some sources. Midrash was a form of rabbinic literature that contained commentary or interpretation of biblical texts. Its origin is after the destruction of the Second Temple (AD 70).

61. Didactic stories were also employed in the New Testament. For example, the temple tax found in the mouth of the fish (Matt 17:24–27). Paying the temple tax appeared to be a problem for Matthew's church. Possibly the cursing of the fig tree was a didactic story (Mark 11:12–25; Matt 21:18–22). Luke 13:6–9 shapes this story as a parable.

62. Stern, *Parables in Midrash*, 197

described above.[63] Jesus' parables are not linked to specific biblical texts that require interpretation or to precise moral situations for which they represent allegorical exemplification.[64] The parables of Jesus do entirely different things than interpret or exemplify.[65] Jesus used figurative language to create participation or involvement.[66] The major feature of his parables is a comparison by employing metaphors or similes.[67] This will become quite clear in the examination of the greater number of Jesus' narrative parables.

Conclusion and Resume

In the previous chapters we saw that Jesus was the charismatic prophet/preacher. He understood himself as the eschatological prophet. The kingdom of God was the centerpiece and content of his mission. His miracles, his mighty deeds, supported the content of his preaching and pointed to the reality of the kingdom. These were carefully evaluated above.

This chapter focused on Jesus as teacher. He was referred to as the halakic Jesus who debated points of law with his contemporaries; he was referred to as teaching wisdom but not as a sage of the Old Testament. Jesus was an itinerant preacher in the mode of the prophets. It is clear from the Gospels that Jesus taught in many different literary genres. These were characteristic in his teaching of the kingdom. The evidence from the Scriptures makes this abundantly evident. It also became clear that Jesus did in fact teach in parables. This is in anticipation of the next chapter which will examine Jesus' parables through the lens of the historical-critical method. Teaching in parables is authentic to the historical Jesus.

The parables were central to Jesus' mission. In spite of the importance of this literary genre in Jesus' teaching, parables were not unique to him. There were antecedents found in the prophetic tradition of the Old Testament. Jesus was steeped in this tradition, and he would have been well acquainted with it. The rabbis contemporaneous with Jesus also taught in parables but their use of the genre is distinguished from that of Jesus. The

---

63. Jesus was a teacher who taught as a poet, and as such, he depended on the metaphor.

64. Crossan, *In Parables*, 20.

65. Stern has provided us with many other references on this subject. See Stern, *Parables in Midrash*, 66–67; 189–99

66. Crossan, *In Parables*, 20.

67. Crossan, *In Parables*, 15. Meier, *Marginal Jew*, 5:37.

rabbis used parable to illustrate a point; Jesus used parable to create participation and involvement. The rabbis were exegetes; Jesus was a prophet. We are now in a position to evaluate the parables of Jesus.

11

A Theological Evaluation of the Parables

Introduction: The Parables Evaluated

THE PREVIOUS CHAPTER PRESENTED the data relative to the parables attributed to Jesus. We are now in a position to examine them from a theological and historical perspective. We know that the Synoptic parables are expressed in figurative language. They are poetic, in a comparative manner of speaking.[1] It is useful for us to examine their relationship to other commonly used literary forms such as allegory, proverbs, and wisdom in order to delineate them from these forms of speech. It is also useful for us to understand how the redactor often shaped the parable to fit the needs of his community. This will help us understand the parable in its original form and allow us to differentiate it from other legitimate literary expressions. After this we will consider a nominal or descriptive definition of the parables.

The Parables and Other Literary Genres

Jesus was a charismatic prophet who was able to draw large crowds by means of his preaching. We can presume that a significant part of his

---

1. Dodd includes the notion of simile in his definition. For our purposes, a parable is a metaphor or simile. The difference is of no particular significance for our discussion.

charism, independent of his message, was that he spoke in an attractive, persuasive manner. We mentioned earlier that Jesus spoke as a poet. His preaching reflected a variety of different literary expressions which were during his time and are even common now. The narrative parable was most notable of the various literary genres Jesus employed and they still have a singular attraction for us. It is useful to compare several of these common literary genres and by so doing deepen our appreciation of the parables. This chapter will differentiate the parable from other common literary genres that Jesus likely used.

The Parables and Wisdom

Wisdom is concerned with prudent behavior. Unlike the proverb, wisdom is not a short, obvious saying.[2] The goal is to teach right conduct, the proper way of living, or how to form character. It is an observation of social convention. Wisdom includes such topics as friendship, choosing a wife, rearing children, warnings on greed, idleness, drunkenness, and other similar themes. This is a common feature of the wisdom literature of the Old Testament. It is based upon human experience as it is in accord with the role of God in everyday life.

The use of the wisdom tradition is not totally neglected by Jesus. This was discussed above.[3] Pheme Perkins tells us that his use of this material was selective.[4] She continues, "But obedience to the Law is an expression of wisdom. It is not surrounded by the complexities of scribal, technical interpretation. Similarly, Jesus addresses the universal experience of humanity as the place in which one finds the truth about God's presence."[5] Whatever the actual content of Jesus' possible teaching in terms of wisdom, one thing seems clear. There are wisdom motifs in the parables.[6] Nevertheless, the parables should be distinguished from the teaching of wisdom. For one thing, there are no parables in

---

2. Wisdom in the Old Testament can be complex. It can be the pursuit of knowledge about the world but more properly it concerns the human response to all of the ethical dimensions of life. It is also seen as a quality of God. Later theology understands wisdom as knowledge of higher things.

3. See chapter 10. Wisdom teaching can be found in the Q sources and in Jesus' teaching on love as well as in other places.

4. Perkins, *Hearing the Parables of Jesus*, 37.

5. Perkins, *Hearing the Parables of Jesus*, 37.

6. Meier, *Marginal Jew*, 5:67n31.

the Old Testament sapiential books. The prime source for narrative parables is not Old Testament wisdom mashal. It is found only in the Old Testament prophetic tradition.[7] Jesus stands more in the prophetic tradition than the sapiential tradition and his narrative parables come out of the prophetic tradition.[8]

The Parables and Proverbs

A proverb is a short saying that expresses an obvious truth.[9] "Spare the rod and spoil the child" and "a stitch in time saves nine" are examples of well-known proverbs. There are many proverbs in the wisdom literature of the Old Testament. They normally express common wisdom.[10]

Jesus used proverbs in his teaching, but they are not very common. There are three conjoined proverbs attributed to Jesus in Luke 9:57–62.[11] He defends his ministry by appealing to a common proverb. "Amen, I say to you, no prophet is accepted in his own native place" (Luke 4:24). He describes those who listen to his words and follows them in terms of a proverb that would sound like "a wise man builds his house on rock" (Matt 7:24//Luke 6:47–49). According to Pheme Perkins, this appears to be a proverb that Jesus has adapted to satisfy a particular instruction. She suggests that at times Jesus reshapes a proverb and expresses it as a

---

7. In general, the narrative parable is not part of the Old Testament except in the written prophetic tradition.

8. Meier, *Marginal Jew*, 5:40. Meier asserts that, "Jesus seems in his parable-telling to have reached back quite consciously to the Former and Latter Prophets of the Jewish Scriptures instead of simply reflecting the more recent apocalyptic or sapiential literature of Israel."

9. Proverb, aphorism, and apothegm are understood as synonyms in this work. Proverbs are a very popular, common literary genre. It is interesting to read the numerous proverbs in Cervantes's *Don Quixote*. This indicates how much delight we get from them. They speak the language of the ordinary person. Cervantes, through the mouth of Don Quixote, tells us that proverbs are "brief maxims drawn from long experience." Cervantes Saavedra, *Don Quixote*, 1008. In another place he tells us that "There is no proverb that is not true, for all proverbs are maxims drawn from experience, the mother of all knowledge." Cervantes Saavedra, *Don Quixote*, 198.

10. As one might expect, the book of Proverbs has many. It is not the only source for Old Testament proverbs. They were evidently very popular.

11. The NABRE refers to these as sayings of Jesus. Their proper literary genre, however, is that of proverb.

parable.¹² In any case, it seems clear that parables and proverbs, as used by Jesus, are quite different both in structure and in content.¹³

The Parables and Allegory[14]

A pivotal moment in the investigation of Jesus' parables came with the work of Adolph Jülicher.[15] Until Jülicher's seminal work on the parables of the New Testament, the fathers of the church, the medieval theologians, and the majority of theologians who followed them interpreted the parables allegorically.[16] These interpretations often employed a great deal of fanciful imagination. Jülicher initiated a new way of understanding the parables. His thesis was that the authentic parables of the New Testament do not admit of allegory. There is but a single point of comparison in the parable and not many as suggested by an allegorical interpretation. This has had a profound impact on our understanding of the narrative parables. While the thesis did counteract previous interpretations which were largely eisegesis, we will see that rejecting all allegory from the authentic parables of Jesus was too extreme.[17] The common or popular notion of allegory that Jülicher reacted to was that the allegory consisted of a string of discrete metaphors.[18] Each discrete metaphor of the allegory, it was thought, points to corresponding realities. Each of the details or discrete metaphors has a figurative meaning. The parable, on

---

12. Perkins, *Hearing the Parables of Jesus*, 39. Perkins suggests that the parable of the Pharisee and publican (Luke 18:9–14) might be a proverb reshaped as a parable. Meier does not list this as a narrative parable. Also note the unjust judge (Luke 18:1–8) or help at midnight (Luke 11:5–8). Some of her suggestions appear to be unlikely or out of the ordinary but nevertheless it is an interesting observation.

13. I have found fifteen proverbs in the Synoptic literature attributed to Jesus but there may be many more.

14. For an excellent and brief explanation of allegory see "The Problem of Allegory," in Meier, *Marginal Jew*, 5:82–87.

15. Jülicher, *Die Gleichnissreden Jesu*.

16. It should be noted that one of the great contributions made by Thomas Aquinas (+1274) was that the proper interpretation of all Scripture was the literal translation. By this he meant that whatever literary form the author intended must be accepted and properly interpreted. A popular legend describes Thomas as interpreting the Song of Songs allegorically on his deathbed. Given his rejection of allegory as a suitable method of interpretation, the story must be relegated to myth.

17. Eisegesis is the process in which the reader imposes his own presuppositions or personal understanding into the text. It is highly subjective.

18. Meier, *Marginal Jew*, 5:82.

the other hand, is an illustrative story with a single point. While this was a tremendous step forward it was ultimately realized that this description of allegory and parable needed some modification.[19] The shortcoming of this description is that it treats allegory too narrowly.

After Jülicher, many rejected the allegorical interpretation of the parables. The parable of the prodigal son, a favorite of the fathers of the church, and the parable of the evil tenants were no longer to be interpreted allegorically. The allegorical interpretations were presumed to be explanations from the experience of the early Christians inserted into the Scriptures and not the authentic teaching of Jesus. Brown challenged this position.[20] He was convinced that Jesus did not make a notable distinction between parable and allegory. His point is that neither do we need to make such a distinction. Did the allegorical interpretation come from Jesus? Brown believes that the allegorical interpretations to three parables did indeed come from Jesus.[21] He is not alone in this opinion.[22]

In general, allegory is a representation of an abstract or spiritual meaning through concrete or material forms; it is a figurative treatment of one subject under the guise of another.[23] An allegorical interpretation of the parables identifies specific characters with Jesus, God, the Jews, and so forth.[24] Meier addresses this issue directly. He asserts that

---

19. This is nicely explained by Brown in *The Gospel According to John*, 1:390. Interestingly, Brown refers to the existence of parables in *The Gospel According to John*, 1:391. It appears, however, that he is referring to metaphors which are understood in an allegorical fashion. It does not seem that these metaphors are equivalent to the narrative parables that we are speaking of here.

20. Brown, *New Testament Essays*.

21. Brown, *New Testament Essays*, 259. The parables are: the sower of seeds (Matt 13:4–9//Mark 4:3–9//Luke 8:5–8) and its allegorical interpretation (Matt 13:18–23//Mark 4:13–20//Luke 8:11–15); the parable of the wheat and darnel (Matt 13:24–30) is explained allegorically (Matt 13:36–43); the parable of the fish net (Matt 13:47–48) is immediately followed by an allegorical interpretation (Matt 13:49–50).

22. The footnote in the NABRE to Matt 13:18–23 supports Brown's opinion. This is a comment on the allegorical interpretation of the sower. The footnote indicates that some scholars believe that "the explanation derives not from Jesus but from the early Christian reflection on apostasy from faith. . . . Others, however, hold that the explanation may come basically from Jesus even though it was developed in the light of later Christian experience." This is a comment on the seed sown on rocky ground and the seed sown among thorns.

23. See Crossan, *In Parables*. Crossan defines *allegory* on page 8 and *metaphor* on page 10.

24. This was commonplace with the fathers of the church, especially with Origen and Augustine.

A THEOLOGICAL EVALUATION OF THE PARABLES

allegory is a broad term.[25] He suggests that it can be found in narrative poetry, lyric poetry, parables, and sometimes in entire novels.[26] It cannot be reduced to any one literary genre. Furthermore, the intention of the author is helpful in understanding the meaning of the parable if it can be determined.[27]

This perspective proposed by Meier is central to a proper understanding of the Synoptic parables. He claims that Jesus used allegorical elements in some of the parables.[28] As we shall see, several important parables which are authentic to the historical Jesus contain significant allegorical traits. Therefore, we shall give this a serious examination.

The church, conscious of having received the parables from Jesus, draws conclusions from them just as any individual might. There are several places in the Synoptic Gospels where the church (the redactor of the parable) has given an allegorical interpretation. These examples in which the allegorical interpretation is obvious are worth noting.[29] The first is the parable of the sower of seeds (Mark 4:3–8//Matt 13:3–8//Luke 8:5–8). Later in the same chapter, the parable is explained allegorically (Mark 4:13–20//Matt 13:18–23//Luke 8:11–15). This allegorical explanation is the work of the church and not the explicit teaching of Jesus.[30] The allegorical interpretation is not a necessary addition, but it resonates with the central meaning of the original. The parable of the wheat and darnel (Matt 13:24–30) follows the same pattern.[31] It is explained allegorically in Matt 13:36–43. A third example is the parable of the net

---

25. Brown claimed that Jülicher and others who followed him had understood allegory and metaphor too narrowly, but he did not devote the time to this issue that Meier has. Brown, *New Testament Essays*, 256.

26. In this regard, Meier spoke of the novel *Animal Farm*. He suggests that a later generation not familiar with the earlier significance of the novel could still gain much from this novel/movie. That statement is precisely the function of the Synoptic parables. Paintings and other art forms can be allegories. Meier, *Marginal Jew*, 5:83–84.

27. In the past, prior to Jülicher, much of the exegesis of the parables and other literary genres was actually an importation, an eisegesis, of the interpreter who imposed his particular ideas on the text.

28. Meier, *Marginal Jew*, 5:146. This would seem clear with the parables of the great supper (Matt 22:1–10//Luke 15:3–7) and the evil tenants of the vineyard (Mark 12:1–11//Matt 21:33–44//Luke 20:9–18).

29. As pointed out above, Brown believed that the allegorical interpretation of these three parables came from Jesus. That view is challenged here.

30. Meier, *Marginal Jew*, 5:85

31. Meier believes that the parable is entirely from Matthew or that Matthew added the allegory. The addition is not part of the original parable. It is an interpretation.

thrown into the sea (Matt 13:47–48). It is immediately followed by an allegorical interpretation (Matt 13:49–50).[32] The supposition or conclusion is that the second part, the explanation, is not original with Jesus but is the church's effort to interpret the parable to match its particular existential situation. We will see below that these explanations would be called *nimshalim* by later rabbinic scholars. It is not impossible that Jesus added these explanations to his parables. Brown has suggested that the allegorical interpretations of the parables may well have been shaped by the early church as reapplications of the original parable. All of this simply reinforces the difficulty in the relation of the parables to possible allegorical interpretation. The three parables mentioned do include allegorical interpretations. The question is this: are they from Jesus or the early Christians?

An example of a parable with allegorical elements is the parable of the wedding feast (Matt 22:1–10).[33] In Luke's version (Luke 14:16–24) it is referred to as the great supper. What makes this an interesting choice is that Meier has established this parable as authentic teaching of the historical Jesus.[34] The notes in the New Jerusalem Bible for this Matthean parable describe it as "a parable with allegorical features."[35] The note continues by giving an allegorical interpretation of the parable: the king is God, the king's son is the Messiah, and so forth. It indicates that the burning of the city is the destruction of Jerusalem, which would certainly be an addition made by the early church. Jerusalem was not destroyed until forty years after Jesus' death. The burning of the city of Jerusalem could hardly have been referred to by him. The note from the NABRE supports this understanding. The editor of the note tells us that it was Matthew who is responsible for the allegorical elements. The note from the NABRE reads, "[Matthew] 22, 1–14: This parable is from Q;

---

32. In this parable it does seem that the explanation of the parable is found on Jesus' lips.

33. Matthew added allegorical features which relate to the destruction of Jerusalem, AD 70. This is an authentic parable. Matt 22:11–14, which is often spoken of as part of the parable of the great supper, is more than likely a separate parable. Meier has suggested that the guest without a wedding garment (Matt 22:11–14) is a parable distinct from the great supper.

34. Meier argues that though this has the appearance of Q, each version of the parable is actually from a different source which he identifies as M and L.

35. The note correctly pointed out that Matthew has probably combined two parables, the wedding feast and the guest without a wedding garment. The second part seems to clearly refer to the early church context. Meier agrees with this position.

see Lk 14: 15–24. It has been given many allegorical traits by Matthew, e.g., the burning of the *city* of the guests who refused the invitation (v. 7), which corresponds to the destruction of Jerusalem by the Romans in A.D. 70. It has similarities with the preceding parable of the tenants: the sending of two groups of *servants* (vv. 3, 4), the murder of the *servants* (v. 6), the punishment of the *murderers* (v. 7), and the entrance of a new group into a privileged situation of which the others had proved themselves unworthy (vv. 8–10)."[36]

This note from the NABRE is clear that the parable in Matt 22:1–10 has been allegorized by the redactor of the Gospel of Matthew. It is easy to read Matthew's version of the great supper allegorically. However, the version from Luke 14:16–24 gives us another point of view. It can easily be read without inferring any allegorizing. Even the reference to the destruction of Jerusalem is absent. One could conclude that this parable in its original form as told by Jesus was not allegorized. The allegorical interpretations, though in the canonical Scriptures, were as a matter of fact the additions of the redactor. The argument which is put forth here is that when Jesus preached this parable, it was not allegorical although it may have lent itself to such an understanding.

What is a Parable? Looking for a Definition

Having distinguished the parable from other literary genres, we are now in the position to better understand the parable as a means of expression. Jesus' parables occupy a prominent place in the Synoptic Gospels. They are central to his preaching of the kingdom of God. Therefore, their proper understanding is a fundamental prerequisite for us. We will examine the narrative parable in the following pages and propose both a nominal definition as well as an explanation of their purpose.

The Parable Define/Explained/Described

We have restricted our discussion to Jesus' narrative parables. We have also referred to these as the Synoptic parables because it is only in the

---

36. According to Meier's examination the sources for this parable appear to be from Q but they are in fact from M and L. This will be further examined below. Meier lists Matt 22:11–14 (guest without a wedding garment) as a distinct parable as the note from the NABRE suggests.

Synoptic Gospels that we find them. We have examined a number of parables and their qualities. It is now possible to give a fuller description or at least a nominal definition of the narrative parable. C. H. Dodd has given us an excellent point of departure for this discussion. He expresses parables in this fashion: "At its simplest the parable is a metaphor or simile drawn from nature or common life, arresting the hearer by its vividness or strangeness, and leaving the mind in sufficient doubt about its precise application to tease it into active thought."[37] While agreeing with Dodd's description, Meier further describes the narrative parable at its foundation as a comparison of one thing to another.[38] It is a metaphor or similitude, which is extended into a self-contained, brief story.[39] This narrative has an implied beginning, middle and end, complete in itself.[40] It is similar to a riddle or paradox in as much as it is puzzling or challenging.[41] It teases the mind into activity. Its meaning is not usually immediately obvious. It is a challenge which requires a reflective response.

In his telling of the parables, Jesus appeals to common human experience. He focused on the individual and a particular situation. The symbolic expression of the parable is concrete and commonplace. These symbols include shepherds and sheep, a good Samaritan, a prodigal son, a lost coin, a net cast into the sea, a pearl of great price, a king, and other similar images. All of these could be found within the possible lived experience of a first century Mediterranean peasant. *The New Jerome Biblical Commentary* describes the parables in the following manner. "As metaphors, the parables of Jesus use concrete and familiar images which touch people in their everyday lives, but which point to a reality (God's reign or kingdom) that transcends definition or literal description."[42] According to this way of describing or defining the parable we consider it in its principle literary form, that is, a metaphor or simile, and we see the parable as stretching this common way of expression. It begins low and moves up; it moves from common human experience to an understanding of God's kingdom.

---

37. Dodd, *Parables of the Kingdom*, 5.
38. Meier, *Marginal Jew*, 5:40, 43.
39. Meier, *Marginal Jew*, 2:146, 5:249.
40. Meier, *Marginal Jew*, 5:37, 242.
41. Crossan, *In Parables*, 10.
42. Brown et al., "Aspects of New Testament Thought," in *NJBC*, 81:68.

A THEOLOGICAL EVALUATION OF THE PARABLES

The parable can also be described as a compressed story.[43] A parable is a story within a larger story. That larger story is Jesus' experience and understanding of God and how God desires us to live. The compressed story requires us to expand it into the fullness of experience of one living in the presence of God.

Thus, the parable can be described as a compressed story or an extended metaphor. Both of these ways of describing a parable have much to recommend them. Taken together they begin to throw light on the nature of a parable as a unique form of storytelling or communication regarding God and our relationship to his presence.

Characteristics of Jesus' Parables[44]

We can discover at least four characteristics of Jesus' parables which will help us to both identify and understand them better. The first characteristic of Jesus' parables is that they require effort to determine their meaning. We have discussed the parables in general and compared them to wisdom and proverbs. Wisdom is an observation of conventional good conduct. Wisdom literature in general addresses prudent behavior. Once one understands the terms of wisdom the truth is immediately intelligible. A proverb is a statement of obvious truth. Once one hears it the meaning is usually quite clear. A parable, however, does not offer an easy or obvious solution. They require effort to determine their meaning. An examination of any parable will verify this. The parables are told in terms of exaggeration, ambiguity, and metaphor. There is no simple, direct meaning. The metaphorical expression makes it difficult to nail down the meaning. It requires effort and introspection.

The second characteristic of the parables is that they create participation or involvement. The parable engages the hearer so that he/she may become involved. We might say that one needs to see the parable from the inside before involvement can be achieved. But it is clear that parables do not give us information. Nor do they give us an immediate action step. We need to become involved in the parable. We need to discover what it communicates concerning God's reign. Only then are we able to obtain understanding. The difficult saying that Jesus did not want

---

43. Perkins, *Hearing the Parables of Jesus*, 24, 47.

44. For a discussion on the characteristics of parables see Brown et al., "Aspects of New Testament Thought," in *NJBC*, 81:72.

others to understand the parables (Matt 13:13) is actually an expression of the early community noting that many did not understand the parable; neither did they get involved in its meaning.[45]

The third characteristic of parables is that they are challenging, provocative; they demand a response.[46] There is no factual information to which one can remain neutral; parables create a moral imperative. Those who reject the parables are not missing information. The response is either to accept or reject the message.

We need to remind ourselves that salvation is freely offered. It is never forced. This is the root of the notion of grace or what we mean by faith. But if it is freely offered and not forced the response must be the same. Salvation must be won in the social and public realm.[47] It puts demands upon us to which we must respond. The parables of Jesus tease us into action. They provoke us to respond. The parables are challenging. The response completes it.

The fourth characteristic is that Jesus does not complete his parables. As expressed, the parables seem to be without a proper ending.[48] The reason for this is that we add the ending or outcome; it requires our interaction. The hearer has the meaning that he/she brings to the parable. This does not mean that the hearer imposes meaning upon the parable, but rather that the parable is a matter of personal address that is responded to out of the experience of the addressee.

The parable's originality is in the fact that one is left to draw a personal conclusion. This makes it different from other literary forms. Jesus addresses the universal experience of humanity.[49] The meaning is found in humanity and human experience. It is in this experience that one discovers the truth about God's presence.[50] This is what is meant

---

45. See Mark 4:1–12//Matt 13:10–15//Luke 8:4–10. This is more than likely the early church's explanation as to way some did not accept the message more than the purpose of the parables.

46. Brown et al., "Aspects of New Testament Thought," in *NJBC*, 81:75, 76.

47. Perkins, *Hearing the Parables of Jesus*, 16.

48. There often appears to be an ending or interpretation which is called a nimshal. We will examine the nimshal below. These are explanatory helps but are not an actual part of the parable.

49. Perkins, *Hearing the Parables of Jesus*, 37.

50. This was a part of the Jewish experience. It realized God's presence and activity in their desert experience; during the exodus; at Jericho; in the Babylonian captivity; and in its suffering when it had remained faithful to the covenant. Revelation was seen in the experience itself. It was not a matter of a simple, clear message come down from heaven; rather it was discovered in human experience.

when we say that the person has the answer. There is a relationship between God and the person; between the parable and the human experience that permits us to interpret or understand it.[51]

Why Teach in Parables? Religious Experience and Its Expression

The experience of God, the Wholly Other in Crossan's expression, cannot be expressed in univocal terms or notional expressions common to our everyday speech of normal human experiences. The experience of God can only be expressed in symbol or metaphor. Symbol is a nonverbal or sacramental way of expressing this experience.[52] For example, the experience of God's presence in the world is expressed as occurring in bread, wine, water, the cross, and many other similar symbolic expressions. The experience of God can also be expressed in metaphor, that is, by using a verbal expression. Examples of metaphor used in this fashion are father, husband, mother hen, kingdom of God as a banquet, and other similar expressions which can be found in the Scriptures.

Jesus' human experience of God is an important consideration in Christology. It is out of that human experience that Jesus is able to express his vision of God, the kingdom, and his ministry in general. There is an intrinsic connection between Jesus' experience of God and Jesus' expression of that experience in parables.[53] Jesus' vision of God, a result of his personal Abba experience, gives him the content of the kingdom or rule of God. It is at the root of both his parables and his authority.

The parables help us understand how we are able to experience God's rule or presence in history. The parables contain an implicit action step, an orthopraxis. There is the need for repentance or metanoia to enable us to live in the presence of God. The parables also point to the fact that human experience has religious dimensions as was discussed above.[54]

---

51. The parable is about a human situation with a religious significance.

52. This addresses the question; how do we know God? Aquinas proposes that God can only be expressed by the analogy of being. See Aquinas, *Summa Theologiae*, I, q. 13, aa., 1–6.

53. Crossan, *In Parables*, 22.

54. This can be related to the notion of the spiritual life. We possess only one life. It should not be divided into compartments, one spiritual and the other secular, as if they were two different lives. Nevertheless, each possesses its own autonomy.

The Purpose of the Parables

For the most part, the parables contain Jesus' vision or understanding of the kingdom.[55] This is central to his preaching. The parables force the reader or hearer to confront the question "what is the mystery of the rule or kingdom of God?" It represents a way in which we make the reign of God present.[56] This is not to suggest that we are making the kingdom present in the way in which Jesus made it present in his word and deed. But we do participate in making its effects visible in the world.

The parables establish a way of looking at the world, of developing a new relationship to it.[57] It asks, "Who are my mother, my brothers and sisters, my neighbor?"[58] These are the questions each disciple must both ask and respond to. The parables are the means to achieve this new view of the world and our human experience.

Christianity tells the story of the parable as its own. If Jesus did not often complete the parables, he did not mean for them not to be completed. That was the entire point. The church continues to preach the parables in a new context different from that of Jesus and it understands or interprets them in a way that fits its current context or situation. The basic story of the parables is that God is active in the world. Parables express the relationship between God and humans within everyday experience. This relationship or contact cannot be conveyed by discursive speech.[59] It is the formation of a new community which is not limited by social and cultural bounds.

In a larger sense, the Gospels were the way in which the early Christians told the story of Jesus Christ in their own situation.[60] These

---

55. Not all of the parables discuss the kingdom directly. But a large number of the parables begin with "the kingdom of God is like . . ."

56. Dodd's study of the parables led him to conclude that the kingdom was only a realized or present eschatology. See Dodd, *Parables of the Kingdom*, 34. In this study we assume that the kingdom is present, and it is also future where it will be experienced in its fullness.

57. This new vision is largely seeing God active in the world for men and women. The metaphor Jesus used is the kingdom of God. This has been extensively discussed in chapter 4.

58. Jesus asks and answers the question "who is my mother? Who are my brothers?" in Matt 12:48–49. The parable of the good samaritan (Luke 10:29–37) addresses the question concerning neighbor.

59. There is something inherent in created nature and God that makes communication and relations with him possible.

60. It has been suggested that Jesus is the story of God as told in the New Testament.

stories, gathered together in the Scriptures, have become normative for us. But it does not preclude us from retelling the story of Jesus in numerous ways in our own day to account for the differing contexts or social situations we presently live in. To put this in a slightly different way, it has been suggested that the Scriptures can be reread as autobiography.[61] The New Testament is the story that the primitive community shared about its experience of Jesus as Savior. As an extension of that primitive community in time, we too can read ourselves into the story.[62] This is especially relevant with regard to the parables, but it is not limited to them. It is our way of understanding that the gospel message is as relevant today as it was two thousand years ago.

The Interpretation of the Parables

The parables are extended metaphors or similes. They are short stories with a beginning, middle and end. Furthermore, they are challenging, teasing the mind into an active search for meaning. And once this meaning is attained there is a need for a response. Thus, it is clear that parables are not simple statements of fact; they require understanding and interpretation. If the meaning is not immediately apparent, how is the understanding or interpretation of the parable achieved?

The Context of the Parables

The Synoptic parables, as extended metaphors, are of their very nature challenging. Their understanding is not immediately apparent. This is compounded by their challenging history. The origin of the parables is in the preaching of Jesus during his ministry. Four decades after his death and resurrection they acquired their written, literary form in the Synoptic Gospels. Their oral history from Jesus' preaching and the literary record in the Gospels was subject to development and this provides a challenge to properly understand them. We need to locate them in their original context.

---

61. Consider the notion of reading the Scripture autobiographically. It permits the reader to bring his contemporary experiences to bear on the biblical text. See McClendon, *Biography as Theology*.

62. This can readily be seen in the cult of the saints. Their lives are recognized as having imitated some aspect of the life of Christ and they did so in a time and era different from that of Jesus.

The context for Jesus' ministry differs from that of the early church. Jesus preached to believers and nonbelievers alike. While his preaching was well received by some it was rejected by others, sometimes with hostility. And still others, we can imagine, heard the message and were not moved by it. The early church, on the other hand, preached to believers who were receptive to Jesus' message and would have received the parables with delight. The written parables reflect this.

There were also historical markers which distinguish the ministry of Jesus and the postresurrection church. One of these is the separation of Christians and Jews soon after the death of Jesus. The early Christians no longer found themselves welcome in the synagogue. A second historical marker is the destruction of the temple in Jerusalem in AD 70. At this point many of Jesus' principal adversaries fade into the shadows of history. Those who survived were often even more hostile.

Thus, there are two distinct contexts in which the Synoptic parables have been told and this presents some small challenge in correctly understanding them. Nevertheless, the context of Jesus' preaching and the context of the early, postresurrection church are distinguishable. We are confronted with discovering the context of the parable in order to understand its intended meaning.

The Interpretive Framework

Dodd indicated that our understanding of the parables is complimented by other statements that Jesus made about the kingdom independent of the parables. He says, "The interpretation of the parables depends upon the view taken of the kingdom of God."[63] Although I challenge his understanding of Jesus' teaching of the kingdom as only realized or present eschatology, his view that other places in Scripture where Jesus speaks of the kingdom will help us to understand the parables makes eminently good sense. They act as a hermeneutical principle. Meier strongly supports this position. He insists that in order to properly understand the parables we need an interpretive framework. The parables' basic interpretive framework is Jesus' overall mission and message.[64] This would include his preaching of the kingdom, the miracle tradition, and the festive meals. It would include all the teaching attributed to him. Thus,

---

63. Dodd, *Parables of the Kingdom*, 142.
64. Meier, *Marginal Jew*, 4:34.

Jesus' words and deeds supply the hermeneutical key to understanding the message of the parables. It might be said that the parables of Jesus and his other teaching interpret each other. These two ideas are paramount in determining Jesus' vision of God.

An Interpretive Addition to the Parable: The Nimshal[65]

As has been discussed above, the parable is a self-contained story complete in itself. It has an implied beginning, middle, and end. However, in some parables, an interpretive literary device to help interpret the meaning of the parable has been added.[66] This was briefly mentioned in chapter 10. It serves as an explanation or commentary on the parable or an application of its intended meaning. Later rabbis referred to this as a nimshal and for clarity we shall follow this tradition. The nimshal is an addition literarily distinct from the parable and whose purpose is to provide an interpretation or explanation of the parable.

Not all parables have a nimshal. When a parable lacks a nimshal, a brief phrase at the beginning of the parable can function as interpretive.[67] This is often a rhetorical question. The identification of the nimshal is relatively easy as can be seen from the examples of the following parables. The evil tenant of the vineyard, the good Samaritan, and the rich fool all possess a nimshal. Examples of parables which possess an introductory explanatory sentence are the wise and foolish builders and the servant placed over a household. There are many parables that have neither a nimshal nor an introductory explanatory verse. Examples of these are the mustard seed, the treasure hidden in the field, and the prodigal son. There is at least one parable, the widow and the unjust judge, which has both a nimshal and an introductory explanatory verse. Beside all of these examples, the parables of the sower and the wheat and weeds have allegorical interpretations which are separate from the parable itself.

---

65. Nimshal is a verb. It means a lesson learned from the mashal or a lesson or moral of the story. It is an explanation. It is not a word found in the Scripture as is mashal, but it is a concept that is frequently found there. Rabbis used the term extensively.

66. Meier, *Marginal Jew*, 5:242–45. Meier notes that the speaker of several Old Testament parables "supplies an interpretation or application of the story to the present circumstances (what Jewish scholars centuries later would call *nimšāl*)." Meier, *Marginal Jew*, 5:37–38. The verb *nimshal* was regularly used by the rabbis. It carries with it the idea of interpretation. See Meier, *Marginal Jew*, 5:64n18.

67. Meier, *Marginal Jew*, 5:242.

The question that this discussion of the nimshal poses is this: Are the nimshalim and explanatory devices typical of Jesus preaching; of his authoritative teaching?[68] Or are these additions by the evangelists? No definitive answer can be given because of the limited number of parables. But the nimshalim are found in all the earliest independent sources (Mark, Q, M, and L).[69] This seems to be sufficient criteria that Jesus used them, but we are not able to identify any specific nimshal or explanatory verse which belongs to Jesus' authentic teaching.

Stern makes the general observation that "the nimshal originated as a device for supplying the mashal's audience with the information necessary to allow them to apply the mashal's rhetorical message to the exegetical occasion behind its composition."[70] He identifies the parable of the wicked tenant and eleven others as narrative parables of Jesus. He lists the nimshal that is connected to each.[71] It is not clear why he lists only twelve narrative parables since it seems clear that the Synoptic Gospels contain many more. In any case, it seems clear that his study supports our understanding of the nimshal.

The Interpretation of the Parables

The interpretation of the individual parables is beyond the scope of this work.[72] We have been given sufficient guides to interpret the parables for ourselves. We will not attempt to give a list of interpretations because our thesis is that, for the most part, the parables are open ended compressed stories that invite us to engage them. There is no one interpretation good for all time that can be deduced from the parables. They can be read autobiographically, that is, we can find ourselves in them. That is the manner in which they address us personally.[73] The parable of the prodigal son

---

68. Meier, *Marginal Jew*, 5:244.

69. This is the same criterion we used to establish that Jesus did in fact teach in parables.

70. Stern, *Parables in Midrash*, 69.

71. Stern, *Parables in Midrash*, 189–200.

72. There are numerous books written about the interpretation of the parables which are valuable reading. Dodd's excellent book *The Parables of the Kingdom* is still worth reading to obtain some direction in understanding the meaning of parables. Jeremias's books *The Parables of Jesus* and *Rediscovering the Parables* should also be included in a reading list. Perkins's *Hearing the Parables of Jesus* is also useful.

73. This approach is far superior to the allegorical interpretation often used in the past and which was evidently not intended by Jesus.

raises numerous questions for the inquisitive reader. Which brother, the prodigal or the elder, do we identify with? In whom do we see ourselves? Can we complete this story for the father? Does he ever bring his sons together? Is this a challenge between being either free-wheeling or conventional? The parable of the good Samaritan tells us something about who our neighbor is. Can we see ourselves as the priest or Levite? Does this address race or religious issues? What sort of challenges do we see in it? Is the parable of the rich man and Lazarus a challenge to the society in which we live? Does it address those of us who enjoy a comfortable, middle-class existence while so many of our neighbors barely subsist? What does this say about wealth, about being wealthy?

We will examine one parable, the parable of the lost sheep, as an example of how the parables might address us in a contemporary setting.[74] In examining this parable, we are confronted with a question: would any shepherd leave his sheep for a single lost one? It doesn't seem likely although it is not impossible. Why would a shepherd risk the safety of the ninety-nine sheep for one who has strayed? This would seem to indicate that the parables are not about prudent action.

What then is the core meaning of the original parable? How does this relate to the Old Testament notion of God as Shepherd? This was certainly a common theme. Another common theme was to consider the leaders of the people as shepherds. Jesus' parable follows this tradition. We have a choice in how we read *shepherd*. We can further raise the question: is this parable looking at the *lost* or at the *ministers* who have been touched by God? God is not out to destroy sinners as is clear in the parable. Bad shepherds will do this. The shepherd in the parable, while appearing imprudent, is acting on behalf of the sheep that has strayed. It well could be that the shepherd is being addressed.[75]

Both Matthew and Luke have edited the parable to help us understand it and to learn how we are to behave toward others. Matthew gives a warning. He extends concern to every member. It is not God's will that anyone be lost (Matt 18:14). Therefore, in like fashion, every member of the community ought to be our personal concern. We might

---

74. This material is heavily dependent on Perkins. Many of the questions raised here were inspired by her.

75. Note the situation with the American church and the scandal revolving around predator priests and the cover-up by their ordinaries. The shepherds in charge largely failed in their duty to care for their flocks. The parable is a fitting commentary on this tragic situation in which the church finds itself today.

come to see the point of this parable as an address to those who have not strayed. Luke stresses repentance and forgiveness in his edit. Who are the sinners? Are they the ones who ignore the law? Note that this is not judgmental. The rejoicing is rejoicing over one who has repented (Luke 15:7). The conclusion would seem to be that if God is not judgmental, neither should we be.

To sum up, we have three actants in this parable: the shepherd, the flock, and the lost sheep. Metaphorically this seems to address a situation in the community that involves those who have strayed from the community, the faithful and the leadership. While it is inviting to interpret this parable allegorically and see the shepherd as God, it can just as easily be seen that the church leadership is being addressed. We can see, however, that the redactions of Matthew and Luke help us to see a number of possible interpretations.

The Authenticity of the Parables[76]

In recent times a consensus existed among biblical scholars that the synoptic parables provided a reliable access to the teaching of the historical Jesus. It was commonly held that all of the Synoptic parables were authentic parables.[77] C. H. Dodd, a singularly noted biblical scholar, could write as late as 1961 that "the parables are perhaps the most characteristic element in the teaching of Jesus Christ as recorded in the Gospels.... Certainly, there is no part of the Gospel record which has for the reader a clearer ring of authority."[78] No clearer statement could be made concerning the belief in the historical authenticity of the parables of Jesus Christ. Jeremias was still promoting this idea a decade later. Meier points out that this was done by most biblical scholars without accounting for the more recent historical-critical scholarship.[79] This confidence in the authenticity of the parables no longer exists. The question now is whether or not we

---

76. It was common in the past to claim that the parables were the most common characteristic element of Jesus' teaching that indicated authenticity. See Meier, *Marginal Jew*, 2:290, 352. He quotes Dodd, *Parables of the Kingdom*, 3, and Jeremias, *Parables of Jesus*, 11, to support this claim.

77. Dodd, *Parables of the Kingdom*; Jeremias, *Parables of Jesus*.

78. Dodd, *Parables of the Kingdom*, 1. Meier gives an exhaustive list of scholars who agreed with Dodd. See Meier, *Marginal Jew*, 5:74–76n54.

79. Meier, *Marginal Jew*, 5:77n54.

A THEOLOGICAL EVALUATION OF THE PARABLES

can find parables that can satisfy the requirements of the historical-critical method. This much, however, is clear: Jesus preached in parables.

How many of the Synoptic narrative parables can be assigned to the historical Jesus? As we shall see below, there are very few parables that can be assigned as authentic. The inability to establish the authenticity of a particular parable, however, does not mean it is not an authentic teaching of Jesus. It simply means that we have insufficient evidence to declare the parable historically authentic. Some of the parables are creations of the early disciples after the death and resurrection of Jesus. Meier believes that at least one is an invention of the evangelist.[80] That is not to deny the authorship of many Synoptic parables to Jesus; it is simply noting that, given our sources, we are not able to say with a high degree of probability, that some of the narrative parables are authentic teaching of the historical Jesus. A number of the parables have been edited by first century Christians. We might assume, however, that since parables were such a principal part of Jesus' teaching that his disciples might well have imitated him in their own preaching of the kingdom.

Having made the above claim it will become clear that, because of the failure to satisfy the criteria already established, there are only four parables that can be established as actually authentic parables of Jesus. These are the parables of the mustard seed, the evil tenants of the vineyard, the great supper, and the talents/pounds.[81] More parables could join this exclusive group but at the present time it is beyond our ability to establish more than four as the authentic teaching of Jesus. It will become clear that some come from the early church.

Conclusion and Resume

The parables are a real treasure in the life of the church, and it is easy to understand that for centuries they were understood as containing an easily accessible part of the teaching of the historical Jesus. Meier pointed out that, even for many modern scholars, the parables were considered to come directly from the historical Jesus.[82] He has seriously and legitimately challenged the view that all of the parables are from the historical Jesus.

---

80. Meier tells us that "he will argue that the parable of the Good Samaritan is a pure creation of Luke the Evangelist." Meier, *Marginal Jew*, 5:51. His argument is given in 5:199–209.

81. See Meier, *Marginal Jew*, 5:231. His discussion on this issue is in chapter 40.

82. Meier, *Marginal Jew*, 5:30.

He believes that only four can match the criteria needed to determine their authenticity.[83] He further proposed that "the parable of the good Samaritan is a creation not of Jesus but of either the early church or Luke himself."[84] Nevertheless, we can readily understand why, after a century of research by Scripture scholars, the parables still stand as a treasure for us. One of the most important achievements of that research is that we no longer understand the parables as allegories, as had been done for centuries. This has helped us to gain a better definition, and to understand them as extended metaphors or as compressed stories. Their meaning includes both a challenge and an invitation to respond.

We have a newfound appreciation for the parables. More recent research has reinforced the understanding that the historical Jesus did indeed teach in parables and that they were central to his teaching. What may have caught many of us off guard is the postulate that we can trace only a few specific parables back to the historical Jesus. However, because we cannot determine by means of the established criteria set down that a parable is an authentic teaching of Jesus, we cannot conclude apodictically that it did not come from Jesus. It is certain that Jesus was a teacher of parables. Many parables do go back to Jesus; but many seem to come from the early church. We can certainly understand that the parables did not come to us pure and without alloy; they came to us through the intermediation of many.

Properly understanding the parables is more important than establishing their origin. The search for a framework to help us understand them seems indispensable. The words and deeds of Jesus provide us with that interpretive framework. Thus, determining the context in which the parable is set is of great importance. It was also pointed out that some of the parables carried with them an interpretive statement, differing in literary genre from the parables, which pointed to the meaning intended. Later usage named this genre nimshal. Some of these are identified with Jesus, others with the evangelist or the early church.

We can readily see that the interpretation of the parables resides with Jesus and his audience; it resides with the early church; and it resides with each of us who hear them anew. We are invited to interpret them just as the evangelists interpreted them for their early communities. Because the parables are open ended, that is, because Jesus

---

83. See Meier, *Marginal Jew*, 5:231.
84. Meier, *Marginal Jew*, 5:199.

never completed them, we complete them. We can read ourselves into the situation of the parable just as we can read ourselves into all of the Scriptures. The parables continue to nourish us because we bring our own situation, our own experience, to the teaching of Jesus.

12

How Jesus Understood Himself

Introduction

THERE CAN BE LITTLE doubt that Jesus was a charismatic person. The scriptural data suggests as much. He could draw large crowds, and they appear to have followed him on his itinerant mission throughout Galilee. The Synoptic Gospels speak of numerous situations in which the crowds were amazed at both his teaching and his healings and exorcisms.[1] Jesus was conscious that he possessed the authority to conduct his mission in the particular manner he chose.[2]

What Are We Looking For

Can we discover anything of Jesus' self-understanding from the scriptural data? In the previous chapters we have examined several themes

---

1. Jesus was recognized as having the authority to perform his mighty deeds and to teach a new teaching unlike others. Amazement is expressed for the deeds Jesus performed in Mark 1:27; 5:20; 5:42; 7:37; in Matt 15:31; and in Luke 4:36; 5:26; 9:43; 11:14. It is also expressed concerning his teaching in Mark 1:27; 6:2; 12:7; in Matt 13:54; and in Luke 2:47 (the boy Jesus in the temple); 4:22. John 7:15 affirms that Jesus' adversaries (the Jews) were amazed at his teaching. This event takes place in the temple precincts during the Feast of Tabernacles.

2. It has been suggested that the temptation in the desert was a time of discernment or reflection for Jesus to define the kind of messiahship his ministry would include. It seems clear that he changed from a baptizer in the company of John the Baptist to an itinerant preacher when he was on his own. See the comments above in chapter 3.

that were prominent in Jesus' mission. We concluded that much of Jesus' teaching and praxis as described in the Scriptures is authentic, that it can be traced back to him with some historical certainty.[3] This present inquiry is about Jesus' personal self-understanding and how he understood his role in the kingdom. We are not addressing Jesus' psychological state or what he was actually thinking at any given moment in his public life. It is not possible to attain either of these from the biblical texts.[4] We cannot discover a person's thought process or psychology from textual evidence. We are attempting to determine Jesus' consciousness about his personal identity and his role in the kingdom.[5]

Why Search for Jesus' Self-Understanding?

Why is this subject important enough to devote a chapter to it? It is clearly not a part of our faith commitment. How Jesus understood himself and his mission has important significance for us in both our devotional and theological lives. Discovering Jesus' self-understanding gives us a better picture of the one whom we have come to call the Christ; it prevents us from imposing on him our personal piety and our political or religious/theological views. This prevents us from creating a false understanding of Jesus based upon an imaginative construct. From a positive perspective, discovering something of Jesus' self-understanding provides us with a valuable means by which we can better understand the Christ of faith. It acts as a basis or grounding for our faith affirmations. This is significant because it serves as a hermeneutic, a way of understanding or interpreting the Jesus of the Gospels more authentically. Let Jesus be Jesus; let him speak for himself.

We are able to discover a considerable amount of Jesus' self-understanding. The flowering of recent biblical studies has provided us with the authentic historical tradition of Jesus. Being able to identify the self-understanding of the historical Jesus brings us closer to understanding Jesus the Christ. Jesus' self-understanding is the reservoir out of which

---

3. Refer to the "indisputable historical facts" discussed in the preface.

4. This cannot be done for any historical character. The texts simply do not permit it. Erik H. Erikson attempted to discover Martin Luther's psychological state from his writings, but the attempt was not entirely successful. See Erikson, *Young Man Luther*.

5. The expression *consciousness* has been studiously avoided because it might lead one to think of the inner working of one's mind. There is no way in which we can discover the inner working of a person's mind. That is beyond our sources.

he acted. It goes to the very center of the person to whom we attach ourselves as his followers.

Jesus' Self-Understanding

This examination will point out what can be defended logically as belonging to Jesus' personal self-understanding. The justification for making this claim is that the manner in which a person expresses himself or the things that a person does gives us some insight into his/her self-understanding.[6] Our words and actions reflect our personal attitudes as well as our personal self-understanding. What is true for us is also true for the Jesus of history. Thus, Jesus' authentic words and deeds, his teaching and praxis, can lead us to make some provisional statement, albeit tentative, concerning his self-understanding. How did he, in his human nature, understand himself and his mission?[7] Furthermore, the way in which he is observed by others may implicitly indicate or support something of his self-understanding.[8]

The Foundation of Jesus' Self-Understanding[9]

A foundation for any of our claims to describe an authentic self-understanding of Jesus of Nazareth can be discovered in the indisputable facts discussed in the preface as well as his authentic teaching and deeds. Jesus' self-understanding and his authentic teaching are intimately joined.[10]

---

6. We are including in this any of Jesus' authentic teachings. Any teaching that can be traced back to Jesus must of necessity be a part of his self-understanding.

7. In her book *Consider Jesus: Waves of Renewal in Christology*, Elizabeth Johnson deals with "Jesus' Self-Knowledge" in chapter 3. This is an excellent examination of whether Jesus understood that he was the Word of God in an ontological sense. In this chapter we are looking at Jesus' self-understanding in his human nature. What did Jesus understand about himself and his role in salvation purely as a grace-filled human being?

8. Keep in mind that we are examining texts which, in many cases, are reports of what the observer witnessed. There are extremely few sayings or narratives that we can actually declare as *ipsissima verba* of Jesus.

9. The following is an examination of the significant scriptural data that indicates something of Jesus' self-understanding and his authority. It is an effort to get behind the christological affirmations which were applied to Jesus as the Christ after the resurrection. We will attempt to be as historical as possible, that is, we are looking for whatever can be judged as authentic to Jesus of Nazareth.

10. Meier, *Marginal Jew*, 2:451. Jesus' authentic teaching will be synthesized and

HOW JESUS UNDERSTOOD HIMSELF

Throughout the previous chapters there were numerous mentions of Jesus' self-understanding. We are going to organize them with the intention of gaining a better, more unified picture of Jesus of Nazareth.

Jesus' Self-Understanding and His Relationship to God

Jesus' self-understanding, his personal consciousness or awareness of himself, was rooted in his intimate, unique relationship to God.[11] Jesus must have had a profound personal experience of the Father which we identified as his Abba experience.[12] This experience is foundational for his self-understanding. His intimate relationship with God provided him with his vision of the kingdom and his own roll in that mission. Jesus was aware of his unique relationship to his Abba.[13]

Although we speak of Jesus' self-understanding as an event at a single moment in his life, it is just as likely that his self-understanding, and his experience of God, his Abba experience, developed over a period of time. It did not come all at once in a single instance. There appears to be several significant shifts in Jesus' thought. It was proposed above that he had a serious commitment to John the Baptist. The first shift which followed this commitment occurred when he changed his mission from a baptizer to an itinerant preacher. The motive for this might have been the imprisonment of John. Unfortunately, we have no way of determining this with any certitude. Another shift was in his preaching of the kingdom. This differs from John in as much as Jesus preached it as an offer of salvation, John as a matter of repentance. His personal understanding of himself as the eschatological prophet developed. When this took place is difficult to determine. It is obvious that it was not a part of Jesus' thought during the time he spent with John. The third shift occurred when he redirected his ministry from Galilee to the final days in Jerusalem. Some have speculated that Jesus was discouraged with the results of his preaching in Galilee, but we have no way of determining this with certitude. It is possible to identify other developments in the life of Jesus. He seems to have shifted his preaching from the house of Israel to one which included

---

developed in chapter 13.

11. Brown, *Introduction to New Testament Christology*, 72.

12. The Abba is also discussed in chapter 5, page 85n3. The subject matter is dispersed throughout the various chapters.

13. Brown, *Introduction to New Testament Christology*, 72.

gentiles. The final events in Jerusalem indicate a dramatic collision with Israel. In any case, it seems evident that Jesus' self-understanding as well as his understanding of his mission developed over time.

Jesus Understood Himself as the Eschatological Prophet[14]

That Jesus was understood as a prophet by the early church seems easy to establish. After his death, the disciples on the way to Emmaus describe Jesus as a prophet (Luke 24:19). More to our point there is sufficient evidence that Jesus was recognized as a prophet by his contemporaries during his public ministry.[15] The evidence is from both Mark 6:15; 8:27–28 par. and Special Luke (Luke 7:39).[16] Fuller suggests that the logia describing Jesus as John *redivivus* (Mark 6:14–16, 28) are genuine memories. It would support the notion that some of Jesus' contemporaries believed he was a prophet.

Did Jesus understand himself as a prophet? He spoke as a prophet in his use of blessings and woes.[17] He acted as a prophet in his prophetic, symbolic acts (Mark 11: 1–19 parr.). Jesus also compared himself to a prophet (Mark 6:4//Matt 13:57//Luke 4:24, Special Luke 13:33; and John 4:44). These are not explicit self-designations; however, Jesus either identifies himself with the activity of the prophets or he implies that he is a prophet.

There is even stronger evidence that he understood himself as the eschatological prophet. This has been treated extensively above.[18] It was argued that Jesus' response to the emissaries sent by John the Baptist indicated that he understood himself as the eschatological prophet and that he was the fulfillment of the prophecy of Isaiah.[19] Luke has

---

14. This was examined at length in chapter 5.

15. Fuller, *Foundations of New Testament Christology*, 126.

16. These two sources (Mark 6:15; 8:27–28 parr. and Luke 7:39) provide us with multiple attestation that Jesus was understood as a prophet.

17. There are numerous references to Jesus speaking in terms of blessings, woes, and warnings. These are typically prophetic expressions. See Mark 12:38–40; Matt 12:23:1–9; Luke 6:20–26 (Sermon on the Plain); 11:37–54; 20:45–47.

18. This entire episode has been treated above in chapter 5. It will be from this understanding that we will ultimately derive our understanding of Jesus as the Christ, the Messiah.

19. The question put to Jesus by the disciples of John is likely rooted in their understanding of the coming of the prophet Elijah which was announced by the prophet Malachi. Malachi was written shortly before 455 BC, but the ideas contained therein

retrojected this historical response into his description of Jesus' inauguration of his Galilean ministry at the synagogue in Nazareth (Luke 4:16–22).[20] Its addition supports the notion that Jesus recognized himself as the prophet who fulfills the prophecy of Isaiah. John Meier concludes that "Jesus saw himself as an eschatological prophet and miracle worker along the lines of Elijah."[21] As the eschatological prophet, "Jesus undoubtedly understands that all he does [is] to be the vehicle of the coming of God in power."[22] While Meier's study is much more scholarly and lengthier than this presentation, the conclusion is the same. That Jesus understood himself as the eschatological prophet is extremely important and it supports the remaining conclusions which will be made concerning his self-understanding.

Jesus' Understanding as the Messiah, the Christ

The title *Messiah* denoted an eschatological agent sent by God in the end-time.[23] Both before and during Jesus public ministry there was a strong messianic expectation.[24] Fitzmyer informs us that there was the development of "a vivid Messianism of different forms, which was current in various types of Palestinian Judaism at the time when Jesus of Nazareth appeared on the scene in the days of Herod the Great and his successors."[25] In general, the Messiah was the expected anointed king of the House of David.[26] The Messiah was understood in both a political and a religious

---

were widespread during the context of Jesus' public life. Elijah is specifically named as the one who is to come in Mal 3:23. He is to prepare for the coming day of the Lord. Jesus quotes Mal 3:23 in reference to John the Baptist as the precursor of the one who is to usher in the day of the Lord. The note in the NABRE indicates that Jesus was quoting from Isa 26:19; 29:18–19; 35:5–6; 61:1. Was this a case where the former teacher (John) heard that the student (Jesus) was going in a new, different direction?

20. Matthew begins Jesus' Galilean ministry in Capernaum (Matt 4:12–17). Mark does not specifically name Capernaum, but it is implied (Mark 1:12–15). Luke shifts the inauguration of the Galilean ministry to Nazareth and inserts Jesus' response to John's disciples into the synagogue scene by using the medium of the scroll from Isaiah.

21. Meier, *Marginal Jew*, 4:415. Meier repeats this idea often. He affirms that this evidence was argued in the first three volumes of his study.

22. Meier, *Marginal Jew*, 3:497.

23. Fitzmyer, *One Who Is to Come*, 2.

24. Fitzmyer, *One Who Is to Come*, 2, 102, 134.

25. Fitzmyer, *One Who Is to Come*, 134.

26. Fitzmyer, *One Who Is to Come*, 132.

sense. He was expected to come at a future time to deliver the people, to subdue their enemies, and to rule over his kingdom.

Shortly after Jesus death and much earlier than the development of the New Testament writings the expression *Christ* (*Christos*, the Greek form of Messiah) became the title par excellence for Jesus in the Greek speaking world.[27] Can we determine whether Jesus understood himself as the Messiah, the Christ? Did others, during his lifetime, identify him as such? There are three blocks of data that address this challenge. They are Peter's confession of Jesus as the Christ (Mark 8:27–30//Matt 16:13–20//Luke 9:18–21); Jesus' trial before the Sanhedrin (Mark 14:53–65//Matt 26:57–68//Luke 22:54–55, 63–71); and Jesus' trial before Pilate (Mark 15:2–5//Matt 27:11–14//Luke 23:2–5). These will be examined below for their possible contribution to resolve our question.

Jesus did not use christological titles such as Messiah/Christ for himself. Did he think of himself as the Messiah? There is no record of Jesus using this title as a self-designation. The title may have been used on rare occasions by others to identify him. One such place (our first block) is in Peter's identification of Jesus as the Messiah which took place at Caesarea Philippi (Mark 8:27–30 parr.). When Jesus asks the disciples the question "who do you say that I am?" Peter responded, "You are the Messiah" (Mark 8:29).[28] Jesus then tells his disciples not to tell anyone. Why were they silenced? While not denying that he is the Messiah, it is possible that Jesus did not want to be identified as a/the Messiah for fear that it could be confused with a militant messianism. Jesus' call for silence may well have been to prevent a misunderstanding of the kingdom as an earthly, political kingdom and that Jesus might be understood as a ruler and conqueror.[29] It could also be that Jesus' silence "may suggest that he [Jesus] did not regard his role or mission as messianic."[30]

Brown is of the opinion that Jesus was actually called Messiah by his followers during his lifetime.[31] Fitzmyer agrees and points out that

---

27. The title Messiah (*Christos* or anointed one) would have had little theological significance outside of Palestine. Other christological titles such as Son of God or Lord became more important. Christ takes on the significance of a proper name.

28. Both the NABRE and the NRSV translate *Christos* as Messiah; the New Jerusalem Bible (NJB) translates it as Christ. Luke is very similar to Mark. Matthew adds "Son of the living God" to the response. It is obvious that the translators have chosen to translate the Greek *Christos* to match the actual situation.

29. This is what is rejected in the narrative of the temptation.

30. Fitzmyer, *One Who Is to Come*, 140.

31. Brown, *Introduction to New Testament Christology*, 79.

whatever Jesus' self-understanding might have been there were some of Jesus contemporaries who thought of him as a messianic figure. Fitzmyer continues, "There is, however, no reason to regard the Gospel accounts as wholly devoid of historical accuracy in this question, even if there is no way of assessing with certainty whether a messianic role would have been part of the consciousness of the Jesus of history."[32] We are forced to conclude that there is no way to determine Jesus' self-understanding from these sources.

The other important block of material which might provide insight into Jesus' consciousness of his identity is the Synoptic version of the trial before the Sanhedrin (Mark 14:53-65 parr.). In Mark's version the high priest asks Jesus, "Are you the Messiah, the son of the Blessed One?" Jesus responds, "I am" (Mark 14:61). Jesus' response in Matthew and Luke are not so clear. In Matthew's version, Jesus responds to the high priest's question by saying, "You have said so" (Matt 26:64). Luke is only slightly different. In Luke's version Jesus responds, "If I tell you [that I am the Messiah], you will not believe" (Luke 22:67). From these responses it is not clear that Jesus considered himself to be the Messiah. Brown believes that Jesus did not deny that he was the Messiah but that he was cautious because of a possible misunderstanding. Neither did he affirm that he was the Messiah.[33] It is likely that the narrative as written was influenced by the conflict between the synagogue and the early postresurrection church.[34] Again we are forced to conclude that there is no way to determine Jesus' self-understanding from these sources.

The third block of material, the trial before Pilate (Mark 15:2-5//Matt 27:11-14//Luke 23:2-5) similarly offers little help in determining Jesus' consciousness.[35] The trial before Pilate is ever so brief. In Luke's version the assembly that brought Jesus to Pilate make the accusation that Jesus "maintains that he is the Messiah, a king" (Luke 23:2b). Luke is alone in including this accusation in the trial. Jesus makes no defense. The question Pilate puts to Jesus is whether he is king of the Jews. He (Pilate) ignores the accusation that Jesus is the Messiah. There is nothing in these pericopes that gives us a hint as to Jesus' personal understanding. There is a conscious effort on the part of the evangelists postresurrection to identify Jesus as Messiah and king. In the primitive church, the titles

---

32. Fitzmyer, *One Who Is to Come*, 140.
33. Brown, *Introduction to New Testament Christology*, 79.
34. Brown, *Introduction to New Testament Christology*, 77.
35. See Fitzmyer, *One Who Is to Come*, 141.

for Jesus develop rapidly because of their need to identify him. But this tells us nothing of Jesus' self-understanding.

It seems clear that there is no way to determine with any degree of certainty that Jesus thought of himself as the Messiah. The early church used the title because there was some basis in his life for its use; the meaning is not taken from a predetermined definition of Messiah. Rather it is from the person of Jesus himself. Jesus' life and death gave meaning to the title. Concerning this Fuller makes the following observation: "For all the Messianic titles mean just this: that God was in Christ, present and active and redeeming. There can be no doubt that this is how Jesus understood himself and his mission. His Messiahship is to be sought, not in his explicit use of Messianic titles (this was the work of the postresurrection church, which transformed its tradition of Jesus' sayings and memory of his doings in the light of its new faith), but in the context of what he said and did."[36]

Jesus' miracles and message are implied in the messianic titles. Jesus connects his miracles with the message that the reign of God is here; and he does so without any messianic claims. Faith in his messiahship is postresurrection. It is how the early church understood him and came to profess him in faith. The church implies the notion of reign of God and miracles in the title Christ. The primitive church modified the title Messiah to fit the reality of Jesus. Jesus' words and deeds define the notion of Messiah.

Jesus' Understanding of His Identity as Son of God

The Son of God is one of the principal christological titles expressed by the primitive postresurrection community. Paul understood Jesus as the preexistent Son of God and the title is prominent in his authentic epistles.[37] An examination of the Gospel use of the title is enlightening. At the annunciation, the angel Gabriel declared Jesus to be the Son of God (Luke 1:35). Luke's genealogy contains the title (Luke 3:38). The title is

---

36. Fuller, *Interpreting the Miracles*, 14.

37. The postresurrection confession of Jesus as the Son of God is well established. The authentic Pauline use can be found in the epistles to the Romans, 2 Corinthians, Galatians, and Philippians. It is clear that Paul made a distinction between the preexistent Son and a son by adoption (Rom 8:14–15). There are three notable poems in the New Testament that confess Jesus as Son of God. They are John 1:1–18; Phil 2:5–11; and Col 1:15–30.

found on the lips of John the Baptist (John 1:34) and of Martha (John 11:27). The disciples who witness Jesus walking on the water profess him as the Son of God (Matt 14:33). Jesus was declared to be the Son of God by the demons.[38] The high priest at Jesus' trial before the Sanhedrin (Matt 26:63//Luke 22:70), the crowd before Pilate (John 19), and the passersby at the crucifixion (Matt 27:40) all refer to Jesus as the Son of God. All of these references appear to be confessional statements more than authentic historical utterances. The early church clearly declared its belief that Jesus is the Son of God in the baptismal narrative (Mark 1:11 par.), in the prologue of the Gospel of John (John 1:14b), and in the conclusion to the Gospel of John (John 20:31).

Is there any scriptural evidence that Jesus used this title for himself? There is no such indication in the Synoptics. The Gospel of John puts the title on Jesus' lips three times: during the Nicodemus narrative (John 3:18), the Samaritan woman narrative (John 5:25), and the raising of Lazarus (John 11:4). Similar to those references mentioned above, these too are obviously confessional and not historical. There are numerous references that Jesus considers himself to be the son of Abba and the son–father theme is prominent in the Gospels. This would provide the basis for the christological title which became a confessional statement after the resurrection. But it would give us no idea of Jesus' understanding.

What would this question mean if it were asked of the historical Jesus? "Are you, Jesus of Nazareth, a/the son of God?" The expression signifies a relationship between Jesus with his God/Abba. This could mean that, in his human nature, he was a child of God by adoption as are all of us.[39] Indeed, he taught us to pray in the same manner that he prayed. He taught us to live in the presence of God as he lived. He clearly understood the relationship between himself and his Abba. This understanding of relationship presents no theological problem. Jesus understood himself as a son of God, a child of God, by adoption. This is a matter of grace and not a union in person as the Council of Chalcedon would declare in the fifth century AD.

---

38. Jesus was declared to be Son of God by the devil during his temptation (Luke 4:3, 9//Matt 4:3, 6), by unclean spirits (Mark 3:11), by the Gadarene demoniac (Matt 8:29), by demons at a healing (Luke 4:41).

39. The theme "child" is employed occasionally in the Gospels to express the relationship of discipleship. It is found in Mark 9:33–37//Matt 18:1–5//Luke 9:46–48 (the greatest in the kingdom) and Mark 10:13–16//Matt 19:13–15//Luke 18:15–17 (blessing of the children). It is clear that Jesus understood that God was his (and his disciples') Father/Abba. Sonship is implied. See chapter 5, above.

However, if this question were asked from the perspective of a high Christology, from the perspective of the declaration of the Council of Nicea, it would not have made a great deal of sense.[40] Would Jesus in his human nature understand himself to be united to God his Father? Would he have understood himself to be a Son of God by divine filiation? Nothing in his mission indicates that he was conscious of this relationship. In the Gospel of John, Thomas declares that the risen Christ is "my Lord and my God [*Theos*]" (John 20:28). This confession would have made no sense during Jesus' earthly life.[41] It can be strongly affirmed that Jesus did not understand himself as equal in nature to the Abba he prayed to and to whom he was obedient.

The consciousness of Jesus as to his divine sonship is a theological question which cannot be answered from the scriptural evidence that describes the preresurrected Christ.[42] There is nothing to indicate what his understanding about this union might have been. One might ask if Jesus was united to God as the council declares, would he have known it? Or would he have had some insight into this union since it is part of his identity? This compelled early theologians to attribute the beatific vision to Jesus. It would be in this direct vision of God in his human nature that he would have known fully who he was. His identity as Son of God would be clear during his historical life. Since the early twentieth century this position has not been widely held and thus the problem of Jesus' knowledge of his true identity becomes a matter of inquiry.[43] Since the early part of the twentieth century a deeper exploration into the Scriptures has reconsidered the question of Jesus' knowledge.

---

40. The Council of Nicea (AD 325) declared that Jesus was true God. This is a doctrine of faith. The Council of Chalcedon (AD 451) declared that Jesus the Christ was one person (the divine) united in two natures (divine and human).

41. This is one of three places in the Scriptures in which Jesus is addressed as God (*Theos*). The other two are John 1:1 and Heb 1:8–9. See Brown, *Jesus God and Man*, 23–28, for a developed discussion.

42. This is not to challenge the reality of the divine sonship of Jesus the Christ. It is a question about his knowledge of this doctrine.

43. Karl Rahner has dealt at length and in depth with this issue. He argues that Jesus, in his humanity, must have had knowledge of his divine union. He attributes "a direct union of his consciousness with God, a *visio immediate*, to Jesus during his earthly life, but this without qualifying, or having to qualify it as 'beatific.'" See Rahner, "Dogmatic Reflections," 203. He asserts that this understanding cannot be simply subconscious or unconscious. It is an illumination. See Rahner, "Current Problems in Christology," 169. For a further discussion on this subject see Von Balthasar, *Theo Drama: Theological Dramatic Theory*, 3:173–83.

Elizabeth Johnson has made a contemporary examination about Jesus' self-understanding in light of his divine sonship.[44] Her reflection is worth reading. Given the denial of the beatific vision to Jesus, is theology able to suppose some sort of knowledge Jesus might have had of his true identity? Unfortunately, there is insufficient evidence to inform us whether this was a part of Jesus' self-understanding. The theological problem will never be definitively resolved.

The Christological Titles

From what has been said above, the Son of God is not a self-designation of Jesus of Nazareth. With the exception of the title Son of Man, the same can be said of the other christological titles.[45] No other christological titles are found on Jesus' lips. They are clearly postresurrection and therefore there is no way of determining Jesus' self-understanding. It is well established that during Jesus' ministry God alone would have been recognized as Savior. References to Jesus as Savior are confessional. While all of these titles are important in the study of Christology, they are not useful in our present examination of Jesus' self-understanding.

Jesus' Understanding of His Authority

It is difficult for us to imagine that Jesus did not have authority to act for God and that he was not fully aware of his authority. Faith would seem to demand such an understanding. Is it possible to establish Jesus' understanding of his authority? Does he ever claim authority either explicitly or implicitly?

---

44. Johnson, *Consider Jesus*, 35–47.

45. For a deeper discussion of the christological titles see Fuller, *Foundations of New Testament Christology*, 102–31. Fuller examines the titles of the Messiah, the Son of David, the Son of God, Kyrios, Son of Man, and the eschatological prophet. See also Brown, *Introduction to New Testament Christology*, 73–102, 133–41. Brown examines the titles Messiah, Son of God, and Son of Man. He also explores the notion of preexistence.

Jesus: The Person and the Mission

Preliminary Considerations: Jesus' Contemporaries and the Early Church

The recognition of the early church as well as the experience of Jesus' contemporaries provides us with a foundation upon which to build. They provide us with an appropriate introduction to discover Jesus understanding of his authority.

The postresurrection Christian community believed that Jesus possessed authority that emanates from God. This was a matter of faith. Scriptural evidence strongly supports as much. The Great Commission, the last narrative in Matthew, describes Jesus acting with and claiming to have all authority (Matt 28:16–20).[46] "All power [*exousia*] in heaven and on earth has been given to me" (Matt 28:18).[47] This powerful missionary statement is postresurrection. What did Jesus do in his lifetime to create this impression?[48]

Jesus' contemporaries recognized Jesus' authority. The number of expressions in the Gospel that indicate Jesus possessed authority, either explicitly or implicitly, is impressive.[49] These expressions are often joined with sayings or narratives that tell us that Jesus' words and deeds caused a great deal of amazement or astonishment.[50] The evangelists often report that the crowds were amazed at Jesus' preaching because he spoke with authority. After beginning his Gospel with the call of the first disciples, Mark records the episode in which Jesus cures a demoniac. We read, "All were amazed and asked one another, 'What is this? A

---

46. The appearance of Jesus to the apostles recorded in John 20:19–23 describes the risen Jesus as having the authority to give his disciples the power to forgive sins.

47. The Greek word for this verse in the critical edition of the New Testament is *exousia*. *Exousia* translates as authority, right, liberty ability, capability, power over. The NAB, NRSV, NJB, and NKJV versions translate *exousia* as authority. The NABRE has chosen to translate it as power. Authority seems a better translation given the context of this pericope. There is another Greek word (*dunamis*) that is translated as power. It could have been used if power, not authority, was meant.

48. This has some significance because the church's claim to authority is based upon the authority of Christ. The amazement of the crowd is almost always followed by a reference to Jesus' teaching or acting with authority.

49. There are more than a dozen independent references in Scripture which refer to Jesus' authority. They are multiply attested in both sources and forms.

50. There are numerous references to amazement shown to Jesus' works or word in the New Testament. There are statements that record that his disciples, the crowds, the chief priests, the scribes and elders, the Pharisees, and even Pilate expressed their amazement at the mission of Jesus. They are found in Mark, John, Q, and L. They are also found in different forms. This supports their historicity.

new teaching with authority [*exousia*]. He commands even the unclean spirits and they obey him'" (Mark 1:27//Luke 4:36).⁵¹ That people were amazed at the words and works of Jesus is well documented.

The many references that Jesus taught with authority are multiply attested both in sources and in forms. This is usually a strong indication that these statements likely go back to the historical Jesus.⁵² This points out something that we more than likely suspected. Jesus, the charismatic, was able to cause amazement among those to whom he preached. That he spoke with authority differentiates him from other religious teachers.⁵³

Jesus Understands That He Has Authority

Is there other textual evidence indicating that Jesus' spoke or acted with authority and was aware of it? The following block of three texts is pertinent to approach this problem.

The first block comes from Jesus' calling and sending the Twelve. Jesus calls the Twelve that he might "send them forth to preach and to have authority [*exousia*] to drive out demons" (Mark 3:14-15).⁵⁴ When Jesus sent them on their missionary appointment, he "gave them authority [*exousia*] over unclean spirits" (Mark 6:7). The parallel version in Matt 10:1 adds authority to "cure every disease and illness." Luke 9:1-2 adds power (*dunamis*) and authority (*exousia*) "over all demons and to cure diseases and he sent them to proclaim the kingdom of God and to heal" (Luke 9:1-2). Jesus gave the Twelve the authority to do what he did. It is clearly implied that he understood himself to have the authority that he gave to his disciples. Meier points out that this text in which Jesus appointed and sent the Twelve consists of a mixture of Mark, Q, and M.⁵⁵ It also shows coherence with Jesus' mission, that is, what he did. Jesus calling

---

51. It is of no little interest that Matthew closes his Sermon on the Mount with this exact verse (Matt 7:28-29). His only change to the verse is the addition that Jesus did not teach like the scribes.

52. An argument which would militate against this conclusion is that these statements do not show discontinuity with the early community. These references to Jesus' authority could be a confessional statement from the early church. It is what was believed.

53. Their technique was to exegete a biblical text, mining it for meaning. Jesus never did. He is always described from a perspective of authority.

54. The Greek word *exousia* and the Latin *potestas* are used synonymously in the New Testament. They mean authority or power.

55. Meier, *Marginal Jew*, 2:432.

disciples and selecting the Twelve is one of the "almost indisputable facts" associated with his mission. It suggests that this narrative of Jesus sending the Twelve is based upon historical fact. Though this does not find Jesus claiming to have authority it strongly indicates that he possesses what he gives. It is one of the sources that implicitly inform us that Jesus understood that he possessed authority and acted upon it.

The second block is a strong reference of Jesus' understanding of his authority. It is the cure of the mute (Matt 12:22–30//Luke 11:14–23). We have already established that this is an authentic miracle of Jesus, and it is the star witness for Jesus referring to the kingdom as a present reality.[56] Jesus' reference to his authority is implicit but very strong. He proclaims to his adversaries, "But if it is by the finger of God that [I] drive out demons, then the kingdom of God has come upon you" (Luke 11:20; brackets in the original). While the appeal to Jesus' understanding that he has authority is implicit, it is exceedingly strong. It would be difficult to imagine that this event occurred without Jesus understanding that he had the authority to heal and to announce the presence of the kingdom.

The third block of material is from Q, the emissaries from John (Matt 11:2–6//Luke 7:18–23). This narrative established Jesus' understanding that he was the eschatological prophet and that his miracles were performed as a sign pointing to the kingdom of God. This implies that Jesus would have understood that he possessed authority from God to fulfill this ministry.

There is one other Gospel reference that we should not neglect in searching for Jesus' self-understanding. The parable of the great supper (Matt 22:1–10//Luke 14:16–14) is an authentic parable and it is quite possibly Jesus' last. Matthew situates it in the temple area shortly after Jesus had cleansed the temple (Matt 21:12–17).[57] Jesus is confronted by the priests and elders (Matt 21:23). The parable explains the hostility towards Jesus as well as his personal understanding of his role. Meier explains that "Jesus dares to make an individual's response to him and his message the determining factor as to whether he or she will be admitted to the eschatological banquet, which is imminent."[58] It is clear that, as eschatological prophet, Jesus understood his role was to usher in the kingdom of God.

---

56. Meier, *Marginal Jew*, 2:399. It is also the most important witness. See Meier, *Marginal Jew*, 3:450.

57. Luke places the parable earlier in Jesus' ministry.

58. Meier, *Marginal Jew*, 5:375.

There is no place in the Scriptures in which Jesus makes a clear, unambiguous, and obvious claim that he has authority. It seems certain that he was recognized as one with authority. The three examples just examined clearly indicate that Jesus was aware of his authority and that it came from God. These support a strong conviction that Jesus' authority was recognized by others and expressed at least implicitly by him.

Jesus Speaks with Authority: The Amen Statements

The expression "amen, I say to you" is found on the lips of Jesus numerous times.[59] Meier estimates it is used approximately seventy-five times in the Gospels.[60] The Old Testament use of *amen* is always responsorial, an expression of approval or agreement to something that was said. In the Gospels, however, it is often characteristic of Jesus in making an authoritative pronouncement.[61] It appears unique to his usage.[62] We remind ourselves, however, that not every instance of the use of *amen* in the Gospels can be traced to Jesus as a historical, authoritative pronouncement. Some of them may have come from the evangelist who would have recognized an authoritative statement of Jesus and emphasized it with the amen. But a significant number can be traced to the historical Jesus.[63] Those that are authentic, and there are many, express a special claim to authority. "Amen, I say to you" is an expression of personal conviction. In using the amen the charismatic Jesus claims to know God's will, to speak with authority.[64] Thus, *amen* is a typical introductory affirmation that Jesus used in many

---

59. Some of the more familiar uses of *amen* are found in Mark 9:1; Mark 13:20; Mark 14:25//Luke 22:18; Matt 5:26//Luke 12:59; Matt 10:23; Matt 23:36; John 13:38; John 14:12. These authoritative statements are found in all four Gospels. Several are from the Q source. In several verses, Luke replaces the Amen with another expression such as "truly I tell you" or simply "for I tell you." There are numerous places in the Gospels where the expression "I say to you" without the amen is used. One instance is when Jesus denounces the Pharisees and scholars (Luke 11:51); another instance is at the Last Supper (Matt 26:29//Luke 22:18).

60. Amen is used thirty-one times in Matthew, thirteen times in Mark, six times in Luke, and twenty-five times in John. In John, amen is often doubled. Amen shows up only six times in Luke because he often substitutes a Greek work *alethos* which means *truly*.

61. This is considered an authentic usage on the part of Jesus because it passes the criteria of continuity and multiple attestations. It is also consistent with him.

62. Meier, *Marginal Jew*, 2:368.

63. Meier, *Marginal Jew*, 2:368.

64. Meier, *Marginal Jew*, 2:370n67.

of his authoritative sayings. The expression *I say to you* that often follows the amen is a "solemn, emphatic introduction to a promise/prediction/prophecy of what Jesus will do in the near future."[65] What is important is that the amen precedes an authoritative utterance.

Meier points out that Jeremias found a striking similarity between Jesus' statement and the Old Testament prophet who would express himself with the expression "Thus says the Lord."[66] My personal judgment is that the Old Testament prophet knew that he was speaking for God. When Jesus employs the expression "I say to you," it appears to be a more direct and profound relationship to his Abba and the revelation. Jesus speaks in his own name and on his own authority. Meier sums up Jesus' use of the expression by saying, "The striking—indeed at his time unparalleled—formula that Jesus used to introduce various [authoritative] pronouncements, 'Amen I say to you,' sums up this claim of the charismatic leader and (more specifically in Jesus' case) the eschatological prophet."[67] This is a particularly significant expression which clearly indicates that Jesus was conscious of his authority. If we were unable to find an explicit claim for Jesus' authority in the miracle traditions, it is clearly expressed with the amen formula. Jesus speaks with authority, and he understands it to be personal. Although the amen statements, similar to the other statements of authority examined above, are not self-designations, they are authoritative.

Conclusion and Resume: Jesus' Understanding of Self and Mission

A considerable amount of Jesus' self-understanding has already been established from a careful examination of the texts. We read the Scriptures from the perspective of faith. That is our principal interest. But we do not exclude the search for a deeper understanding. In our reading of the texts, we attempted to discover that which can be grounded in fact, in history. If we gather together several of the events examined above, we

---

65. Meier, *Marginal Jew*, 2:306.
66. Meier, *Marginal Jew*, 2:368n62.
67. Meier, *Marginal Jew*, 4:655. Meier discusses *amen* and the authoritative statement it introduces in *Marginal Jew*, 2:306, 367n62, 370n67. Much of this discussion relies on his position on Jesus' authoritative statements. Meier is very cogent and convincing on this subject.

get a fairly clear picture of the way in which Jesus understood himself, his mission, and his role in it.

The Grounding of Jesus' Self-Understanding and Authority

From what has been examined so far it seems clear that the foundation of Jesus' understanding of self and his mission as well as his recognition of the authority he possessed to fulfill this mission was rooted in his personal experience and deep union with God, his Abba.[68] This was the source of his preaching charism and authority.[69] Jesus' closeness to God, his charismatic nature, helps us to understand better his self-understanding.[70] What is being described here in terms of Jesus' personal union with his Abba is better explained as a matter of grace. It is a gift open to every human. In Jesus' case we claim that he has received its fullness.[71]

Jesus the Eschatological Prophet

Jesus understood that he was called to be a prophet.[72] More than a prophet, we concluded that Jesus understood himself as the eschatological prophet. "Jesus saw himself as an eschatological prophet and miracle worker working along the lines of Elijah."[73] This is our principal

---

68. There would need to be some form of revelation to ground Jesus' behavior, to preach a new mode of salvation. This experience of God I have named Jesus' Abba experience. It is not possible to determine when this experience actually occurred and whether it occurred over a period of time. We simply lack the data.

69. From a theological perspective, Jesus' charism is described as a matter of grace. In the past, some theologians wondered why Jesus needed grace since he was united to the Word. Thomas Aquinas responded by saying that if Jesus Christ, in his humanity, did not have grace, then he was lacking something that other humans possess.

70. This needs to be compared to an older Christology that dealt with this issue by attributing to Jesus, in his humanity, the beatific vision. This was based upon dogmatic perspectives. This older position is no longer popular.

71. For an excellent discussion on the grace of Christ as a human see Aquinas, *Summa Theologiae*, III, q. 7, aa. 1–13. The beatific vision as knowledge attributed to Christ is treated in III, q. 10, aa. 1–4.

72. Fuller, *Foundations of New Testament Christology*, 125–29. Fuller argues that Jesus understood himself as a prophet, but he did not do so explicitly. He continues, "Jesus does not identify himself *expressis verbis* with the eschatological prophet in any of the current forms of Jewish expectation. But he does interpret his mission in terms of eschatological prophecy." Fuller, *Foundations of New Testament Christology*, 129.

73. Meier, *Marginal Jew*, 4:415.

discovery and, in some sense, it grounds our understanding of him in his mission as the charismatic agent of the kingdom. This is Jesus' basic self-understanding but, like so many others, it is not explicit.

The implicit figure of the eschatological prophet gives unity "to all Jesus' historical activity."[74] Jesus' personal understanding of himself as the eschatological prophet, which we have already established as historical, imperated all of his historical activity. It governed his mission, his words, and his deeds. Nevertheless, it is not our definitive understanding of Jesus' person. This affirmation does not exhaust our total understanding of Jesus.

It is unclear whether Jesus recognized himself as the Messiah. He did not want to be identified with many of the popular messianic descriptions of his day. We concluded that we are not able to determine if the notion of Messiah was a part of Jesus' self-understanding. The early Christians referred to Jesus as the Messiah, but they understood that the definition of the expression actually came from his life. It is what Jesus did and said that gives meaning to the term Messiah/Christ and not any popular first century understanding.

It is also evident that Jesus never understood his human consciousness in the manner in which he was confessed at the Councils of Nicea or Chalcedon.

Jesus' Authority to Speak for God

Our curiosity was first raised by numerous reports in the Gospels that referred to the crowd's amazement; Jesus spoke with an authority that was unlike any of his contemporaries. His personal understanding of his authority is more implicit than explicit. As the eschatological prophet, Jesus understood himself as the one who was to inaugurate the kingdom of God. Jesus spoke for God.[75] This is clearly expressed in his preaching, the major theme of which was the kingdom of God. Jesus recognized his authority to speak for God. This authority is evident throughout his ministry. He understood that his healings and exorcisms were a sign of the kingdom. His festive meals which belongs to Jesus authentic history supported this understanding.

---

74. Fuller, *Foundations of New Testament Christology*, 130

75. The Gospel of John has described Jesus as clearly the one who speaks for God. He is from God and will return to God. This description of Jesus speaking for God, however, is more theological than historical.

HOW JESUS UNDERSTOOD HIMSELF

We are not totally devoid of statements in which Jesus spoke with authority. It has been established that many of his amen statements were both authentic and authoritative. They were rooted in his Abba experience. Jesus spoke authoritatively and understood he had the authority to do so.

In chapter 13, we will examine a number of occasions in which Jesus changed or modified the law. In commenting on this Meier suggests that Jesus' self-understanding as the *Elijah-like* prophet explains "why he [Jesus] dares to appropriate to himself the authority to make startling decisions about the Law, with no priestly status or formal scribal training on which to base his authority."[76] The change in the law was somewhat dramatic since it contradicted long standing traditions of divorce and oaths. Jesus accepted the validity of Sabbath worship, and he interpreted it in a way that was more humane than the strict observance of his contemporaries.

Even more dramatic than his change of the law in regard to oaths and divorce was his conflict in the temple precincts. This reflects his most mature self-understanding since he consciously appears to be calling for the end of temple worship. The kingdom will make this a reality and evidence for this becomes even more prominent at the Last Supper. Jesus understood he had the authority to break with the temple, which in fact he did.

In Summary: Why This is Important

Jesus' self-understanding can be found in the events of his authentic ministry. This is of great significance in grounding his words and deeds in their historical expression. Even though the basis of the Scriptures is faith and not history, the scriptural texts permit us to discover much of what Jesus understood about himself, his relationship to God, and his mission. There is an identity between Jesus' self-understanding and its expression in the Scriptures. A considerable amount of material has been examined to explore Jesus' self-understanding. The conclusions are summarized above. We have established a clear picture of Jesus' self-understanding and it is impressive.

Foundational for all that we have discovered is Jesus' conviction that he was the eschatological prophet. This is his unique understanding of

---

76. Meier, *Marginal Jew*, 4:656.

his person, his mission, and his authority. This understanding governed his entire mission. But he did not become aware he was the eschatological prophet in a single moment. It seems evident that this awareness developed after his time with John the Baptist. This is a radical departure from an older Christology. As important as Jesus' self-understanding as eschatological prophet is, it does not exhaust all that can be said of him. While it is not the final word, it is the best first word. The christological affirmations are conceptually understood in the foundational title of eschatological prophet.

The self-understanding of the Jesus of history directed his ministry and the Jesus of history grounded the faith of those who followed him. The memories of this experience were translated into the written Scriptures. There is coherence between our research and the fullness of our faith convictions. What we have discovered permits us to use Jesus' self-understanding as a hermeneutic to achieve a deeper understanding of the confessional statements that fill out the scriptural data. It also provides us with a defense against a docetic description in which the divinity of Jesus subsumes his humanity.[77] It prevents us from creating our own picture of the Jesus of faith. The self-understanding of Jesus and his authentic teaching anchors us and provides boundaries for our faith and theological reflection.

It is clear that the self-understanding of Jesus as eschatological prophet is well grounded in history. Jesus understood himself to have the authority to act for and usher in God's kingdom. His authority reaches its full development in the Last Supper. The Last Supper (which anticipates his death) is the culmination of his mission as eschatological prophet. It fully expressed Jesus' authority and self-understanding.

The same historical grounding of Jesus serves our present-day faith and reflection. It guards against the accusation that the early church created the Jesus we believe in. This is certainly important for contemporary Christians in their attempt to be faithful to one to whom they commit themselves; to understand the Christ of faith.

---

77. It also eliminates the tortured explanations of the past in which Jesus had experiential knowledge in spite of his beatitude. There is no need to defend this or explain the older position, in spite of the brilliance of the older theologians.

13

Jesus the Teacher: Authentic Themes and Sayings

Introduction

SEARCHING FOR THE AUTHENTIC teaching of the historical Jesus is not intended to be a rejection or diminution of the truths revealed in the Scriptures or tradition.[1] The historical Jesus and his authentic teaching, that is, the teaching that can be attributed to Jesus of Nazareth in his historical ministry, is a valuable hermeneutical tool. It can help us understand the Jesus of the Gospels and the truths of the Scriptures.[2] It prevents us from remaking Jesus in our own image and likeness. The search for the historical Jesus and his authentic teachings is an important undertaking and their discovery is a real treasure. It should be of interest to anyone committed to Jesus as the Christ.

Jesus recognized the validity of the Old Testament and, for the most part, he did not teach contrary to its basic tenants. Indeed, they

---

1. We presuppose the validity of Scripture and tradition as our point of departure. This study is a serious attempt to distinguish the Jesus of history from the Jesus of the Gospels. In no way is this a rejection or challenge to the faith expressed in the Scriptures or by the church, which is joyously accepted.

2. The justification for identifying Jesus' authentic teaching is given in chapter 2. Significant authentic themes and activities are attributed to the Jesus of history. They are distinguished from sayings or deeds that either cannot be established as historical or those that do not in fact go back to the historical Jesus. We have already affirmed that the Scriptures are the authentic source for this study.

are the matrix for his preaching. He taught the great prophetic insights and he must be seen within that prophetic tradition. He taught as a poet, using various literary genres which were attractive to those who heard him.[3] Meier beautifully and accurately describes Jesus when he says that "He [Jesus] was not a systematic teacher, scribe, or rabbi; he was a religious charismatic."[4] Jesus did not leave any personal written record of his teaching nor is his teaching organized or categorized in any systematic way in the Gospels. It is possible, however, to discover and thematize Jesus' authentic teaching.

Much of the authentic teaching of the Jesus of history has already been explored in the chapters above. Therefore, this chapter may appear redundant. The purpose of this chapter is to organize and comment on Jesus' authentic teaching.[5] The Gospels are a rich collection of his authentic teaching. They are also an early Christian reflection on it. The historical Jesus and his teaching are precisely what his first disciples experienced. It is the logical beginning for all that followed, including the composition of the Scriptures. It was necessary for the first disciples to understand the teaching of Jesus and apply it to the situation in which they found themselves after his death and resurrection. It is assumed that there is a valid conceptual development between Jesus' teaching and what is reflected in the Scriptures.[6]

---

3. We have already identified narratives, parables, sayings (among which are antithetical parallelism and chiasms), amens, and blessings which are included in Jesus' authentic teaching.

4. Meier, *Marginal Jew*, 4:415; see also 4:655. From a theological perspective this charism is a matter of grace. Meier repeated this observation numerous times in the earlier three volumes.

5. The expression *authentic teaching* used throughout our study is a shorthand way to indicate teaching that can be traced back to Jesus of Nazareth in his historical ministry.

6. The development of doctrine has always been a part of the Catholic tradition. Saint Vincent of Lerins (+445) proposed the following: "Is there to be no development of religion in the Church of Christ? Certainly, there is to be development and on the largest scale.... Who can be so grudging to men, so full of hate for God, as to try to prevent it? But it must be truly development of the faith, not alteration of the faith. Development means that each thing expands to be itself, while alteration means that a thing is changed from one thing into another." Catholic Book Publishing, *Liturgy of the Hours*, 363. Doctrinal development was articulated extremely well in modern times by Cardinal Newman in his *An Essay on the Development of Christian Doctrine*, originally published in 1845. Development must be recognized as occurring between the authentic teaching of Jesus and its recording in the New Testament.

JESUS THE TEACHER: AUTHENTIC THEMES AND SAYINGS

Jesus' authentic teaching is presented here in three distinct categories. The first includes themes of Jesus authentic teaching. The second articulates his authentic teaching on the law. The third is a collection of narratives and sayings that can be established as authentic to the Jesus of history.

Authentic Themes: The Teaching of the Jesus of History

Just as there are several events in Jesus' life that are considered to be indisputable (his baptism, his miracle tradition, his festive meals, his death by crucifixion, etc.), so also there is a growing consensus around a collection of themes integral to Jesus' authentic teaching.

The Kingdom of God[7]

Jesus preached the kingdom of God as the core or central vision of his mission. It can be found in the very beginning of his mission in Galilee, and he concludes his life professing it at the Last Supper. It is found in his narratives, his parables, and the beatitudes. It is supported by his miracles and his festive meals. He never explains the meaning of the expression since it seemed obvious that those who heard him preach would have understood it. Jesus' vision of the kingdom was rooted in his experience of God and his understanding of the Old Testament. In general, the kingdom is a way of describing the reign or rule of God. It indicates when and where God is present to men and women. It also points out the sinful condition of this world and the need for the reversal of its values. The King (God), unlike the despots of Jesus' time, will reign like a loving father.

The kingdom of God is suitably described by several characteristics. The first and major characteristic is Jesus' understanding of the kingdom as an offer of a new mode of salvation.[8] Fitzmyer informs us that "His [Jesus'] mission differed too [from the Old Testament notion] because it was no longer deliverance in a political or economic sense, but solely in

---

7. This theme, the preaching of the kingdom of God, was examined in chapters 4, 5, and 6 above.

8. See Fitzmyer, *Christological Catechism*, 45. This is his first and primary theme attributed to Jesus.

a spiritual sense."[9] This new mode of salvation is both explicit in the sayings and parables of Jesus as well as implicit in his miracles and deeds.[10] It is an offer directed to all human beings.[11]

A second characteristic of the kingdom is that Jesus taught it as both a present and future reality;[12] it is both earthly and heavenly.[13] This is an advance over previous understandings. The kingdom as present addresses how we should organize our social and religious lives on earth. It is clear this was not intended to be a replacement for various forms of political or cultural life. However, since Jesus clearly teaches that this new mode of salvation is a present reality, it is obvious that it is not totally spiritual as suggested by Fitzmyer.

Israel's initial recognition of salvation was this—worldly, here and now. Jesus taught a salvation that extended beyond our earthly boundaries. This authentic understanding cannot be doubted. We are fortunate to possess an authentic pericope recorded in Mark in which the Jesus of history describes his vision of the future kingdom. Meier informs us that "it [Mark 12:18–27] alone preserves from some pre-Gospel source an account of one particular clash between Jesus and the Sadducees."[14] Jesus argument with the Sadducees is an actual incident that occurred in Jerusalem.[15] Meier argues that "Mark 12:18–27 is a unique and precious relic that allows us to appreciate more fully Jesus' own views on what the future coming of the kingdom would mean."[16] It seems clear that Jesus' vison of the future kingdom transcends all earthly considerations. He quotes from the Scripture and refers to God as the God "of the living" (Abraham, Isaac, and Jacob). This is an obvious reference to a future, heavenly reality.

---

9. Fitzmyer, *One Who Is to Come*, 183.

10. Fitzmyer, *Christological Catechism*, 45.

11. Fitzmyer, *One Who Is to Come*, 183.

12. The eschatology of the kingdom is rather complex. Jesus describes the kingdom as a future reality, an immanent event, and as being already present.

13. This was discussed at length in chapter 5. See Luke 11:20 and Luke 17:20–21.

14. Meier, *Marginal Jew*, 3:412; see also 3:433. The entire pericope is examined in Meier, *Marginal Jew*, 3:411–44.

15. Meier, *Marginal Jew*, 3:443.

16. Meier, *Marginal Jew*, 3:443. This event should be associated with authentic prophecy from the Last Supper in which Jesus refers to the kingdom. The prophecy is found in Mark 14:25 and parallels. See Meier, *Marginal Jew*, 2:302–9.

JESUS THE TEACHER: AUTHENTIC THEMES AND SAYINGS

A third characteristic of this new kingdom is Jesus' extension of it to include all persons regardless of ethnic identity or social status.[17] His teaching gave it a universal character.[18] The Jews who lived in the first century understood that when Israel would be restored some gentiles would also be included with them. The restoration Jesus envisioned went far beyond this. It included those who were ordinarily excluded (sinners, tax collectors, etc.). The inclusion of gentiles becomes abundantly clear in two authentic parables which are literarily placed at the end of Jesus' ministry. The one is the parable of the evil tenants (Mark 12:1–11//Matt 21:33–44//Luke 20:9–18) and the other is the great supper (Matt 22:1–10//Luke 14:16–24).

God as Father (Abba)[19]

Jesus had a very special relationship with God such that he refers to him as his Father/his Abba, a term which had not been used previously as a personal address for God. The term *Father* is placed on his lips by the evangelists more than 150 times. We proposed a deep *Abba experience* in which Jesus saw his Father in a special relationship. When this experience first occurred is difficult to determine. We place the beginnings of this experience sometime before Jesus' public appearances, but it could have occurred or deepened after.

How did Jesus describe his Father, his Abba?[20] This was elaborated upon above at some length in the discussion on the kingdom of God. What seems clear, however, is that much of Jesus' understanding of God is derived from the Old Testament tradition. God was referred to as *Father* in the Old Testament multiple times but nowhere is he addressed as *Father*. What seems new is Jesus' understanding of the God of the Old Testament as his Abba, with whom he shares a very personal relationship. Jesus was unique in addressing God as his Father/Abba. This distinguishes Jesus from his contemporaries.

---

17. This is clear from his table fellowship. See Fitzmyer, *One Who Is to Come*, 182–3.

18. This provides us with the basis for our notion of *preferential option or concern for the poor* as well as the idea of social justice.

19. See Meier, *Marginal Jew*, 2:358n20.

20. Jesus' use of the expression Abba is recorded only once in the Gospels. It is found in Mark 14:36 during his agony in Gethsemane. Paul uses the expression in Rom 8:15 and Gal 4:6.

We have already established that the manner Jesus referred to his Father/Abba in prayer was authentic. Jesus taught his disciples that they too should pray to him as their Father/Abba.[21] It was argued that the Lord's Prayer is the authentic teaching of the historical Jesus.[22] Jesus taught that God as Abba is intimate and personal, the God and Father of all humans.

A New Emphasis on Love

Our examination of the theme of love in the Gospels may seem disappointing at first since it is not often attributed to the Jesus of history in the Synoptic Gospels.[23] Furthermore, teaching the doctrine of love is neither unique to Jesus nor to his followers. Judaism taught love as foundational. The notion of love is found in nearly all of the Old Testament books. It was a common rabbinical teaching. The Hellenistic world, and various religious movements of the day, also taught love of fellow human beings. Thus, the teaching of love would not have been unique to Jesus.

There are two significant teachings on love that can be traced to the historical Jesus. The first is the double command: to love God and to love neighbor.[24] To the question proposed by the scribe as to which of the commandments was the greatest, Jesus replied, "The first is this: 'Hear, O Israel! The Lord our God is Lord alone! You shall love the Lord your God with all your heart, with all your soul, with all your mind, and with all your strength.' The second is this: 'You shall love your neighbor as yourself.' There is no other commandment greater than these" (Mark 12:29–31).[25]

---

21. The authenticity of this was argued for in Meier, *Marginal Jew*, 2:291–4.

22. The version of the Lord's Prayer that we use liturgically and in personal prayer is from Matthew's version (Matt 6:9–13). The word *debt* is a metaphor for sin and reflects an Aramaism. Luke's version of the Our Father, although shorter than Matthew's, is considered by many to be closer to the original words of Jesus.

23. It may well be that love is often expressed under different concepts, different manners of speaking.

24. See the brilliant exposition of Meier, *Marginal Jew*, 4:478–576. This could have been categorized as Jesus halakic teaching since it is his commentary on the law, however it is better placed as a major theme. See also Fuller, *Essays on the Love Commandment*.

25. The parallels are in Matt 22:34–40 and Luke 10:25–28. While Luke differs somewhat in the manner in which this command is revealed, the substance of these parallels is the same. Another form of this can be found in Matt 19:16–19. See also Rom 13:9, Gal 5:14, and James 2:8.

JESUS THE TEACHER: AUTHENTIC THEMES AND SAYINGS

This double command is the joining of two individual commandments from the Old Testament law: the Shema from Deut 6:4–5 and the verse on loving one's neighbor from Lev 19:18. These individual commands are integral to the Judaism of the Old Testament. Jesus joins together these two commands which share the same word, love. This method later became a common Jewish method referred to as *gezera sawa*.[26] Meier argues that this joining of the love of God and love of neighbor is an authentic saying of the historical Jesus.[27] It is unique to Jesus since there is no evidence that any other person joined these two original commandments in this fashion.

The double command to love God and love of neighbor encompasses the supreme command of the entire law.[28] This is a very special emphasis on the notion of love. The double command to love is both an authentic and unique teaching of the Jesus of history.

The second significant teaching is Jesus' extension of the concept of love of neighbor (Lev 19:18) to love of ones enemies (Matt 5:43–48//Luke 6:27, 32–36).[29] This teaching is discontinuous with the law (Judaism).[30] Jesus declared this on his own authority. No one is excluded from the Father's love for his grace falls on both the good and the evil alike.[31] If God loves those who sin so also should others love them. Love of enemies is an

---

26. *Gezera sawa* (or *shawa*) means an "equal category," according to which an obscure passage might be illuminated by reference to another containing the same key term. See Meier, *Marginal Jew*, 4:493.

27. Meier, *Marginal Jew*, 4:519. Meier proposes that *neighbor* meant another member of Israel. It should be pointed out that the law included proper behavior toward the alien. Was the law to be observed in such a limited manner as Meier seems to suggest? Furthermore, Jesus extended the kingdom to include gentiles. See Meier, *Marginal Jew*, 4:651.

28. Jesus gives these commands his personal theological stamp by joining them in the manner that he does.

29. This is from the Q source. The Johannine literature is not helpful in this issue. Is it possible that 1 John 4:20–21 reflects the authentic Jesus? Meier concludes that "in all likelihood, it does not go back to the historical Jesus." See Meier, *Marginal Jew*, 4:572.

30. In the book of Proverbs we read, "Rejoice not when your enemy falls, and when he stumbles, let not your heart exult, lest the LORD see it, be displeased with you, and withdraw his wrath from your enemy. Be not provoked with evildoers, nor envious of the wicked; for the evil man has no future, the lamp of the wicked will be put out" (Prov 24:17–20). This teaching enjoins upon us not to take delight in the fall of our enemy. Unlike Jesus' teaching, it does not call for love of enemies.

31. Luke introduced the parable of the good Samaritan which appears to be his creation (Luke 10:29–37). This universalizes the object of love for Christians to all men and women. Unfortunately it is not one of Jesus' authentic parables.

authentic teaching of the historical Jesus. This is also reflected symbolically in his festive meals in which even sinners are included.

Personal, Individual Forgiveness

The notion of forgiveness is foundational in the Old Testament which is filled with expressions of God's forgiveness. It appears in almost every book. An examination of the Old Testament, however, reveals that almost every case involves God granting forgiveness or an intercession for God's forgiveness. To find a reference which enjoins one Israelite to forgive another is nearly impossible. Making atonement for one's sins is clearly articulated. Personal forgiveness of another is surprisingly absent.[32]

There is one significant exception in the Old Testament that enjoins forgiveness on one who has been offended. "Forgive your neighbor the wrong done to you; then when you pray, your own sins will be forgiven" (Sir 28:2).[33] This may well be the only place in the Old Testament which calls for personal forgiveness of an offender. This injunction is followed by several conditions necessary for one to be forgiven by God. Forgiveness from God of one's personal sins requires

---

32. This brief excursus on forgiveness in the Jewish tradition would be incomplete without mentioning Yom Kippur. Yom Kippur, also known as the Day of Atonement, is the holiest day of the year in Judaism. The entire chapter 16 in Leviticus is dedicated in great detail to the proper way of keeping this day. It concludes with the injunction "this, then, shall be an everlasting statute for you: once a year atonement shall be made on behalf of the Israelites for all their sins" (Lev 16:34). But there is no indication in this chapter of forgiving another. Its entire focus is on asking God's forgiveness for personal sins. It should be noted that modern day Judaism enjoins on its adherents the command that if anyone has offended another, he must ask for forgiveness from the one he offended. This duty is taken seriously. From Rosh Hashanah to the preceding day or evening of Yom Kippur, prayer, asking others for forgiveness and acts of charity are enjoined upon the devout. The tradition can be found in the Mishnah the written text of the oral tradition. This can be dated to the second century AD. It calls for repentance and making amends. It is unclear what the oral tradition might have been in the first century AD.

33. The book of Sirach (Wisdom of Ben Sira), named after its author Yeshua (Jesus), son of Eleazar, son of Sirach, was composed in Hebrew by one author during the third and early second centuries BC (200–175 BC). It is also referred to as Ecclesiasticus (*Liber Ecclesiasticus*) and the name is thought to come from its frequent use as a church book by the primitive Christian community. Sirach is one of the deuterocanonical books. However, it is not included in the Hebrew Canon. It is found in the Catholic and Orthodox Bibles. The Protestants excluded it because no Hebrew version was found, and it was considered a product of Greek culture. However, it was included in the original King James Version. A Hebrew version (several manuscripts) was found in the Dead Sea Scrolls.

a proper attitude. One must not nourish anger, refuse mercy, or harbor vengeance against another.[34] "Remember the commandments and do not be angry with your neighbor; remember the covenant of the Most High, and overlook faults" (Sir 28:7).[35]

Personal forgiveness is not mentioned explicitly elsewhere in the Hebrew Bible, but it is not totally absent; it is implied in several places. The book of Leviticus counsels against hating another and then encourages love: "You shall not bear hatred for your brother in your heart. Though you may have to reprove your fellow man, do not incur sin because of him. Take no revenge and cherish no grudge against your fellow countrymen. You shall love your neighbor as yourself. I am the Lord" (Lev 19:17–18). The command joins a rejection of hatred with the promotion of love of neighbor. This is an important text which was quoted by Jesus. However, while love is enjoined, there is no mention of personal forgiveness, that is, of forgiving another for an offense received or asking forgiveness for an offense committed although it may be implied.

Jesus' teaching on forgiveness appears frequently in the Gospels and in other New Testament writings. There are numerous references in the Synoptic Gospels to Jesus both forgiving and teaching his disciples to forgive.[36] This is an authentic teaching of the Jesus of history. To borrow a phrase from Meier from an earlier discussion, the *star witness* in our search for Jesus' authentic teaching on forgiveness is found in the Lord's Prayer (Matt 6:9–13//Luke 11:2–4). This is an essential witness to the understanding that Jesus taught his disciples to forgive one another. The Lord's Prayer has already been established as authentic teaching of the historical Jesus.[37] The petition from Matthew reads, "And forgive us our debts, as we forgive our debtors" (Matt 6:12). The parallel verse found in Luke 11:4 is almost identical. The reference to *debts* is an Aramaism for sins. Meier describes the second half of the petition as provisional. God will forgive us if we forgive those who have

---

34. Sirach 28:3–5. Sirach continues with his counsel. "Think of the commandments, hate not your neighbor; [think] of the Most High's Covenant, and overlook faults" (Sir 28:7). Given these verses, there is little else in the Hebrew Scriptures that deals with asking another for personal forgiveness. The NRSV is a clearer translation of these verses. It translates *remember* for *think*.

35. The commandment referred to in this verse is from Lev 19:17.

36. Jesus forgives and teaches forgiveness. Consider Matt 6:12–15, 18:21; Mark 11:25; Luke 11:4, 17:3–4; and John 20:23. The cure of the paralytic (Mark 2:1–12//Matt 9:2–8//Luke 5:18–26) is particularly pertinent.

37. The prayer is from the Q source.

offended us.[38] Repentance is a necessary condition in order to receive God's forgiveness. An apology from the offender is not required. This is a significant departure from the Jewish tradition.

The Lord's Prayer is followed by a significant addition from M. "If you forgive others their transgressions, your heavenly Father will forgive you" (Matt 6:14). It should be noted that forgiveness is enjoined upon the injured party. The Old Testament, as near as we can tell, enjoined the offending party to seek forgiveness. Jesus' teaching of forgiveness turns our normal way of thinking on its head. Mark 11:25 is a parallel to M. "When you stand to pray, forgive anyone against whom you have a grievance, so that your heavenly Father may in turn forgive you your transgressions" (Matt 6:14). These are two distinct sources.[39]

There are other references which support the theme that Jesus taught forgiveness. Notable among these is Luke 17:3–4 and Matt 18:15, 21–22, (Q source). Luke's version states, "If your brother sins, rebuke him; and if he repents, forgive him" (Luke 17:3). Matthew's version repeats this injunction. The need for repentance of the offender is implied in Matthew's version.[40] One important element in this common pericope is that it refers to the community situation. It speaks of a brother sinning against another member of the community. The Greek word in question is *adelphos*. Literally, *adelphos* means brother. The NRSV has translated this word in Luke as *disciple* and in Matthew as *another member of the church*. In this situation brother is understood as a fellow believer. It is clear that the NRSV recognizes that this Q pericope has been edited to account for a communal postresurrection situation. Nevertheless, this is seen as consistent with the teaching of Jesus as expressed above.

The teaching of forgiveness attributed to Jesus is authentic. It is attested in multiple sources. This basic teaching is in Mark, the Q source, and M.[41] It is also evident in multiple forms. It is consistent with the things that Jesus did. The command to forgive certainly appears to come from Jesus and his teaching on forgiveness ought to be added to

---

38. See Meier, *Marginal Jew*, 2:292n12, 357n12. Compare this with the conditions from Sir 28:3–6.

39. Matthew 6:14 is from M and therefor a source distinct from Mark 11:25. See Meier, *Marginal Jew*, 2:890.

40. In Luke's version of this pericope, Jesus enjoins forgiveness seven times a day. In Matthew's version, Jesus enjoins forgiveness seventy-seven times. For this particular number see Gen 4:24.

41. Meier, *Marginal Jew*, 2:357n12.

the list of significant authentic themes. It seems to be closely connected to his vision of God and salvation. Jesus forgave and taught his disciples to forgive as well.

Jesus and the Law: The Halakic Teaching

Jesus must be seen in his Mediterranean Jewish context in which he makes eminently good sense.[42] Jesus the Jew was completely immersed in the Jewish tradition. He was "first, last, and always a product of the Judaism native to the land of Israel."[43] He was also totally immersed in the teaching of the law.[44] During his public ministry, Jesus entered into typical rabbinical debates over the law. It is what we should have expected. Meier is clear in his assessment that "the historical Jesus is the halakic Jesus, that is, the Jesus concerned with and arguing about the Mosaic Law as well as the questions of practice arising from it."[45] Halakic refers to the interpretation of the law.[46] Jesus was deeply involved in the debates that took place with the rabbis on various points of the law. He was not systematic in his teaching.[47] Nevertheless, Jesus reflected on the totality of the Torah. We discussed the double command of love above.[48] At this point, we will examine Jesus' interaction with the scribes and Pharisees

---

42. It has been argued in the introduction and chapter 1 that it would be a serious mistake to decontextualize Jesus. He must be seen in his social and religious context to properly understand him.

43. Meier, *Marginal Jew*, 4:574.

44. To support this, the temptation is to quote Matt 5:17. "Do not think that I have come to abolish the law or the prophets. I have come not to abolish but to fulfill." This passage, however, is the creation of Matthew or his church. See Meier, *Marginal Jew*, 4:41, 65–89, 68n68, and 120–24.

45. Meier, *Marginal Jew*, 4:8. The expression halakic Jesus is found in numerous places. See also 4:297 and 4:649.

46. This is variously spelled. Halacha (halakha, halakah) refers to the body of Jewish law derived from the written and oral tradition of the Torah. It is a noun. It refers to the entire body of Jewish law and tradition. Halakic (halachic, halakhic) is the adjectival form.

47. The Gospel of Matthew, most especially the Sermon on the Mount, arranges Jesus' teaching in a systematic manner. Matthew attempted to organize an ethic for his community. It is thought by many that the resource for Matthew's Sermon on the Mount came from an already existent, organized body of Jesus' teaching.

48. This was examined above on pages 242–244 when we discussed the double commandment to love God and love neighbor. See Meier, *Marginal Jew*, 4:575. See Fuller, *Essays on the Love Commandment*.

and determine if some of the debates referred to in the Gospels can be established as going back to the authentic Jesus tradition.

Ritual Purity and Dietary Laws

There are several references in the Gospels which describe Jesus commenting on the purity laws.[49] However, a careful exegetical examination of Mark's text (and others) finds that it does not go back to the authentic Jesus tradition. Meier concludes that "the authentic Jesus tradition is completely silent on the topic of ritual purity in stark contrast to debates in the early church."[50] Most of these disputes belong to the early church and not to Jesus' ministry. No significant pronouncement on dietary rules can be found in the Gospels.[51] On the other hand, there are many references to them in the Epistles of Paul. It is clear that circumcision and dietary laws especially vexed the early Christian community. Their challenge was to determine what Jewish observances should be practiced by a Jewish convert to Christianity. The dispute between Peter and Paul found in Gal 2:11–14 is especially informative. The conflict with the Judaizers, those who insisted on following the dietary laws and other Jewish customs, is well known. These disputes can be seen as the growing pains of the nascent Christian movement as it entered more fully into the gentile world and into conflict with the synagogue. Jesus had no articulated position on either ritual purity or dietary laws.

The Observance of the Sabbath

The attack on Jesus curing on the Sabbath is more than likely a Christian polemic.[52] For one thing, there were no prohibitions in the law from curing

---

49. See Mark 7:1–21. This passage refers to these traditions. With the exception of the reference to *qorban* (Mark 7:10–12) this pericope does not reflect the authentic teaching of Jesus. See Meier, *Marginal Jew*, 4:413. It should be understood that the teaching on the commandment to honor father and mother and the rejection of the qorban interpretation is authentic. We could hardly accept the interpretation of the Pharisees and scribes.

50. Meier, *Marginal Jew*, 4:414.

51. Meier, *Marginal Jew*, 4:411.

52. There are a number of cures recorded as happening on the Sabbath and which provoked conflict. See Mark 32:23–28 parr.; Mark 3:1–6; Luke 13:10–18; Luke 14:1–6; and John 5:1–18.

on the Sabbath.⁵³ The same can be said of eating grain plucked in the fields on the Sabbath. On the other hand, Meier argues that the Sabbath sayings came from the halakic Jesus, the Jesus who would engage in debate with his contemporaries over questions of the law.⁵⁴ These debates significantly reflected the Jewishness of Jesus. Jesus never annulled the Sabbath; neither was he overly strict about its observance.⁵⁵ He presupposed and affirmed this sacred institution. But he rescued it from the rigorism of an overly strict interpretation. Jesus expressed a common-sense attitude. He wanted to make the Sabbath more livable for contemporaries. For Jesus, "The sabbath was made for man, not man for the sabbath" (Mark 2:27). This reflects an understanding of the observance of the Sabbath that fits better with human nature and rejects an attitude that borders on scrupulosity. Jesus proposed a more moderate, humane, common-sense approach to the Sabbath observances. However, the laws are relaxed or interpreted more leniently by Jesus in order to make the common person's life more humane.⁵⁶ This is judged authentic.⁵⁷ Schillebeeckx observes that "what is striking about Jesus is his liberating 'humanization' of religion which nevertheless remains the service of God."⁵⁸

Prohibition of Divorce

Divorce was a common and permitted practice during the time of Jesus. The Mosaic law legitimated divorce and only required a writ of divorce and sufficient cause to make it legal (Deut 24:1). Permission to divorce is also found in Leviticus and Numbers.⁵⁹ Ezek 44:22 forbids marriage to a divorced woman, which presumes an acceptance of divorce in general. Isaiah 50:1 and Jer 3:8 speak of divorce as a metaphor explaining the relationship between Israel and the Lord. The one lone minority position

---

53. Meier, *Marginal Jew*, 4:294.
54. Meier, *Marginal Jew*, 4:283.
55. The law which declared the observance of the Sabbath was quite strict. The family, their slaves, strangers, and even the animals were obliged to rest on the Sabbath. See Exod 20:8–11; 23:12; 31:12–17; Lev 23:3; and Deut 5:12–15.
56. See Mark 2:23–28//Matt 12:1–8//Luke 6:1–5; Mark 3:1–6//Matt 12:9–14//Luke 6:6–11; Luke 13:10–18; and Luke 14:1–6.
57. Meier, *Marginal Jew*, 4:294.
58. Schillebeeckx, *Church with a Human Face*, 24.
59. Lev 21:7, 14; 22:13 indicate that divorce was socially acceptable. Numbers 30:9 expresses legal permission to divorce according to the law.

that contradicts permission to accept divorce is found in Malachi. "For I hate divorce, says the Lord, the God of Israel" (Mal 2:16a).

Even so, Jesus' authentic teaching on marriage and divorce repudiates the law and what was then permissible. There are a number of sayings in the Gospels in which Jesus forbids divorce. They are found in Mark 10:2–12; Matt 5:31–32; 19:3–9; and Luke 16:18. Mark and Luke describe Jesus' teaching prohibiting divorce as an absolute. His authentic teaching can be summed up in his own words. "Therefore what God has joined together, no human being must separate" (Mark 10:9).[60]

Matthew's Gospel contains sayings which appear to permit divorce under certain circumstances (Matt 5:32; 19:9). These sayings are referred to as the exceptive clauses. They are understood by some as a "modification of the absolute prohibition."[61] The exceptive clauses are an addition from the community of Matthew and it was not an authentic teaching of Jesus. Jesus' teaching against divorce is absolute. This needs to be seen as opposing the prevailing teaching that divorce was permissible.[62] Jesus' apparent rationale is that in the beginning of creation divorce was not permitted but that the later (human) tradition had accepted it. His teaching is rooted in the creation narrative and the formation of humans as found in Gen 1–2 and is expressed in Mark 10:9. Meier concludes his examination by saying that "Jesus absolutely forbade divorce and branded divorce and remarriage as the sin of adultery."[63] This is how Jesus' teaching would have been understood in his context.

Jesus' teaching against divorce is part of the authentic Jesus tradition. There are multiple attestations found in the Gospels. Paul's teaching, which forbids divorce, is supported by his claim that it is from the Lord (1 Cor 7:10–11). The exception to the absolute prohibition is attributed to the situation in Matthew's community. If it is true that the absolute prohibition of divorce goes back to the authentic Jesus tradition, then it would be clear that Jesus taught a position contrary to the Mosaic law as it was understood during his time.

---

60. Meier argues that this is an authentic teaching of Jesus. See Meier, *Marginal Jew*, 4:125. The entire chapter 32 examines this material. See also Luke 16:18//Matt 5:32; Matt 19:9; and 1 Cor 7:10–11.

61. See the note in the NABRE for Matt 5:31–32. The note also points out that "there are other sayings of Jesus about divorce that prohibit it absolutely." (See Mark 10:11–12; Luke 16:18; cf. 1 Cor 7:10–11b.)

62. Meier, *Marginal Jew*, 4:126.

63. Meier, *Marginal Jew*, 4:126.

Jesus' condemnation of divorce presents considerable problems for the contemporary theologian who must deal with societal factors in which divorce and remarriage among Catholics is commonplace. This is a serious and considered approach to discover the authentic teaching of the historical Jesus and how to apply it to a contemporary situation.

The Prohibition against Oaths

It seems clear that the Hebrew Scriptures permit the taking of oaths. We are told, "You shall not swear falsely by my name, thus profaning the name of your God. I am the Lord" (Lev 19:12). The presumption is that there is a proper way to make an oath. Exodus 20:7 and Deut 5:11 repeat the same command in their respective versions of the Decalogue. Taking the name of the Lord in vain means the "false use of an oath in legal proceedings."[64]

Jesus forbade taking oaths (Matt 5:34–37). The parallel passage is found in James 5:12. It appears that James has incorporated part of the authentic Jesus tradition into his epistle. Interestingly, both the Pauline Epistles and the Epistle to the Hebrews approve of taking oaths. Therefore we must conclude that the prohibition against oaths is multiply attested and it is discontinuous from Paul and Hebrews.[65] This supports the idea that Jesus actually rejected a part of the Mosaic law. Meier writes, "I conclude that the prohibition of oaths can take its place alongside the prohibition of divorce as a second example of the historical Jesus' revocation of individual institutions and/or commandments of the Mosaic Law."[66] Even though Jesus was steeped in the law, his prohibition of oaths is a significant place in which he modifies it. We can conclude that Jesus' personal understanding of his authority permits him to change the law.

Meier explains the possible reason for the restriction against oaths and divorce in this manner. "We probably have here another example of the eschatological prophet proclaiming the rules of conduct binding on those who already live proleptically in the kingdom of God."[67] Whether or not this explanation is totally satisfactory, the one thing Meier consistently points out is that Jesus is a charismatic prophet. The source

---

64. Clifford, "Exodus," in *NJBC*, 3:33.
65. This satisfies the requirement for historical authenticity.
66. Meier, *Marginal Jew*, 4:205.
67. Meier, *Marginal Jew*, 4:205–6.

of his understanding is not the normal one for a rabbi. Theologically we propose that Jesus had a profound vision of his Father and was the recipient in his human nature of the movement of grace similar to that which any mystic would experience.[68] Contemporary theology is better served by identifying Jesus as a charismatic moved by God's grace rather than by an infused beatific vision.

Conclusion: Jesus Modifies the Mosaic Law[69]

The scriptural tradition informs us that Jesus made specific pronouncements on divorce, oaths, and Sabbath observances. Only Jesus' teaching on divorce and oaths deviates significantly from the Torah. Meier sums up this conclusion:

> When it comes to the sabbath, Jesus presupposes and affirms this sacred institution enshrined in the Torah, all the while arguing against sectarian rigorism and in favor of a humane, moderate approach to detailed questions of observance. Yet when it comes to divorce and oaths, two key social institutions permitted and regulated by the Torah, Jesus totally forbids both divorce and swearing—two prohibitions that, as far as we can tell, were unheard of among the various competing Jewish parties and sects of his day.[70]

Concerning Sabbath observances Jesus' intention is to reform practices that are often burdensome. He liberalizes them to accommodate the life of the common person. Regarding oaths and divorce, Jesus appears to teach significant modifications to the Mosaic law. His position extends beyond an interpretation that deviated from the norm. He changed the law, and he did it on his own authority.[71]

In conclusion, it seems likely that there were many other halakic statements made by Jesus. The Scriptures, however, do not tell us more

---

68. As has been pointed out earlier, until the early 1900s most Catholic theologians would have posited the beatific vision as the source of all knowledge of Jesus beyond normal experiential knowledge. The more contemporary understanding would be to treat this epistemological problem as a matter of grace or divine inspiration.

69. See Meier, *Marginal Jew*, 4:647.

70. Meier, *Marginal Jew*, 4:297.

71. An examination of the authentic teaching of the Jesus of history reveals that he never appeals to the authority of anyone or anything else. His authentic teaching is often preceded by the phrase "amen, I say to you . . ." It is the nature of a charismatic to know the mind of God intuitively.

JESUS THE TEACHER: AUTHENTIC THEMES AND SAYINGS

about these rabbinical debates than what has already been referred to. Regarding ritual purity and dietary laws there is silence.[72] Jesus had little or no interest in these. Furthermore, they were of no interest to the gentile world. Much of what we read in the New Testament on these matters reflects the experience of the early church in a Jewish-Palestinian context. It is more a description of the conflict between the synagogue and the nascent church than of Jesus and his contemporaries. From what has been said above, it is clear that Jesus did in fact change the law and he understood that he had the authority to do so.

Other Important Authentic Teaching[73]

So far in this chapter, we have covered several major themes as well as teachings on the law that are associated with the authentic teaching of the historical Jesus. The themes and halakic teachings examined above are central and important but they do not exhaust all of the authentic teaching that can be attributed to the historical Jesus. There are other narratives and sayings which are authentic and important. We will organize them for convenience sake much as we did for the major themes discussed above.

The Call to Discipleship

The authentic teaching of Jesus included the invitation to become a disciple and to follow him (Mark 1:17).[74] In this Jesus was no different from John the Baptist who called disciples and instructed them. The call of the Twelve and other disciples is clearly an authentic historical invitation.[75] It is a consequence which follows upon Jesus' preaching the kingdom of God.

---

72. Meier, *Marginal Jew*, 4:414.

73. Meier has given a challenging list of sayings that are considered authentic to the historical Jesus. See Meier, *Marginal Jew*, 4:330n1451. All of these sayings share the characteristic of antithetical parallelism and chiasm. Other authentic sayings can be found in the conclusions to various sections found in his five volumes. Unfortunately for us, Meier does not summarize them in a single place.

74. Evidence for this can be found in Mark, Q, L, and John. See Meier, *Marginal Jew*, 3:50–51.

75. Concerning the call of the Twelve, see Meier, *Marginal Jew*, 3:128–47. The Twelve as well as disciples are listed in the "almost indisputable facts" referred to in the preface.

Disciples must also be prepared to endure persecution. Jesus said, "Whoever wishes to come after me must deny himself, take up his cross, and follow me. For whoever wishes to save his life will lose it, but whoever loses his life for my sake and that of the gospel will save it" (Mark 8:34-35 parr.).[76] This is an authentic teaching of the Jesus of history. Even the Twelve are not exempt from persecution. The ambition of John and James to obtain places of honor is met with the promise of persecution. Jesus tells them that "The cup that I drink [passion and death], you will drink, and with the baptism with which I am baptized, you will be baptized" (Mark 10:39 par.).[77] Jesus challenged the ambition of his disciples.

Jesus' disciples are called to dedicate their lives to the kingdom. This requires a proper attitude, to focus on the values of the kingdom and to reject the distractions of this present life. He exhorts them not to be anxious about food, clothing and other similar objects. What is necessary to become a disciple is the need for dependence on God (Matt 6:25-34//Luke 12:22-31).[78] The sense of this very poetic passage is to trust in God and all else will be taken care of. This establishes a proper attitude toward God. This is an authentic teaching of Jesus. The kingdom is a life lived with God.[79]

The Beatitudes

There are numerous antecedents to the expression *blessed* (beatitude) or *happy* in the Old Testament.[80] It is found prominently in both the Psalms and the book of Proverbs. In these sources, beatitude or happiness is described as a reward for the one "who does what is right" (Ps 106:3); "whose way is blameless" (Ps 119:1); who is "concerned for the poor" (Ps 41:1); and who "fears the Lord" (Ps 112:1). It is conceived of as a reward for proper behavior.

---

76. Both of these verses are authentic teaching of Jesus. They are found in Mark, Q, and John. See Meier, *Marginal Jew*, 3:55-66.

77. See Meier, *Marginal Jew*, 3:216-20. Meier supports the basic historicity of Mark 10:35-40. The authenticity seems obvious since it is found in Mark, Q and John. See Meier, *Marginal Jew*, 3:220.

78. See Meier, *Marginal Jew*, 3:517. This is an authentic narrative found in the Q source.

79. See Meier, *Marginal Jew*, 3:517.

80. The expressions *blessed* and *happy* are used in both the Old and New Testament translations. They signify the same concept.

JESUS THE TEACHER: AUTHENTIC THEMES AND SAYINGS

It is clear that Jesus' use of the expression *blessed* is not unique to him.[81] Given the prominence of this literary genre in the Old Testament, it would seem more than probable that Jesus would have been familiar with it and would have used it. As was noted earlier, Jesus spoke in the language of beatitude. The expression is found in the Q source, M, L, and the Gospel of John.[82] This multiple attestation of the expression supports the conclusion that it is historically certain that it was used by Jesus.

What is more challenging, however, is to determine if any individual beatitude can be traced to Jesus. Matthew's Sermon on the Mount and the parallel material in Luke's Sermon on the Plain provide us with the most probable material to support his use. They are the four beatitudes of Luke's list (Luke 6:20-22) and the first, second, fourth and ninth beatitudes in Matthew's list (Matt 5:3, 4, 6, 10). These are parallels.[83] This material can be traced to two differing versions of the Q source in Matthew and Luke. Luke appears to reflect the original version best. These Beatitudes can be established with a high degree of probability as authentic Jesus' teaching.[84] Several other beatitudes from Matthew's list are more than likely candidates to be added to this list of authentic sayings. There is another blessed saying that is worth mentioning here because of its importance in establishing the authenticity of the miracle tradition. Jesus declared that those who have been eyewitnesses to his miracles are blessed. "Turning to the disciples in private he said, 'Blessed are the eyes that see what you see. For I say to you, many prophets and kings desired to see what you see, but did not see it, and to hear what you hear, but did not hear it'" (Luke 10:23-24 parr.). This saying has already been established as authentic.

Blessed is Jesus' way of announcing that the hearer should be happy or fortunate.[85] The Beatitudes are addressed to those who are poor

81. As was noted earlier, Jesus spoke in the language of beatitude. Matthew begins his Sermon on the Mount with what is correctly called the Beatitudes. A complete exposition of this material can be found in Meier, *Marginal Jew*, 2:317-36.

82. See Matt 16:17; Luke 11:28; 14:14; 23:29; and John 13:17.

83. See Meier, *Marginal Jew*, 2:318-23.

84. Meier has established that the first three beatitudes of Luke and their parallels in Matthew are authentic. One has to be inclined to believe that the same could have been done for the fourth beatitude in Luke and its parallel in Matthew. The first three share common characteristics. They begin with the expression *blessed* (*makarios, -ioi*) and are very compact. They are thought to have been a collection of three when received by Matthew and Luke. It is somewhat easy to establish that these three beatitudes are authentic teachings.

85. It is of some interest that this expression is not unique to Jesus. There are

(*anawim*), who mourn and who hunger. This would seem to reflect the situation of much of the population during first-century Palestine. There is an eschatological reason for this happiness declared in the beatitudes. The kingdom of God will reverse these inhumane conditions when it comes. Those who heard this message would have expected it to happen by an act of God who would reign as king. The kingdom of God is meant for the poor, those who mourn, and those who hunger.[86]

Teaching on Wealth (Mammon)

Much of Jesus' teaching concerned the things of earth that are impediments to the kingdom.[87] Among these is wealth (mammon). Jesus warned that one cannot serve both God and mammon.[88] Wealth is not only a danger, but it conflicts with the kingdom and the following of God. "No one can serve two masters. He will either hate one and love the other or be devoted to one and despise the other. You cannot serve God and mammon" (Matt 6:24//Luke 16:13).[89] Riches are a serious impediment to discipleship. In the narrative of the rich man (Mark 10:17–31//Matt 19:16–30//Luke 18:18–30), it is revealing that he could obey the commandments but was unable to give up his wealth to follow Jesus. This is obviously a difficult challenge for anyone. Jesus says, "How hard it is for those who have wealth to enter the kingdom of God!" (Mark 10:23//Matt 19:23//Luke 18:24). This narrative is followed by an authentic saying. "It is easier for a camel to pass through [the] eye of [a] needle than for one who is rich to enter the kingdom of God" (Mark 10:25; brackets in the original).[90]

---

numerous antecedents to it in the Old Testament. We also find this expression in M, L, and John. See Matt 16:17; Luke 11:28; 14:14; 23:29; and John 13:17. This multiple attestation supports the historicity of Jesus' use.

86. Meier points out that this is not a matter of a change in concrete social and political reform. This is unlike the prophets of the Old Testament who often addressed the social and political ills of their day. Jesus saw this as the definitive arrival of God's reign. See Meier, *Marginal Jew*, 2:331. Amos is a clear example of this.

87. The parable of the sowing of the seed contains several impediments to the kingdom. It was shown that this parable was not listed among those that could be identified as authentic, but it reflects the disciples' understanding.

88. Mammon is an Aramaic word which means money or wealth. Both Matt 6:24 and Luke 16:13 employ this word rather than its Greek equivalent.

89. See Meier, *Marginal Jew*, 3:517–18. This saying is from Q.

90. See Meier, *Marginal Jew*, 3:515.

JESUS THE TEACHER: AUTHENTIC THEMES AND SAYINGS

Of all the New Testament sources, Luke seems to be the one who describes the evil of wealth most vividly. His first woe (Luke 6:24) declares "Woe to you who are rich, for you have received your consolation." Similar ideas that suggest that wealth is an impediment to the kingdom can be found in the parable of the rich fool (Luke 12:16–21), the parable of the rich man and Lazarus (Luke 16:19–31), and the Zacchaeus narrative (Luke 19:1–10). These parables and narrative are unique to Luke. They are the early church's reflection on the authentic teaching of Jesus. It seems clear that this teaching conflicts with many contemporary ideologies.

Comments on the Sermon on the Mount[91]

The Sermon on the Mount deserves special attention because of its contribution to our understanding of Jesus' authentic teaching. Matthew's Gospel is beautifully organized. It is divided into five books each possessing a narrative and a discourse section. The Sermon on the Mount is the first discourse section, and it is Matthew's masterpiece. The entire three chapters of the sermon portray Jesus as the preacher or teacher par excellence. It is accurately described as follows: "The Sermon is a Matthean construction, pieced together from material scattered in Q (cf. Luke 6:20–49), Mark, and other material. There is no reason to doubt that most of this material derives from Jesus himself; but each case must be weighed on its own merits, and the sayings have undergone revision."[92] In general, the subject matter of the sermon is a collection of teachings on ethical behavior designed to shape the Christian life; it is a Christian orthopraxis.[93]

There is a considerable amount of teaching in the Sermon that can be traced to the Jesus of history as authentic. The list includes the beatitudes (Matt 5:3–4, 6), Love of enemies (Matt 5:44b), The Lord's Prayer (Matt 6:10), the saying on God and mammon (Matt 6:24//Luke 12:22–11) and the exhortation against anxiety (Matt 6:25–34). It is clear that, although much of this Sermon has been edited, it is a significant repository of Jesus' authentic teaching. Those narratives and sayings

---

91. For a good explanation on the Sermon on the Mount (Matthew) and on the Plain (Luke) see Meier, *Marginal Jew*, 4:613n173.

92. Viviano, "Gospel According to Matthew," in *NJBC*, 42:22.

93. It appears that Matthew possessed a source that was already a structured collection of sayings of Jesus.

which can be established as authentic teaching of Jesus provide a better understanding of his message. The authentic teaching reinforces our general understanding of the Gospel message.

We need to be aware of Matthew's editing. Therefore, it was of some value for us to indicate what can be traced back to him with some historical certitude. Enough has been discovered to put them into a fairly long authentic column. There is also some material that cannot be authenticated as historical and seems more appropriately designated as a creation of a postresurrection Christian community. This will be discussed in the next section.

False Friends: Inauthentic Teaching

A false friend is one who appears loyal but in fact is just the opposite.[94] We can identify places in the Scriptures where we are misled by passages that appear to be authentic teaching of Jesus but in fact are not. They may well be interpretations of or additions by the evangelist.

It has already been noted that the evangelists edited their sources or at times proved to be very creative in expressing their faith. We mention a few. The Golden Rule, so named from the eighteenth century, is a well-known saying. "Do to others whatever you would have them do to you" (Matt 7:12a//Luke 7:31). One could easily imagine that the Golden Rule and the double love command as well as the command to love one's enemies are cut from the same cloth. They certainly make a unified theological statement. What may come as a surprise is that the Golden Rule is not an authentic saying of the historical Jesus. It fails the historical test. Meier believes that "there are no solid grounds for affirming that the Golden Rule was ever uttered by the historical Jesus."[95] There are several reasons for this conclusion. It fails to satisfy the criterion of discontinuity. It is found in both pagan and Jewish sources prior

---

94. The expression is often used in the study of language when a word from the language being studied seems to have an obvious meaning based on the language of the learner, but it does not. An example of a false friend is when we confuse the English word embarrassment for the Spanish word *embarazada* which means pregnant. Some false friends are also false cognates but not all.

95. Meier, *Marginal Jew*, 4:552, 557. He argues that it has a "pagan or a-theistic" origin. Meier, *Marginal Jew*, 4:651. It should not be presupposed, however, that all of Jesus' thoughts must be identified with the Torah. As a charismatic his thoughts could also appeal to reason.

JESUS THE TEACHER: AUTHENTIC THEMES AND SAYINGS

to Christ. There is no multiple attestation since it appears only in the Q source. And there is no likely coherence.[96]

The latter half of the verse, "this is the law and the prophets" (Matt 7:12b) is thought to be a Matthean addition. This verse is the last part of an inclusion; the first part is "do not think that I have come to abolish the law or the prophets. I have come not to abolish but to fulfill" (Matt 5:17). These two verses include or "sandwich" a major part of Matthew's Sermon on the Mount.

We have already pointed out that many of the parables could not be authenticated. It is thought that the parable of the good Samaritan (Luke 10:29–37) was the creation of Luke.[97] The exceptive clauses of Matt 5:32a is also thought to be a creation of Matthew.

The final verses of the Sermon on the Mount (Matt 7:28–29) require a brief comment. "When Jesus finished these words, the crowds were astonished at his teaching, for he taught them as one having authority, and not as their scribes." This is almost an exact quotation of Mark 1:22. "The people were astonished at his teaching, for he taught them as one having authority and not as the scribes." It seems apparent that Matthew borrowed this verse from Mark to indicate the authority he believed the sermon possessed.

Conclusion and Resume

In the last chapter, we explored Jesus' self-understanding. In this chapter, we explored his authentic teaching. There was considerable overlap between these chapters. We also appealed to previous chapters to support our conclusions. In this chapter we raised several hypothetical questions. What teaching can be identified as authentic, that is, what can be traced back to the historical Jesus with some degree of historical certainty? What teaching attributed to Jesus in the Scriptures actually belongs to the postresurrection editing and interpretation of the evangelist and the early church? We realize that the authors of the Scriptures inserted polemical and christological material into their writings. They edited the material to address the situation in which they lived, and which often differed considerably from the original context in which

---

96. Meier, *Marginal Jew*, 4:557.
97. Meier, *Marginal Jew*, 5:199–209.

Jesus conducted his mission.[98] The message begins in a Jewish-Palestinian context, moves to a Jewish-Hellenistic context and then finally finds its last home in the Hellenistic world. This created no small difficulty in locating the teaching of the historical Jesus.

The answer to these rhetorical questions which were raised above is actually a good deal of teaching can be traced back to the Jesus of history as authentic. The result of this chapter is evidence of that. There has been no attempt to arrange Jesus' teaching in a chronological order, an impossible task. It was given here in some sense of its importance.

We have covered several major themes that represent the authentic teaching of the historical Jesus. We also examined Jesus' theological debates with his contemporaries and noted his halakic teaching. In an ancillary way we also explored various other teachings that are authentic but by no means did we exhaust all the possibilities that could be discovered as authentic.[99] What we have discovered, however, has significance in our understanding, not only of the historical Jesus but it may also lead to a deeper understanding of the Jesus of faith. Keep in mind the distinction between the message revealed in the Scriptures (the writings accepted by the church as the authentic revelation proposed for our salvation) and the results of our search for the historical Jesus. These two important areas are distinct, but they are not separate. They intersect: the latter cannot exist without the former. It was the Jesus who lived and taught during his public life who was ultimately accepted as the Christ of faith.[100] This distinction is not without its pitfalls, and we should keep that in mind. As theologians we are primarily interested in the data of Scripture properly

---

98. We have discussed the rules that help us to arrive at the historical or authentic teaching above in chapter 4. The missionary activity from the Jewish world to the Hellenistic world required serious reframing of the message. This required a good deal of inculturation.

99. There are several significant authentic sayings of Jesus which were not discussed in this chapter but were discussed earlier. These are Jesus' response to the emissaries of the Baptist (Matt 11:5–6//Luke 7:22–27), Jesus declares that John the Baptist is the greatest in the kingdom (Matt 11:11 parr.), the saying that refers to Jesus is a winebibber and a glutton (Matt 11:18–19), Jesus declares the kingdom as present. "For behold, the kingdom of God is among you" (Luke 17:20b–21a), and Jesus' saying that "if it is by the finger of God that [I] drive out demons, then the kingdom of God has come upon you" (Luke 11:19–20; brackets in the original). There are several brief statements that are authentic. Among these are the eunuch saying (Matt 19:12), the coin of tribute (Mark 12:17 parr.) and the *qorban* saying (Mark 7:10–12). These and others are authentic sayings of Jesus.

100. Until Jesus' death we can only speak of a Jesusology. Christology proper does not come into existence until after the resurrection.

JESUS THE TEACHER: AUTHENTIC THEMES AND SAYINGS

understood but we are also deeply interested in recovering something of the historical Jesus. Jesus, as his first disciples experienced him, was the basis of their faith which continued after his death and resurrection. The context in which Jesus preached the kingdom of God and the context in which the Scriptures were written differed. But there is continuity in the original experience and the written expression which followed.

We make the claim that the historical Jesus and his authentic teaching, that is, the teaching that can be attributed to him in his ministry, is a valuable hermeneutical tool which can help us understand the Jesus of the Gospels and the truths of the Scriptures. These prove to be invaluable in our interpretation or understanding. They prevent us from remaking Jesus in our own image and likeness; from engaging in *eisegesis*.

What we have identified as authentic is limited. As mentioned above, much of that which belongs to the historical Jesus is found in his words (sayings, parables, narratives, and other literary genres) and deeds (miracles, table fellowship). There are many other teachings that belong to the historical Jesus. There are many more authentic sayings than those presented here; but these are a product of a serious application of the historical critical method in an effort to discover the authentic teaching of Jesus. Our inability to determine whether a teaching or a deed is authentic in no way lessens its value relative to our faith.

Our intention was to be as faithful to the Jesus of history as possible since he is the origin of all that follows. This can help us in appreciating the Scriptures as we have received them and most especially the work of the evangelists and their inspired work. They accomplished what we would call inculturation. They made the original preaching of Jesus make sense at a later time and in a different context and culture. We can also see the beginnings of doctrinal development in both Jesus' explanation of the Torah and his understanding of his Abba as well as in the composition of the New Testament. In fact, this continuity is what is demanded in faith. There is what we call a conceptual development, and this is one of our very strong presuppositions. Our faith in Christ was not an invention of the early church.[101] It was the development of those committed to him and to his teaching.

---

101. The thought of Saint Vincent of Lerins seems to express this well. He says that "in the Catholic Church itself, every care should be taken to hold fast to what has been believed everywhere, always, and by all" (*Quod ubique, quod semper, quod ab omnibus creditum est*). Vincent of Lerins, *Commonitories*, 270.

14

Jerusalem: The Final Act

Introduction

THE BAPTISM OF JESUS in the Jordan by John the Baptist and the final events of Jesus' life in Jerusalem serve as bookends for his entire ministry.[1] Jesus' baptism was logically the first event in his public life. The passion was not only historically the last of the events, but it was also the first to be formally written in the Scriptures.[2] These "bookends" provide us enormous insight into the person and message of Jesus of Nazareth.

The final events of his life are a rich source of discovery of Jesus' understanding of his mission and his role in preparing the way for the coming of the kingdom.[3] In a sense, it interprets all that came before. Jesus is the Elijah-like eschatological prophet who ushers in the end time. As we would expect, his final words and actions are of special

---

1. Because of the nature of our sources, no chronology of events in the life of Jesus can be definitively established. At best, we can offer a general framework. The events between the baptism and the passion have been examined thematically as is clear from the previous chapters.

2. It was indicated above that the passion narratives were the first formal writings of the Gospels. Events that occurred during Jesus' mission were later appended to them. The resurrection and infancy narratives were added last.

3. The fifth primary criterion of the historical-critical method proposed by Meier is named the "Criterion of Rejection and Execution." It examines what Jesus did and said that would bring about his death. Meier, *Marginal Jew*, 1:177. The entrance of Jesus into Jerusalem and the temple incident would certainly be significant both in understanding what brought about Jesus' death as well as giving us some insight into his personal understanding.

JERUSALEM: THE FINAL ACT

import. They are foundational. Three specific events, which occur in the last week of Jesus' life are especially significant.[4] The first is Jesus' entrance into Jerusalem. The second is the temple incident often referred to as the cleansing of the temple. The third is Jesus' Last Supper with his disciples.[5] All three events are directed in a distinct way to the coming of the kingdom, and all three provide critical insight into the authentic Jesus tradition. There is widespread support that these three events are authentic historical events of Jesus' life.[6] We add a fourth, the crucifixion and death of Jesus. This event is historically certain, and is interpretive of the meaning of Jesus' life. We will exam this in chapter 15.

The Symbolic Acts of the Last Week

The entrance of Jesus into Jerusalem and the temple incident which follows shed considerable light on Jesus' self-understanding. These two prophetic acts are historically authentic. What was Jesus' motive for carrying out these events in the manner that he did?

Jesus' Entrance into Jerusalem

Jesus began his last week in Jerusalem just prior to the celebration of the Passover. It was a historical event reported in all four Gospels.[7] There

---

4. The chronology of the last week of Jesus' life is taken from the Gospel of Mark. The other Gospels make no attempt to give a chronology. It was a convenient structure for Mark to recount Jesus' last days. See Borg and Crossan, *Last Week*. Using the framework provided by the Gospel of Mark, the authors give a day-by-day account of Jesus' last week from Palm Sunday to Easter Sunday.

5. Jeremias includes the entire last week of Jesus' life in the passion narrative. This includes the entrance into Jerusalem as well as the temple Incident. This corresponds to what is referred to as passion week. *The New Jerome Biblical Commentary* and *The Paulist Biblical Commentary* identify the Passion Narrative as Mark 14:1—15:36, Matt 26:1—27:66; Luke 22:1—23:56; and John 18:1—19:42.

6. Jesus' entrance into Jerusalem, the temple incident, and the Last Supper are included in the "almost indisputable facts." The complete list was given in the preface, xin9 above. In their book *The Last Week*, Borg and Crossan examine the last week of Jesus' life but do so from a careful reading of the text and not from an historical examination. They rely on the very carefully structured narrative found in Mark's Gospel. Meier also believes that these events are historical. For his position on the two prophetic acts, see Meier, *Marginal Jew*, 3:575n26.

7. The references for Jesus' entrance into Jerusalem are in Mark 1:1–11//Matt 21:1–9//Luke 19:29–38; and John 12:12–19. The event is considered to be historical.

would be a considerable number of pilgrims in Jerusalem at this time. The number has been estimated as three hundred thousand to four hundred thousand.[8] Jesus' entered Jerusalem of his own initiative and he is described as coming on a colt that had not yet been ridden.[9] This is an allusion to the prophet Zechariah. "Exalt greatly, O daughter Zion! Shout for joy, O daughter Jerusalem! Behold: your king is coming to you, a just savior is he, humble, and riding on a donkey, on a colt, the foal of a donkey" (Zech 9:9). All four Gospels describe the crowd as shouting a verse from Ps 118:26. In his Gospel, Luke reshapes the verse to refer to Jesus as "the king who comes in the name of the Lord" (Luke 19:38).[10]

Sanders understands Jesus' entry into Jerusalem as a prophetic act.[11] He admits there are many who do not believe Jesus' entry was historical, but he is inclined to think that it was.[12] Kinman argues persuasively that Jesus' entry into Jerusalem is historical.[13] He understands this as a royal entry. Jesus is king.[14] He does not come in power and as a conqueror. Neither is he declared directly as the Messiah. Meier describes this as a "symbolic claim to messianic status."[15] It represented a peaceful king. It also represented the conflict between the Imperial kingdom and the kingdom of God. It is the beginning of the eschatological events. This conflict will continue into the temple.

How was this prophetic act received by those who observed it? How was it received by the Romans and the Jewish authorities? Borg

---

8. Sanders, *Historical Figure of Jesus*, 249. Sanders comments on the feast are worth reading. The size of the crowd that welcomed Jesus has been variously described by commenters as both large and small.

9. The Gospel of John seems to deviate from the Synoptic tradition on this point. In John's version, Jesus appears to be riding a full-grown animal.

10. Pilate interrogated Jesus with the question, "Are you the king of the Jews?" (Mark 15:2 parr.).

11. Sanders, *Historical Figure of Jesus*, 253. Sanders also enumerates similar prophetic acts found in the Old Testament.

12. Sanders, *Historical Figure of Jesus*, 254. Meier says much the same thing. See Meier, "Jesus," in *NJBC*, 78:44.

13. Kinman, "Jesus' Royal Entry into Jerusalem." The conclusions to this study are found on pages 257–60.

14. Meier supports this. See Meier, *Marginal Jew*, 2:885. Meier describes the entry of Jesus into Jerusalem as royal—he is king. This act confronts both Roman and Jewish systems of oppression. The use of Zech 9:9 understands the nature of Jesus entrance as one of humility and not of power. See also Meier, *Marginal Jew*, 3:496; Meier, "Jesus Christ," 15.

15. Meier, "Jesus Christ," 15.

and Crossan draw an insightful comparison in *The Last Week* between Jesus' entrance into the city, and an imaginary Roman legion entering the city through another gate.[16] The contrast is instructive. Jesus' prophetic act would have been very provocative to the Romans, and one wonders why Jesus was not immediately arrested by the political powers. It seems obvious that Jesus was sending a message to both the Roman and Jewish authorities.

The Temple Incident

The entrance of Jesus into Jerusalem in the manner he chose can only be understood in conjunction with what is often referred to as the cleansing of the temple.[17] Sanders and Herzog refer to this as a controversy. Herzog adds that it is a disturbance, which is certainly how it is portrayed in the Gospels.[18] The temple incident was not simply a pious act on Jesus' part. The narrative describes Jesus as having perceived that his Father's house had been desecrated.[19] We are perhaps misled by the statement that "you [money changers and sellers of sacrificial animals] have made [my father's house] a den of thieves" (Mark 11:17 parr.).[20] These functions were necessary for the operation of the temple.[21] Jesus' driving out those selling animals and overturning the tables of the money changers was a prophetic act and not simply an act of piety.[22] The words associated with

---

16. Borg and Crossan, *Last Week*, 2–5, 30. Borg and Crossan speak of two processions, a peasant procession and an imperial procession.

17. The NABRE describes this event as the "Cleansing of the Temple." The NRSV describes it as "Jesus Cleanses the Temple." The New Jerusalem Bible uses the headline "The expulsion of the dealers." As we shall see these expressions may be somewhat misleading.

18. One of the "almost indisputable facts" enumerated by Sanders and supported by Herzog is that Jesus engaged in a controversy about the temple. This narrative can be found in Mark 11:15-17; Matt 21:12-13; Luke 19:45-46; and John 2:13-17. Interestingly enough, the Gospel of John situates the cleansing of the temple early in Jesus' ministry, following the wedding feast of Cana.

19. In the Synoptic version of this narrative, Jesus is described as alluding to Isa 56:7 or Jer 7:11. John's version of the incident seems to allude to Ps 29:10.

20. This verse (Mark 11:17 parr.) refers to Isa 56:7 and Jer 7:11.

21. The animals were for the sacrifice called for by the law. The exchange of money was to enable pilgrims to pay the temple tax.

22. Sanders indicates that "the action of overturning symbolized destruction rather than cleansing as an act of moral reform." Sanders, *Historical Figure of Jesus*, 257. John's version (John 2:13-22) describes the incident to be even more dramatic than the

this act are no longer available to us but it seems likely they concerned the destruction of the temple.[23] It is possible the passage relating to the destruction of the temple had been separated from the dramatic action of Jesus and placed elsewhere in the Gospel text.[24] But in this action, Jesus exercises the authority to call the temple into question. This was not a call for reformation.[25] Turning over tables was a deliberate act of destruction. It was the end of the old order including the temple. Jesus was establishing a revolutionary form of worshiping God.[26] This act would have been offensive to all who witnessed it, and Jeremias believes that Jesus risked his life by doing it.[27] It is a clarion call to live out the demands of the kingdom which signifies a marked departure from the old way. It is certainly clear that Christians understood Jesus, in his person, as replacing the Temple. The note in the NABRE for Matt 21:12–17 is as follows: "Thus Jesus' attack on those so engaged [in selling and buying] and his charge that they were making God's house of prayer a den of thieves (vv. 12–13) constituted a claim to authority over the religious practices of Israel and were a challenge to the priestly authorities."[28] In my judgment this act was more than a challenge to the authorities. This was an end to temple worship, a practice Jesus was devoted to during his lifetime. This dramatic symbolic act signifies a change in the covenant as will become clearer when we examine the Last Supper.

Synoptic version. Jesus formed a whip and drove the money changers and those who sold animals out of the temple area. He spilled the coins and overturned the tables of the money changers.

23. Meier, "Jesus," in *NJBC*, 78:74.

24. See Mark 13:1–2//Matt 24:1–2//Luke 21:5–6. It is thought that this prophecy about the destruction of the temple might actually have been connected to the cleansing of the temple narrative and then later moved to another place in the Gospel. The motive for this edit would have been that after the actual destruction of the temple in AD 70, the prophecy joined to the prophetic act would have been problematic.

25. Meier sees this as a call for radical change and not an act calling for reform. It is a challenge to a "corrupt and unpopular hierarchy in Jerusalem." Meier, "Jesus," in *NJBC*, 78:74.

26. Jesus' message was originally directed to all of Israel. This symbolic act seems more directed to the authorities, and it would have been understood by them as such. Borg and Crossan point out that "It [the conflict] was not Jesus against Judaism, or Judaism against Jesus. Rather his was a Jewish voice . . . about what the loyalty to the God of Judaism meant." Borg and Crossan, *Last Week*, 30.

27. Jeremias, *New Testament Theology*, 279.

28. This supports the answer to the question as to whether Jesus changed the law. This goes beyond the various discussions on the law above.

Jesus performs both of these prophetic acts at his personal initiation and authority and, most significantly, at his peril. They give us a privileged insight into his understanding of his ministry and authority. Jesus initiates the eschatological event, and he does so fully conscious of the meaning of his actions.

The Final Solemn Acts: The Last Supper

Jesus understood himself as the eschatological prophet. He preached the immanent coming of the kingdom and performed healings and exorcisms to support his message.[29] His entire ministry was a prelude to the Last Supper.

The History of the Last Supper[30]

The Last Supper is one of the indisputable events associated with the historical Jesus.[31] Meier tells us that "the historicity of a final meal held by Jesus with his disciples is generally accepted by scholars across the spectrum, since its existence is supported both by the criterion of multiple attestations and the criterion of coherence."[32] It is clearly attested in all the Gospels as well as in Paul's first letter to the Corinthians.[33]

The event of the Last Supper is historically grounded. Jesus's words over the bread and wine are also historically authentic. Meier tell us that

---

29. Jesus also preached the kingdom as present. This creates a tension for the interpreter. This was discussed earlier in chapter 5.

30. The Last Supper continues Jesus' table fellowship. These festive meals celebrated during Jesus' lifetime were a symbolic enactment of the divine banquet in the kingdom of God. The Last Supper also looks proleptically to the divine heavenly banquet. Jesus' table fellowship with sinners is supported by the criteria of embarrassment and discontinuity with the early church. See Meier, *Marginal Jew*, 2:965–67.

31. It is not found on Sanders' list, but it has been added by Herzog. There are good reasons for adding it.

32. Meier, *Marginal Jew*, 2:302.

33. Our principal sources include the following. Paul's first letter to the Corinthians (1 Cor 11:23–26) is the earliest written tradition. Paul probably received it about AD 33. It was verified on his first trip to Jerusalem. Mark 14:22–26 is the most primitive of the Synoptic tradition. Matt 26:26–30 depends upon Mark. Luke 22:14–20 possibly relied on Mark but seems to be more dependent upon Paul. It is also possible that he relied on his own source, L. John 6:22–59 is the bread of life discourse. The most significant verses for our purposes are John 6:35, 51, and 53–56. See Meier, *Marginal Jew*, 4:71n79.

"among the best attested sayings of Jesus are the 'Eucharistic words' of Jesus over the bread and wine at the Last Supper (with four different formulations).... Jesus had an opportunity to say them only once before his arrest and execution."[34] The prophecy that followed the cup words is important since it expresses Jesus' personal understanding. "Amen, I say to you, I shall not drink again the fruit of the vine until the day when I drink it new in the kingdom of God" (Mark 14:25 parr.).[35] Both Meier and Fuller believe this is an authentic saying of the historical Jesus.[36] Thus the event and the narratives of the Last Supper are historically authentic. This provides us with an extremely important source to discover the personal understanding of the historical Jesus.

The Last Supper: A Passover or a Farewell Meal

The Last Supper was a memorable meal held by Jesus with his disciples in Jerusalem around AD 30. It was a prelude to his death. As the eschatological prophet, Jesus was fully aware of a prophet's death. There are numerous references which support that Jesus both anticipated and predicted his impending death.[37] Jeremias tells us that "there can be no doubt that Jesus expected his suffering and death."[38]

Jesus initiated the Last Supper with the expectation that it would be his last meal. In fact, he prophesied his death at the supper.[39] The Last Supper is meant to be understood as the last of a series of meals,

---

34. Meier, *Marginal Jew*, 4:71 n.79.

35. Meier, *Marginal Jew*, 2:302-9.

36. Fuller, *Mission and Achievement of Jesus*, 75-76; Meier, *Marginal Jew*, 2:302-9 and 1036n317.

37. Jesus' death is predicted three times in the Synoptic Gospels (Mark 8:31-33 parr.; Mark 9:30-32 parr.; Mark 10:32-34 parr.). Jesus alludes to his possible death in the authentic parable of the wicked tenants (Mark 12:1-12 parr.). In John 7:1 and 5:18 we read that "the Jews were trying to kill him." Jeremias argues that Jesus forecast his death. See Jeremias, *New Testament Theology*, 280-86. Fuller, however, argues that the texts do not supply us with Jesus' understanding of his death. See Fuller, *Foundations of New Testament Christology*, 118-19. He says, "So we cannot use the Marcan passion predictions as evidence for Jesus's self-understanding." John Meier tells us that "Jesus would have had to be a simpleton not to have foreseen the possibility of a violent death when visiting the capital at Passover." Meier, "Jesus," in *NJBC*, 78:45-50.

38. Jeremias, *New Testament Theology*, 286.

39. Luke positions the prophecy before the meal. Mark joins it to the cup saying. See Meier, *Marginal Jew*, 2:307. The significant texts are Mark 14:25//Matt 26:29//and Luke 22:18.

all of which intended to celebrate the joy of the heavenly banquet.[40] The final farewell is generally accepted by scholars as belonging to the authentic historical tradition.

Given its historical authenticity, the Last Supper provides us critical insight into Jesus' self-understanding. The question that immediately confronts us is whether the Last Supper was a Passover meal or a farewell meal in the style of Jesus' festive meals (the table fellowship meals). Answering this question will help us discern the meaning Jesus intended for this meal.

Was the Last Supper a Passover Meal?

According to the Jewish manner of reckoning time, days were measured from sundown to sundown. Thus, the new day began at sundown. According to the tradition, the Passover meal was prescribed in Exod 12:8 to be eaten in the evening after sundown of 15 Nisan, the first month of the Jewish calendar.[41] The lambs for the meal were sacrificed early in the day, between 3:00 p.m. and 5:00 p.m. Therefore, according to the Jewish calendar, the lambs were slain on 14 Nisan and the Passover was celebrated on 15 Nisan.[42]

The Synoptic tradition leads us to presume that this meal was a Passover because the Gospel narrative indicates that Jesus sent his disciples to prepare for one.[43] Both Jeremias and Fuller argue that the Last Supper was a Passover meal though in diverse ways. Jeremias accepts the Synoptic chronology as historical.[44] The roots of the Last Supper are in the festive meals of Jesus. In *The Eucharistic Words of Jesus*, Jeremias goes

---

40. Concerning a discussion of the banquet theme, see Meier, *Marginal Jew*, 2:1036n317. Footnote 317 refers to pages 965–67 in the text.

41. The Passover ritual is described in Exod 12:1–28, 43–50.

42. By way of explanation, it should be noted that the Feast of Unleavened Bread began on 14 Nissan and ended on 21 Nissan. It was a seven-day celebration in which the first day, Passover, and the last day were celebrated with great solemnity. The day before Passover is known as the day of preparation. This is recorded in Exod 12:1–20. It is repeated in Deut 16:1–8. It is a perpetual memorial (Exod 12:14, 17) that signifies the salvation of the Hebrews from the Egyptians and their wandering in the desert.

43. Mark 14:12–16//Matt 26:17–19//Luke 22:7–13 refer to the preparation for the Feast of Unleavened Bread. This reference occurs only once and is not likely to be historically authentic. During the meal, Luke 22:15 specifically identifies the meal as a Passover. This is the only reference that refers to the meal as a Passover.

44. Jeremias' argumentation can be found in *Eucharistic Words*, 15–84.

to great lengths to defend his thesis and to respond to its critics.[45] His main argument focuses on Jesus' interpretation of the bread and wine. He says, "This is the fixed part of the Passover ritual."[46] Jesus, acting as the head of the household, gave the Passover meal a new interpretation. The bread and wine of the Passover meal became his body and blood.[47] There is some theological cogency to this argument.

Fuller agrees with Jeremias that the Last Supper was a Passover meal. He posits, however, that Jesus anticipated its celebration. He did not celebrate the Passover meal on the day the liturgy called for.[48] Like Jeremias, Fuller also argues from his knowledge of the nature of a Passover meal. As was the custom, a Passover meal always began with a discourse. The observance of the Passover Feast included the question of the children, "What does this rite of yours mean?" (Exod 12:26; Deut 6:20–25).[49] This preceded the supper. The one who led the celebration, normally the head of the house, then explained the salvific event of the Passover.[50] We can imagine that the Last Supper was similar. Most likely, Jesus instructed his disciples before the meal which would have been the custom of anyone leading the Passover Seder service.[51]

Fuller suggests that the discourse which preceded the sharing of the bread and wine had the nature of the Haggadah.[52] He believes that the verse "amen, I say to you, I shall not drink again the fruit of the vine until the day when I drink it new in the kingdom of God" (Mark 14:25) is an

---

45. Jeremias, *Eucharistic Words*, 41–84.

46. Jeremias, *Eucharistic Words*, 56.

47. Jeremias, *New Testament Theology*, 290. It was the head of the house who explained the significance of the Passover meal. See Exod 12:26 and 13:8. At the Last Supper, Jesus gave a new interpretation to the Passover meal.

48. Fuller, *Mission and Achievement of Jesus*, 70.

49. The question is asked by the youngest person at the Passover Seder. It is responded to by the Seder leader who would explain the events of salvation which occurred in the exodus. See Exod 12:20; 13:8, 14; Deut 6:20–25.

50. Jeremias, *New Testament Theology*, 290. Jeremias believed this was a Passover meal. Others are not so sure. Meier says that there is nothing "that demands that we consider the Last Supper a Passover meal." Meier, *Marginal Jew*, 1:397. Only Luke describes the meal as a Passover.

51. The Scriptures indicate that there was a meal tradition which preceded the sharing of the bread and wine. This tradition can be found in Mark 14:17–21; Luke 22:15–16; the Farewell Discourse of John.

52. Fuller, *Mission and Achievement of Jesus*, 71. The Haggadah is a text that sets out the order of the Seder meal. While Jeremias does not refer to the Haggadah, he does speak of Jesus acting as the head of the household. Jeremias, *New Testament Theology*, 290–92. The Haggadah was not written before AD 170.

interpretive addition which represents the mind of Jesus.[53] It would have been expressed at an earlier stage of the meal. This authentic, genuine memory would have been added later to the words of bread and wine by the (Aramaic-speaking) community.[54] This is an intriguing idea.

Was the Last Supper a Farewell Meal?[55]

Both the Synoptic Gospels and the Gospel of John agree that the Last Supper meal took place on Thursday evening and that Jesus was crucified on Friday. But they disagree on the date of Passover. Let us consider the Synoptic chronology first. If the lambs were prepared on Thursday, which was required by law, and eaten at Passover on Thursday evening after sundown, Jesus' crucifixion and death would have been placed on the day of Passover. It seems unlikely that Jesus' arrest and trial by the Sanhedrin would have occurred on the Passover. The chronology of the Gospel of John is markedly different. John 18:28 describes Jesus as having been brought from Caiaphas to the praetorium in the morning. This would have been on Friday after the meal had been eaten on Thursday evening according to the Synoptic tradition. The narrative tells us that they "did not enter the praetorium, in order not to be defiled so that they could eat the Passover" (John 18:28b). John's telling of the events indicates clearly that the Passover meal had not yet been eaten by observant Jews, Caiaphas, or the Jewish authorities. It would be eaten that evening (Friday, 15 Nisan). Jesus had been taken down from the cross around 3:00 p.m. before the Passover festival began. According to the chronology provided by John, Friday after sundown would be 15 Nisan, the beginning of Passover. Passover day and the Sabbath coincided during this year.[56] John places Passover on the Sabbath, a more reasonable assumption than that of the Synoptics.

---

53. Luke 22:18 is a parallel. According to Meier, this is an authentic saying of Jesus. See Meier, *Marginal Jew*, 2:305, 309. It is totally discontinuous with the early church for whom the death was not recognized as a failure.

54. The argument above holds even if this was not a Passover meal.

55. Meier's calculation of the date of Last Supper and the crucifixion can be found in Meier, *Marginal Jew*, 1:386–401.

56. The chronology in the Gospel of John put Thursday on 13 Nisan, Friday on 14 Nisan, and Saturday on 15 Nisan. Jesus was taken down from the cross before sundown on 14 Nisan, that is, before the beginning of Passover and the Passover meal.

The supper, viewed in itself, gives no indication that it was a Passover meal.[57] Meier offers that "the context of the Passover meal is rather a theological framework created by Mark and followed by Matthew and Luke."[58] The Gospel of John places Jesus' death on preparation day, that is, the day before the Passover (John 19:31). He also describes that Jesus' body was put in the tomb on preparation day (John 19:41). We should understand that preparation day is the time the lambs are slaughtered. Passover does not begin until after sundown.

The chronology of John seems more likely than that of the Synoptics. While the Synoptic tradition may have sound theological reasons for situating the Last Supper on Passover, its chronology creates problems. The Synoptic Gospels describe Jesus' arrest as having occurred at night after which he was brought before the Sanhedrin. Luke speaks of this meeting as occurring "when day came" (Luke 23:66). Mark describes Jesus as having been brought before Pilate "as morning came" (Mark 15:1). The Synoptics agree. There is no mention of becoming unclean should they enter the praetorium. That they would engage Pilate on Passover, and that Jesus would be put to death on the same day thus seems highly unlikely. Meier concludes that the Last Supper was a memorable farewell meal and not a Passover.[59] Raymond Brown agrees.[60]

The Last Supper then was most likely not a Passover meal. It was the last in the line of many festive meals celebrated by Jesus with his disciples, tax collectors, and sinners. It is possible, however, that Jesus celebrated this last meal in anticipation of the feast of Passover.[61] By design, Jesus prepared his disciples for his impending death. The question remains: did Jesus anticipate celebrating a Passover meal or was it simply the last of his festive meals with his disciples?

Fitzmyer argues well for both chronologies, but concludes that we cannot determine which one is factual.[62] It should be noted that the evangelists had theological reasons for situating the Last Supper as

57. Luke 22:15 refers to the meal as a Passover. In Luke's version, before Jesus spoke the words over bread, the following statement is attributed to him. "I have eagerly desired to eat this Passover with you before I suffer." This is Luke's edit. It is not found in Mark or Paul. If this verse were removed, the eucharistic tradition would give no indication that the Last Supper was a Passover.

58. Meier, "Eucharist at the Last Supper," 344.

59. Meier, *Marginal Jew*, 1:386–401.

60. Brown, *The Gospel According to John*, 2:555–58.

61. Fuller, *Mission and Achievement of Jesus*, 70–71. This is Fuller's position.

62. Fitzmyer, *Gospel According to Luke*, 2:1382.

they did. The Synoptics identify the Last Supper with the Passover. Jesus reinterpreted the Passover Feast just as Moses interpreted the events that led to the original feast. On the other hand, the Gospel of John places Jesus' death at the time when the lambs were sacrificed for the Passover.[63] Both choices have merit from a theological-literary perspective.

The Sources: Some Significant Features[64]

The events of the Last Supper and its associated narratives are accepted as historical. However, Paul and the evangelists describe the words and gestures differently. There are two important traditions to consider. The first is Mark 14:22–25, thought by many to be the oldest tradition and most likely dependent upon an earlier pre-Marcan tradition. Matt 26:26–29 is dependent on Mark and the differences between their narratives are attributed to Matthew's editing. The second principal source is 1 Cor 11:23–25. Paul wrote this authentic epistle around AD 55. It should be noted that Paul's first letter to the Corinthians is the earliest text in the New Testament that mentions the eucharistic tradition. It is likely that Paul received this tradition in Damascus shortly after his conversion which would be circa AD 33.[65] Luke is more difficult to situate. It is certain that Luke is in general dependent upon Mark, and had this Gospel at his disposal. However, Luke also worked in a Pauline church and could have been dependent on the Pauline tradition. Fitzmyer proposes a more radical solution. He speculates that Luke had an independent source L (Luke Special) which he substituted for Mark's version.[66] This is an indication of how complex these texts are. It is likely that the bread words and the cup words were originally separated as they are in Paul and Luke. They are joined in Mark and Matthew. There is little balance between the

---

63. John identifies Jesus with the "Lamb of God." See John 1:29, 36. This identification corresponds to his chronology of the Last Supper.

64. We will follow the common practice of referring to the words of institution as bread words and cup words.

65. Fuller, *Mission and Achievement of Jesus*, 66. See Acts 9:20–31 and Gal 1:17–18. It is also possible that he received it when he first visited Jerusalem a few years later but this seems less likely.

66. Fitzmyer argues that Luke's substitution for Mark is certainly from the L (Luke Special) "for vv. 15–17 and 19cd, 20, and probably also for v. 18." He continues, "It is impossible that vv. 15–18 are a mere reworking of Mark 14:25." Fitzmyer, *Gospel According to Luke*, 2:1386. Jeremias seems to find Luke's entire narrative dependent upon L with Mark woven in. Jeremias, *Eucharistic Words*, 97.

bread words and the cup words in either tradition. The order would have been the bread broken and shared at the beginning of the meal and the cup of wine would follow the meal. Oddly enough, Luke added a second cup at the beginning of the meal which is absent from our other sources. He alone refers to this meal as a Passover. The bread and cup words appear to be substantially the same in all of the traditions.

The different traditions found in the Gospels and in Paul represent the liturgical practices used in the various early communities before the early church arrived at a more uniform formula.[67] Liturgical use brought these traditions together and moved toward balance that was not in the original meal. The original words of Jesus would be hard to determine, although Meier has offered his conjecture which will be examined below.

The attempt to reconstruct the tradition and to understand the editing of the evangelists and Paul is to get closer to the original bread and cup words of Jesus. This should assist us in establishing the authentic meaning. We will follow Meier's reconstruction.

The Meaning of the Last Supper

We have not often been treated to a historical event in the life of Jesus in which the entire narrative is considered his authentic teaching. The Last Supper is one such episode. As the eschatological prophet, Jesus celebrated numerous festive meals with his disciples, tax collectors, and sinners.[68] The Last Supper is the last of these meals and is the culmination of Jesus' earthly ministry.[69] We can presume that it was also the event at which he gave his final instructions to his disciples. During the meal Jesus took the initiative and acted on his personal authority. Jesus offered the bread and wine as symbolic of himself, his entire life. The Last Supper narrative can be conveniently divided into the words of Jesus over the bread, the words

---

67. John's tradition is found in the Bread of Life Discourse, John 6:22–59. The parallel to the bread and cup are John 6:53–56. John did not narrate the institution of the Eucharist.

68. During his lifetime Jesus did not proclaim himself; he proclaimed the kingdom of God. In the preceding chapters, we discovered some of Jesus' self-understanding even though it was with much difficulty. It was often implied in what he said and did. Jesus understood himself as the eschatological prophet, the one who initiated the coming of the kingdom. It also seems clear that this was his self-understanding at the Last Supper. Jesus' prediction of his death cannot be separated from his prophetic ministry.

69. The Last Supper is linked to Jesus' festive meals. See Jeremias, *New Testament Theology*, 290

over the wine, and the prophecy that immediately follows. We will deal with the bread words, the cup words, and the prophecy in order.[70]

The Words of Institution: The Bread Words and Cup Words

It seems clear that the breaking of the bread occurred at the beginning of the meal. This would have been normal were it a Passover meal or one of Jesus' festive meals. Jesus' words over the bread are consistent in all of the traditions and their variations.[71] Each tradition contains a blessing (or a giving thanks), the breaking of the bread, and Jesus' pronouncement that "this is my body."[72] Jesus identified the bread as his body.[73] In this context, body means Jesus' person, his life.

The words that Jesus spoke when offering the cup are more developed than the bread words. Meier's reconstruction reads as follows. "He [Jesus] took bread, and giving thanks [or: pronouncing a blessing], Broke [it] and said: 'This is my body.' Likewise also the cup, after supper, saying: 'This cup is the covenant in my blood.'"[74] It is important to note that the expressions "which will be shed for many/for you" (Mark 14:24; Matt 26:18; Luke 22:20) along with Paul's expression "that is for you" (1 Cor 11:24b) are absent from Meier's reconstruction.[75] The same should also be noted for the expression "do this in memory/in remembrance of me"

---

70. The words of Jesus over the bread and wine are found in the two principal sources: Mark 14:22-24 and 1 Cor 11:23-25. The prophecy which follows the bread and cup words can be found in Mark 14:25//Matt 26:29; and Luke 22:18.

71. See Fitzmyer, *Gospel According to Luke*, 2:1393.

72. This agrees with Meier's reconstruction.

73. The Aramaic retroversion would read flesh in place of body.

74. Meier, "Eucharist at the Last Supper," 347; brackets in the original. Meier also gives a reconstruction in "Jesus," in *NJBC*, 78:51. The *NJBC* was published in 1990. This is five years prior to the article published in *Theology Digest*. It differs only slightly from the version quoted above. The *NJBC* version is "this is my flesh [body]," and "this [cup?] is [= contains, mediates] the covenant [sealed] by my blood." This echoes Exod 24:8. It is of some interest that Mark 14:24 and Matt 26:28 refer to a "covenant." Luke 22:20 and 1 Cor 11:25 both refer to a "new covenant." This difference will be discussed below.

75. The NRSV translates v. 20 as "poured out for you." The NABRE and NRSV translations of v. 20 are conceptually identical. Is this Lukan verse from his L source or is it borrowed from Mark? There is some dispute about this. It would lend some weight to its historicity if v. 20 is from L. This would be theologically significant. There is something vicarious expressed in these verses. If these are two independent sources, Paul and L, then an argument could be made that these are from the Jesus of history. Even if these are not authentic, they imply Jesus' understanding of his death as both vicarious and salvific.

(Luke 22:19; 1 Cor 11:24, 25). These too are absent from Meier's reconstruction. Paul repeats the injunction "do this . . . in memory of me" over the cup words which he had attached to the bread words. He alone has this phrase attached to the cup. In the mind of Paul, this is clearly a rite that is to be repeated.[76] These expressions are not in Meier's reconstruction. He does not consider them authentic to the Jesus of history. As we shall see, Jeremias has a different view which we will discuss below.

The cup is offered at the end of the meal as suggested by Paul and Luke; Mark has closely aligned the bread and cup words together.[77] Even though it is likely that all those in attendance had a personal cup of wine at the Last Supper, Jesus shares one cup with the entire group.[78] This is a significant action. It identifies solidarity between Jesus and those who shared in the meal/cup. The meal pointed to the future kingdom and the covenant inaugurated by Jesus' death.[79] Sharing in the bread and cup signified participation of all those sharing the meal in the eschatological banquet and its benefits.[80]

The Covenant

Each of our four sources reveals that when Jesus shared the cup with his disciples, he associated it with the covenant. The word itself should draw our attention because of its significance in affirming the relation between God and his people. In Mark's version, after Jesus had offered

---

76. According to Fitzmyer, "the vicarious and soteriological character of Jesus' reinterpretation comes out still more clearly in his words over the cup after the meal." Fitzmyer, *Gospel According to Luke*, 2:1391. The identification of the vicarious and soteriological nature of Jesus words over the bread and cup is significant for both faith and theology.

77. The present liturgy of the Catholic Church refers to the cup following the meal. "In the same manner when supper was over." The one exception is in Eucharistic Prayer IV which makes no reference to any elapsed time between the bread and cup words.

78. See Mark 14:24//Matt 26:27//Luke 22:17; and 1 Cor 11: 25. The disciples all drink from the one cup offered by Jesus. This is a symbolic way of expressing the disciples share in this atoning power of his death. See Jeremias, *New Testament Theology*, 292. Meier does not refer to the atoning power of Jesus death. Instead, he describes the disciples' sharing of the one cup of Jesus as an action which "contains, mediates, communicates that basic relationship between God and Israel . . . which Jesus is about to renew and bring to consummation" with his death. See Meier, "Eucharist at the Last Supper," 349.

79. Sanders, *Historical Figure of Jesus*, 264.

80. Jesus invites the disciples to share in the effects of the event about to transpire.

the bread as his body, "he said to them, 'This is my blood of the covenant'" (Mark 14:24//Matt 26:28).[81] This is an early tradition in which the death of Jesus was clearly anticipated. Paul's tradition differs only slightly. "This cup is the new covenant in my blood" (1 Cor 11:25// Luke 22:20). Both of the principal sources, Mark and Paul, refer to the cup as Jesus' death (vicarious sacrifice?), which he anticipated.[82] The future kingdom and his covenant, which are intimately linked concepts, would be inaugurated by his death.[83]

What meaning did Jesus intend to communicate by this reference to covenant? It is clear that the Old Testament often makes mention of covenants. God made a covenant with Noah (Gen 9:9), and another covenant with Abraham (Gen 17:7). The most significant covenant is the one God made with Moses and the Israelites (Exod 19:3–8).[84] This followed the fundamental saving act of God with his people the Israelites. There is a relation between the exodus from Egypt and the covenant made on Mount Sinai (Horeb). The words Jesus said over the cup reflect the ratification of the covenant as found in Exod 24:8. After reading the covenant to the people, Moses sprinkled the blood of the sacrifice on them. The words are informative. "Then he [Moses] took the blood and splashed it on the people, saying, 'This is the blood of the covenant which the LORD has made with you according to all these words'" (Exod 24:8). The cup words in Mark are almost identical to the words in Exodus. What seems clear is that Jesus interpreted his last meal with his disciples in reference to the original covenant with Moses. He gave the meal, the bread and cup words, a special significance. He understood that his death would

---

81. The reconstruction of Meier reads, "This cup is the covenant in my blood." This was discussed above. See above, 275n74. This verse is considered an authentic historical statement of Jesus. Paul and Luke refer to a "new" covenant. This will be discussed below. Fuller believes that the covenant language was the authentic language of Jesus, but it was actually spoken at the Haggadah in anticipation of the meal. The expression was added to the cup words by the Aramaic speaking community. He believed that Luke 22:29 is the actual expression spoken by Jesus. For his arguments see Fuller, *Mission and Achievement of Jesus*, 69–74.

82. It also indicates that his life is being offered for those who follow him. This will be discussed below when we discuss *atonement*.

83. Sanders, *Historical Figure of Jesus*, 264. Meier, "Jesus," in *NJBC*, 78:51.

84. These verses narrate God's initiation of the covenant with Israel on Mount Sinai. Exodus 24:1–8 narrates the ratification of the covenant. It is the symbolic or liturgical way of making concrete this agreement. The covenant is also expressed in Deut 5:1–4. Deuteronomy names the mountain as Horeb.

restore the covenant.[85] In so doing, Jesus pointed to a tradition with which he would have been abundantly familiar. Moses sprinkled the blood of the sacrifice on the people as a sign of the ratification of the covenant. At the Last Supper, Jesus' blood is offered as the "sacrifice of salvation" which would be accomplished in his death.

The expression *new covenant* was a common prophetic expression. There are several references in the Old Testament that speak of a "new covenant" or that the covenant would be renewed or reestablished.[86] At no time did the prophetic tradition indicate the abrogation of the original Sinai covenant. As a devout Jew, Jesus would have been familiar with this tradition and its various forms of expression.

In the context of the Last Supper, the covenant expression reflects the original covenant made between Yahweh and the people of Israel at Sinai. The question we need to address is whether this is a complete disjunction between the old covenant and the new.[87] Or is it a continuation, a perfection of the old? It is clear that Jesus intended his death to be the inauguration of the covenant and the kingdom. The temple Incident, which preceded the Last Supper, indicates that the covenant Jesus associated with his death was not intended to be a reform of the old. It is something much more dramatic. Jesus intended an end to the present state of affairs. It was a rejection of the way the covenant had been *taught and lived* by the authorities. The covenant that Jesus refers to is not entirely new since the early church sought Jewish converts and attended the synagogue.[88] It kept the Hebrew Bible as its own. The church, however, did not seem to be attracted to the temple. It devolved quickly in its missionary activity to the gentiles. The covenant is not an abrogation or replacement of the old. It is a continuation, a consummation, a perfect fulfilment of the Sinai covenant. It will form a new people which will include both Jews and gentiles.[89]

---

85. Meier, "Jesus," in *NJBC*, 78:51.

86. The following references will support these concepts. See Jer 31:31–33; 32:40; Bar 2:35; Ezek 16:60–62; 34:25; 37:26; and Hos 2:18–22.

87. The prophet Jeremiah refers to a new covenant (Jer 31:31). The Letter to the Hebrews 8:1–13 also speaks of a new and an old covenant. Hebrews 8:12 is a quotation of Jer 31:31–34. The note in the NABRE speaks of an old and a new testament in the prophetic tradition.

88. The Christians were ejected from synagogue services quite late.

89. See Meier, "Eucharist at the Last Supper," 349.

The Meaning of Jesus' Passion and Death[90]

Both in its liturgy and its theology, the church has consistently affirmed that the death of Jesus was the cause of our salvation, our reconciliation with God.[91] Scripture uses numerous metaphors to explain the salvation wrought by Jesus the Christ.[92] Jesus predicted his death several times during his ministry and anticipated it during the Last Supper. What significance did Jesus attach to his death? We can presume that he understood its meaning since he accepted it freely. Can we discover the authentic understanding of Jesus?

In order to answer these questions, we once more turn our attention to the Last Supper as we did earlier in examining the meaning of the covenant.[93] While Jesus anticipated his death, he never explicitly explained its meaning. What can we discover from the Last Supper narrative? The words of institution communicate "the whole saving event of Jesus' death and ultimate vindication."[94] It seems, therefore, if we are to answer our question it will be by an examination of the Last Supper narrative.

As we search for Jesus' understanding of his death, we can anticipate what it does not mean. It is certain that God the Father did not require a blood sacrifice of his son to initiate redemption or salvation.[95] This idea is inconsistent with our understanding of God and Jesus' relationship to him. In the proper sense, Jesus' sacrifice occurred because of his total

---

90. Theologically speaking, our focus here is on Jesus of Nazareth and how he understood his role in salvation history. This precedes the resurrection.

91. Among the New Testament references, we can list Rom 5:10–11; 2 Cor 5:18–19; Eph 1:7; 2:13, 16; Col 1:20; 1 John 1:7; and Heb 9:12. In the liturgy, the Eucharistic Prayers make specific mention that Jesus' death is the cause of our salvation. It is a matter of *lex orandi, lex credendi*. We pray what we hold in faith. Theologically, there is a long history of reflection on this subject. Anselm's *Cur Deus Homo* is a classic atonement theory based on satisfaction.

92. Some of the metaphors found in the Pauline corpus are reconciliation, atonement, redemption, expiation, purchased, salvation, justification, sanctification, freedom and transformation. See Fitzmyer, "Pauline Theology," in *NJBC*, 82:67–80.

93. There are references in the Scriptures, other than the Last Supper, which could help us in this regard. However, we will limit ourselves to the Last Supper.

94. Meier, "Eucharist at the Last Supper," 350.

95. Fitzmyer tells us that, "One should not invoke such passages as 1 Thess 1:10; Rom 5:9 to suggest that the shedding of Christ's blood has actually appeased the Father's wrath." Fitzmyer, "Pauline Theology," in *NJBC*, 82:73. These and similar passages could lead us to falsely conclude that Jesus' death was a punishment, or that God desired a blood sacrifice.

dedication to his Abba.[96] He did not desire to die. This seems clear from the narrative preceding his arrest. He acceded to his death and accepted it freely because he was obedient to the will of his Abba. As the eschatological prophet, Jesus' intention was to usher in the kingdom, not to be immolated to satisfy God. God did not demand a blood sacrifice.

What significance then did Jesus attach to his death? Did he understand it as a reconciliation of the people with God? Did he understand it as atonement for sin? His use of covenant language suggests his acceptance of both concepts.[97] The research of Jeremias and Meier are most illuminating on this point, and there are good reasons to examine and compare these two scholars. Jeremias published his academic work at the beginning of the new historical-critical method.[98] The German edition of his *New Testament Theology* was published in 1971.[99] The beginning of the new historical-critical method was around 1970. Meier published the first volume of *A Marginal Jew* in 1991, twenty years later. The comparison of these two investigations will prove beneficial and enlightening for our personal understanding because of their differing points of view and conclusions.

---

96. For a suitable description see Rahner and Vorgrimler, "Sacrifice." This entry fits the sacrifice of Jesus perfectly.

97. The language of reconciliation is not expressed verbally in the Hebrew Bible, but it is found there conceptually. The idea of atonement is closely associated with reconciliation. Atonement is expressed in Leviticus and Numbers but not frequently elsewhere. The rules for the Day of Atonement, one of Israel's most holy feast days, are found in Leviticus 16:1–34. Fitzmyer tells us that "this idea of reconciliation is the same as 'atonement' when that word is understood rightly as at-one-ment." Fitzmyer, "Pauline Theology," in *NJBC*, 82:72. Reconciliation and atonement are not to be confused with expiation (to make satisfaction) and propitiation. These terms reflect quite different concepts. See Fitzmyer, "Pauline Theology," in *NJBC*, 82:72. This is an important distinction. The origin of the word atonement is from the sixteenth century and its Old English equivalent is at-one + ment. At-one reflects the meaning of union or reconciliation as does the word atonement. The syllable *-ment* comes from the Latin and it signifies the result or object of an agent. Its root is the Latin *-mentum*.

98. This was twenty years after Bultmann and the debate that followed him (1941–1953). Bultmann's position was that the historical quest was futile because the sources were written from faith and not from history. They could not provide us with history.

99. The third edition of Jeremias' *The Eucharistic Words* was published in 1960, much closer to Bultmann and the demythologizing dispute which raged until around 1953. This ushered in a new phase of the historical-critical method beginning with Käsemann, a student of Bultmann. In his *New Testament Theology*, published in 1971, Jeremias begins on page one with his discussion on "the historical problem of Jesus." The most recent phase of the historical critical method began around 1970.

Jeremias: Jesus Understood His Death as Atonement

Jeremias observed that the early church understood that Jesus suffered for others and attributed atoning powers to his death.[100] He is quite confident that this was the mind of Jesus. He tells us that in the bread and cup words, Jesus alluded to his death as a vicarious shedding of his life, a sacrificial death.[101] "Jesus describes himself as a sacrifice."[102] The question is whether Jesus in fact understood his death as atoning for others. Jeremias' point-of-departure to establish this theological conclusion is his conviction that the Last Supper was both a historical event and a Passover meal. These presuppositions serve as a framework for his reflection and are foundational for his argument. Jeremias believed that at the Last Supper, Jesus would have functioned as the head of the household (*paterfamilias*). It was "a likely assumption" that Jesus interpreted the Passover lamb in terms of himself during the Passover devotion which preceded the meal.[103]

Jeremias concludes that at the Last Supper, Jesus was "most probably speaking of himself as the paschal lamb."[104] He describes himself as the saving lamb sacrificed and prefigured on Sinai. The parallel is unmistakable. At Sinai, Moses "took blood and splashed it on the people, saying, 'This is the blood of the covenant which the Lord had made with you according to all these words'" (Exod 24:8). Jesus would have been familiar with this text. He understood himself to be the sacrificial lamb and by so doing he sealed a covenant with God. The parallels between the sacrificed lamb and Jesus are unmistakable. "By comparing himself with the eschatological paschal lamb, Jesus describes his death as a saving death."[105]

---

100. Jeremias, *New Testament Theology*, 287. Jeremias enumerates several of the references in *Eucharistic Words*, 237. Included in this list are 1 Cor 10:16 (the Eucharist is participation in Jesus' death); Rom 3:25 (Jesus' death is expiation); 5:9 (we are justified by his blood); Eph 1:7 (redemption and forgiveness is by his blood); and Eph 2:13 (the gentiles were alienated but now are united by the blood Christ). There are other references that could be appealed to.

101. Jeremias, *Eucharistic Words*, 221–23. The bread and cup words which speak of flesh and blood refer to the entire person of Jesus.

102. Jeremias, *New Testament Theology*, 290. Jeremias, *Eucharistic Words*, 220.

103. Jeremias, *Eucharistic Words*, 221–22.

104. Jeremias, *Eucharistic Words*, 223. This is not a strong argument, but it is one more that Jeremias added to support his position.

105. Jeremias, *Eucharistic Words*, 225. Earlier, Jeremias argued that this idea can be found in pre-Pauline language, which he finds in Pauline corpus, 1 Peter, Hebrews, 1 John, and Revelation. See Jeremias, *Eucharistic Words*, 223.

Just as the sacrificed lamb brought salvation, so also Jesus' death brings salvation. Jeremias proposes that this was certainly the basis for its later formulation by the early postresurrection church.

Jeremias' reconstruction of the primitive form of the words of institution read as follows. "Take! This [is] my body/my flesh. This [is] my blood of the covenant which [will be shed] for many."[106] He accepts this verse as authentic. "Jesus uses this phrase (shed for many) to signify that he knows he is the servant of God who goes to his death as the representative of others."[107] *Shed for many* must be seen in conjunction with the suffering servant of Isa 53. As a devout Jew, Jesus would have understood that the language of atonement or suffering for another comes from Isa 53.[108] Jeremias believes that without this understanding, Jesus' shedding his blood for many "remains incomprehensible."[109] He concludes that Jesus understood himself as the suffering servant whose death was atoning. This is Jeremias' answer to our original question.

Jeremias has made several presuppositions which have been challenged. If the Last Supper was not a Passover (the chronology of the Gospel of John) does the strength of the argument hold? Most critical is whether his argument hinges upon the historicity of the cup words "which will be shed for many." This is almost identical to the form in Mark 14:24.[110] Failing this, can we actually arrive at Jesus' understanding of his death or are we simply creating a theological model supported by postresurrection testimony? Finally, can we be so certain that Jesus would have accepted the general understanding of atonement as found in Isa 53?

---

106. Jeremias, *Eucharistic Words*, 173; brackets in the original. Jeremias, *New Testament Theology*, 289. The expression *for many* is not intended to exclude anyone. The word *many* is a Semitism designating the collectivity. It is equivalent to *all*. See Jeremias, *New Testament Theology*, 291. The notes in the NABRE for Matt 20:28 repeat the same idea.

107. Jeremias, *New Testament Theology*, 291.

108. Jeremias saw that Jesus, as a ransom for many, was equivalent to an atoning offering for many. In order to make the point that Jesus understood he was a ransom, Jeremias appealed to an earlier passage from Mark. "For the Son of Man did not come to be served but to serve and to give his life as a ransom for many" (Mark 10:45//Matt 20:28). Jesus serves by surrendering his life as an atonement offering. See Jeremias, *New Testament Theology*, 292–93.

109. Jeremias, *New Testament Theology*, 291.

110. This is critical. See Jeremias, *Eucharistic Words*, 173.

Meier: Does Jesus Understand His Death as Atonement?

Meier followed Jeremias by twenty years. By this time, the rules for the historical-critical method had been more fully developed. Meier's method is more restrictive than Jeremias's. It is purely historical and limited itself to the Jesus of history. He says, "My method follows a simple rule: it prescinds from what Christian faith or later Church teaching says about Jesus without either affirming or denying such claims."[111] What has Meier concluded by a rigorous application of the more developed criteria?

The Synoptic Gospels indicate that Jesus' words and gestures over the bread and cup are followed by a prophecy which foreshadows his impending death.[112] Meier argues that Jesus' prophecy is authentic.[113] It was Jesus' personal expression about his immanent death; it does not include or involve others.[114] Jesus' final recorded statement (the prophecy) at the Last Supper is "amen, I say to you, I shall not drink again the fruit of the vine until the day when I drink it new in the kingdom of God" (Mark 14:25).[115] The amen which usually precedes an authoritative, emphatic statement is supportive of the authenticity of this verse.[116] From a human perspective, Jesus' ministry was a failure. Israel did not accept his message. The kingdom did not come in its fullness as he had anticipated. His ministry would end with his death which he had foreseen. In spite of his failure, Jesus had faith that God would bring about the kingdom and that he would be vindicated. Meier can see no cause and effect between Jesus' death and the coming kingdom.[117] In this prophecy, it is the kingdom that is central and not Jesus. Jesus' death is not described as either atoning or salvific. Jesus had faith that God would save him and seat him

---

111. Meier, *Marginal Jew*, 1:1.

112. Jesus had previously expressed his anticipation of this event during his ministry, but he does it again at the Last Supper.

113. Meier, *Marginal Jew*, 2:307.

114. One could imagine that when Jesus refers specifically to his impending death, he would have shared his personal understanding with his disciples during the meal.

115. Mark 14:25//Matt 26:29; and Luke 22:18. Fitzmyer has suggested that Luke 22:18 is from L. If accurate, this would give two independent sources for this important statement. Meier suggested the same conclusion. See Meier, *Marginal Jew*, 2:304.

116. See Meier's discussion on the amen sayings in *Marginal Jew*, 2:367n62. See also Jeremias, *New Testament Theology*, 35–36.

117. Meier, *Marginal Jew*, 2:308.

at the heavenly banquet.[118] Jesus is "the one saved. No more, no less."[119] Meier proposes the following: "Jesus is convinced that his cause is God's cause and that therefore, despite Jesus personal failure and death, God will in the end vindicate his cause and his prophet by bringing in his kingdom and seating Jesus at the final banquet, to drink the festive wine once again."[120] Meier continues, "There is no hint of Jesus' death as an atoning sacrifice, to say nothing of an explicit affirmation of his resurrection, exaltation, or parousia."[121] Does Meier's judgment apply to Jesus' entire self-consciousness, or does it apply only to this prophecy, a single verse, concerning his death? Can we discover other references which could shed new light on this matter?

To understand Meier's position more fully we must return to the bread and cup words to see if anything in them suggest Jesus understood his death as salvific or atoning. Meier has already construed the primitive form of the words of institution. It is repeated here for convenience. "He [Jesus] took bread, and giving thanks [or: pronouncing a blessing], broke [it] and said: 'This is my body.' Likewise, also the cup, after supper, saying: 'this cup is the covenant in my blood.'" He tells us that the words of institution "may well go back to Jesus himself."[122] This construction is missing several passages from the scriptural versions.[123] "Do this in re-

---

118. Meier, *Marginal Jew*, 2:349.

119. Meier, *Marginal Jew*, 2:308. Meier's argument for this statement may be true (Mark 14:25) but there may well be other arguments which support Jesus' understanding as atoning.

120. Meier, *Marginal Jew*, 2:308. Schillebeeckx offers a theological treatment of what Meier did exegetically. Schillebeeckx proposed that Jesus, in his humanity, is defined by his relationship to God. Jesus reveals the divine; he reveals the true nature of our humanity. He continues, "God's cause is our cause." Schillebeeckx, *Church: The Human Story*, 122. Mary Catherine Hilkert, writing on Schillebeeckx, says that "Schillebeeckx wanted to retell the story of Jesus as disclosing the mystery of a God 'bent toward humanity' in compassion, not a God who demanded suffering and death as recompense for sin. In one of his memorable ways of capturing this mystery, Schillebeeckx wrote: 'God's cause is the human cause' (and the cause of all of God's creation)." Hilkert, "Edward Schillebeeckx," January 7, 2011.

121. Meier, *Marginal Jew*, 2:308. Meier's commentary on the prophecy (Mark 14:25) can be found in *Marginal Jew*, 2:306–9. The First Letter of Peter might lend support to Meier on this point. The verse reads, "For Christ also suffered for sins once, the righteous for the unrighteous, that he might lead you to God" (1 Pet 3:18). This suggests an imitation and not an atonement. On the other hand, Saint Paul's Epistles contains a considerable amount of atonement language.

122. Meier, "Eucharist at the Last Supper," 347; brackets in the original.

123. This was pointed out earlier.

membrance of me" is found in Paul after both the bread and cup words (1 Cor 11:24, 25); it is found in Luke only after the bread words (Luke 22:19). It is not in either Mark or Matthew. Meier believes that this is an early Christian addition to the original.[124] We find in Mark, Matthew, and Luke a statement that more directly addresses our present concern. It speaks of the blood of Jesus "which will be shed for/on behalf of many" (Mark 14:24; Matt 26:29) and "which will be shed for you" (Luke 22:20).[125] Again, Meier informs us that this is a Christian addition.[126] It is the early church's confession that the death of Jesus atoned for sin. But it does not tell us if Jesus believed that his death was a representative one suggesting atonement as did Jeremias. In his article "Jesus" in the *NJBC*, Meier teases us with a very brief statement concerning this matter. He says, "Jesus therefore interpreted his death as the (sacrificial? atoning?) means by which God would restore the covenant with Israel at Sinai."[127] Unfortunately, Meier never explains why he put the words *sacrificial* and *atoning* in parentheses with question marks. Does he believe it possible that Jesus may have understood his death as atoning? Is Meier leaving this an open question? In an article published five years after "Jesus," Meier again raises the question of whether Jesus understood his death as reconciling or atoning.[128] After examining the bread and cup words in depth, Meier concludes with the statement "the hallowed bread and wine first of all mediate or communicate ... the whole saving event of Jesus' death and ultimate vindication."[129] He continues. "Jesus the final prophet sees his words and symbolic gestures not as empty signs but as

---

124. Meier, "Eucharist at the Last Supper," 345. Luke has added the phrase "which will be given for you" to the bread words (Luke 22:19).

125. The NRSV translates the phrase *shed for* as *poured out for us*. There is no significant difference in meaning.

126. Meier, "Eucharist at the Last Supper," 341, 347. Jeremias accepted this as historically authentic. This partly explains why he and Meier depart so greatly in their final conclusions. As mentioned earlier, the phrase is found in all of the Eucharistic Prayers presently in use by the Catholic Church. This expresses the faith of the church, which is also expressed in the Scriptures.

127. Meier, "Jesus," in *NJBC*, 78:51. This article was published in the *NJBC* in 1990. "The Eucharist at the Last Supper" was written five years after the article in the *NJBC* and would indicate that Meier had reached the same conclusion. See Meier, "Eucharist at the Last Supper," 349.

128. Meier, "Eucharist at the Last Supper." This article was published after Meier had completed two volumes of *A Marginal Jew*.

129. Meier, "Eucharist at the Last Supper," 350.

symbols charged with the power of the events they proclaim."[130] Does this not indicate that Jesus understood the meaning of his death as a saving event? A preceding statement of Meier is worth quoting in full. Jesus "goes to his death, giving his flesh, his whole self, his very life, even unto suffering and death to bring about the restoration of Israel in the end time. The one person willingly surrenders himself to death to give life to the many."[131] Is this not a vicarious giving, one life for the lives of many? Doesn't Jesus see himself as mediating the covenant found in the cup words? This requires further examination.

Does Jesus understand his death only as the occasion that brings salvation and not its cause? While this may give us pause as to whether we should attribute reconciliation or atonement to Jesus understanding of his death, this was certainly not the case with his disciples postresurrection. Are we confronting the same experience and understanding of Jesus that his disciples did?

It is clear that God alone reconciles or brings about the atonement of others with himself. He is the principal cause and initiator. It is also clear that Jesus is the mediator of God's reconciliation or atonement. It is difficult to both discover and understand the mind of Jesus. He never spoke directly about reconciliation or atonement. He did, however, express his insight into his personal role in salvation history. Meier indicates that in both his words and gestures, Jesus mediated or communicated the saving event. In his words and gestures, Jesus brings about the restoration of Israel. Does this not connote reconciliation or atonement? Would not Jesus have understood as much? A compelling case can be made that what Meier denies to the prophecy of Jesus (atonement) can be affirmed by other words and gestures of Jesus. This remains the work of theology.

Conclusion and Resume: Jesus' Understanding of His Last Formal Meal

We have examined two significant scholars in our attempt to secure a deeper comprehension of Jesus' self-understanding of his suffering and death. Both have provided us with considerable appreciation of this problem. Jeremias presumed that the Last Supper was a Passover meal,

---

130. Meier, "Eucharist at the Last Supper," 350. One has to ask whether this statement is not saying the same thing that is said in Mark 14:24.
131. Meier, "Eucharist at the Last Supper," 349.

and he accepted the historicity of Jesus' statement over the cup that "this [is] my blood of the covenant which [will be shed] for many."[132] Both of these observations, however, have been significantly challenged. Many doubt that the Last Supper was a Passover meal. Most notably, the expression "will be shed" is not included in Meier's reconstruction because he believes it is a later addition and not authentic. Jeremias also provided considerable background information to the Last Supper. He proposed that the use of sacrificial and atonement language was common in first century Palestine and Jesus would have been acquainted with its use. He would also have been well acquainted with the Scriptures. Jeremias argues that this evidences that Jesus saw himself as the suffering servant reflected in Isa 53, one who vicariously suffered for others.

If Jeremias proposed that Jesus affirmed the atonement of his death, Meier is much more reticent. Meier focused his search on what the texts could provide from the historical-critical method. Though Meier argued there was no indication that Jesus understood his death as atonement in the prophecy (Mark 14:25 parr.), he was less clear about the meaning of the words of institution. One can surmise that Meier considered the words of institution as evidence that Jesus understood his death as atonement for sin, but he does not say this directly.

Jesus believed that his Father/Abba would vindicate him. His mission and preaching of the kingdom would be justified and validated. The question is this: did Jesus understand his death as an atonement for sin? Jesus' understanding is not an easy question to answer. The bread and cup words (the words of institution) are Jesus' conscious, authentic statements prior to and foreshadowing his death. While they carry considerable weight in determining his self-understanding, so far, our task has proven elusive. There may be arguments discovered in other places in the life of Jesus that could support his consciousness about his death as one of atonement.[133]

The resurrection experience of the early church provided a new hermeneutic for Jesus' disciples. It was not Jesus' intent to proclaim himself as the Christ, but rather to proclaim the kingdom of God both as present and future realities. The early church understood Jesus' historical words and deeds through the eyes of faith. It spoke of his atonement and mediation. It proclaimed Jesus as the Christ. Jesus never made

---

132. Jeremias, *Eucharistic Words*, 173; brackets in the original.
133. Jeremias argued in this fashion. There is legitimacy in his method.

such a claim, or if he did he did so in a way that is difficult for us to see and understand. The disciples' understanding was based on their experience of Jesus during his public ministry. It was not invented. Jesus did not need to claim to be Savior or Messiah to be recognized as such after the resurrection. It was implicit in his earthly activity.[134] The resurrection event provides a hermeneutic to understand the historical Jesus in a new way, but offers little assistance in helping us grasp Jesus' personal understanding. The nature of our sources provides us with serious difficulties in determining Jesus' personal understanding regarding atonement. All of this presents a serious challenge that only study and contemplation can adequately address, if not meet.

---

134. This relates to what will be called the development of doctrine in later theology.

15

The Passion and Death of Jesus

Introduction[1]

THE CRUCIFIXION AND DEATH of Jesus are indisputable, historical facts that were enumerated earlier.[2] Our sources indicate that shortly after the Last Supper, Jesus and his disciples retired to "a place called Gethsemane."[3] All the Gospel narratives imply that Jesus' arrest occurred at night. John 18:3 indicates that those who came to arrest Jesus were carrying lanterns and torches. It seems clear from what has already been discussed that Jesus foresaw these events. Those who come to arrest him are variously described as a "crowd with swords and clubs who had come from the chief priests, the scribes and the elders" (Mark

---

1. The passion of Christ is often understood as the story of Jesus Christ's arrest, trial, and suffering, which ends with his execution by crucifixion. This is the picture given in the Gospel of John. The Synoptics begin the passion with the conspiracy against Jesus by the "chief priests and the scribes" followed by his anointing by a woman at Bethany.

2. It seems clear that Jesus anticipated his death. His motive for this dramatic last week of his life was to initiate the kingdom of God. He had faith that he would be vindicated, and the kingdom would be inaugurated. It is not clear in what fashion he saw his role as the initiator. It was God who was the prime cause. See Meier, "Jesus," in *NJBC*, 78:45–50.

3. Both Mark 14:32 and its parallel in Matt 26:36 refer to Jesus' place of agony as Gethsemane. This is the only mention of Gethsemane in the Gospels. In Hebrew and Aramaic, it means "winepress" and designates an olive orchard on the western slope of the Mount of Olives. Luke 22:39 refers to the place as the Mount of Olives. John 18:1 is the only source that refers to this place as a garden. John also indicates that it was the custom of Jesus to visit this place (John 10:2). It is located between Bethany and Jerusalem. See Murphy-O'Conner, *Holy Land*, for a fuller description of the area.

14:43//Matt 26:47), a crowd which included "chief priests and temple guards and elders" (Luke 22:47, 52), and a "band of soldiers and guards from the chief priests and the Pharisees" (John 18:3). A few verses later, John describes a "band of soldiers, the tribune and the Jewish guards" (John 18:12). The location and timing of Jesus' arrest suggest that it was designed to minimize any public disturbance.

After his arrest, Jesus is taken before the Sanhedrin for what is sometimes described as a trial, sometimes as an inquiry.[4] Caiaphas is the high priest who presided.[5] It is implied that this event took place late at night, certainly before Peter becomes aware of his denial of Jesus at cock crow, that is, before dawn.[6] Luke alone identifies this event as occurring "when day came" (Luke 22:66). It is difficult to determine precisely the time and nature of the trial and how many of the Sanhedrin were present on such short notice. But there is complete agreement among our sources that Jesus was brought before the Sanhedrin and found guilty of an offense serious enough to bring him before the Roman prefect Pontius Pilate at the praetorium.[7] All of the Gospel sources indicate that this was in the morning.[8] Pilate conducted a trial which concluded with Jesus being hastily condemned, scourged, and mocked.[9] After the trial, Jesus is forced to carry his cross to the place of his execution as a criminal. The actual execution was carried out by the Romans in the Roman way, by crucifixion. Meier fixes the date precisely as April 7, AD 30. Jesus died

---

4. See Sanders, *Historical Figure of Jesus*, 272–73 for a discussion on the trial of Jesus. See "Historical Reconstruction of the Arrest and Trial of Jesus" in Brown, *Gospel According to John*, 2:791–802.

5. Matthew 26:57 and John 18:24 identify Caiaphas as the high priest. Josephus supports this in his *Antiquities*. Caiaphas was high priest from AD 18 to AD 36. For more details on Caiaphas, see Brown, *Death of the Messiah*, 1:404–11.

6. Mark 15:72; Matt 26:75; and John 18:27.

7. John 18:28 is the only Gospel to mention the praetorium but this would be the logical place to bring Jesus for a Roman trial. It was the palace of Pontius Pilate when he was in Jerusalem. Herod the Great had built it as one of his residences. The emperor Tiberius appointed Pilate the Roman prefect of the Roman province of Judaea circa AD 26. An inscription found at Caesarea Maritima described Pilate as *praefectus Judaea*. He was not a procurator as many scholars incorrectly note. Pilate remained in office until AD 36 when he was called to Rome because of his heavy-handed suppression of Samaritans on Mount Gerizim. Nothing is known of his history or what happened to him after this. His reputation was that he was excessively cruel.

8. Mark 15:1; Matt 27:1; and John 18:28. Luke implied that it was in the morning.

9. The trial and surrounding events are difficult to establish with absolute historical certainty.

THE PASSION AND DEATH OF JESUS

and was taken down from the cross before sundown which was the beginning of the celebration of the Feast of Passover.

Who Was Responsible for Jesus' Death?[10]

There were two major participants in this drama: Caiaphas the high priest in collusion with the Sanhedrin and Pontius Pilate the Roman prefect. They represent the major Jewish and Roman powers. But who was responsible for Jesus' execution?[11] At the outset of this discussion the nation of Israel must be exonerated. It is evident that many Jews admired Jesus; others did not.[12] Jesus' ministry in Galilee makes this abundantly clear.[13] Those who were angered or displeased with his preaching or prophecy had no power or authority to bring him to trial. There is no recorded hostility from the people in general. Even though John 18:3 mentions there were Pharisees in the arresting group, it seems clear that the Pharisees, as a group, played no role in Jesus' trial or crucifixion. It was the Sadducees who were more likely to be in conflict with Jesus. The remote hostilities to Jesus in Galilee did not rise to the level of a moral or legal denunciation.[14] The Sanhedrin was the major player in Jesus' judicial condemnation. While Raymond Brown does not find all members of the Sanhedrin worthy of condemnation, he concludes that "some were

---

10. It should be noted at the outset, that there have been many sins committed against the Jewish people at the hands of Christians throughout the centuries. However, there is nothing in the teaching of Jesus of Nazareth that would justify this shameful behavior.

11. See Sanders, *Historical Figure of Jesus*, 272–73. Sanders gives a very brief description of the motives behind the authorities who wanted Jesus out-of-the-way.

12. The Synoptics report that entire towns rejected Jesus (Matt 11:20–24//Luke 10:12–15).

13. Much of the hostility experienced by Jesus while in Galilee was from those who came from Jerusalem. Many of the conflicts experienced from Galileans were of the nature of the typical rabbinic disputes in which Jesus engaged.

14. Jeremias argues otherwise. He believes that the conflict with the synagogue was over the law and that this alone could have put Jesus' life in danger. See Jeremias, *New Testament Theology*, 278–79. Meier finds these conflicts to be typical rabbinical theological arguments. Meier, *Marginal Jew*, 4:8. At the conclusion of volume 4, Meier informs us that "the legal material that can be reasonably traced back to the historical Jesus is distressingly sparse and scattered." It is the preaching of the kingdom and the healing activity of Jesus that is most pronounced. Meier, *Marginal Jew*, 4:652.

undoubtedly acting selfishly and without much probing of conscience, in order to protect their vested interest in the *status quo*."[15]

It seems clear that Caiaphas and the Jewish officials in Jerusalem (the Sanhedrin) were responsible for bringing Jesus to Pilate and that they would accept no less than a death sentence. Pilate obliged them. Caiaphas and the Sanhedrin were the conspirators, Pontius Pilate the enabler. Pilate presided over Jesus' trial, sentenced him to death, and ordered his crucifixion.

Jesus' Execution: The Motive of the Jewish Authorities

It is clear that Caiaphas and the Jewish authorities, in conjunction with Pilate, were responsible for Jesus' death. What motive can be attributed to them for wanting Jesus out of the way? Blasphemy appears to be the charge of the Sanhedrin in Mark 15:63 and Matt 26:65. It is implied in Luke 22:70–71. John makes no reference to blasphemy. In the Gospel of John, Jesus is handed over to Pilate as a criminal, a danger to the state. Because these accusations reflect an understanding of a high Christology, it is likely that this is a postresurrection understanding. It is unlikely that these accusations were the true motive for Jesus' death.

There are numerous references in the Synoptic Gospels indicating that Jesus, while still in Galilee, had attracted considerable attention of the authorities who resided in Jerusalem. His preaching of the kingdom was unsettling to the them, but hardly rose to the level of a capital crime. Nevertheless, it may have been seen as creating unrest among the people

Jesus' entry into Jerusalem, however, may have raised more serious concerns, especially if the crowds recognized him as a king. It was provocative and possibly intended to be so. "Jesus' entry to Jerusalem and his teaching about the kingdom" could well have been contributing causes.[16] These events would have caused grave concern for the Jewish authorities. Sanders proposed that "the Temple action sealed his fate."[17] This was a prophetic action symbolizing the destruction of the temple.[18] It would have been even more serious if we accept the possibility that Jesus may

---

15. Brown, *Gospel According to John*, 2:802.
16. Sanders, *Historical Figure of Jesus*, 272.
17. Sanders, *Historical Figure of Jesus*, 265.
18. The temple incident was a prophetic utterance indicating that the "Temple was about to be destroyed to make way for a new and perfect one." Meier, "Jesus," in *NJBC*, 78:44.

have made a statement about the destruction of the temple during this prophetic act. However this statement might be understood, whether the physical destruction of the Temple or some other mode, this action would have been offensive even to pious Jews. Caiaphas would have seen this as both an attack on his authority and the possible escalation of public unrest. It served his purposes to maintain order and rid himself of Jesus as the cause of a disturbance. Sanders proposes that Caiaphas "had Jesus arrested because of his responsibility to put down trouble-makers, especially during festivals."[19] Sanders continues, "Jesus was dangerous because he might cause a riot, which Roman troops would put down with great loss of life."[20] Sanders proposed that "Caiaphas made only one decision: to arrest and execute Jesus. . . . He did not act because of theological disagreement, but because of his principal political and moral responsibility: to preserve the peace and to prevent riots and bloodshed."[21] The temple incident was the straw that broke the camel's back. The ruling body of Jews would have seen in Jesus someone who could bring down their house by means of his kingdom. The officials, both religious and political, would need to protect the status quo for their own benefit.

Jesus' Execution: The Motive of Pilate

Pilate became the prefect of the province of Judea in AD 26. He had the reputation of being extremely cruel. Herod Agrippa I described him as "inflexible by nature and cruel because of stubbornness" and accused him of "grafts, insults, robberies, assaults, wanton abuse, constant execution without trial, unending grievous cruelty."[22] He was responsible for the slaughter of Samaritans on Mount Gerizim for which he was recalled to Rome. Pilate did not require a great deal of motivation to put one more troublesome Jew to death. He had already done so, too many times to mention. The motive of the Roman governor was more than likely to halt any sedition. It should be noted that the disciples were not hunted down after Jesus was arrested. They were not considered a threat. Mark tells us that after Jesus' arrest, all the disciples "left him and fled" (Mark 14:50// Matt 26:56b). Jesus the charismatic was the only threat.

19. Sanders, *Historical Figure of Jesus*, 269.
20. Sanders, *Historical Figure of Jesus*, 272.
21. Sanders, *Historical Figure of Jesus*, 273.
22. Quoted by Fitzmyer et al., "History of Israel," in *NJBC*, 75:168.

Comments on the Passion Narratives

At the beginning of chapter 14, Jesus' baptism and his passion and death were described as bookends to his life. The baptism of Jesus ushered in his public life. It defined his mission and set the stage for the prophetic ministry that followed. The passion and death were the completion or fulfillment of Jesus' life and mission. Our effort has been to discover as much as we could of the historical Jesus that fell between these bookends, which we examined thematically in the above chapters. This thematic presentation provided us with a well-developed understanding of the Jesus of history through his authentic words and deeds. We learned that the foundation of Jesus' personal understanding and his vision of the kingdom of God were shaped by his profound attachment to his Abba. Jesus not only acted as God's prophet, he lived the life of God. God's presence is manifested in everything that Jesus of Nazareth said and did. His proclamation of the kingdom and the miracle tradition that supported this message reflected God's presence.

From this initial experience in his ministry, Jesus came to understand that he was the charismatic, eschatological prophet in the mode of Elijah the miracle worker.[23] Jesus' understanding of his mission developed during his Galilean mission. It led him to realize that his proclamation of the kingdom of God would demand of him no less than his life.[24]

This chapter and chapter 14 focused on the final week of Jesus' life, his passion and death.[25] These events are integrally related and extremely important.[26] The events that comprised the earthly life of Jesus point to his passion and death. He came to realize that his ministry in Galilee was not a success.[27] His entrance into Jerusalem brought him into further conflict with the authorities who had recognized Jesus as a threat even before he journeyed there.

---

23. We spent considerable effort to discover Jesus' self-understanding, an interesting exercise in itself. All of this will be commented on in our next chapter and will give us a more complete picture of the Jesus of history.

24. See Meier, "Jesus," in *NJBC*, 78:45.

25. The entrance into Jerusalem and the temple incident are indicators of the drama that occurred at the Last Supper.

26. The Passion narratives were the first formal written narrative in the Gospels. This indicates its importance for the primitive community. It forms the framework for the last week of Jesus life.

27. This is often referred to as the Galilean crisis. At some point Jesus turned his attention to Jerusalem as if looking for a climax to his mission.

THE PASSION AND DEATH OF JESUS

Jesus' final meal with his disciples is a continuation of his festive meals (table fellowship) he celebrated frequently during his public ministry. But this Last Supper was also unique. It provided the opportunity for Jesus to impart his final instructions to his closest disciples. To speak of this as his last will and testament has substance. The bread and cup words were the centerpiece of this meal. It is clear this was not intended to be a liturgical ritual separated from the activity of his life and the proclamation of the kingdom.[28] Jesus declared that his death would usher in the Sinai covenant anew. His disciples, in sharing in the one cup, participated in this covenant. Jesus' words and deeds contain what they symbolize. Jesus had faith that God's kingdom would come. He understood he would be vindicated by his Father in spite of his apparent failure.

We are left with several vexing questions that have no clear answer.[29] Can we discover the understanding of the historical Jesus concerning his death? Two questions are worth briefly noting. We discussed Jesus' understanding of his role in salvation history above. As eschatological prophet, he looked for the fullness of the arrival of the kingdom. As a charismatic, he understood his mission and he determined how to initiate it. He was going to his death freely in obedience to his heavenly Father.[30] But did he understand his death as causative of the kingdom? His prophecy (Mark 14:2) would seem to cast some doubt on this. What value did the Jesus assign to his death? Did the Jesus of history understand or express his death as salvific? The postresurrection community certainly did. They found that his death was salvific in the words of institution.

Conclusion and Resume

The passion and death of Jesus is the unique event in salvation history. This event cannot be separated from Jesus' public life which preceded it. Jesus' passion and death was the fulfillment of his mission. It interpreted

---

28. Jesus understood his death as the means to establish a new covenantal relationship with God.

29. The vexation is in understanding the historical Jesus. These are not vexing for faith since what we understand in the words of Scripture has been expressed with the interpretation of the postresurrection faith.-

30. Jesus made the ultimate sacrifice. This was in obedience to the Father. It was done in solidarity with his disciples and with us. Words and gestures reflect a self-understanding.

the events that preceded it and supplied their authentic meaning. In general, the Last Supper and Jesus' death serve as an interpretation of his mission. This is the culmination of the development that can be found in the life and death of Jesus of Nazareth.

Jesus' death brings our search for the historical to a close. We have been blessed with the specific events of the last week of his life. They provide us with a deeper way of understanding his proclamation of the kingdom that preceded it. The resurrection of Jesus is the final blessing. It provided those first followers with a new hermeneutic, a new way of interpreting the life and death of the Jesus of history who came to be professed as the Christ. The resurrection now becomes a part of our final comments. It provides us with a Christology in the proper sense. It is clear, however, that the Jesus of history served as the foundation for the faith statements which followed his death. We are now in a position to better understand that early experience of the first disciples. It was the historical Jesus that his followers experienced. It was also the historical Jesus that his followers enlightened by the resurrection experience identified as the Christ. There is a necessary connection between faith and fact. We are now free to theologize. This was the goal of our study. We are not able to leave aside what we have discovered of this experience any more than we can leave aside our assimilation of contemporary biblical studies.

16

Afterword: Concluding Comments

Introduction: A Final Word

We have come to the end of our search. A final word of explanation, an afterword, is now appropriate. We have attempted to discover the authentic history of Jesus of Nazareth, his authentic words and deeds. This chapter is an evaluation of what we have accomplished.

The Jesus of history has had a profound impact on our world. He left us a rich tradition which extends beyond the boundaries of Christianity. It seems natural that we should show a keen interest in him and his mission. For believers this goes beyond purely historical or social interests. Our point of departure is an expression of the believer's attachment to the person of Jesus Christ. This is a matter of faith, a personal relationship. It creates a way of life and a distinct vision of the world. The story of this person, Jesus Christ, is recounted in the Scriptures and continues in a lived tradition in the church. It has its beginning, however, in the life and death of Jesus of Nazareth, the Jesus of history.

Our purpose for this study is articulated above in the preface and the introduction. It will be briefly summarized here for the readers' convenience. Our primary goal is to gain a fresh perspective on how Jesus' disciples experienced him during his public life. The Gospels were our principal source. We are more than fortunate to have available the historical-critical method in the search for the Jesus of history.

This work does not intend to answer all relevant theological or faith questions about our subject matter. Its intention is much more modest. This project is an introduction, a foundation, for further study of Jesus. Its intention is to avoid replacing biblical metaphors with theological metaphors. In the Gospel of John, we read "His [Jesus'] disciples said, 'Now you are talking plainly, and not in any figure of speech'" (John 16:29). This present work is intended to speak plainly in imitation of Jesus in order to get at the meaning of the Scriptures. A considerable amount of material has been made available for the interested reader. Our goal is to serve both the faith of the believer and the study of Christology for the beginner.

The Jesus of history is the foundation for Jesus the Christ of faith. Each of these realities is related to a different historical context. There is continuity between the two, however, as the latter is based on the former. Therefore, our focus has been on two important historical periods: the first encompasses the public life and mission of the Jesus of history; the second is postresurrection, the time of the early church's preaching of the Christ and the writing of the Scriptures. Each context must be accounted for. Not to do so can only lead to failure in accomplishing our goal.

Jesus of Nazareth: What Have We Accomplished?

We began our study with a brief examination of the sources. A discussion of the method that was employed followed.[1] We hoped to attain an accurate picture of Jesus as he began and ended his ministry of preaching the kingdom of God. This established a foundation for any future Christology.

Principal Goal of this Study[2]

Theology views the Scriptures through the eyes of faith in order to deepen understanding and articulate its meaning for believers. Theology and faith were always present in our examination. Our task, however, was to separate the Jesus of history conceptually from the Christ of faith. We did so by examining the sources available to us and we arrived at a clearer understanding of the Jesus of history. Our goal was to distinguish authentic history from the faith affirmations of Scripture. We were able to distinguish Jesus' authentic teaching and deeds from

---

1. This material can be found in chapters 1 and 2 above.
2. A more complete explanation can be found in the preface and the introduction.

the report of the evangelists who relied upon their personal experience in recounting the words and deeds of Jesus.[3] It is apparent that much of the Gospel material is a creation of the early church. By *creation* we do not mean a falsification of Jesus in his ministry; we do mean that the evangelists did not intend to communicate the truth in historical categories. Good storytellers never do.

What Kind of History or Biography Could We Now Write?

Given what we have discovered in the previous chapters, what sort of story of Jesus' public life could we write? We were unable to establish a strict chronology of Jesus' public life because of the nature of our sources. But we were able to establish what is essential to his mission with a high degree of historical certainty.

We have no knowledge of the manner in which Jesus the tekton became Jesus the prophet. He was a first century Jew who was deeply committed to the faith of Israel.[4] Furthermore, the charismatic Jesus had a profound experience of God which we referred to as his Abba experience. It was this experience that gave him his deep and unique understanding of God and his kingdom.[5] Jesus' relationship with his Abba, his Father, was a special bestowal of grace for upon him.[6] He lived God's life in history. As a disciple of John, he shifted his ministry from a baptizer to an itinerant preacher. He came to understand himself as the eschatological prophet and taught the coming presence of the kingdom. He was not a social reformer, a teacher of ethics, nor was he a sage. He taught a praxis, a way of living in anticipation of the kingdom.[7] He interpreted the law with authority, and in several instances,

---

3. It is unlikely that the evangelists were eyewitnesses to the events of Jesus' life. They passed on what they had received (the oral tradition) from those who experienced Jesus during his lifetime.

4. Jesus' commitment to the faith of Israel is an important source for properly understanding him. It is a significant part of his context.

5. Later church faith statements saw in this the basis for referring to Jesus as the Christ, the Messiah.

6. To speak of a moment of grace is not intended to reduce this to a point in time. Jesus' understanding more than likely occurred over a period of time.

7. There were members of the primitive community who expected the return of Jesus immanently. See Mark 13:24–27//Matt 24:29–31//Luke 21:25–28 and 1 Thess 4:13–17. The First Epistle to the Thessalonians is an authentic Pauline Epistle and was composed around AD 50. It is the earliest written book in the New Testament. The

significantly modified it. He was known as a miracle worker, a healer. In this calling he imitated the prophet Elijah.

We identified many of Jesus' authentic teachings that can be traced back to him with historical certainty. Prominent among these are the themes of the kingdom of God, the forgiveness of sin, and a new emphasis of love.[8] As a poet, he taught in parables and other literary forms.[9] His preaching was at first limited to the house of Israel but toward the end of his mission he universalized his message. God is the God of all men and women. Most significantly, Jesus did not preach of himself as the early church did; he preached the kingdom of God. Jesus' identity as Christ, as well as other christological or honorific titles, is only recognized postresurrection.[10]

There is still more to be accomplished both in the discernment and assimilation of the authentic Jesus material. This study stands at the beginning of this process. It looks forward to further scholarship. What is implicit in the Scriptures and tradition must now be made explicit.

Jesus as the Christ: The Postresurrection Faith[11]

A significant shift occurred after Jesus' death and resurrection. The importance of the resurrection experience cannot be overstated.[12] What followed was an understanding of Jesus of Nazareth as Jesus the Christ. christological titles were assigned to him as a product of this new, deeper understanding. These were an attempt by the primitive community to construct a description that corresponded to their experience and how

---

early church's understanding of the praxis that it was to follow can be found in Matthew's Sermon on the Mount (Matt 5:1—7:28) and Luke's Sermon on the Plain (Luke 6:20–49).

8. Jesus' teaching to love enemies is a unique teaching.

9. He used the expression *blessed are those* and often began pronouncements with an authoritative *amen, I say to you*.

10. Jesus' use of the title Son of Man is an exception.

11. There is an identity between Jesus of Nazareth and the Jesus of the Gospels. The disciples of Jesus, however, acquired a more profound understanding of the Jesus of history after the resurrection.

12. We should be aware that this experience, powerful as it was, still required the faith of the disciples. The resurrection was not a proof in the general sense. See Aquinas, *Summa Theologiae* III, q. 55, a. 5. His position is that the experience of the first postresurrection Christians gave them no advantage over us because they too required faith in what they experienced. It was not a proof or demonstration that one could not deny.

they came to understand him in his union with God.[13] These titles are not pure inventions of the disciples. They are found in the Palestinian environment.[14] They have Jewish roots which support their validity.

From Jesus of Nazareth to the Christ of Faith

The resurrection experience of those early disciples was critical for the understanding of Jesus that followed. We can presume that those who experienced Jesus in his resurrection appearances had followed him during his ministry.[15] This brought about a dramatic shift in understanding for the first disciples. The resurrection experience replaced a disastrous ending to the ministry of Jesus with an understanding of success and resurgence. The historical Jesus was no longer present to the primitive church as he was prior to his death. The resurrection appearances provided a new experience, a hermeneutical principle, which shaped both the preached and written expression of Jesus. During his lifetime, Jesus preached the kingdom of God. In their experience of Jesus, risen from the dead, the early disciples identified him as the Christ, the Messiah. And in preaching him and writing about him in the Scriptures, Jesus of Nazareth was seen through this new lens.[16] The community experience and preaching identified Jesus as the Christ, the Messiah. As Christ, the risen Jesus gradually replaced the preaching of the kingdom.[17] This accounts for the most significant development in the faith of the early disciples.[18] Our effort in the previous chapters was to discover the Jesus who existed prior to this new experience.

---

13. Paul is a good example of this. He speaks of Jesus in his person as Christ/Messiah, Son of God (1 Thess 1:10), and Savior (Phil 3:20). He also speaks of what Christ has done for us. He used such expressions as justified us, saved us, reconciled us, redeemed us, sanctified us, transformed us, expiated for us, and atoned for us. A later theological effort to do something similar can be found in Anselm's *Cur Deus Homo*.

14. This is certainly true of Paul's usage. See Fitzmyer, *According to Paul*, 11. See also Fuller, *Foundations of New Testament Christology*, and Cullmann, *Christology of the New Testament*.

15. This is apparent in the choice of Judas' successor. See Acts 1:15–26.

16. The justification for this was given above in chapter 4.

17. While the expression *kingdom* or *kingdom of God* is not totally missing from the Acts of the Apostles and the Epistles, its use is significantly reduced.

18. Furthermore, development came about from the need for inculturation. The new context, the Hellenistic world, differed from the original Palestinian context. This change in contexts came about early in the church's missionary activity.

The liturgical practices of the early community were coterminous with the primitive oral tradition. No time existed after Jesus' death when the Lord's Supper and baptism were not a part of the communal life of the earliest Christians. It seems clear that the early church continued what we now call the Eucharist. It also followed the practice of baptism for initiation into the community. These practices preserved the community belief.

Paul proposed that faith in Christ is foundational. Jesus never did. Paul employs several important christological hymns in his Epistles. These are found in Phil 2:6-11 and Col 1:15-20.[19] Another well-known christological hymn is found in John 1:1-14.[20] Paul also contains references to the institution of the Eucharist (1 Cor 11:23-32). He is an important witness to the oral tradition prior to its written expression in the Gospels. These written traditions were composed out of a need to preserve the message, the oral tradition, for the future. They also reflect the development that followed the resurrection of Jesus.

Continuity: Development from the Jesus of History to the Written Text[21]

It now seems abundantly clear that there is a significant development between the preaching of the disciples from the time of their resurrection experience to the writing of the Epistles and Gospels.[22] It was necessary to adapt as they moved from a Palestinian-Jewish environment to a more Hellenistic one. Contemporary theology would describe this as inculturation, an adaptation to a new culture. The Jesus of history is the foundation for Jesus the Christ. To put this in another way, Jesus the Christ is the preached historical Jesus. The postresurrection reflection on the experience of the Jesus of history was to identify him by

---

19. The Epistle to the Philippians is an authentic Pauline epistle, composed between 54-58 AD. It is unlikely that Paul wrote the Epistle to the Colossians. It is dated between AD 70 and AD 80.

20. These hymns express the preexistence of Christ, a faith/theological perspective impossible to express prior to the resurrection.

21. There is a need to support this new understanding. The early church was conscious of the identity between Jesus of history and the Christ of faith.

22. Doctrinal development is a well-established teaching in the church. It defends or explains that the later teachings of the church that are proposed for universal belief are in continuity with the original revelation received either in Scripture or in tradition. The church developed doctrinally.

affirming christological titles such as Messiah, Savior, Redeemer, and so forth.[23] These are expressions intended to make him intelligible to those to whom he was preached.

This study has indicated that there was a development within the primitive community as it came to understand the full dimensions of Jesus as the Christ. This was preceded by a development within the life of Jesus and his mission.[24] There was a development in Jesus' words and deeds as well as in his self-understanding. Such developments should be expected. Nevertheless, there is continuity between the Jesus of history and the written word as well as the tradition that followed. This is a conceptual development.[25] It is a necessary presupposition. Our theological reflection must both presuppose this continuity and be faithful to it. Conceptually, we can say no more nor less than the Scripture. Thus, the Jesus of history is clearly a hermeneutic for correctly understanding the written words of our sources.

Justification for This Study

This theological examination has attempted to do two things: first to remain faithful to the data of Scripture and the affirmations of faith; and second to discover as much of the historical Jesus as possible to give us scholarly means of understanding the Christ we believe in. A few comments on each of these is warranted.

Some Reflections on Scripture

The Scriptures have an intrinsic value in themselves. They support the Christian life of faith. They carry with them a meaning that is immediately intelligible to the believer.[26] This is especially true for the Gospels.

---

23. For a good discussion on the christological or honorific titles applied to Jesus, see Fuller, *Foundations of New Testament Christology*, and Cullmann, *Christology of the New Testament*.

24. See Komonchak et al., "Development of Doctrine," 280–83.

25. See Marin-Sola, *Homogeneous Evolution of Catholic Dogma*.

26. This is not to suggest that there are no parts of the Scriptures that are not without some difficulty to understand. The medieval discussion on preaching referred to the hard parts and the easier parts of Scripture. The Scriptures were, however, written to be understood in a religious, nonscholarly atmosphere. The faithful read them without research and with great spiritual benefit.

JESUS: THE PERSON AND THE MISSION

The reading of and meditating on the Scriptures has served us well for centuries both personally and communally. A significant part of the liturgy, the Eucharist as well as the Divine Office, is based on the Scriptures. The individual practice of *lectio divina*, the monastic practice of reading, meditating, and praying the Scriptures has proven both popular and profitable. Having moved beyond the walls of the monastery *lectio divina* has become a widespread practice among the laity. There are many other examples of the manner of reading the Scriptures that have nourished the life of faith.[27] They are in themselves valuable. Stories move minds and hearts, and they inspire.

While the Scriptures possess an intrinsic value in themselves, they did not fall from heaven, clear and unalloyed, with an immediately apparent meaning. Discernment of their meaning requires considerable effort. The authors of the Scriptures left their personal imprint on what they wrote.[28] The evangelists gathered their material, both oral and written, structured the Gospel according to their own designs, and employed their own vocabulary. These sacred writings are an interpretation created by the evangelists out of their experience of the early Jesus tradition. An example of this creativity is Luke's historicizing of the resurrection event as he recorded it in the Acts of the Apostles. The note in the New American Bible indicates that "what should probably be understood as one event (resurrection, glorification, ascension, sending of the Spirit—the paschal mystery) has been historicized by Luke when he writes of a visible ascension of Jesus after forty days and the descent of the Spirit at Pentecost."[29] The paschal event is retold in a literary manner to make a theological point, not a historical one. This is a clear example of the evangelist using his literary skill to shape the tradition he had received.

There are numerous other examples which illustrate the editing of the evangelists. The infancy narratives provide us with an excellent example of a theologoumenon.[30] These narratives are creations

---

27. Another practice that has proven useful is to read the Scriptures as autobiography. It is possible that we can read ourselves into the narrative of the biblical text. The parable of the good Samaritan (Luke 10:29–37) is an excellent example. We can see ourselves as the priest, the Levite, or the Samaritan (the good neighbor). The prodigal son (Luke 15:11–32) is another example which is easily understood as autobiography. Who are we? Do we see ourselves as the prodigal son, the elder son, the father?

28. There is considerable evidence to indicate the editing and additions by the evangelists.

29. See the notes in the NABRE to Acts 1:3.

30. Theologoumenon is a theological construct to explain some event or idea. See

of Matthew and Luke. Their purpose is not intended to be a historical report on the birth of Jesus; they are a statement of doctrine. It is unlikely that the flight into Egypt to escape the wrath of Herod the Great is factual. The historicity of these narratives may be called into question but the truth they communicate is not. Jesus is proclaimed Son of God, an affirmation that is postresurrection.

Meier proposed that the parable of the good Samaritan (Luke 11:29–37) is more than likely a creation of Luke, fashioned out of whole cloth.[31] It cannot be listed with the authentic parables of Jesus. It is a response to the question "who is my brother?" The narrative of the final judgment found only in Matt 25:31–46 also appears to be a narrative developed by Matthew or the early church. The "exceptive clause" in Matthew is his addition to Jesus' authentic teaching on divorce. Matthew addressed a problem that had developed in his community postresurrection. This narrative is a creation of the evangelist and not necessarily an authentic report of a historical event.

Besides these literary devices used by the evangelists, there are faith affirmations about Jesus in the Scriptures not made during his lifetime. The christological titles and the claim for Jesus' divinity are two of these.[32] The postresurrection experiences of the evangelists and other early followers of Christ were instrumental in forming these faith statements.

These examples illustrate a crucial point. The Scriptures in general and the Gospels in particular are complex in their composition.[33] They are often based upon the creative imagination of the authors. Because of this, the meaning of the Scriptures is not always immediately clear. Study and research necessarily follow upon reading and meditating on the Scriptures. While personal reflection is profitable, it invites, it even demands, study and research. This is part of the ancient tradition. The church and her theologians have engaged the Scriptures for centuries. They did so, however, without the benefits of more recent contemporary biblical studies or the historical-critical method. The theology of the past

---

Meier, *Marginal Jew*, 1:237n41, Kasper, *Jesus the Christ*, 65–66, and Schillebeeckx, *Jesus*, 752. Other possible literary genres might properly identify the infancy narratives.

31. See Meier, *Marginal Jew*, 5:199–209.

32. The disciples engaged in numerous conflicts after Jesus' death. This influenced the way in which Jesus is described in the Gospels.

33. It is difficult to distinguish the authentic Jesus of history material from other faith statements.

is a treasure. But there are now methods which have replaced the older ones and permit a deeper understanding of this treasure.

Recent biblical research has proven invaluable. It provides new interpretations of the Scriptures which were not available in the past. This is a part of a legitimate development and an opportunity to present the faith in a more meaningful way to our contemporaries. As a practical matter, we are doing what theologians and biblical scholars have done for centuries before us. We simply have new tools which, if we are serious in our efforts, we cannot avoid using. The discovery of literary forms that are neither historical narratives nor authentic teaching of Jesus does not diminish their truth. As valuable as the Scriptures are in themselves as faith documents, they require an exegesis to obtain their deeper meaning. This is a long-standing tradition in the intellectual life of the church. The search for the historical is predicated upon biblical exegesis. It provides the authentic Jesus material. The historical-critical method moves beyond these other exegetical methods. Its importance is apparent.

A Brief Justification for This Study

In no way does historical-critical research impoverish the Scriptures. Neither does it detract or lessen the value of its poetry or its literary character. The search for the Jesus of history is in no way intended to be a diminution of Holy Scripture which holds pride of place in our faith. We are not looking for a historical truth that reduces the value of the biblical narratives.[34]

What then are the reasons for the introduction of the Jesus of history into our effort to articulate a contemporary Christology? The search for the historical Jesus has been preceded by an examination of the Scriptures using all the tools presently available. This was the task enjoined upon Scripture scholars and theologians by Pius XII with his well-known encyclical letter, *Divino Afflante Spiritu*, published in 1943. The task to incorporate this more recent biblical effort into theology and Christology continues. The historical-critical method is a more recent part of this task. Earlier in this study we justified the search for the historical

---

34. It was suggested above that the narrative stories move minds and hearts and inspire much more than bare history.

AFTERWORD: CONCLUDING COMMENTS

Jesus, and it will not be repeated here.[35] But the historical-critical method changes our theological reflection in several ways.[36]

First, the historical study is not intended to be a ressourcement, a return to the beginnings. It does not replace the biblical Jesus by another earlier, more primitive, picture of him. The result of the historical methodology improves our understanding of the written Scripture and our faith. We need to establish a serious conversation between the Jesus of history and the Christ as found in the Scriptures. This is more than a mere recovery of the past.

Second, it places us closer to the experience of the earliest disciples. It gives us a fuller presentation of the human activity of Jesus his disciples witnessed. We can see Jesus more fully in his humanity. This will certainly impact the way we do our theological reflection since much of the past theological reflection was imperated by the notion of the Word of God and not the humanity of Jesus.

Third, it provides the basis for the original written text. We can better understand the original experience which is the basis for the postresurrection affirmations. The results of the historical-critical method support what is written in the Scriptures. For one thing, the miracle tradition is not an invention of the early church. It has its basis in the history of Jesus. The historical-critical method has established this. It supports what the Scriptures teach as valid and truthful.

Fourth, the success of the present search for the historical Jesus is a safeguard against an inadequate picture of Jesus that we might create. It prevents us from imposing our own ideas onto the text. What stands out among the reasons given in the introduction is that an understanding of the Jesus of history, his authentic teaching and deeds, prevents us from using the Jesus that we read about in the pages of Scripture as a cipher that we can fill with our own personal presuppositions or ideas. It prevents manipulation of the Jesus of the Gospels to fit personal images of him. It requires fidelity to the Jesus as discovered by the historical-critical method.

Fifth, the Jesus of history in conjunction with the data of Scripture gives us a better, truer description of the Jesus of our faith. The historical Jesus, his words and his deeds, is also interpretive, a valuable

---

35. It can be found in the introduction.

36. In using the historical-critical method, we are not looking for bare, historical facts. We are attempting to discover what can be identified as authentic in the life and mission of Jesus.

hermeneutical tool. This helps us to understand the Jesus of faith more deeply. It supports the Gospel picture of the Jesus of history, witnessed by the apostles and first disciples, who were the first preachers of the Christ and who shaped their memories of him in their evangelization. These memories and practices were the material that the evangelists relied on to produce the Gospels. There is an intimate connection between the historical Jesus of Nazareth as he performed his mission, those who experienced him during his earthy life and then later preached him as the postresurrection Christ, and those who authored the canonical Scripture.[37] The Jesus of history draws us closer to the lived experience of his first followers. Furthermore, there must be continuity between the Jesus experienced by the first disciples and what was written about him by the postresurrection church.

The Authoritative Statements of the Church

The authoritative statements of the church are both fundamental in our belief and guides for the theologian.[38] The early councils declared that Jesus was true God and true man. He was like us in all things but sin. He possessed everything that a true human being possesses, that is, he possessed an integral human nature. The historical-critical method offers no challenge to the validity or truthfulness of these doctrines. It thoroughly rejects both Adoptionism and Docetism, the two enemies of the councils.

There were significant consequences for the theological process following these councils. The focus was most often on the divine in Jesus Christ as the Word of God.[39] Because of this high Christology, Jesus was understood not only as a true, integral man, he was also understood as a

---

37. There is a connection between the experience of Jesus' first disciples and the postresurrection disciples. See Acts 1:15–26. Matthias was chosen to replace Judas Iscariot because "it [was] necessary that one of the men who accompanied us the whole time the Lord Jesus came and went among us, beginning from the baptism of John until the day on which he was taken up from us, become with us a witness to his resurrection" (Acts 1:21–22).

38. The Councils of Nicaea (AD 325) and the Chalcedon (AD 451) are most important in this regard. Much of the theological reflection on these councils was done from a high Christology. This was the basis for attributing the beatific vision to the Jesus of history. It was a generally accepted position until the early part of the twentieth century.

39. This was often a corrective to an adoptionist perspective, but it often led to a view that appeared Docetist. Briefly, Adoptionism is the position in which Jesus is Son of God by adoption only. It denies his preexistence. Docetism is the position that the Christ only appeared to be human. Both these positions must be rejected.

perfect man to whom all the perfections possible for a human being were attributed. This was not a biblical position but rather it was based on the dogmatic position of the Word of God united with human nature. Thus, a high Christology dominated theological speculation for centuries.

An older Christology taught that Christ, from the moment of conception, possessed the beatific vision. Without going into all of the theological arguments, Jesus would have seen God and all things related to his mission directly.[40] Although this did create theological difficulties, this position was common until the fifteen hundredth anniversary of the Council of Chalcedon at which time the council was assiduously reexamined. While the dogmatic statements of the council were not challenged, its classical theology was. And for good reasons. If Jesus possessed the beatific vision, he would have had no need for faith. He would have seen the divine directly and he would have understood who he was and what his mission was. It would also have influenced the way he conducted his mission.

Any discussion about what Jesus said and did during his lifetime was absent from the council's declarations.[41] This present study intends to complete the picture. It can give us a more holistic view. Jesus was a man of faith who was like us in all things but sin.[42] There is no change in our

---

40. A few observations are needed on the beatific vision. It was an early christological affirmation. Fulgentius of Ruspe (462–533) was an early proponent. As late as 1950 it was taught as a necessary theological conclusion. This was proposed as an explanation and not a proof. It was always described as fitting (*conveniens*), a consequence of the hypostatic union. It was not based on the Scriptures. The Council of Chalcedon asserted that Jesus possessed an integral human nature. Later theologians proposed that Jesus possessed a perfect human nature. Christ possessed the fullness of grace because he was near to the source (Aquinas, *Summa Theologiae*, III, q. 7, a. 1). He was intimately joined to the Word in his human nature. The argument is from closeness of human nature to the divine. He had perfections in act and not potentially because he was the cause of these perfections (Aquinas, *Summa Theologiae*, III, q. 9, a. 2). It should be noted that Hans Urs von Balthasar denied this position. Elizabeth Johnson raised this question: wouldn't Jesus know who he was? Her answer is given in chapter 3 of *Consider Jesus*. If the beatific vision is assumed, Jesus would have lacked faith. The object of faith would have been possessed in act.

41. The councils answered the questions about Jesus' true identity. They did not discuss his earthly activity, that is, what he did in his ministry. But in reality, we know who a person is by what a person does.

42. The grace of Christ is an interesting parallel to the beatific vision. Jesus was a man of grace. Fullness of grace is a theological judgment because of his union with the divine. If he did not possess grace in his soul, he lacked something that we have. The christological question is what would a human nature be like united to the divine? The answers must of necessity be one of *conveniens*.

understanding of the Christ as the Son of God but there is a fuller understanding of him as Son of Man. The historical-critical method deepens our understanding of the dogmatic statements of the councils.

The primitive community first experienced Jesus in his earthly life, in what he did and what he said. From their experience of Jesus raised from the dead, they came to understand his true identity. These two experiences are part of the same mystery. One in the context of his mission and the other as raised from the dead.[43] The one requires the other. They can be distinguished but cannot be separated. By their nature they are coterminous. The historical-critical method attempts to correct the failure to account for Jesus' actual human life.

This Is Not the Last Word

This study is not merely descriptive of the Jesus of history, as satisfying as that may be. It is a propaedeutic, a point of departure, for any future Christology. Its goal is an in-depth analysis of the scriptural data which addresses the meaning of the person of Jesus the Christ. It achieves its goal by consciously beginning with what it can attain of the Jesus of history. The Gospels are dynamic sources and are a continuation of the life story of the Jesus of history.[44] This process begins by setting Jesus in his original earthly context. The context of any event is of itself interpretive and contributes to our understanding. To decontextualize the earthly Jesus, to remove him from his earthly context, is an implicit rejection of the Incarnation.[45]

What will this accomplish for the beginner or the interested reader? The intention is to reinforce and deepen the biblical narrative.[46] The challenge is to reflect a faithful understanding of an authentic Jesus for a contemporary audience. It attempts to include much of what was missing from the doctrinal declarations of Nicea and Chalcedon. The principal concern

---

43. Christology (who Jesus is) and soteriology (what Jesus did) were not distinguished or separated in early Christology. Aquinas and other medievalists are witnesses to this. They should be kept together even though they may be distinguished.

44. It recognizes the dynamism of the Scriptures as it records the life of Jesus.

45. An event cannot be removed from its context without doing serious harm to its proper understanding. This study strongly rejects any effort to decontextualize the events of the life of Jesus recorded in the Scriptures.

46. But even that which is not historical in the Scriptures is accepted as part of the revelation.

of these councils, especially Chalcedon, was the person of Jesus Christ. What Jesus did and said were not a significant part of their purview. But this is what contemporary Christology must now account for.[47]

Conclusion and Resumé: Jesus the Human Face of God

To say that we have devoted a good deal of time and effort on the search for Jesus of Nazareth and his authentic words and deeds would be an understatement. His historical importance should be clearly understood. It was Jesus, the man from Nazareth, who was experienced by his disciples and many others during his public ministry.[48] This experience provided the foundation for the postresurrection faith experience. Thus, Jesus of Nazareth has special importance for faith and for Christology. We propose three important concepts that express faith in Jesus the Christ which have been constructed from material found in the previous chapters. They summarize important faith observations and provide a general framework upon which to develop the authentic words and deeds of Jesus as well as the Christology that follows. Our study suggests the following three concepts.

Jesus, in His Humanity, Is a Unique Manifestation of God[49]

In his earthly, human existence, Jesus appeared as any other human being. There was something attractive in his teaching and his deeds that gave rise to faith in him. His disciples came to understand him as the human face of God. We have come to recognize Jesus as the authoritative locus

---

47. Sanders articulates the general point well. He says, "There are two aspects to 'Christology': the person of Christ and the work of Christ, that is, who he was and what he did. In the third, fourth, and fifth centuries a lot of effort was expended on statements of who he was, but the creeds and other christological formulations of those centuries, which are still accepted throughout Christianity, are largely negative, in that what they forbid is clearer than what they permit. A doctrine of the work of Christ was never achieved, and one can speak only of theories of the atonement. Christians agree that Christ 'saves' in some way or other, but not necessarily on how he does it." Sanders, *Paul*, 77. This present work is an effort to achieve a Christology that includes the deeds and words of Jesus Christ.

48. The same experience is open to all our contemporaries through faith.

49. This material is dependent upon Schillebeeckx, *On Christian Faith*. There is a British version with the title *Jesus in Our Western Culture*.

in which we can understand God most deeply.⁵⁰ Seeing Jesus through the eyes of faith is to see God and to understand God's relationship to humankind. We are obviously referring to Jesus' humanity as this special place. This metaphorical expression, the face of God, is an analogical way of moving from the human to the divine.

There is considerable scriptural support for the theological concept that Jesus is the means to experience God. Consider the following passages from the Gospel of John. In the recapitulation of the Book of Signs in this Gospel we read that Jesus said, "Whoever believes in me believes not only in me but also in the one who sent me, and whoever sees me sees the one who sent me" (John 12:44–45). Later in the Gospel, Philip asked Jesus to "show us the Father and that will be enough for us." Jesus responded, "Whoever has seen me has seen the Father" (John 14:8–9). There is a similar statement attributed to Jesus in the Q source. "No one knows the Son except the Father and no one knows the Father except the Son and anyone to whom the Son wished to reveal him" (Matt 11:27//Luke 10:22).⁵¹ These statements reflect the faith of the early Christians.⁵² Jesus is understood as the face of God. Contemporary ecclesial documents also offer support for this biblical position. While commenting on the dignity of man, *Gaudium et Spes* affirmed that "Christ the Lord, Christ the new Adam, [is] the very revelation of the mystery of the Father and of his love."⁵³ Jesus, in his human nature, reveals the true nature of God to man.

The person of Jesus Christ is the historical revelation of salvation from God. This is a statement of faith. God is manifest in Jesus' teaching and praxis. Jesus acts as God acts on our behalf in his teaching and praxis providing for us an example to imitate.⁵⁴ He wants us to act like God acts; to be like God.⁵⁵ This program places new demands on our

50. He is also the manifestation of true humanity. See Flannery, *Gaudium et Spes*, no. 22. The document affirms that his humanity reveals something of our true humanity.

51. See John 3:35; 6:46; 7:28; 10:15. Adolph von Harnack believed that this Q quote was a pivotal christological passage in the Synoptics. It resonates with the Gospel of John in its high christological significance.

52. No attempt is made to establish the historical authenticity or certitude of these statements. It is clear that they profess what is believed.

53. Flannery, *Gaudium et Spes*, no. 22.

54. Schillebeeckx expresses this in another way: The cause of humans is the cause of God. It is sometimes expressed as God's cause is the cause of humans.

55. This concept is reflected in the eucharistic liturgy when the chalice is prepared at the offertory. The priest or deacon pours a small amount of water into the wine, and

behavior and attitudes. God acts towards us as he wants us to act toward one another. Jesus is the agent who communicates this to us because he is the unique point of contact between the divine and human.[56]

Jesus Is a Contingent Manifestation of God[57]

Salvation always occurs in a historical context. Edward Schillebeeckx makes the following perceptive observation. "Thus salvation from God comes about first of all in the secular reality of history and not primarily in the consciousness of believers who are aware of it."[58] God manifests himself in the historical, the contingent. This is a profound insight for it helps us understand the very nature of God's revelation. For Christians, Jesus is the unique, contingent manifestation of God.

Our claim that Jesus is the human face of God does not mean that Jesus exhausts all that we can understand about God. Jesus is a limited, contingent human being. Therefore, the revelation of God made in and through him is of its nature limited. Furthermore, Jesus' ministry was limited in time and place. God, however, is not limited. In faith we affirm that there is a special, unique relationship between Jesus and God, but it is not the only possible relationship. As human, Jesus is necessarily a contingent, therefore limited, being.[59] He does not exhaust other revelations from God, nor does he reveal all that can be known about God.

Jesus Understood as True Mystery

The expression *mystery* does not mean mysterious. It refers to something hidden from our immediate view but that is accessible to us. It can be discovered. The concept of mystery as applied to Jesus means that something is both hidden and revealed in his person. For Christians, Jesus is clearly the revelation of God. But it seems just as obvious that not everything about him is immediately evident or compelling.

---

he quietly says, "By the mystery of this water and wine may we come to share in the divinity of Christ who humbled himself to share in our humanity."

56. This reflects the very nature of the incarnation.
57. Schillebeeckx, *On Christian Faith*, 3.
58. Schillebeeckx, *On Christian Faith*, 9. Schillebeeckx affirms that the secular event undergirds the religious experience. Revelation presupposes human events. Confer the exodus (Deut 26:5–9).
59. Schillebeeckx, *On Christian Faith*, 3.

Jesus' parables were heard by many, so also were his miracles witnessed by many. But not all of those who heard or who witnessed accepted him. Some accepted the validity of Jesus' mission, while others did not. Even though he reflects the mystery of God, Jesus is not so compelling to human experience that he cannot be denied or rejected. This reflects the very nature of faith. It requires an acceptance and a response. We need to enter freely into the mystery.[60]

Jesus both reveals and conceals in his person. This notion of hiddenness and revealedness permits us to refer to the unique place where divinity and humanity are joined. It is in Jesus himself, in his humanity, that God is revealed. Jesus lived the God life. The true, authentic nature of man is also revealed in the person of Jesus. "In reality it is only in the mystery of the Word made flesh that the mystery of man truly becomes clear. . . . [Christ] fully reveals man to himself and brings to light his most high calling."[61] In this statement Vatican Council II made clear something implicit in Catholic theology. Christ not only reveals God to us, but he also reveals in his person what restored human nature looks like. Jesus is "the perfect man who has restored in the children of Adam that likeness to God which had been disfigured ever since the first man."[62] In this sense Jesus is both revealer and intermediary. Having drawn these conclusions from our biblical search it becomes clear how the early church could assign christological or honorific titles to the Jesus of history. What was implicit in Jesus' mission the early church made explicit.

The Final Statement

This afterword has attempted to summarize the complexities found in the text. It concludes that the authoritative preaching and praxis of the Jesus of history which have been articulated in this search are not only useful in creating a Christology, but they are absolutely necessary. Once having been established, they can no longer be ignored. Central to this statement

---

60. This was suggested for the parables in chapter 11, 203–205. Crossan makes an interesting observation when he says, "Jesus proclaimed God in parables, but the primitive church proclaimed Jesus as the Parable of God." Crossan, *In Parables*, xiv.

61. Flannery, *Gaudium et Spes*, no. 22. Christ is described as the New Man. Both Paul and Irenaeus speak of all things being subsumed into Christ. He stands at the center of humanity.

62. Flannery, *Gaudium et Spes*, no. 22. The reference to "perfect man" is not identical to what the medieval or classical theology meant by the expression.

AFTERWORD: CONCLUDING COMMENTS

is the fact that we can now identify much of what, in substance, pertains to the Jesus of history.[63] And the Jesus of history is the foundation for our faith affirmations. These authentic statements provide a framework to construct a truly contemporary Christology, one that is both faithful to the Scriptures and to dogmatic faith statements of the church. This body of information is a treasure. It supports faith. It gives a more accurate and understandable human picture of Jesus. It prevents us from incorrectly using the hermeneutic of the word as past theology did. This was our stated goal. We have searched for the authentic words and deed of Jesus of Nazareth and now we are in a position to bring the project to completion by constructing a new, contemporary Christology.

---

63. Much has been discovered that is authentic, that is, it can be taken back to the Jesus of history. More will be discovered with time.

Works Consulted

Achtemeier, Paul J., ed. *The Harper Collins Bible Dictionary*. Rev. ed. San Francisco: HarperSanFrancisco, 1985.
Anselm, Saint. *Saint Anselm: Basic Writings*. 2nd ed. Translated by S. N. Deane. La Salle, IL: Open Court, 1962.
Aquinas, Thomas. *Summa Theologiae*. 60 vols. Edited by Thomas Gilby. New York: McGraw Hill, 1964–1981.
Aristotle. *Poetics*. Translated by Gerald Else. Ann Arbor, MI: University of Michigan Press, 1967.
Barrett, C. K., ed. *The New Testament Background*. Rev. ed. San Francisco: HarperCollins, 1989.
Benedict XVI, Pope. *Deus Caritas Est (God is Love)*. AAS 80 (2006).
Bettenson, Henry, and Chris Maunder, eds. *Documents of the Christian Church*. 4th ed. Oxford: Oxford University Press, 2011.
Boadt, Lawrence. "Ezekiel." In *The New Jerome Biblical Commentary*, edited by Raymond E. Brown et al., 305–28. Englewood Cliffs, NJ: Prentice Hall, 1990.
Borg, Marcus J., and John Dominic Crossan. *The Last Week: A Day-by-Day Account of Jesus's Final Week in Jerusalem*. San Francisco: HarperSanFrancisco, 2006.
Brown, Raymond E. *The Birth of the Messiah*. New updated version. New York: Doubleday, 1993.
———. *The Churches the Apostles Left Behind*. New York: Paulist, 1984.
———. *The Death of the Messiah: From Gethsemane to the Grave*. 2 vols. New York: Doubleday, 1994.
———. *The Gospel According to John*. 2 vols. The Anchor Bible 29–29A. Garden City, New York: Doubleday, 1966–1970.
———. *The Gospel and Epistles of John*. Collegeville, MN: Liturgical Press, 1988.
———. *An Introduction to New Testament Christology*. New York: Paulist, 1994.
———. *An Introduction to the New Testament*. New York: Doubleday, 1997.
———. *Jesus God and Man*. New York: Macmillan, 1967.
———. *New Testament Essays*. London: Geoffrey Chapman, 1965.
———. *Responses to 101 Questions on the Bible*. New York: Paulist, 1990.
———. *The Virginal Conception and Bodily Resurrection of Jesus*. New York: Paulist, 1973.

WORKS CONSULTED

Brown, Raymond E., et al. "Aspects of New Testament Thought." In *The New Jerome Biblical Commentary*, edited by Raymond E. Brown et al., 1354–81. Englewood Cliffs, NJ: Prentice Hall, 1990.

———. eds. *The New Jerome Biblical Commentary*. Englewood Cliffs, NJ: Prentice Hall, 1990.

Butler, Trent C., ed. *Holman Bible Dictionary*. Nashville: Holman Bible, 1991.

Catholic Book Publishing. *The Liturgy of the Hours: According to the Roman Rite*. Vol. 4. Translation by the International Commission on English in the Liturgy. New York: Catholic Book Publishing, 1975.

Cervantes Saavedra, Miguel de. *Don Quixote of La Mancha*. Rev. ed. Translated by Walter Starkie. New York: A Signet Classic, 1964.

Chilton, Bruce. *Pure Kingdom: Jesus' Vision of God*. Grand Rapids: Eerdmans, 1996.

Chiu, Jose Enrique Aguilar, et al., eds. *The Paulist Biblical Commentary*. New York: Paulist, 2018.

Clifford, Richard J. "Exodus." In *The New Jerome Biblical Commentary*, edited by Raymond E. Brown et al., 44–60. Englewood Cliffs, NJ: Prentice Hall, 1990.

Crossan, John Dominic. *The Historical Jesus: The Life of a Mediterranean Jewish Peasant*. San Francisco: HarperSanFrancisco, 1991.

———. *In Parables: The Challenge of the Historical Jesus*. New York: Harper & Row, 1973.

Cullmann, Oscar. *The Christology of the New Testament*. Rev. ed. Philadelphia: Westminster, 1963.

———. *Salvation in History*. New York: Harper & Row, 1967.

Danker, Frederick William, ed. *A Greek-English Lexicon of the New Testament and Other Early Christian Literature*. 3rd ed. Chicago: University Press, 2000.

Dodd, C. H. *The Apostolic Preaching and Its Development*. New York: Harper & Row, 1962.

———. *The Coming of Christ*. Cambridge: Cambridge University Press, 1954.

———. *The Founder of Christianity*. London: Macmillan, 1970.

———. *The Parables of the Kingdom*. Rev. ed. New York: Charles Scribner's Sons, 1961.

Dowell, Mark Allan, ed. *The HarperCollins Bible Dictionary*. 3rd ed. New York: HarperCollins, 2011.

Dunn, James D. G. *Jesus and the Spirit*. Grand Rapids: Eerdmans, 1975.

———. *Jesus Remembered*. Christianity in the Making 1. Grand Rapids: Eerdmans, 2003.

———. *The Theology of Paul*. Grand Rapids: Eerdmans, 1998.

Ellacuria, Ignacio, and Jon Sobrino, eds. *Mysterium Liberationis: Fundamental Concepts of Liberation Theology*. Maryknoll, NY: Orbis, 1993.

Erikson, Erik H. *Young Man Luther: A Study in Psychoanalysis and History*. New York: W. W. Norton, 1958.

Feldman, Asher. *The Parables and Similes of the Rabbis: Agricultural and Pastoral*. London: Cambridge at the University Press, 1924.

Fitzmyer, Joseph A. *According to Paul: Studies in the Theology of the Apostle*. New York: Paulist, 1993.

———. "The Biblical Commission's Instruction on the Historical Truth of the Gospels." Theological Studies 25.3 (September 1964) 386–408.

———. *A Christological Catechism*. New York: Paulist, 1991.

———. *The Gospel According to Luke*. 2 vols. The Anchor Bible 28-28A. Garden City, NY: Doubleday, 1981-1985.

———. *The Impact of the Dead Sea Scrolls*. New York: Paulist, 2009.

———. *The Interpretation of Scripture: In Defense of the Historical-Critical Method*. New York: Paulist, 2008.

———. *The One Who Is to Come*. Grand Rapids: Eerdmans, 2007.

———. "Pauline Theology." In *The New Jerome Biblical Commentary*, edited by Raymond E. Brown, 1385-416. Englewood Cliffs, NJ: Prentice Hall, 1990.

———. *Scripture and Christology: A Statement of the Biblical Commission with a Commentary*. New York: Paulist, 1986.

Fitzmyer, Joseph A., et al. "History of Israel." In *The New Jerome Biblical Commentary*, edited by Raymond E. Brown et al., 1219-222. Englewood Cliffs, NJ: Prentice Hall, 1990.

Flannery, Austin, ed. *Ad Gentes Divinitus (Decree on the Church's Missionary Activity)*. In *Vatican Council II: The Conciliar and Post Conciliar Documents*. Rev. ed., 813-62. Collegeville, MN: Liturgical, 1996.

———, ed. *Dei Verbum (Dogmatic Constitution on Divine Revelation)*. In *Vatican Council II: The Conciliar and Post Conciliar Documents*. Rev. ed., 750-65. Collegeville, MN: Liturgical, 1996.

———, ed. *Gaudium et Spes (Pastoral Constitution on the Church in the Modern World)*. In *Vatican Council II: The Conciliar and Post Conciliar Documents*. Rev. ed., 903-1001. Collegeville, MN: Liturgical, 1996.

———, ed. *Vatican Council II: The Conciliar and Post Conciliar Documents*. Rev. ed. Collegeville, MN: Liturgical, 1996.

Francis, Pope. *Laudato Si' (On Care for Our Common Home)*. AAS 107 (2015).

Freedman, David Noel, et al., eds. *Eerdmans Dictionary of the Bible*. Grand Rapids: Eerdmans, 2000.

Fuller, Reginald H., ed. *Essays on the Love Commandment*. Philadelphia: Fortress, 1978.

———. *The Foundations of New Testament Christology*. New York: Charles Scribner's Sons, 1965.

———. *Interpreting the Miracles*. Philadelphia: Westminster, 1963.

———. *The Mission and Achievement of Jesus*. London: SCM, 1954.

Gutierrez, Gustavo. *A Theology of Liberation*. Rev. ed. Translated and edited by Caridad Inda and John Eagleson. Maryknoll, New York: Orbis, 1988.

Harrington, Daniel J. "The Gospel According to Mark." In *The New Jerome Biblical Commentary*, edited by Raymond E. Brown et al., 596-629. Englewood Cliffs, NJ: Prentice Hall, 1990.

Herzog, William R. *Prophet and Teacher: An Introduction to the Historical Jesus*. Louisville: Westminster John Knox, 2005.

Hilkert, Mary Catherine. "Edward Schillebeeckx: A herald of God among us." *National Catholic Reporter*, Jan 7, 2011.

Hollenback, Paul W. "Jesus, Demoniacs, and Public Authorities: A Socio-Historical Study." *Journal of the American Academy of Religion* 49 (December 1981) 567-88.

Horsley, Richard A. *Jesus and Magic: Freeing the Gospel Stories from Modern Misconceptions*. Eugene, OR: Cascade, 2014.

Jeremias, Joachim. *The Eucharistic Words of Jesus*. 3rd ed. Translated by Norman Perrin. Philadelphia: Fortress, 1977.

———. *New Testament Theology: The Proclamation of Jesus*. New York: Charles Scribner's Sons, 1971.
———. *The Parables of Jesus*. 2nd rev. ed. New York: Charles Scribner's Sons, 1963.
———. *The Problem of the Historical Jesus*. Translated by Norman Perrin. Philadelphia: Fortress, 1964.
———. *Rediscovering the Parables*. New York: Charles Scribner's Sons, 1966.
John Paul II, Pope. *Novo Millennio Ineunte (At the Beginning of the New Millennium)*. AAS 93 (2001).
Johnson, Elizabeth. *Consider Jesus: Waves of Renewal in Christology*. New York: Crossroad, 1991.
Jülicher, Adolf. *Die Gleichnissreden Jesu*. 2 vols. Freiburg, Germany: Mohr, 1889.
Kasper, Walter. *Jesus the Christ*. The Collected Works of Walter Kasper 3. New York: Paulist, 2018.
Kinman, Brett. "Jesus' Royal Entry into Jerusalem." *Bulletin for Biblical Research* 15.2 (2005) 223–60.
Komonchak, Joseph A., et al. "Development of Doctrine." In *The New Dictionary of Theology*, 280–83. Wilmington, DE: Michael Glazier, 1987.
Kummel, Werner Georg. *Introduction to the New Testament*. 17th ed. Nashville: Abingdon, 1992.
Küng, Hans. *On Being a Christian*. Garden City, NY: Doubleday, 1976.
Lane, Dermot. *Christ at the Centre*. Dublin: Veritas, 1990.
Lohfink, Gerhard. *Jesus of Nazareth*. Collegeville, MN: Liturgical, 2012.
Luttenberger, Gerard H. *An Introduction to Christology*. Mystic, CT: Twenty-Third, 1998.
Mackey, James P. *Jesus: the Man and the Myth*. New York: Paulist, 1979.
Macquarrie, John. *Jesus Christ in Modern Thought*. London: SCM, 1990.
Mandonnet, Pierre. *Saint Dominic and His Work*. Saint Louis: B. Herder, 1944.
Manson, Thomas Walter. *The Sayings of Jesus: As Recorded in the Gospels According to St. Matthew and St. Luke*. London: SCM, 1971.
Marin-Sola, Francisco. *The Homogeneous Evolution of Catholic Dogma*. Translated by Antonio T. Pinon. Manila, Philippines: Santo Tomas University Press, 1981.
McClendon, James. *Biography as Theology: How Life Stories Can Remake Today's Theology*. Maryland: Abingdon, 1974.
McIntyre, John. *The Shape of Christology: Studies in the Doctrine of the Person of Christ*. 2nd ed. Edinburgh: T&T Clark, 1998.
Meier, John P. "The Bible as a Source for Theology." Paper presented at the Forty-Third Annual Convention of the Catholic Society of America, Toronto, Ontario, June 1988.
———. "The Eucharist at the Last Supper: Did It Happen?" *Theology Digest* 42.4 (Winter 1995) 335–51.
———. "Jesus." In *The New Jerome Biblical Commentary*, edited by Raymond E. Brown et al., 1316–28. Englewood Cliffs, NJ: Prentice-Hall, 1990.
———. "Jesus Christ in the New Testament: Part One: The Historical Jesus behind the Gospels." *Dialogue: A Journal of Mormon Thought* 30.4 (Winter 1997) 1–18.
———. *A Marginal Jew: Rethinking the Historical Jesus, Volume 1; The Roots of the Problem and the Person*. The Anchor Bible Reference Library. New York: Doubleday, 1991.

———. *A Marginal Jew: Rethinking the Historical Jesus, Volume 2; Mentor, Message, and Miracles*. The Anchor Bible Reference Library. New York: Doubleday, 1994.

———. *A Marginal Jew: Rethinking the Historical Jesus, Volume 3; Companions and Competitors*. The Anchor Bible Reference Library. New York: Doubleday, 2001.

———. *A Marginal Jew: Rethinking the Historical Jesus, Volume 4; Law and Love*. The Anchor Yale Bible Reference Library. New Haven: Yale University Press, 2009.

———. *A Marginal Jew: Rethinking the Historical Jesus, Volume 5; Probing the Authenticity of the Parables*. The Anchor Yale Bible Reference Library. New Haven: Yale University Press, 2016.

Murphy-O'Conner, Jerome. *The Holy Land*. Oxford: Oxford University Press, 2008.

Newman, John Henry Cardinal. *An Essay on the Development of Christian Doctrine*. Edited by Charles Frederick Harrold. New York: Longmans, Green, 1949.

Perkins, Pheme. "The Gospel According to John." In *The New Jerome Biblical Commentary*, edited by Raymond E. Brown et al., 942–85. Englewood Cliffs, NJ: Prentice Hall, 1990.

———. *Hearing the Parables of Jesus*. New York: Paulist, 1981.

Perrin, Norman. *Jesus and the Language of the Kingdom*. Philadelphia: Fortress, 1976.

Pius XII, Pope. *Divino Afflante Spiritu (By the Divine Inspiration of the Spirit)*. AAS 35 (1943).

Pontifical Biblical Commission. *Instruction Concerning the Historical Truth of the Gospels (Sancta Mater Ecclesia)*. Translated by Joseph A. Fitzmyer. *Theological Studies* 25.3 (September 1964) 402–8.

Leo I, Pope. *The Letters and Sermons of Leo the Great, Bishop of Rome*. Translated by Charles Lett Feltoe. The Nicene and Post-Nicene Fathers of the Christian Church 12. Second Series. 1894. Reprint, Grand Rapids: Eerdmans, 1979.

Rahner, Karl. "Current Problems in Christology." In *God, Christ, Mary and Grace.*, 149–200. Theological Investigations 1. New York: Seabury, 1964.

———. "Dogmatic Reflections on the Knowledge and Self-consciousness of Christ." In *Later Writings*, 193–215. Theological Investigations 5. New York: Seabury, 1966.

Rahner, Karl, and Herbert Vorgrimler. "Sacrifice." In *Theological Dictionary*, edited by Cornelius Ernst, translated by Richard Strachan, 418–19. New York: Herder and Herder, 1965.

———. *Theological Dictionary*. Edited by Cornelius Ernst. Translated by Richard Strachan. New York: Herder and Herder, 1965.

Rice, Anne. *Christ the Lord: Out of Egypt*. New York: Alfred A. Knopf, 2005.

Roberts, Alexander, et al., eds. *The Apostolic Fathers with Justin Martyr and Iranaeus*. The Ante-Nicene Fathers 1. 1885. Reprint, Grand Rapids: Eerdmans, 1981.

Sanders, E. P. *The Historical Figure of Jesus*. London: Allan Lane, 1993.

———. *Jesus and Judaism*. Philadelphia: Fortress, 1985.

———. *Paul*. Oxford: Oxford University Press, 1991.

Schillebeeckx, Edward. *Church: The Human Story of God*. New York: Crossroad, 1990.

———. *The Church with a Human Face*. New York: Crossroad, 1985.

———. *Jesus: An Experiment in Christology*. New York: Seabury, 1979.

———. *On Christian Faith: The Spiritual, Ethical, and Political Dimensions*. New York: Crossroad, 1987.

Smith, Morton. *Jesus the Magician*. San Francisco, CA: Harper & Row, 1978.

WORKS CONSULTED

Sobrino, Jon. *Jesus the Liberator: A Historical-Theological Reading of Jesus of Nazareth.* Translated by Paul Burns and Francis McDonagh. Maryknoll, New York: Orbis, 1993.

Stern, David. *Parables in Midrash: Narrative and Exegesis in Rabbinic Literature.* Cambridge, MA: Harvard University Press, 1991.

Vawter, Bruce. "Introduction to Prophetic Literature." In *The New Jerome Biblical Commentary*, edited by Raymond E. Brown et al., 186–200. Englewood Cliffs, NJ: Prentice Hall, 1990.

Vermes, Geza. *Jesus the Jew: A Historians Reading of the Gospel.* Philadelphia: Fortress, 1973.

Vincent of Lerins. *The Commonitories.* Translated by Rudolph E. Morris. The Fathers of the Church 7. New York: Fathers of the Church, 1949.

Viviano, Benedict T. "The Gospel According to Matthew." In *The New Jerome Biblical Commentary*, edited by Raymond E. Brown et al., 630–74. Englewood Cliffs, NJ: Prentice Hall, 1990.

———. *The Nativity: History and Legend.* New York: Doubleday, 2007.

Voltaire. *Candide.* Translated by Lowell Bair. New York: Bantam, 1959.

Von Balthasar, Hans Urs. *Theo Drama: Theological Dramatic Theory.* Vol. 3. Translated by Graham Harrison. San Francisco: Ignatius, 1988–1989.

Wright, N. T. *Jesus and the Victory of God.* Minneapolis: Fortress, 1996.

Index

Abba experience, 59, 74–75, 85, 108, 130, 205, 219, 233, 235, 241, 299
Acts of the Apostles, 79, 103–4, 132–34, 136, 160, 165, 304
actual Jesus. *See* Jesus of history
agent of the kingdom, Jesus' role as, 113
allegory, 186, 188, 197–201
amen statements, 180, 231–32, 235
Anselm, Saint, 9–10
apologetics, 8–9
Aquinas, Thomas, 11, 65, 69–70
atonement, 281–86
authenticity of the parables, 212–13
authentic teachings of Jesus, 87–97, 114, 200–201, 218, 237–61, 300, 305–6
authoritative statements of the church, 308–10
authority, Jesus', 227–36

banquet in the kingdom, 89–90, 102, 117, 284
Baptism of Jesus, 47–75, 262
beatitudes, 90, 114, 254–56
bread and cup words, 275–76, 281–86, 295

Caiaphas, 291–93
call story, 154
canonical Gospels, 21–25, 36, 201
catechesis, 8–9
changing water into wine at Cana, 149

characteristics of the parables, 203–5
christological titles, 29, 74, 77, 110, 222, 224–25, 227, 300, 303, 305
Christology, 1–18, 19–20
   attempt to make a unified, 32
   Baptism of Jesus, 55–56
   contemporary, 310–11, 315
   definition, 11–13
   experience of God, 6–7
   human experience, 73, 205
   Jesus of history, 37
   presuppositions, 30
   recent developments, 3–4
   recovering the Jesus of history, 44–45
   sources, 25–27
   temptations, 69
cleansing of the temple, 265–67
coherence, criterion of, 41, 267
compressed story, 203
consequences of the kingdom for contemporary life, 17–18
contemporaries of Jesus, 228–29
contemporary theology, 13
context of the parables, 207–8
core of miracles which are historical, 168–72
Council of Chalcedon, 19–20, 73, 111, 225, 234, 309, 310–11
Council of Nicea, 226, 234, 310–11
covenant, 276–78, 295
Cross-Gospel theory, 21–22

INDEX

cure of the mute, 230
curse miracles, 152–53

destruction of the temple, 178, 208, 266, 292–93
dietary laws, 248, 253
discipleship, call to, 253–54
disciples of John the Baptist, 60–62
discontinuity, 40–41, 66
divorce, prohibition of, 249–51
double command of love, 242–44

early church and Jesus' contemporaries, 228–29
earthly Jesus, 35, 310. *See also* Jesus of history
embarrassment, criterion of, 39–40, 55
entrance into Jerusalem, Jesus', 263–65, 292–93, 294
epiphany miracle, 150–51
Epistle to the Hebrews, 66, 160, 251
eschatological prophet, 163–64, 220–21, 230, 233–36, 267–68, 274, 280, 294–95, 299
eschatology, 106–7
evil, 116–21
execution of Jesus, 289–93
exorcisms, 94–96, 99, 144–45, 173–75
experience of God, 6–7
extrabiblical miracle tradition, 131–32, 159–60

faith, 8–11, 166–67, 175
faith statements, 3, 16, 23, 32, 305, 315
false friends, 258–59
farewell meal, 271–73. *See also* Last Supper
feeding the multitude, 149–50
festive meals, 74, 79, 88, 98, 102, 114, 117, 166, 239, 244, 269, 272, 274, 275
final events of Jesus' life in Jerusalem, 219–20, 262–88
forgiveness, 244–47

Galilean Ministry, 70–71
gentiles, 101–4, 241
God as Father (Abba), 241–42

God's presence, 105, 129, 166, 294
God's reign, 112–13
Golden Rule, 258–59
Gospels, 8, 14, 19–32, 303–6, 310
    amen statements, 231
    as Christologies, 27
    composition of, 28
    divorce, 250
    exorcisms, 144–45
    extrabiblical expressions for miracle, 159–60
    forgiveness, 244–47
    healing miracles, 145–46
    Jesus as teacher, 180
    kingdom of God, 113–14
    love, 242–44
    miracles as special part, 134–36
    parables, 179, 206–7
    raisings from the dead, 146–48
    ritual purity and dietary laws, 248
    sources, 25–27
    stages of development, 28–30
grace, 122–23
Greek New Testament, 150–51, 160

halakic teaching of Jesus, 247–52
healing miracles, 145–46
healings, Jesus', 173–75
Hebrew Bible, 160–61
high Christology, 49, 64, 150–51, 226, 308–9
Hillel, 190–91
historical-critical method, 5–6, 20, 36, 38–39, 54–55, 66, 136, 144–45, 147, 150, 155, 158, 168–72, 175–76, 212–13, 280, 305–10
    primary criteria, 39–42
    secondary criteria, 42–43
human nature of Jesus, 16–17

imminent-future eschatology, 99
inculturation, 110, 302
infancy narratives, 30, 48–50, 304–5
intercalation, 153

Jesus curses the fig tree, 152–53
Jesus of history, 33–46, 294–95, 297–98, 306–8

INDEX

agent of the kingdom, 113
amen statements, 231–32
authenticity of the parables, 212–13
authentic teachings, 114, 200–201, 237–61
and Christ of faith, 3, 8, 36, 43–44, 301–2
for Christology, 37–38
contemporary Christology, 310–11
core of miracles which are historical, 168–72
feeding the multitude, 150
forgiveness, 245
Golden Rule, 258
healing miracles, 146
importance of searching for, 43–45
Jesus as teacher, 180–82
Jesus of the gospel, 3, 14, 29, 31, 35–36, 179
kingdom as future, 114
kingdom as present, 96
Last Supper, 267–68
method of the rabbis, 190–92
role in the kingdom, 98–99
self-understanding, 216–36, 303
Sermon on the Mount, 257–59
significance of, 34–38
true mystery, 313–14
unique manifestation of God, 311–13
to the written text, 302–3
See also eschatological prophet; public ministry
Jesus stilling of the storm, 151–52
Jesus walks on the water, 150–51
Jewishness of Jesus, 5, 186, 249
Johannine Jesus, 36
John the Baptist, 48–74, 92–94, 115, 147, 163

kerygmatic, miracles as, 164–65
kingdom of God, 17–18, 239–41
  characteristics of, 125–27
  discipleship, call to, 253–54
  eschatology, 86, 106–7
  fundamental notion, 113–14
  God's presence, 105
  God's reign, 112–13
  interpretative framework for parables, 208
  is an offer of salvation, 115–16
  Jesus' role in, 98–99
  Jesus' understanding of, 85–86
  liberation from evil on a collective or social level, 117–18
  liberation from forces of evil, 116–21
  liberation that permits us to become fully human, 120
  message of the kingdom demands a response, 128
  personal and social sin, 119–20
  preaching of the, 44–45, 76–78, 108–9
  preliminary considerations, 76–107
  as present, 114–15
  present/future reality, 87–97, 106–7, 114, 129–30, 240
  primitive church context, 109–11
  recovery of, 111–12
  requires an ethical component, 123–25
  salvation is historical, 121–23
  and the secular world, 129
  theophany, 58
  wealth (mammon), 256–57
  when the kingdom would arrive, 99–101

Last Supper, 236, 267–86, 295
liberation from the forces of evil, 116–21
liberation theology, 45
literary genres, 194–95
Lord's Prayer, 88, 246

mashal, 187–88
Messiah, Jesus' understanding, 221–24, 234
Midrash, 190–91
miracles, 158–76
  biblical tradition associated with Jesus in the Gospels, 134–40
  biblical tradition outside the Gospels, 132–34
  core of miracles which are historical, 168–72

INDEX

miracles *(continued)*
    cultural environment of the New Testament, 138–39
    extrabiblical expressions for, 159–60
    extrabiblical miracle tradition, 131–32
    of Jesus, 142–57
    kerygmatic, 164–65
    meaning or significance of miracle tradition, 162–63
    miraculous catch of fish, 154
    nature miracles, 148–53, 175–76
    New Testament expressions for, 161–62
    non-miracles, 154–55
    Old Testament expressions for, 160–61
    Pauline testimony regarding, 133–34
    Petrine kerygma in the Acts of the Apostles, 133
    preliminary considerations, 131–41
    purpose of, 166–67
    represent a special part of Jesus' activity, 134–36
    rescue miracles, 151–52
    theological conclusion, 172–76
Mosaic law, 249–53
multiple attestations, 41

nature, 138–40
nature of the temptations, 66–67
New Testament: miracles in, 137–39; parables in, 183, 189–90
nimshalim, 200, 209–10

oaths, prohibition against, 251–52
Old Testament: miracles in, 160–61; parables in, 187–88
oracles of Isaiah, 163–64

Palestinian Judaism, 109–10
parables, narrative, 177–93, 194–215, 314
    and allegory, 197–201
    defined, 201–3
    characteristics of, 203
    interpretation of, 207–12
    Jesus as teacher, 180–82
    literary genres, 194–95
    locating the, 178–79
    method of the rabbis, 190–92
    New Testament, 183, 189–90
    number and distribution in Synoptic parables, 184
    Old Testament, 189–90
    and proverbs, 196–97
    purpose of, 206–7
    scriptural background, 186–92
    significance and importance of, 178
    transmission of, 185–86
    and wisdom, 195–96
passion and death of Jesus, 262–88, 289–95, 300–301
Passover meal, 269–71
Pauline Epistles, 132–33, 160
Pauline testimony regarding miracles, 133–34
personal Christology, 18
personal forgiveness, 244–45
personal relationship, 2–3, 7, 297
personal sin, 116–20
Peter's mother-in-law and her fever, 155
Petrine kerygma in the Acts of the Apostles, 133
Pontius Pilate, 223–24, 291–93
preaching of the kingdom of God, 44–45, 76–78, 108–9
presuppositions, 30–32
primary criteria, 39–42
prophecy, Jesus', 283–86
prophetic acts, 56–57, 178, 267
proverbs, 196–97
public ministry, 28–29, 36, 47–75
    Baptism of Jesus, 47–75
    beginning of movement, 74–75
    change in, 71–72
    Galilean Ministry, 70–71
    human experience, 73–74
    infancy narratives, 48–50
    itinerant preacher, 62, 67, 68, 70–74, 126, 192, 219, 299
    schematic history, 73
    temptations, 64–70
    See also John the Baptist

rabbis, 190–92; rabbinical cures, 132
raisings from the dead, 146–48, 175
reality of the temptations, 65–66, 69
real Jesus, 34–35. *See also* Jesus of history
recovery of the kingdom, 5, 111–12
recovery of the mythological in the life of Jesus, 4–5
rejection and execution, criterion of, 42
religious experience, 205
responsibility for Jesus' execution, 289–93
ritual purity, 248, 253

Sabbath, observance of, 248–49
salvation, kingdom of God, 115–21, 239–40
salvation history, 72, 80–81, 121–23, 286, 295
Sanhedrin, 223, 291–93
schematic history, 43, 73
Scripture and tradition, 3, 7–8, 14, 30
secondary criteria, 39, 42
secular and noncanonical sources, 21–22
self-understanding, Jesus', 269
Septuagint, 160, 161, 187
Sermon on the Mount, 257–59
Son of God, Jesus' identity as, 224–27
Son of Man statements, 100–101, 106
soteriology, 13, 46
sources, Last Supper, 273–74
statements of faith, 8–9, 46
Synoptic Gospels
    Baptism of Jesus, 57
    charismatic Jesus, 216
    exorcisms, 144
    expression for miracles, 161–62
    forgiveness, 245–46
    itinerant preacher, 71
    Jesus as disciple of John the Baptist, 61
    Jesus' prophecy, 283–86
    Last Supper, 269–74
    miracles, 164–65
    nimshal, 210
    parables, 179
    public ministry, 48
    responsibility for Jesus' execution, 292
    Synoptic parables, 184, 194, 199–200, 207–8, 212–13
    temptations, 64–65, 67–68

Talmud, 190–91
teaching and parables, Jesus', 180–82
temple tax, 154–55
temple worship, 81, 153, 235, 266
temptations of Jesus, 64–70
theologoumenon, 48, 152–53, 304–5
theology/theological method, 8–11
theophany, 57–59
tradition, 7–8
true Jesus, 35. *See also* Jesus of history
Twelve, Jesus' calling of, 79, 229–30

Vatican Council II, 2, 12, 16, 20, 314

wealth (mammon), 256–57
wedding feast, 149, 200–201
wisdom, 181–82, 195–96
wonder-worker, 136–37, 159–60, 166–67